STREAMS
IN THE
DESERT
—2—

Books by Mrs. Cowman—

STREAMS
IN THE
DESERT
—2—

Mrs. Charles E. Cowman

ZondervanPublishingHouse
Academic and Professional Books
Grand Rapids, Michigan

A Division of HarperCollins*Publishers*

Requests for information
should be addressed to:
Zondervan Publishing House
1415 Lake Drive S.E.
Grand Rapids, Michigan 49506

Streams in the Desert — 2

ISBN 0-310-22430-6

Printed in the United States of America

91 92 93 94 / AF / 62 61 60

This edition is printed on acid-free paper and meets the American
National Standards Institute Z39.48 standard.

PUBLISHER'S FOREWORD

It was with a deep feeling of responsibility and mission that plans were made for this second volume of *Streams in the Desert*. During the time of her final illness (1957–1960), Mrs. Charles E. Cowman entrusted her files to an associate and it is from these personal papers, writings, and books that the devotionals in this volume have been prayerfully selected. Now, these selections, loved and preserved by Mrs. Cowman, may be shared with the world that so welcomed the first volume.

Because of her intimate knowledge of Mrs. Cowman through working with her on an earlier book, Mrs. Nulah Cramer was chosen to bring together and edit these devotional meditations. We are greatly indebted to Mrs. Cramer and her associate, Miss Marie Taylor, for their sensitivity in the selection of material and in preserving the same deeply inspirational and spiritual qualities that have made *Streams in the Desert*, Volume One, a world-recognized devotional classic for more than forty years.

To the readers of the more than two million *Streams in the Desert* now in print, this new volume will be a recognized companion. To all who discover "Streams" treasures for the first time in this edition, there is a rich store of daily guidance and inspiration. It is our prayer that Volume Two will take its place alongside the earlier book and extend even further the great ministry of Christian nurture in the personal and family life of God's people everywhere.

The Publishers

Forgetting the past . . . I press onward (Phil. 3:13, 14).

One of God's glorious gifts to mankind is to bestow upon him the dawn of a new year. New opportunities and challenges are before him. A chance to try again, to make another endeavor to successfully accomplish the ambitions which were perhaps cast aside with discouragement in the year past. Life is full of beginnings. As one stands at the gate and with doubtful hand draws aside the curtain and peers into the unknown, he begins today by taking his first step across the threshold of the new year. It is already a beautiful year because it is another year of our Lord.

Gazing at the far horizons and half wondering what the coming months will bring, pause but a moment to reflect over the old volume of three hundred and sixty-five days just ended. The pages may have been marred by mistakes and torn by intentions, but a few more miles have been covered on the upward climb, pressing toward the mark.

> Through many dangers, toils and snares
>   We have already come,
> 'Twas grace that brought us safe thus far,
>   And grace will lead us Home.

It has not been our own achievement. Great has been our Father's faithfulness; new every morning have been His mercies. He faileth never!

It is part of our nature to want to live in the yesterdays of life, in "the days that come not back again." We would rather relive the strifes, the bad habits, the heartaches, and stumbling steps than to face the uncertain. With tenacity the past does cling, and like barnacles, would hinder us from pushing out from the shore and launching into the deep.

> Old Past, let go, and drop in the sea!
> Till fathomless waters cover thee;
> For I am living, but thou art dead;
> Thou drawest back, I strive ahead
>   The Day to find.
> Thy shells unbind! Night comes behind,
> I needs must hurry with the wind
>   And trim me best for sailing.

Standing at the parting of the ways, there is a choice to make, some road to take, we must consider which. How is it that we intend to live? Will it be repetitious of the past?

"I do not see my way: I do not care to: but I know that He sees His way, and that I see Him." Shining destinies are ahead! We must keep our eyes upon Jesus as we now face the dawn.

JANUARY 2 _____

And the Lord shall guide thee continually . . . (Isa. 58:11).

. . . and he will make my feet like hinds' feet, and he will make me to walk upon mine high places (Hab. 3:19).

Advance into this new year on your knees. Faith does not concern itself with the entire journey. One step is enough. That first step is all that is needed. Breathe a prayer for courage to fill your legs as well as your heart as you face the unknown, the unexpected. What matters that you know not your destination? Put your hand into the hand of God. He gives the calmness and serenity of heart and soul. As He endures, you too can endure the climb over sharp rocks and crags. Climb with Him to the end of the year—yea, even to the end of life's trail. "The peak that is nearest the storm-cloud is nearer the stars of light." He gives the courage for which you pray to rise above the valley. Heed the Master's voice and press bravely on to the fulfillment of your task. You have a whole year to scale.

> A Voice said "CLIMB." And he said, "How shall I climb?
> The mountains are so steep that I cannot climb."
> The Voice said, "CLIMB or DIE."
> He said, "But how? I see no way up those steep ascents.
> This that is asked of me is too hard for me."
> The Voice said, "CLIMB or PERISH, soul and body of thee, mind and spirit of thee. There is no second choice for any son of man. CLIMB or DIE."

Some of the bravest of mountaineers have related incredible tales concerning their climbs up the hills of earth. Sometimes they were aware of the presence of a Companion who was not among the earthly party of climbers on the mountains.

How much more positive is the presence of the Heavenly Guide as God's mountaineers climb the high places of the Spirit!

God's mountain climbers are created to walk in precarious places, not on the easy levels of life.

Do not limit the limitless God! With Him face the new trail and follow on unafraid, for you walk not alone!

JANUARY 3

And he said unto me, My grace is sufficient for thee; For my strength is made perfect in weakness . . . (2 Cor. 12:9a).

. . . Most gladly therefore will I rather glory in my infirmities that the power of Christ may rest upon me (2 Cor. 12:9b).

> God hath not promised
>   Skies always blue
> Flower-strewn pathways
>   All our lives through;
> God hath not promised
>   Sun without rain,
> Joy without sorrow,
>   Peace without pain.
>
> But God hath promised
>   Strength for the day
> Rest for the labor,
>   Light for the way,
> Grace for all trials,
>   Help from above,
> Unfailing sympathy,
>   Undying love.
>   *Annie Johnson Flint*

We never prize the precious words of promise," said Mr. Spurgeon, "til we are placed in conditions in which their suitability and sweetness are manifested." We all of us value those golden words: "When thou walkest through fire thou shalt not be burned, neither shall the flame kindle upon thee," but few, if any of us, have read them with the delight of the martyr Binney. To him this passage was a mainstay while he was in prison awaiting burning at the stake. His Bible, still preserved in the library of Corpus Christi College, Cambridge, has the passage marked with a pen in the margin.

Doubtless if all were known, every promise in the Bible has borne a special message to some one Christian, and so the whole volume might be scored in the margin with mementos of Christian experience, every one appropriate to the very letter.

> Every promise in the Book is mine;
> Every chapter, every verse, every line.

"Whereby are given unto us exceeding great and precious promises" (2 Peter 1:14).

"The promises of God are certain, but they do not all mature in ninety days." *A. J. Gordon*

JANUARY 4

The Lord is good unto them that wait for Him . . . (Lam. 3:25).

Wait on the Lord: . . . He shall strengthen thine heart (Ps. 27:14).

Wait on the Lord, . . . and He shall exalt thee . . . (Ps. 37:34).

Slow me down, Lord! Ease the pounding of my heart by the quieting of my mind. Steady my hurried pace with a vision of the eternal reach of time. Give me, amidst the confusion of my day, the calmness of the everlasting hills. Break the tensions of my nerves and muscles with the soothing music of the singing streams that live in my memory. Help me to know the magical, restoring power of sleep. Teach me the art of taking minute vacations . . . of slowing down to look at a flower, to chat with a friend, to pat a dog, to read a few lines from a good book. Remind me each day of the fable of the hare and the tortoise that I may know that the race is not always to the swift; that there is more to life than increasing its speed. Let me look upward into the branches of the towering oak and know that it grew great and strong because it grew slowly and well. Slow me down, Lord, and inspire me to send my roots deep into the soil of life's enduring values that I may grow toward the stars of my greater destiny. In Jesus' name, Amen. *Unknown*

We must learn to wait. When we do not know what to do we must simply do nothing. Wait till the fog clears away. Do not force a half-open door; a closed door may be providential. Ability to hold steady under pressure gives God unlimited sway. A hurried spirit is always from beneath (and out of breath). "He that believeth shall not make haste."

There is grace supplied for the one who waits. The psalmist knew this secret. He experienced this grace. "I wait for the Lord," he declared in Psalm 130:5. Waiting is a great part of life's discipline and therefore God often exercises the grace of waiting in the anxious hurrying person. "Waiting has four purposes," says Dr. James Vaughan. "It practices the patience of faith. It gives time for preparation for the coming gift. It makes the blessing the sweeter when it arrives. It shows the sovereignty of God—to give just *when* and *as* He pleases.

JANUARY 5

. . . called to be saints: . . . (Rom. 1:7; 1 Cor. 1:2).

Why were the saints, saints?
It is quite simple.

> Because they were "Cheerful" when it was difficult
>   to be Cheerful.
> Because they were "Patient" when it was difficult
>   to be Patient.
> Because they pushed on when they wanted to stand still.
> Because they kept silent when they wanted to talk.
> Because they were agreeable when they wanted
>   to be disagreeable.   *Selected*

What is a saint?
That was all!

> A JEWEL in disguise,
> A PRINCE in peasant's garbs.
> An immortal LIFE in dying flesh.
> An AMBASSADOR of the King Eternal, detained on
>   foreign soil.
> A MONARCH at the foot of the throne, waiting for
>   his crown.
> A ROYAL SLAVE in a prison of clay, preparing for
>   a mansion.
> A TRAVELER on a rocky road, bound for the streets

of gold.

A WATCHMAN on the midnight hills, to greet the everlasting Day,

A DIAMOND in the rough, being polished to shine as the stars.

A NUGGET of gold in the crucible, to be refined from its dross.

A PEARL in the oyster, to be delivered from the body of flesh.

A LAMP in a dark, dark night, soon to blaze forth with everlasting light.

A STRANGER in the midst of enemies, hurrying on to live in everlasting fellowship.

A FLOWER in a garden of briars, soon to unfold its petals where the Rose of Sharon blooms.   *Unknown*

JANUARY 6 _____

He is a refuge in desperate hours (Ps. 9:9, MOFFATT).

A well-known businessman would drop into our office every few days. His visits were ever times of spiritual refreshing. His face was always wreathed in smiles. He had an elastic tread. He radiated victory. A few minutes in his presence and one felt the lifting tides of God, for victory acts as a contagion. The old prophets knew this secret when they wrote of the carpenter *encouraging* the goldsmith, and the goldsmith *encouraging* those that beat out the tongs, etc.

Recently this same man shuffled into our office, sank down in a chair, buried his face between his hands, and burst into tears. What had happened to this child of God? He had *fainted in the day of adversity.* He experienced a great calamity which swept away his home, his business, his money. Then he began to worry, and, in consequence, he lost his health and is now a physical wreck. Here was Satan's opportunity, and he was not slow to avail himself of it. He came with the insidious question: "How are you going to face the world?" He led this triumphant Christian to the very edge of the precipice, and told him to cast himself down. Everything was dark, pitch dark.

The Father cares when He sees His children in the teeth of a blinding storm, but He knows that faith grows in the tempest. He will hold our hands bidding us not to try to *see* the next step we are to take. He who knows the paths of a hundred million stars, *knows the way* through the whirlwind and the storm, and has promised, "I will never let go your hand!"

There is unquestionably a grave danger of many becoming *spiritually paralyzed* by depression. The forces of darkness are so imminent, the magnitude of the crisis is so great that many are being tempted to cry out with the disciples, "Lord, carest thou not that we perish?" Yet He who may appear to be "asleep upon a pillow" is riding upon the storm in all His divine majesty. The great need is for more faith in the omnipotent God.

Mrs. Charles E. Cowman

JANUARY 7

The effectual fervent prayer of a righteous man availeth much (James 5:16).

The Lord's answers to prayer are infinitely perfect, and they will show that often when we were asking for a stone that *looked like bread*, He was giving us bread that to our shortsightedness *looked like stone.*

J. Southley

THE UNANSWERED PRAYER

She asked to be made like her Saviour;
　He took her right then at her word,
And sent her a heart-crushing burden
　Till the depths of her soul were stirred.

She wanted a meek, lowly spirit—
　The work He gave answered that cry,
Till some who had once been companions,
　With a pitying smile passed her by.

She asked to lean hard on her Saviour,
　He took human props quite away,
Till no earthly friend could give comfort,
　And she could do nothing but pray.

She had prayed to be made like the Saviour,
　And the burdens He gave her to bear
Had been but the great Sculptor's teaching;
　To help answer her earnest prayer.

Unknown

13

The life of fellowship with God cannot be built up in a day. It begins with the habitual reference of all to Him, hour by hour. It then moves on to more and longer periods of communion; and it finds its consummation and bliss in days and nights of intercession and waiting.   *F. B. Meyer*

JANUARY 8

... He will be silent in His love ... (Zeph. 3:17).

There is a beautiful story told of how one Christian dreamed that she saw three others at prayers. As they knelt the Master drew near to them.

As He approached the first of the three, He bent over her in tenderness and grace, with a smile full of radiant love and spoke to her in accents of purest, sweetest music. Leaving her, He came to the next but only placed His hand upon her bowed head, and gave her one look of loving approval. The third woman He passed almost abruptly without stopping for a word or glance. The woman in her dream said to herself, "How greatly He must love that first one, to the second He gave His approval, but none of the special demonstrations of love He gave the first; and the third must have grieved Him deeply, for He gave her no word at all and not even a passing look.

"I wonder what she had done, and why He made so much difference between them?" As she tried to account for the action of her Lord, He Himself stood by her and said: "O woman! how wrongly hast thou interpreted Me. The first kneeling woman needs all the weight of My tenderness and care to keep her feet in My narrow way. She needs My love, thought and help every moment of the day. Without it she would fail and fall. The second has stronger faith and deeper love, and I can trust her to trust Me however things may go and whatever people do.

"The third, whom I seemed not to notice, and even to neglect, has faith and love of the finest quality, and her I am training by quick drastic processes for the highest and holiest service. She knows Me so intimately, and trusts Me so utterly, that she is independent of words or looks or any outward intimation of My approval. She is not dismayed nor discouraged by any circumstance through which I arrange that she shall pass; she trusts Me

14

when sense and reason and every finer instinct of the natural heart would rebel;—because she knows that I am working in her for eternity, and that what I do, though she knows not the explanation now, she shall understand hereafter.

"I am silent in My love because I love beyond the power of words to express, or of human hearts to understand, and also for your sakes that you may learn to love and trust Me in Spirit-taught, spontaneous response to My love, without the spur of anything outward to call it forth." *Pittsburgh Bible Institute Publications*

JANUARY 9

A man that hath friends must shew himself friendly: and there is a friend that sticketh closer than a brother (Prov. 18:24).

The only way to have a friend is to be one. *R. W. Emerson*

A blessed thing it is for any man or woman to have a friend; one human soul whom we can trust utterly; who knows the best and the worst of us, and who loves us, in spite of our faults; who will speak the honest truth to us, while the world flatters us to our faces, and laughs at us behind our backs; who will give us counsel and reproof in the day of prosperity and self-conceit; but who, again will comfort and encourage us in the day of difficulty and sorrow, when the world leaves us alone to fight our own battles as we can.

If we have had the good fortune to win such a friend, let us do anything rather than lose him. We must give and forgive; live and let live. If our friends have faults we must bear with them. We must hope all things, believe all things, endure all things rather than lose that most precious of all earthly possessions—a trusty friend. And a friend once won, need never be lost, if we will only be trusty and true ourselves. *Charles Kingsley*

There is a Friend, a Friend who sympathizes,
And in each sorrow, dries the falling tear;
His is the love, unchanging it remaineth,
Our lives to bless, to brighten, and to cheer.
F. B. (Ambassador Verse Cards. No. 1, G. F. Vallance, publisher of Christian literature, Goodmayes, Essex)

The wilderness and the solitary place shall be glad for them; and the desert shall rejoice, and blossom as the rose (Isa. 35:1).

I will give waters in the wilderness, and rivers in the desert, to give drink to my people, my chosen (Isa. 43:19, 20).

The desert shall blossom as a rose. When traveling across certain areas of the western United States, it is a never failing thrill to pass out of the hot, dry, barren area into the lush green of cultivated acres. What is responsible for this marvelous transformation in the countryside? Water—and loving care and hard work on the part of industrious, enterprising people. To those who are spiritually minded a spiritual analogy always comes to mind in such a situation.

Those full-flowing irrigation ditches resemble the water of life that makes the hot, barren desert of the sinful heart to blossom as a rose.

However, no effort on the part of the desert could have made it bloom. It required the love and care of those who knew its possibilities and could bring it water and transform it into a fruitful, productive place.

It is so with God and the desert of the human heart. Not through our own efforts, but through His kindness and love He brings to us the water of life. It is ours to respond and yield to Him all our latent capacities of heart and mind. These He takes and transforms— brings to life. He uproots the cacti and bush of sin, clears the debris from a barren desert life, and plants His own life in the heart that has been thus prepared by Him. Nurtured by the constant flow of His life-giving water, the once-barren life begins to yield fruitfully—some sixty, some a hundred-fold.

"The transformed life brings joy and relaxation and delight to all who pass by." *Selected*

Be thou my strong habitation, whereunto I may continually resort: for thou art my rock and my fortress (Ps. 71:3).

Near the capitol in Rome there stands an ancient building, built when Christianity was still very young in the world. In one of its corridors is a stone bench where the little pages sat waiting calls from their masters. On the wall, right over the bench, is scratched a rude cross with an outstretched figure on it. Beneath it the mischievous artist had cartooned one of his companions and had written, "Silly Aleximos worships Christ." The other boys thought it strange that Aleximos should look up to Jesus Christ as his King. For, as someone has pointed out, the world had never seen a King who had no possessions. . . . At His birth Jesus was born in a borrowed manger. He preached a sermon in a borrowed boat. He rode into Jerusalem on a borrowed beast. He ate His last supper with His disciples in a borrowed room. He was buried in a borrowed grave. Yet He stands, the living, risen Son of God, stripped of all earthly possessions, saying, "All authority has been given Me in heaven and earth."

Other kings have always needed to be propped up; have needed to lean against many supports: gold in the treasury to buy men's souls; a host of marching legions to destroy all opposition; games in the arena to keep the crowds in good humor; bread to food the hungry to keep them from becoming dangerous. But Jesus Christ leaned on none of these supports. He leaned only on the eternal God, the unseen and everlasting Father. And, while the supports of other kings had always crumbled in the end, the Supporter of Jesus stood firm as Pilate growled, "Behold your King!"; stood unshaken as the mob yelled, "Crucify Him! Crucify Him!" Then Easter came, and the centuries began to file by; and the world began to see that true kingliness needs no gold or armies to hold it up. Men began to see that a kingly spirit stands unbroken, unbreakable, before all the blows of life, because the Spirit of the living God within a man is stronger than any enemy there is!   *St. Stephen's Protestant Episcopal Church Bulletin*

JANUARY 12 _____

But there is a God in heaven that revealeth secrets (Dan. 2:28).

Whenever your adversary pours in upon you like a flood suggesting all kinds of impossibilities and improbabilities, what are you to do and how are you to go forward? Take down the old Book; sit far into the night; read the promises and the prophecies. Read again the heartwarming words of Daniel: "There is a God in heaven that revealeth secrets." Your night will unveil new stars never seen by day. On the black thundercloud a rainbow will appear—God's everlasting covenant—and you will find a sunrise at midnight.

"There's acres of blue up there," he said,
    Beyond all these clouds and rain;
There's oceans of joy and love somewhere,
    Apart from sorrow and pain.

"There's millions of stars that man's never seen
    Where life can begin anew;
There's perfect calm where the ends of a rainbow
    Dip into acres of blue."   *Selected*

What shall you do? Act as people who have no faith, no light, no discernment? You cannot be like the unbelievers caught in the whirlpool and sink beneath the swirling waters of doubt and despair. You are a pilgrim of the day; a pilgrim of the light, guided by a glow as soft and tender as it is warm and luminous. Thank God for the assurance of divine guidance, and pray that you may stand in the right relationship to all the impossibilities and improbabilities.

"Trust in the dark brings Triumph at dawn."
                                    Mrs. Charles E. Cowman

Faith finds her path through
    Many a starless night;
And without wonder, meets
    The coming dawn—
With confidence she journeys
    Toward the light,
And as she goes, the darkness
    Is withdrawn.   *Selected*

JANUARY 13 _____

O taste and see that the Lord is good; blessed is the man that trusteth in Him (Ps. 34:8).

18

Often you cannot get at a difficulty so as to deal with it aright and find your way to a happy result. You pray, but have not the liberty in prayer which you desire. A definite promise is what you want. You try one and another of the inspired words, but they do not fit. You try again, and in due season a promise presents itself which seems to have been made for the occasion; it fits exactly as a well-made key fits the lock for which it was prepared. Having found the identical Word of the living God you hasten to plead it at the throne of grace saying, "Oh Lord, Thou hast promised this good thing unto Thy servant; be pleased to grant it!" The matter is ended; sorrow is turned to joy; prayer is heard.

C. H. Spurgeon

Faith, mighty faith, the promise sees
    And looks to God alone,
Laughs at impossibilities,
    And cries, "It shall be done."

Try all your keys! Never despair! God leaves no treasure house locked against us!

An old Negro's prayer: "O Lord, help me to remember that nothin's goin' to happen to me today that You and me together can't handle."

Mr. Babson, one of the world's greatest statisticians, says: "The greatest undeveloped resource of our country is *faith;* the greatest unused power is *prayer.* "   *Handley Moule, bishop of Durham*

A stauch soldier of the cross said that he loved to sit at the feet of the old heroes of faith in Hebrews the eleventh chapter, hear them relate their experiences, tell of the darkness of their night, the humanly impossible extremities and situations in which they so often found themselves. It was in those dark places that they were taught the strength of omnipotence.

JANUARY 14 _____

They that wait upon the Lord shall mount up with wings as eagles (Isa. 40:31).

Many are the lessons to be learned from the present chaotic world condition. We are taught the way of simple faith as we are driven back to the Word of God and prayer. We should make use of these adverse conditions! There is a lesson for us to learn from the eagle who sits on the edge of the precipice and watches the dark clouds overhead filling the sky with blackness. There he sits perfectly still, turning one eye and then the other towards the storm as the forked lightnings play back and forth. He never moves a feather until he feels the first burst of the breeze. It is then that he knows the hurricane has struck him. With a scream he swings his breast to the storm. It is the storm itself that he uses to soar upward into the black sky. He goes borne upon it. God wants this experience to take place in the lives of every one of His children! He wants us to "mount up on wings as eagles!" We can turn the storm clouds into a chariot!

We never get anywhere nor do conditions and circumstances change by looking at the dark side of life. A well-known man of God once made this statement: "My religious organs have been ailing for a while past. I have lain, a sheer hulk in consequence. But I got out my wings, and have taken a change of air." It is so often true—we do not use our wings! We walk along the road of life as mere pedestrians, and we tire so easily—for the ugliness of our circumstances burdens us down. In many different ways we can be put on the shelf or become bedridden—and "our religious organs are in danger of becoming sickly; of losing their brightness, both in mood and discernment."

We who keep too close to the road of life and do not respond to the upward calling do not have time to breathe the lofty air of the heavenlies! But we who turn unto the Lord, the Omnipotent One, have the power of wings, and we rise from our tiresome journey into the higher heavens of the glories of our most high God.

> I watched a bird upon a fragile stem;
> It seemed it would surely break with him;
> He did not seem to worry or to mind,
> For all his swaying in the wind.
> He sat erect and sang his lilting song,
> He felt so very sure, so very strong.
>   FOR HE HAD WINGS! *Selected*

JANUARY 15 _____

God [the greatest lover] so loved [the greatest degree] the world [the greatest number] that He gave [the greatest act] His only begotten Son [the greatest gift] that whosoever [the greatest invitation] believeth [the greatest simplicity] in Him [the greatest person] should not perish [the greatest deliverance], but [the greatest difference] have [the greatest certainty] everlasting life [the greatest possession] (John 3:16).

Jim Bickford was a master of the ax and a deeply religious man. He lived in Birch Intervale in New Hampshire, in the last decades of the nineteenth century, and was widely respected, both for his fabulous skill with his ax, and for his deep down everyday Christian faith. He practiced his faith, and thought about it, between Sundays and prayer meetings.

One day Jim's pigs broke out, and they gave him a peck of trouble. He knew where they belonged, where they were safest—and they seemed bound to go always in the opposite direction. All the time he was struggling with them, Jim was thinking of Jesus' teaching, especially about the Gadarene swine. Finally he herded them back, only to have them break out again. He thought a lot of those pigs, so once more he painstakingly, patiently herded them back; still thinking, and saying his prayers. That night he stood up in prayer meeting and testified. I do not know his exact words, but I believe that at last he knew how God feels about His people— "How oft would I have gathered them. . . ." He thought of those pigs, Jim did, and he declared, "The devil was in those swine!" At last he truly understood God's feeling about His children's stubborn resistance against His loving will for them. I'm sure that those who listened to Jim's testimony in the Wonalancet Chapel that night never forgot it; and opened their hearts to let God draw them home.

Said Billy Bray, the Cornish evangelist: A farmer in England placed on the wind indicator on his barn the words, "God is Love." A friend asked him, "Do you mean that God is as changeable as the wind?" "No," replied the farmer, "I mean God is Love no matter which way the wind blows!"   *Selected*

JANUARY 16 _____

Who is this that cometh up from the wilderness, leaning upon her beloved? (Song of Sol. 8:5)

Yea, I will uphold thee with the right hand of my righteousness (Isa. 41:10).

21

When the storm's a rumblin'
And our strength's a crumblin'
And Oh! so sore we're tried,
When the wind's a blowin'
And our spirit's lowerin'
O Lord, support us, on the leanin' side!

When the loved one's taken
And the heart's a'breakin'
And sorrow's multiplied,
When we're crushed and grievin'
And our hope's a leavin'
O Lord, support us, on the leanin' side!

When the thunder's roarin'
And the torrent's pourin'
And sweepin' in, the tide,
When we're rowin', rowin'
And our courage goin'
O Lord, support us, on the leanin' side!

When we're weak and fallin'
And we need recallin'
Be Thou our Stay, our Guide;
As we're heav'nward hiein'
When a livin, dyin',
O Lord, support us, on the leanin' side!   *Edith L. Mapes*

JANUARY 17

Lord, increase our faith (Luke 17:5).

A crowd of five thousand men, besides an uncounted number of women and children, were gathered on a hillside in Galilee overlooking the little lake. In this great host of people who had come to listen to the Master was one small boy who wanted to be of help. Just one boy would not seem to matter much. Yet because of his faith and obedience people all over the world for two thousand years have marveled at the incident in which he played a major role.

The sun was just setting. The people had been listening all day to Jesus as he mingled with them. It was no wonder that the children were restless and hungry. They had had no food for the entire day. The disciples concerned themselves with preparations for a meal. Jesus had mentioned that the crowd must have something to eat before starting homeward. Feed them—with what? There was no place nearby where they could get food.

Hoping some would share if they had brought lunches with them, the disciples moved through the throng asking for food. A small lad tugged on Andrew's arm. "Here is my basket. There are but five loaves and two fishes." Utterly amazed, Andrew took the basket to Jesus. Andrew had begun to despair for carrying out such an obviously empty gesture in obedience to the commands of his Master. In the hands of the Master, the small basket of lunch became enough to feed the whole multitude. After all had eaten, there were still twelve baskets full of the leftovers!

Who are we to judge what God can or cannot do? He made the world! He made all that is in it! He made the laws of nature! He rules the whole of creation as He wills! *We are the created, not the creators!*

Emerson so fittingly penned these words: "All I have seen teaches me to trust the Creator for all I have not seen."

> I have nothing to do with tomorrow,
>   My Savior will make that His care;
> Its grace and strength I can't borrow,
>   So why should I borrow its care. *Major D. W. Whittle*

JANUARY 18

God will allow no suffering, no trial above what you are able to bear (see 1 Cor. 10:13).

In an old book written by the blind Scotch preacher, George Matheson, we found some very heartening words. We quote a few excerpts:

"There is a time coming in which your glory shall consist in the very thing which now constitutes your pain. Nothing could be more sad to Jacob than the ground on which he was lying, a stone for his pillow! It was the hour of his poverty. It was the season of his night. It was the seeming absence of his God. The Lord was in the place and he knew it not. Awakened from his sleep he found that the day of his trial was the dawn of his triumph! Ask the great ones of the past what has been the spot of their prosperity and they will say, 'It was the cold ground on which I was lying.' Ask

Abraham; he will point you to the sacrifice on Mount Moriah. Ask Joseph; he will direct you to his dungeon. Ask Moses; he will date his fortune from his danger in the Nile. Ask Ruth; she will bid you build her monument in the field of her toil. Ask David; he will tell you that his songs came from the night. Ask Job; he will remind you that God answered him out of the whirlwind. Ask Peter; he will extol his submersion in the sea. Ask John; he will give the path to Patmos. Ask Paul; he will attribute his inspiration to the light which struck him blind. Ask *one more!*—the Son of God. Ask Him whence has come His rule over the world; He will answer, 'From the cold ground on which I was lying—the Gethsemane ground— I received my sceptre there.' Thou too, my soul, shall be garlanded by Gethsemane! The cup thou fain wouldst pass from thee will be thy coronet in the sweet by and by.

"The hour of thy loneliness will crown thee. The day of thy depression will regale thee. It is thy *desert* that will break forth into singing. It is the trees of thy silent forest that will clap their hands. The last things will be first, in the sweet by and by. The thorns will be roses. The vales will be hills. The crooks will be straight lines, the ruts will be level. The shadows will be shining. The losses will be promotions. The tears will be tracks of gold. The voice of God to thine evening will be this: 'Thy treasure is hid in the ground, where thou wert lying.' "

JANUARY 19

And lead us not into temptation . . . (Matt. 6:13).

When tempted:

> Forget the slander you have heard,
> Forget the hasty, unkind word;
> Forget the quarrel and the cause,
> Forget the whole affair, because,
> Forgetting is the only way.
> Forget the storm of yesterday.
> Forget the chap whose sour face
> Forgets to smile in any place.
> Forget that you're not a millionaire,
> Forget the gray streaks in your hair.
> Forget the coffee when it's cold.
> Forget to kick, forget to scold,

Forget the plumber's awful charge,
Forget the doctor's bill is large;
Forget the repair man and his ways,
Forget the winter's blustery days.
Forget the neighbor's wagging tongue.

BUT DON'T

Forget God when day is done.   *Unknown*

A dear old saint was asked what she would do if a fierce temptation overtook her. Her quick reply was, "I would lift up my hands to the Lord and say, 'Lord, your property is in danger. Take care of it quick!' Then I'd forget about it 'til I was tried again."

Are you worsted in a fight?
Are you cheated of your right?
   Laugh it off.
Don't make tragedies of trifles,
Don't shoot butterflies with rifles—
   Laugh it off.
Does your work get into kinks?
Are you near all sorts of brinks?
   Laugh it off.
If it's sanity you're after,
There's no recipe like laughter—
   Laugh it off.   *From* Modern Methods

JANUARY 20 _____

Casting all your care upon him; for he careth for you (1 Peter 5:7).

I have a Friend, whose faithful love
Is more than all the world to me,
'Tis higher than the heights above,
And deeper than the soundless sea:
   So old, so new,
   So strong, so true,
Before the earth received its frame
He loved me—Blessed be His name!   *Unknown*

John Bunyan Smith wrote, "Let us turn our fears into faith, and quit worrying over the thing that has not and never will happen."
Don't let tomorrow use too much of today!
The refusal to worry does not mean lack of concern. Too many

people have that. But though one cares greatly, when he has done all he can to prevent the evil or bring the good to pass, he has a right to trust in God.

It is not the work, but the worry
   That makes the world grow old,
That shortens the years of many
   Before half their life is told.
It is not the work, but the worry
   That places on life a band,
The cares and fears that crowd the years
   That break the heart of man.   *Unknown*

"It is good that a man should both hope and quietly wait for the salvation of the Lord" (Lam. 3:26).

JANUARY 21 _____

Who shall separate us from the Love of Christ? (Rom. 8:35).

He had anxiously waited for the day when the Man of Galilee would come to his town. He had delayed making an important decision until with his own eyes he could behold Jesus. Now he saw the Man. Jesus passed by. Nothing had happened.

They were almost out of sight. Was it too late? Gathering up his robes about him he ran. Upon reaching the group he knelt at the Master's feet. In desperation, before he again changed his mind, the young ruler asked, "Good Master, what shall I do to inherit eternal life?" Jesus discussed the keeping of the law. The rich man said he had kept it: "But what lack I yet?"

Then Jesus beholding him loved him, and said unto him, "One thing thou lackest: go thy way, sell whatsoever thou hast, and give to the poor, thou shalt have treasure in heaven: and come, take up the cross, and follow me."

And he was sad at that saying, and went away grieved: for he had great possessions.

The heart of Jesus was grieved also. The rich young ruler had everything but strength of character.

God give us strength to rid ourselves of any allurement which separates us from Thee!

Longfellow could take a worthless sheet of paper, write a poem on it, and make it worth $6,000—*that's genius.*

Rockefeller could sign his name to a piece of paper and make it worth a million dollars—*that's capital.*

Uncle Sam can take gold, stamp an eagle on it, and make it worth $50—*that's money.*

A mechanic can take material that is worth only $5 and make it worth $50—*that's skill.*

An artist can take a fifty-cent piece of canvas, paint a picture on it, and make it worth $1,000—*that's art.*

God can take a worthless, sinful life, wash it in the blood of Christ, put His Spirit in it, and make it a blessing to humanity—*that's salvation.*   *Unknown*

JANUARY 22 _____

I can do all things through Christ which strengtheneth me (Phil. 4:13).

The story is told of a small boy trying very hard to lift a heavy object. His father coming into the room and noting the son's struggle asked him, "Are you using all your strength?" "Yes, of course I am," the boy impatiently exclaimed. "You are not," the father answered. "You haven't asked me to help you."

If the burden is too heavy to bear, it is time to ask our Heavenly Father for help. Our own puny supply of power is so often insufficient for the disappointments and difficulties we have to face. Let us form the habit of asking for God's help. God will allow no suffering, no trial above what we are able to bear. For He says in 1 Corinthians 10:13, "God is faithful, who will not suffer you to be tempted above that ye are able; but will with the temptation also make a way to escape, that ye may be able to bear it."

There is an old, old legend of a time when the people of the earth made loud lament. Every man felt that he had been given a heavier load to bear than his neighbor, and that, if he could trade troubles with his fellowman, life would be easier. The clamor went on so long that the gods decided that they must do something about it. It was arranged that, on a given day, each man should bring his burden to a certain place, and there shed it forever. But it was also arranged that each man must choose for himself one of the lighter loads he had so enviously watched others carry.

What a day that was! People came and threw down their old burdens, the aches and pains, problems, responsibilities, besetting sins. And then they pawed over the vast heap, each person weighing one and then another, only to find it heavier and more uncomfortable than his old load. In the end, it is said, each man took back his own familiar burden! The simple fact is that any burden is heavy if it is carried the wrong way. And any load, however light, becomes intolerable if you keep thinking about its heft. Jesus said, "Come unto Me, all ye that labor and are heavy-laden, and I will refresh you. Take My yoke upon you and learn of Me . . . and ye shall find rest unto your souls."

St. Stephen's Protestant Episcopal Church Bulletin

JANUARY 23 _____

But he that cometh after me is mightier than I (Matt. 3:11).

I have fought a good fight, I have finished my course, I have kept the faith (2 Tim. 4:7).

The best any of us can do in this world is but a fragment. "The old prophet thought his work had failed because Baalism was not yet entirely destroyed. Then he was told of three other men, who would come after him—two kings and then another prophet, who each in turn would do his part, when at last the destruction of the great alien 'idolatry' would be complete. Elijah's faithfulness had not failed, but his achievement was only a fragment of the whole work.

"We are not responsible for finishing everything we begin. It may be our part only to begin it; the carrying on and finishing of it may be the work of others. They may be those we know or do not know and perhaps others not yet born. We all enter into the work of those who have gone before us, and others who come after us shall in turn enter into our work. Our duty simply is to do well and faithfully our own little part. Why fret over what we *cannot* do when that which we can do will occupy all our time. What we cannot do is not our responsibility. It belongs to some other worker, waiting even now, perhaps, in some obscure place, who at the right moment will come forth with new zeal and dedicated skill, anointed for his task."

J. R. Miller, D.D.

Of youth and the waiting worker it is said:

> They to the disappointed earth shall give
> The lives we meant to live,
> Beautiful, free, and strong;
> The light we almost had
> Shall make them glad;
> The words we waited long
> Shall run in music from their voice and song.

JANUARY 24

And when He had thus spoken, He showed them his hands . . . (Luke 24:40).

In the hands of Jesus there is certainty! There is providence! There is majesty! The hands of Jesus are human hands. They were once baby hands! Did not the angels from the realms of glory bid the shepherds to hasten to Bethlehem to behold those infant hands? For the fullness of time had come. The pagan empires had unknowingly set the stage. This great moment of which the prophets had spoken and the psalmists had sung had arrived! A body had been prepared for Him to permit the Godhead to be veiled in flesh.

In the course of time those tiny hands became toiling hands. He who fashioned the stars toiled in a carpenter's shed! His workmanship would be thorough. "We are His workmanship," cries Paul. He knew! Those hands that hewed rough timber into useful objects of beauty and usefulness had transformed him from a despot to a disciple, motivated not by law but by love.

The hands of Jesus are generous hands—generous in tender care. His hands were laid upon the little children in blessing when the stern disciples dared to drive them away.

His hands were generous in cleansing. He laid aside His robes and with His own hands He began to wash His disciples' feet. When Peter protested, He replied, "Except I wash thee, thou hast no part with me." Those hands are even today at our disposal when we need cleansing.

The hands of Jesus are saving hands. The Bible describes every type of sin but declares that the Lord delivers from them all.

His hands can save only because they are pierced hands. The

only things in heaven that man has made are the five wounds which are born in His body. His wounded hands plead at the throne of grace for all who call upon the name of the Lord.

His saving hands are secure hands. Of all who come to Him, He said: "I will give them eternal life, and they shall never perish, neither shall any man pluck them out of my hand." They are able to hold secure for time and eternity all that we commit to Him.

JANUARY 25

Why beholdest thou the mote that is in thy brother's eye, but considereth not the beam that is in thine own eye! (Matt. 7:3).

If you confer a benefit, never remember it. If you receive one, never forget it."

How wilt thou say to thy brother, Let me pull out the mote out of thine eye; and, behold a beam is in thine own eye? Thou hypocrite, first cast out the beam out of thine own eye; and then shalt thou see clearly to cast out the mote out of thy brother's eye (Matt. 7:4, 5).

The following was written by Miss Mary Stewart of Washington, D.C., a good many years ago, and has been adopted by many business and professional women's organizations all over the United States, as their official prayer:

"Keep us, O God, from pettiness, let us be large in thought, in word, in deed.

"Let us be done with faultfinding and leave off self-seeking.

"May we put away all pretense and meet each other face to face—without self-pity, and without prejudice.

"May we never be hasty in judgment and always generous.

"Let us take time for all things; make us to grow calm, serene, and gentle.

"Teach us to put into action our better impulses, straightforward and unafraid.

"Grant us to realize it is the little things that create differences, that in the big things of life we are as one.

"And may we strive to touch and know the great, common woman's heart of us all, and, O Lord, let us forget not *to be kind*.

"Write injuries in the dust, but kindness in marble."

"We must overcome our enemies by gentleness, win them over

30

by forbearance. Let us not at once wither the big tree from which a more skillful gardener may yet entice fruit."

St. Gregory Nazianzen

"All heaven listens when we send up a heartfelt prayer for an enemy's good."

JANUARY 26

As the eagle stirreth up her nest, fluttereth over her young, spreadeth abroad her wings, taketh them, beareth them on her wings—so the Lord . . . (Deut. 32:11–12).

The mother eagle had tried by every means to induce the little one to leave the nest, but he was afraid.

Suddenly, as if discouraged, she rose well above him. I held my breath, for I knew what was coming. The little fellow stood on the edge of the nest, looking down at the plunge he dared not take. There was a sharp cry from behind, which made him alert, tense as a watch spring. The next instant the mother eagle had swooped, striking the nest at his feet, sending his support of twigs and himself with them out into the air together.

He was afloat now, afloat on the blue air in spite of himself, and flapped lustily for life. Over him, under him, beside him, hovered the mother on tireless wings, calling softly that she was there. But the awful fear of the depths and the lance tops of the spruces was upon the little one; his flapping grew more wild; he fell faster and faster. Suddenly, more in fright, it seemed to me, than because he had lost his strength—he lost his balance and tipped head downward in the air. It was all over now; he folded his wings to be dashed in pieces among the trees. Then like a flash the old mother eagle shot under him, his despairing feet touched her broad shoulders, between her wings. He righted himself, rested an instant, found his head; then she dropped like a shot from under him, leaving him to come down on his own wings. A handful of feathers, torn out by his claws, hovered slowly down after them.

It was all the work of an instant before I lost them among the trees far below. And when I found them again with my glass, the eaglet was in the top of a great pine, and the mother was feeding him.

And then, standing there alone in the great wilderness, it flashed upon me for the first time just what the wise old prophet meant; though he wrote long ago in a distant land, and another than Cloud-wings had taught her little ones, all unconscious of the kindly eyes that watched out of a thicket—"As the eagle stirreth up her nest, fluttereth over her young, spreadeth abroad her wings, taketh them, beareth them on her wings—so the Lord."

Christabel Gladwell
12 and 14 Gandy St., Exeter, England,
from the leaflet The Bible and Testament Depot

JANUARY 27

The Lord is good unto them that wait for Him, to the soul that seeketh Him. It is good that a man should both hope and quietly wait for the salvation of the Lord (Lam. 3:25, 26).

It was the hour when defeat seemed inevitable that Joshua stood alone in prayer to God, and the answer was a glorious victory over the five kings.

It was the hours Elijah communed with God that brought fire from the sky which convinced Ahab that the Lord was God. It was the hours Jonah spent with Him in the deep sea when in the belly of the whale that prepared him to preach repentance to the people of Nineveh. It was the hours Daniel spent in the upper chamber alone with God that made him a prince among men, and also saved him in the den of lions. It was the hours the disciples spent in the upper room waiting upon the Lord which enabled them to preach three thousand souls into the Kingdom at Pentecost. It was the hours the Apostle Paul spent alone in prayer that enabled him to make Felix tremble and to make King Agrippa exclaim, "Almost thou persuadest me to be a Christian!" It was the hours Gladstone spent alone with God in prayer that made him the wise and safe leader of England. It was the hours Spurgeon spent alone in prayer that made him the greatest preacher since the days of Paul. It is the hours Billy Graham spends confiding in God that makes him the world's most influential revivalist today.

Mrs. Charles E. Cowman

The real victory in all service is won in secret beforehand by prayer. Service is gathering up the results.

I have a treasure which I prize,
  Its like I cannot find;
There's nothing like it on the earth—
  'Tis this, a QUIET MIND.

Unknown

JANUARY 28 ———————————————————————

We are journeying unto the place of which the Lord said, I will give it you . . . (Num. 10:29).

I saw a way-worn trav'ler
  In tatter'd garments clad,
And struggling up the mountain
  It seem'd that he was sad;
His back was laden heavy,
  His strength was almost gone,
Yet he shouted as he journeyed,
  Deliverance will come.

The summer sun was shining,
  The sweat was on his brow,
His garments worn and dusty,
  His step seem'd very slow:
But he kept pressing onward,
  For he was wending home;
Still shouting as he journeyed,
  Deliverance will come.

The songsters in the arbor
  That stood beside the way
Attracted his attention,
  Inviting his delay:
His watchword being "Onward!"
  He stopped his ears and ran,
Still shouting as he journeyed,
  Deliverance will come.

I saw him in the evening,
  The sun was bending low,
He'd overtopped the mountain,
  And reached the vale below:
He saw the golden City—

His everlasting home—
And shouted loud, Hosanna,
Deliverance will come!

While gazing on that city,
  Just o'er the narrow flood
A band of holy angels
  Came from the throne of God:
They bore him on their pinions
  Safe o'er the dashing foam;
And joined him in his triumph—
  Deliverance has come!

I heard the song of triumph
  They sang upon that shore,
Saying, Jesus has redeemed us
  To suffer nevermore:
Then, casting his eyes backward
  On the race which he had run,
He shouted loud, Hosanna,
  Deliverance has come!   *Rev. John B. Matthias, 1836*

The man who walks with God always gets to his destination.

JANUARY 29 ─────────────────────────────

*Though I walk through the valley of the shadow of death, I will fear no evil:
for Thou art with me; Thy rod and Thy staff they comfort me (Ps. 23:4).*

It is a great art to learn to walk through the shadowy places. Do
not hurry; there are lessons to be learned in the shadow that
can never be learned in the light. You will discover something
about His ministries you never knew before. His rod and His staff
they will comfort you—the one to guide, the other to protect you,
and the sheep that are nearest will know the most of both.

When we go into the valley of the shadow of death we come so
near Him that we look into His face and say, not "He is with
me"—that is too formal, too far away—but "Thou art with me."
The need and the usefulness of Christ is seen best in trials.
                                            W. Y. Fullerton, D.D.

Through the wearisome hours of a sorrowful night
  I have prayed for the morning to break;
Till there came—not the morn—but this broad beam of

light:
   He knoweth the way that I take.
He knoweth the way! and the way is His own,
And I take it with Him—not alone, not alone!

And so, as I journey through darkness and light
   Till the valley's dark shades overtake,
And the city of rest lifts its towers on my sight,
   He knoweth the way that I take.
He knoweth the way! and the way is His own,
And I take it with Him—not alone, not alone!

Mrs. S. M. Walsh,
At the Beautiful Gate, *1879*

Do not pray for easy times. Pray to be stronger men! Do not pray for tasks equal to your powers. Pray for powers equal to your tasks.   *Phillips Brooks*

JANUARY 30

Everyone that exalteth himself shall be abased; and he that humbleth himself shall be exalted (Luke 18:14).

"Excelsior" is a very well-known motto and has been used throughout history. Look well to the mode of interpreting it. "He that exalteth himself shall be abased." If man is to be governed by the rules of God's kingdom, he shall find that the only way up is to go down. The One who now occupies the very highest place in heaven is the One who voluntarily took the very lowest place on earth.

O, who like Thee so humbly bore
The scorn, the scoffs of men before?
So meek, so lowly, yet so high,
So glorious in humility.   *Selected*

At the dinner table of one of the well-known millionaires who had done much for the public good, discussion turned upon the value of prayer. The millionaire said that he did not believe in it. He had everything he wished for, so there was no need for him to pray for any favors.

The principal of a Scottish university, who was present, said, "There is one thing that you might pray for."

35

"What is that?"

"You might pray for humility."

Whatever our possessions, we shall be all the happier if we pray for the humble spirit which can thank God for His mercies.

From The Sunday School Times

JANUARY 31 —————————————————

For God hath caused me to be fruitful in the land of my affliction (Gen. 41:52).

A nd the twelve gates were twelve pearls." Dr. Edward T. Sullivan once took for his text: "every gate a pearl! Every entrance into the heavenly life is through a pearl! What is a pearl? A wound is made in a shell. A grain of sand, perhaps, gets imbedded in the wound. And all the resources of repair are rushed to the place where the breach has been made. When the breach has been closed, and the process of repair is complete, a pearl is found closing the wound. The break calls forth unsuspected resources of the shell and a beauty appears that is not otherwise brought out. A pearl is a healed wound! No wound, no pearl!"

He went on to show how, in our lives, misfortune can be transformed into blessing, hurts changed into pearls of precious value. Even a grievous handicap may become a lifesaving power. He tells a story of Nydia, the blind flower girl in the *Last Days of Pompeii.* She had not become bitter about her blindness; nor had she sulked or sat at home. She had gone about the business of living and had earned her livelihood as best she could. Then came the awful day of the eruption of Vesuvius, with "The doomed city as dark as midnight beneath a thick pall of smoke and falling ashes; the terror-stricken inhabitants rush blindly to and fro, and lose themselves in the awful blackness." But Nydia does not get lost; because of her cross of blindness, she had learned to find her way by touch and hearing, and now she could go straight to rescue the life of the one she loved best. By learning to walk swiftly and surely in the dark, she had made of her handicap a treasure and a God-send in the dark hour.

"Every gate a pearl!" Every misfortune, every failure, every loss, may be transformed. God has the power to transform all "misfortunes" into God-sends. So Jesus transformed the cross from a criminal's badge of shame into the sign of the love of God. Often it takes a wound to transform a denying Peter into a fearless rock of a man. "No wound, no pearl!"—out of life's buffetings may come our richest rewards.

Whether life grinds down a man, or polishes him, depends on what he is made of.

FEBRUARY 1

The prayer of the upright is his delight (Prov. 15:8).

Because you prayed—
God touched our weary bodies with His power
And gave us strength for many a trying hour
In which we might have faltered, had not you,
Our intercessors faithful been, and true.

Because you prayed—
God touched our lips with coals from altar fire,
Gave Spirit-fulness, and did so inspire
That, when we spoke, sin-blinded souls did see;
Sins' chains were broken;
Captives were made free.

Because you prayed—
The dwellers in the dark have found the Light;
The glad good-news has banished heathen night;
The message of the Cross, so long delayed,
Has brought them life at last—
Because you prayed.   *Charles B. Bowser*

It is not the arithmetic of our prayers, how many they are; nor the rhetoric of our prayers, how eloquent they may be; nor the geometry of our prayers, how long they be; nor the music of our prayers, how sweet our voice may be; nor the logic of our prayers, how argumentative they may be; nor the method of our prayers, how orderly they may be—which God cares for. Fervency of spirit is that which availeth much.

There is nothing that makes us love someone as praying for him, and when you can do this sincerely for anyone, you have fitted your soul for the performance of everything that is kind and civil toward him. Be daily on your knees in a solemn, deliberate performance of this devotion, praying for others in such form, with such length, importunity and earnestness as you use for yourself; and you will find all little, ill-natured passions die away, your heart will grow great and generous. *William Law*

The prayers of godly men and women can accomplish more than all the military forces in the world. "Prayer-craft is greater than aircraft!"

FEBRUARY 2

Be strong and of a good courage. . . . He it is that doth go with thee (Deut. 31:6).

There is something very encouraging in the idea of a new start. We should keep short accounts with God, and live not only day by day but moment by moment. Thus the staleness will disappear from life. His mercies will be new every morning, and each experience will come to us like living waters fresh from the fountains of His love and grace.

There is something most attractive in the idea of a new discovery, an unexplored land, a fresh advance on new territory, and new achievements. How it lures the adventurer to the frigid zones and the dangerous tropics! God has for each of us great and mighty things which we know not, and visions of truth and attainment which "eye hath not seen nor ear heard, neither hath it entered into the heart of man, the things which God hath prepared for them that love Him."

Let us press farther on! *Dr. A. B. Simpson*

Life is too short to nurse one's misery. Hurry across the lowlands, that you may spend more time on the mountaintops. *Phillips Brooks*

John Bunyan, by trade a tinker and by nature headstrong and passionate, lived a carefree and reckless life—until he became a Christian. Then he turned his immense energies into publicly preaching the gospel that had redeemed him—until he was thrown into jail. (It was contrary to English law for dissenters from the state religion to hold public meetings.) Even in the face of imprisonment the freedom-loving nature did not despair. During the twelve years of confinement in Bedford jail, Bunyan supported his family by making shoelaces, and affirmed his Christian faith by writing *Pilgrim's Progress*. His book became the most popular and effective tract in propagating Christianity ever written.

From the lowliest depth there is a path to the loftiest height.

Carlyle

The greater the difficulty, the greater the glory.   *Cicero*

Never despair, but if you do, work on in despair.

Edmund Burke

FEBRUARY 3

So shall my word be that goeth forth out of my mouth: it shall not return unto me void, but it shall accomplish that which I please, and it shall prosper in the thing whereto I sent it (Isa. 55:11).

The life is not in the sower, but in the seed. Even if an infidel scattered the Scriptures, he would only be exploding his own battlements.

For in scattering divine literature we liberate thistledown, laden with precious seed, which, blown by the winds of the Spirit, floats over the world. The printed page never flinches, never shows cowardice; it is never tempted to compromise; it never tires, never grows disheartened; it travels cheaply, and requires no hired hall; it works while we sleep; it never loses its temper; and it works long after we are dead. The printed page is a visitor which gets inside the home, and stays there; it always catches a man in the right mood, for it speaks to him only when he is reading it; it always sticks to what it has said, and never answers back; and it is bait left permanently in the pool.

Luther wrote a pamphlet on Galatians which, falling into Bunyan's hands, converted him; and several hundred translations of *Pilgrim's Progress* have been issued. More than 150,000,000 copies of Spurgeon's sermons have gone into circulation. Nor is even the political influence of the printed page measurable. A young Frenchman who had been wounded at the siege of Saint Quentin was languishing on a pallet in the hospital when a tract that lay on the coverlet caught his eye. He read it and was converted by it. The monument of that man may be seen before the Church of the Consistory in Paris, standing with a Bible in his hand—Admiral Coligny, the leader of the Reformation in France. But the tract had not yet finished its work. It was read by Coligny's nurse, a Sister of Mercy, who penitently placed it in the hands of the Lady Abbess, and she, too, was converted by it. She fled from France to the Palatinate, where she met a young Hollander and became his wife. The influence which she had upon that man reacted upon the whole continent of Europe, for he was William of Orange, who became the champion of liberty and Protestantism in the Netherlands.

The printed page is deathless: you can destroy one, but the press can reproduce millions; as often as it is martyred, it is raised: the ripple started by a given tract can widen down the centuries until it bears upon the great white throne. Its very mutilation can be its sowing. *M. P. Panton*

FEBRUARY 4

Who shall change our vile body, that it may be fashioned like unto his glorious body, according to the working whereby he is able even to subdue all things unto himself (Phil. 3:21).

There is a legend of an artist who long sought for a piece of sandalwood, out of which to carve a madonna. At last he was about to give up in despair, leaving the vision of his life unrealized, when in a dream he was bidden to shape the figure from a block of oakwood which was destined for the fire. Obeying the command, he produced from the log of common firewood a masterpiece. In like manner many people wait for great and brilliant opportunities for doing the good things, the beautiful things, of which they dream, while through all the plain, common days, the very opportunities they require for such deeds lie close to them in the simplest and most familiar passing events and in the homeliest circumstances. They wait to find sandalwood out of which to carve madonnas, while far more lovely madonnas than they dream of are hidden in the common logs of oak they spurn with their feet in the woodyard. *J. R. Miller, D.D.*

It is very noticeable in all history that the larger part of great men in every department have sprung from the common people, so far as the absence of wealth or rank or great ancestry can make them common.

> And Gideon was nothing,
>   Was nothing in the frey.
> But just a suit of working clothes
>   The Spirit wore that day.   *Unknown*

Apostles are made from common men.

FEBRUARY 5

They began to pray Him to depart (Mark 5:17).

Of all the passages in the Bible, this one is perhaps the saddest. One can hardly conceive of any person asking Jesus to depart from them. The Son of God had come to the coast of the Gardarenes to perform acts of healing and blessing. It has been said that "His hands were full of golden gifts." The Son of God had power to heal the sick and afflicted, to open blind eyes, to scatter miracles of blessing among the inhabitants of the land. The instant He landed on the coast he began His work of grace by healing the most terrible malady—demon possession. He was most willing to do more than this, to continue His acts of love, but they besought Him to depart. Because the means of their existence was threatened—the loss of their swine—they did not want Christ's miracles to go any farther.

There are individuals today who feel the same way as these Gardarenes when some work of grace affects their means of support. They oppose the spreading of Christianity because it interferes with their progress in the community. Bars, certain places of recreation, some civic organizations, even several religious groups perhaps oppose revivals. When Satan is hindered these places are less frequented and business drops off. They are against the spreading of Christianity because Christianity is against them. When Christ interferes with our hopes and cherished plans, we are apt to want Him to depart.

Jesus did not remain when these apprehensive people asked Him to go. He does not stay where He is not wanted. He carried back the "golden gifts" He had come to leave with them. The afflicted remained miserable, the lame continued to hobble, the demoniacs stayed, and the hopeless passed away.   *M. Taylor*

> Thou the Spring of all my comfort,
>   More than life to me;
> Whom have I on earth beside Thee?
>   Whom in heav'n but Thee?
>   *Fanny J. Crosby*

FEBRUARY 6

But they that wait upon the Lord shall renew their strength (Isa. 40:31).

Every true Christian life needs its daily "silent times," when all shall be still, when the busy activity of other hours shall cease, and when the heart, in holy hush, shall commune with God. One of the greatest needs in Christian life is more devotion. Ours is not an age of prayer as much as an age of work. The tendency is to action rather than worship; to busy toil rather than to quiet sitting at the Savior's feet to commune with Him. The keynote of our present Christian life is consecration, which is understood to mean devotion to active service. On every hand we are incited to work. Our zeal is stirred by every inspiring incentive.

The truest religious life is one whose devotion gives food and strength for service. The way to spiritual health lies in the paths of consecrated activity. It is related in monastic legends of Saint Francesca, that although she was unwearied in her devotions, yet if during her prayers she was summoned away by any domestic duty, she would close her book cheerfully, saying that a wife and a mother, when called upon, *must quit her God at the altar to find Him in her domestic affairs.* Yet the other side is just as true. Before there can be a strong, vigorous, healthy tree, able to bear much fruit, to stand the storm, to endure the heat and cold, there must be a well-planted and well-nourished root; and before there can be a prosperous, noble, enduring Christian life in the presence of the world, safe in temptation and unshaken in trials, full of good fruits, perennial and unfading in its leaf, there must be a close walk with God in secret. We must receive from God before we can give to others, for we have nothing of our own with which to feed men's hunger or quench their thirst. We are but empty vessels at the best, and must wait to be filled before we have anything to carry to those who need. We must listen at heaven's gates before we can go out to sing the heavenly songs in the ears of human weariness and sorrow. Our lips must be touched with a coal from God's altar before we can become God's messengers to men. We must lie much upon Christ's bosom before our poor earthly lives can be struck through with the spirit of Christ and made to shine in the transfigured beauty of His blessed life. Devotion is never to displace duty—it often brings new duties to our hands—but it fits us for activity.   *J. R. Miller, Silent Times, 1886*

FEBRUARY 7

He knoweth what is in the darkness . . . (Dan. 2:22).

I will even make a way in the wilderness . . . (Isa. 43:19).

About a century ago South Africa was opened to a simple missionary, named Shaw, and his family, who went to Capetown with the intention of entering the interior as a missionary. The Boers discouraged him and gave him no assistance. Every door seemed closed. At last he and his wife got into an ox-cart and resolved to go just wherever the oxen might draw them. Day after day they followed on over the pathless veldt, until they had traveled three hundred miles at the guiding of a mysterious providence, when, lo, upon the distant plain they saw a company of native travelers approaching them. As they drew near, they found it was a band of Hottentots on their way to Capetown, seeking for a missionary. There in the wilderness they met, and God began His mighty work among these African tribes.

There is a guide that never falters,
    And when He leads I cannot stray,
For step by step He goes before me,
    And marks my path, He knows the way.

Oft-times the path grows dim and dreary,
    The darkness hides the cheering ray,
Still I will trust, tho' worn and weary,
    My Saviour leads, He knows the way.

He knows the evils that surround me,
    The turnings that would lead astray,
No foes of night can ere confound me,
    For Jesus leads, He knows the way.   *A. B. Ackley*

For whosoever would save his life will lose it, and whosoever loses his life for My sake will find it (Matt. 16:25).

The following parable brings home the truth of our Master's words:

There are two seas in Palestine. One is fresh and there are fish in it. Slashes of green adorn its banks. Trees spread their branches over it and stretch out their thirsty roots to sip of healing water. Along its shores the children play as children played when He was there. He loved it. He could look across its silvery surface when He spoke His parables. And on a rolling plain not far away He fed the five thousand people.

The River Jordan flows on south into another sea. Here is no splash of fish, no fluttering leaf, no song of birds, no children's laughter. Travelers choose another route, unless on urgent business. The air hangs heavy above its waters, and neither man, nor beast, nor fowl will drink.

What makes this mighty difference in these neighbor seas? Not the River Jordan. It empties the same good water into both. Not the soil on which they lie. Not the country round about.

This is the difference. The Sea of Galilee receives but does not keep the Jordan. For every drop that flows into it, another drop flows out. The giving and receiving go on in equal measure.

The other sea is shrewder, hoarding its income jealously. It will not be tempted into generous impulse. Every drop it gets, it keeps.

The Sea of Galilee gives and lives. The other sea gives nothing. It is named the Dead Sea.

There are two kinds of people in the world.

There are two seas in Palestine.

Only the persons who continue full of life are like the Sea of Galilee, which gives and lives!

> Sail forth! Steer for the deep waters only!
> Reckless, O soul, exploring, I with thee, and thou with me;
> For we are bound where mariner has not yet dared to go,
> And we will risk the ship, ourselves and all.
> O, my brave soul!
> O, farther sail!
> O, daring joy, but safe! Are they not all the seas of God!
> O, farther, farther, farther sail.

Faith must be tested. The ships God builds are sent to sea.
From Christian Triumph

FEBRUARY 9

. . . yet not I, but Christ liveth in me . . . (Gal. 2:20).

I cannot say "our" if I live in a watertight spiritual compartment.
I cannot say "Father" if I do not demonstrate the relationship in
daily life.

I cannot say "which art in heaven" if I am so occupied with the
earth that I am laying up no treasure there.

I cannot say "hallowed be thy name" if I, who am called by His
name, am not holy.

I cannot say "thy kingdom come" if I am not doing all in my
power to hasten its coming.

I cannot say "thy will be done" if I am questioning, resentful of,
or disobedient to His will for me.

I cannot say "in earth, as it is in heaven" if I am not prepared to
devote my life to His service.

I cannot say "give us this day our daily bread" if I am living on
past experience or if I am an under-the-counter shopper.

I cannot say "forgive us our trespasses, as we forgive those who
trespass against us" if I harbor a grudge against anyone.

I cannot say "lead us not into temptation" if I deliberately place
myself in a position to be tempted.

I cannot say "deliver us from evil" if I am not prepared to fight it
in the spiritual realm with the weapon of prayer.

I cannot say "thine is the kingdom" if I do not accord the King
the disciplined obedience of a loyal subject.

I cannot say "thine is the power" if I fear what men may do or
what my neighbors may think.

I cannot say "for ever" if my horizon is bounded by the things
of time.   *From* The Christian Messenger

FEBRUARY 10

*The sacrifices of God are a broken spirit: a broken and a contrite heart, O
God, thou wilt not despise (Ps. 51:17).*

Lord, I have laid my heart upon Thy altar,
But I cannot get the wood to burn;
It is hardly flames ere it begins to falter,
And to the dark return.

Old sap, or night-fallen dew, has dampened the fuel;
In vain my breath would flame provoke.
Yet, see! at every poor attempt's renewal,
To Thee ascends the smoke.

'Tis all I have—smoke, failure, foiled endeavor,
Coldness and doubt and palsied lack;
Such as I have I send Thee, perfect Giver—
Send Thou Thy lightning back!
George MacDonald, from Thoughts for the Thoughtful

Your sacrifice is burning on the altar, and all around you the temple of life is filled with smoke, and no light comes in through the windows, and the very walls you cannot see, but you know where you are; for as long as you suffer you are nigh the altar. That you know, and by that knowledge hold fast. Be quiet, fear not; and be you sure that, when the sacrifice is over, one after the other the windows that open into the infinite—faith and hope— will show themselves, and the air about you will be the clearer and the sweeter for having been so darkened a while.

William Mountford, from Thoughts for the Thoughtful

Laid on Thine Altar, oh my Lord Divine,
Accept my gift this day for Jesus' sake.
I have no jewels to adorn Thy shrine,
Nor any world-famed sacrifice to make.
Yet here I bring within my trembling hand
This will of mine—a thing that seemeth small,
But Thou alone, O Lord, canst understand
How, when I yield Thee this, I yield Thee all.
Hidden therein, Thy searching eye can see
Struggles of passion, visions of delight,
All that I have, and am, and fain would be,
Fond hope, deep love and longing infinite.
It hath been wet with tears and dimmed with sighs,
Clenched in my grasp till beauty it hath none.
Now from Thy footstool, where it vanquished lies,
The prayer ascendeth, "May Thy will be done."
Take It, O Father, ere my courage fail,
And merge it so in Thine own will, that e'en

If in some desperate hour my cries prevail,
And Thou give back my will, it may have been
So changed, so purified, so fair have grown,
So one with Thee, so filled with peace divine,
I may not know it, feel it as mine own,
But gaining back my will, may find it Thine.

Unknown

FEBRUARY 11 _____

Most gladly will I glory in my infirmities (2 Cor. 12:9).

Make allowance for the infirmities of the flesh, which are purely physical. To be fatigued, body and soul, is not sin, to be in "heaviness" is not sin.

Christian life is not a feeling, it is a principle, when your hearts will not fly, let them go, and if they will neither fly nor go be sorry for them and be patient with them, and take them to Christ as you would carry your little lame child to a tenderhearted, skillful surgeon. Does the surgeon, in such a case, upbraid the child for being lame?   *Elizabeth Prentiss*

Three men were walking on a wall,
Feeling, Faith, and Fact,
When Feeling got an awful fall,
And Faith was taken back.
So close was Faith to Feeling,
He stumbled and fell too,
But Fact remained,
And pulled Faith back,
And Faith brought Feeling too.

From The Miracle Hand Around the World

FEBRUARY 12 _____

It is good for me that I have been afflicted (Ps. 119:71).

God, pity those who can not say:
"Not mine, but Thine"; who can pray
"Let this cup pass," and cannot see
The purpose in Gethsemane.   *Unknown*

G od seems to ask greater depths of experience of us as we go along the heavenly pathway. First the water of trial is ankle deep, then knee deep, and later loin deep with waters to swim in. Swimming on top of trouble would never be possible in ankle deep waters. How good that the Lord graduates our trials, which though severe all issue well. *W. M. Wadsworth, D.D.*

One man upon entering the national scene was an expert in experiencing defeat and failure. Had it not been for his determination to serve his fellow countrymen and his God, history would not have recorded him as one of the greatest American presidents. His failures were his victories.

Abraham Lincoln met his first political failure when he lost the seat in the Illinois legislature. Friends persuaded him to venture into business. Failing at this he spent nearly twenty years paying off debts. His next failure was the loss of the young woman he was to marry. He later married a woman who proved to be a "thorn in his side"—another failure for happiness.

Congress was his second political goal. Not only did he miss it, but the United States Land Office and the United States Senate both were claimed by opponents. Most men would lose their courage after so many defeats. But Mr. Lincoln pursued even higher attainments. He believed he could gain the vice presidency in 1856. Failing to take the office he tried once more in 1858 and lost to Douglas.

One failure after another—severe and disastrous failures. Who has not heard of Abraham Lincoln? Yet he is a man *not known* for his failures! *M. Taylor*

"In all things we are more than conquerors through Him that loved us" (Rom. 8:37).

FEBRUARY 13 _____

I know whom I have believed, and am persuaded that he is able to keep that which I have committed unto him against that day (2 Tim. 1:12).

W hen the great chemist, Sir Michael Faraday, was on his deathbed, some journalists questioned him as to his speculations concerning the soul and death. "Speculations!" said the dying man, in astonishment; "I know nothing about speculations; I am resting on certainties!"

> I want the proved certainties
>   To soothe the soul's deep cries;
> And not man's vain philosophies
>   Based only on surmise.
>
> I want a book that is inspired
>   In which to posit faith;
> And not some mutilated scroll,
>   Or literary wraith.
>
> I want the calm assurance of
>   A voice beyond the dust.
> A voice from out eternity
>   In which to place my trust.
>
> For when I come, at eventide,
>   To Jordan's swollen stream,
> I want the tested verities,
>   And not some mystic dream.
>
> This mortal life is far too brief,
>   Eternity too vast,
> To follow human sophistries
>   And lose the soul at last!
>
> Then give me back the Holy Book
>   By inspiration penned;
> I'm through with fabled falsities,
>   And allegoric trend.   *M. D. Clayburn*

If an angel should fly from heaven and inform the saint personally of the Savior's love, the evidence would not be one whit more satisfactory than that which is borne in the heart by the Holy Ghost.   *Spurgeon*

FEBRUARY 14 _____

A friend loveth at all times (Prov. 17:17).

What is the secret of your life?" asked Mrs. Browning of Charles Kingsley. "Tell me, that I may make mine beautiful, too." He replied: "I had a friend."

WHAT IS A FRIEND?

A group of friends were gathered together for a time of social fellowship. The conversation drifted to the subject of friendship and an athlete said: "In my opinion, a friend is a balancing pole that enables us to walk the tightrope of life without falling."

Said a physician, "I believe a friend may be likened to a soft bandage and a soothing ointment for the cuts and bruises of life."

To a botanist it seemed that "a friend is a vine that clings to us and hides the discrepancies and rough places of life;" to which a florist added: "Yes, and the greater the ruin, the closer a friend clings."

"A friend is a golden link in the chain of life," said a jeweler.

A woman in mourning responded, "A friend is one who comes in when the whole world goes out."

"The best friend of all," said a white-haired man of eighty, "is Jesus, who said, 'Greater love hath no man than this, that a man lay down his life for his friends.' "   *From* Illustrated Incidents

Love much. There is no waste in freely giving;
  More blessed is it, even, than to receive.
He who loves much, alone finds life worth living;
  Love on, through doubt and darkness; and believe
There is no thing which Love may not achieve.
Ella Wheeler Wilcox

A friend is one who knows all about you and loves you all the same.   *Charles Kingsley*

You cannot buy a friend. They are God-given and their friendship lasts throughout eternity.

FEBRUARY 15

Whoso hearkeneth unto me shall dwell safely, and shall be quiet from fear of evil (Prov. 1:33).

The Christian faith began among thorny difficulties. It began with an inndoor closed in the face of an unborn Babe. It continued with flashing swords which sought to liquidate the Holy Child. It went on with a flight in the night, as Joseph and Mary sped away to carry their Babe to the safety of distant Egypt. A few years passed, and the breadwinner, Joseph, died, and the Oldest

Son took up the burden of providing for that large family. So the Christian faith went on, through the ranks of the angry, hostile Scribes and Pharisees, through the desertions and denials and betrayals, through Gethsemane to Calvary itself. The Christian way seemed to have a genius for landing in grave difficulty, and an equal genius for overcoming it!

So Christian folk have always felt at home in difficulty. You may remember in the unforgettable *Uncle Remus* stories how Br'er Fox was determined to bring Br'er Rabbit's career to an end. Br'er Rabbit very shrewdly pleaded with the fox not to throw him in the briar patch; let Br'er Fox do anything else to him, but, please, not that! So the fox threw him plumb into the middle of the briar patch, with all its brambles and thorns; and Br'er Rabbit scrambled to his feet, shouting joyfully, "Bred en bawn in de briar patch, Br'er Fox! Bred en bawn in de briar patch!" The fox should have remembered that Br'er Rabbit was quite at home in the difficulties of the briar patch, for he had grown up there.

Someone has said that, if you try to be a Christian, you will always be in difficulties. That is true. You will always be deep in the difficulties of others, because you care enough about them to help them work their way out. You will always be finding yourself on steep paths, because Christ has a way of leading His people up to high joys and far views; and that always takes climbing. But the Christian, like the mountain climber, is at home in difficulties. He loves the far view, the glory of overcoming tough slopes; the thrill of knowing that, with Christ as guide, no difficulty can lick him.
St. Stephen's Protestant Episcopal Church Bulletin

Don't worry. Let us be of good cheer remembering that the misfortunes hardest to bear are those which never come.   *Lowell*

FEBRUARY 16 ————————————————————

. . . For I have learned, in whatsoever state I am, therewith to be content (Phil. 4:11).

> Your time is far too brief
>   For cruel act or words that sting,
> For worthless grief
>   At Fortune's slight.

Let your heart sing!
  'Twill soon be night.

Your days are far too few
  For faulty wish, or deed, that bring
No happiness to you.
  Keep your shield bright,
With Honour ring!
  'Twill soon be night.

Susan Holton

HAVE YOU EVER NOTICED—

When the other fellow acts that way, he is *ugly;* when you do, it is *nerves.*

When the other fellow is set in his ways, he is *obstinate;* when you are, it is just *firmness.*

When the other fellow does not like your friend, he is *prejudiced;* when you do not like his, you simply are showing that you are a *good judge* of human nature.

When the other fellow takes time to do things, he is *dead slow;* when you do, you are *deliberate.*

When the other fellow spends a lot, he is *spendthrift;* when you do, you are *generous.*

When the other fellow picks flaws in things, he is *cranky;* when you do, you are *discriminating.*

When the other fellow is mild in his manners, he is *weak;* when you are, you are being *gracious.*

When the other fellow gets destructive, he is *tough;* when you do, you are *forceful.*

From The King's Highway

FEBRUARY 17

I take pleasure in infirmities, in reproaches, in necessities, in persecutions, in distresses for Christ's sake (2 Cor. 12:10).

It is indeed hard for any person to face infirmities, reproaches, persecutions, or any manner of distress. One must be trained in this type of school. One has to experience over and over again such acts of unkindness against himself to even begin to recognize their coming and cope with them. No victory is an easy victory. Sometimes after facing the warrior for but a moment, it seems an age. For he who wars against us and righteousness is a bitter foe. It takes all the forces of heaven's hosts to combat such evil. When victory comes, we can acclaim with hearts filled to overflowing praise the faithfulness of God's presence through the conflict.

We know that Christ gives victory over suffering. The best that pagan religions of the world and the philosophies of men can offer to those who suffer is a fatalistic resignation and endurance. That army is continually defeated. Who would join forces with it? But Christ offers His constantly abiding presence to those who suffer. His presence enables men to handle the obstacle of suffering with triumph and victory. It was the presence of Christ which enabled Paul and Silas to sing songs of praise at the midnight hour, while bound in stocks and chains in the Philippian jail. It was the presence of Christ which enabled Paul to give a triumphant testimony in the midst of suffering. He says: "Therefore I take pleasure in infirmities, in reproaches, in necessities, in persecutions, in distresses for Christ's sake: for when I am weak, then am I strong." Strong? Yes, because the God of strength is in our ranks.

M. Taylor

O God of the impossible
  When we no hope can see,
Grant us the faith that still believes
  All possible to Thee;

That stands upon Thy Word, Thy Name,
  And will not let Thee go,
Till Thou Thy mighty power hath shown
  Love's blessing to bestow!   *J. H. S.*

FEBRUARY 18

He shall sit as a refiner and purifier of silver . . . and purge them as gold and silver, that they may offer unto the Lord an offering in righteousness (Mal. 3:3).

God is the refiner, the purifier. He tries, proves, and establishes those who yield to His molding. It is a slow process; not hurried. He sits down to His work, He takes plenty of time. He is even willing to wait years with His subject to perfect it into the ideal image. It depends upon content. Some individuals take a long time to learn a single lesson, and the Refiner is perfectly willing to wait until that lesson is learned. Others He will get through with at once, if they are willing to take a quicker process—through the hotter fire.

O what love! How touching that He takes so much trouble with all the little matters. No wonder Job exclaimed: "Lord, what is man that Thou shouldest magnify him? and that Thou shouldest set Thine heart upon him? and that Thou shouldest visit him every morning and try him every moment?" (Job 7:17, 18).

Every moment of every day the great Refiner is waiting to add some new touch to your strength and beauty and fit you for a higher place in His eternal kingdom. So prone is man to think that trials and sufferings are but mere accidents, incidents, mishaps, or personal injuries from personal hands; but after a while, he learns that His hand is above every other hand and His love above every hateful blow. He is molding and making a perfect image.

If the one being tried by fire could understand life as the Heavenly Refiner does, he would see nothing but His hand in every circumstance. If the sufferer could meet the gracious Purifier in every circumstance, he would see nothing but His ever-abiding presence. Every unfriendly blow of the hammer would be warded off if the one being beaten down would have a shield of faith that nothing can pierce. Out of every fiery trial he could shout with the great Apostle, "None of these things move me." Beloved, they will come until they don't move you. "For unto you it is given in the behalf of Christ, not only to believe on Him, but also to suffer for His sake" (Phil. 1:29). "That He might present to himself a glorious church, not having spot or wrinkle or any such thing, but that it should be Holy and without blemish" (Eph. 5:27). "Not as though I had already attained, . . . I press toward the mark" (Phil. 3:12, 14).
                                                                    M. Taylor

> My life was like an uncut gem
>   All rough and angles sharp,
> Its brilliance dimmed as by a veil
>   No gleam or sheen, all dark.
> But the Master's hand worked miracles,
>   Each pain and woe or trial or test
> A facet cut upon my soul,
>   He watched the work and blest.
>
> And even when it seemed to me
>   No other facet could He add
> That pain and suffering had wrought
>   A gleam and sheen that made Him glad.

Still other processes there were
   To polish, and the gem to set,
For now become a gleaming jewel rare,
   I must be made ready for His service yet.
                                    Mabel M. Brown

FEBRUARY 19 _____

. . . in quietness and in confidence shall be your strength (Isa. 30:15).

Do you know what Luther said? "Suffer and be still and tell no man thy sorrow; trust in God—His help will not fail thee." This is what Scripture calls keeping silent before God. To talk much of one's sorrows makes one weak, but to tell one's sorrows to Him who heareth in secret, makes one strong and calm.
                                    Tholuck

   The little sharp vexations
      And the briars that catch and fret,
   Why not take all to the Helper
      Who has never failed us yet?
   Tell Him about the heartache,
      And tell Him the longings, too;

   Tell Him the baffled purpose
      When we scarce know what to do.
   Then, leaving all our weakness
      With the One divinely strong,
   Forget that we bore the burden,
      And carry away the song.   *Margaret Sangster*

FEBRUARY 20 _____

And the work of righteousness shall be peace; and the effect of righteousness quietness and assurance for ever (Isa. 32:17).

Your life needs days of retirement, when it shuts the gates upon the noisy whirl of action and is alone with God.

   I need wide spaces in my heart
   Where faith and I can go apart
   And grow serene.

Life gets so choked by busy living,
Kindness so lost in fussy giving,
That love slips by unseen.

I want to make a quiet place
Where those I love can see God's face,
Can stretch their hearts across the earth.
Can understand what spring is worth,
Can count the stars,
Watch violets grow,
And learn what birds and children know. *Selected*

The most tempestuous wind cannot disturb the quiet serenity of
the stars. *Unknown*

The world is too much with us; late and soon,
Getting and spending, we lay waste our powers:
Little we see in nature that is ours;
We have given our hearts away, a sordid boon!
William Wordsworth

FEBRUARY 21 _____

I will bless the Lord at all times (Ps. 34:1).

The twin keys that unlock the doors to His treasure chest:
PRAISE and PRAYER! Keys that open the windows of
heaven and let the showers of heaven descend! Oh, the power of
prayer and praise! It can open every prison door and set the
prisoners free. What it did for Peter and Paul and Silas it can do for
us no matter where that confinement may be.

Show me a more wretched captive than a worrying Christian
whose song has been stilled by Satan. The song of praise and the
voice of prayer would open the prison for him, even though it be
midnight in the soul.

To the natural man "In nothing be anxious; but in everything by
prayer and supplication with thanksgiving" may seem an impossible injunction. But the Christian is a supernatural man: "Christ
liveth in me."

"By prayer and supplication with thanksgiving" (Phil. 4:6).

We do not understand that we are to give thanks for evil in itself, but we may offer praise for the overruling of it for good. Again, many things that we regard as misfortunes are blessings. Trials and crosses are often among the greatest blessings in disguise, for it is only through such disciplinary processes that the character is perfected. When we consider that the disagreeable is indispensable enrichment and strengthening of character, we see that we should offer thanks for this phase of experience, as well as the agreeable. What a change would be wrought in our lives if we thus acted!

George Matheson, the well-known blind preacher of Scotland, now with the Lord, said: "My God, I have never thanked Thee for my 'thorn!' I have thanked Thee a thousand times for my roses, but never once for my 'thorn'; I have been looking forward to a world where I shall get compensation for my cross, but I have never thought of my cross as itself a present glory. Teach me the glory of my cross; teach me the value of my 'thorn.' Show me that I have climbed to Thee by the path of pain. Show me that my tears have made my rainbow." *From* Pittsburgh Christian Advocate

FEBRUARY 22

Therefore all things whatsoever ye would that men should do to you, do ye even so to them (Matt. 7:12).

This universal language is the *language of action.* I understand that you have a kind heart, because your kindness takes shape in a friendly letter or deed—I can *see* your kindness. I understand how much you love your family because your love for them takes form in hard-working devotion to their needs. In the same way we come to know the love of God. For long centuries God in His wisdom spoke to men through words, on the lips of prophets and priests and sages and saints, and men could not be sure what God was like. Then when they were ready, He spoke to them in a new way: "And the word was made flesh, and dwelt among us, and we beheld his glory, full of grace and truth." God's love took form in a life which we could *see,* in a death upon a cross which we *beheld;* and ever since then, men have said, "God is like Jesus Christ. God's love is like the cross." This was the "incarnation," taking shape in flesh before the eyes of people. God had spoken, at last, in the universal language of action!

George Washington, one day, had a tempting opportunity to preach a sermon on loving your neighbor. He was riding across the farmlands with a company of gentlemen, when the last horse over a stone fence knocked over a number of stones, leaving a large opening. Washington suggested that they stop and repair it, but the others shrugged their shoulders; so he said nothing more, and rode on with them. When the party disbanded, one of them, riding homeward, found Washington back at the farmer's fence, carefully replacing the stones. "Oh, General," chattered the man, "You are too big a man to be doing a thing like that." "No," answered Washington, gravely inspecting his work, "I'm just the right size." Washington was preaching his sermon in the universal language of action. Words would have bored the farmer no end, but that deed of neighborliness spoke for itself.

If you want, with all your heart, to tell someone that you love them, say as little as possible about it, and show them in loving deeds.　　　　*St. Stephen's Protestant Episcopal Church Bulletin*

FEBRUARY 23

As dying and behold we live (2 Cor. 6:9).

I had a bed of asters last summer, that reached clear across my garden in the country. Oh, how gaily they bloomed. They were planted late. On the sides were yet fresh blossoming flowers, while the tops had gone to seed. Early frosts came, and I found one day that that long line of radiant beauty was seared, and I said, "Ah! the season is too much for them; they have perished"; and I bade them farewell.

I disliked to go and look at the bed, it looked so like a graveyard of flowers. But, four or five weeks ago one of my men called my attention to the fact that along the whole line of that bed there were asters coming up in the greatest abundance; and I looked, and behold, for every plant that I thought the winter had destroyed there were fifty plants that it had planted. What did those frosts and surly winds do?

They caught my flowers, they slew them, they cast them to the ground, they trod with snowy feet upon them, and they said, leaving their work, *This is the end of you.* And the next spring there were for every root, fifty witnesses to rise up and say, *By death we live.*

And as it is in the floral tribe, so it is in God's kingdom. By death came everlasting life. By crucifixion and the sepulchre came the throne and the palace of the eternal God. By overthrow came victory.

Do not be afraid to suffer. Do not be afraid to be overthrown.

It is by being cast down and not destroyed; it is by being shaken to pieces, and the pieces torn to shreds, that men become men of might, and that one a host; whereas men that yield to the appearance of things, and go with the world, have their quick blossoming, their momentary prosperity and then their end, which is an end forever.   *Beecher*

> Measure thy life by loss and not by gain,
> Not by the wine drunk, but by the wine poured forth.
> For love's strength standeth in love's sacrifice,
> And he who suffers most has most to give.   *Unknown*

FEBRUARY 24

My soul, wait thou only upon God (Ps. 62:5).

A Christian man of intense business enterprise and activity was laid aside by sickness. He who never would intermit his labors was compelled to come to a dead halt. His restless limbs were stretched motionless on the bed. He was so weak that he could scarcely utter a word. Speaking to a friend of the contrast between his condition now and when he had been driving his immense business, he said, "Now I am growing. I have been running my soul thin by my activity, now I am growing in the knowledge of myself and of some things which most intimately concern me." No doubt there are many of us who are running our souls thin by our incessant action without finding quiet hours for feeding and waiting upon God.

Blessed, then, is sickness or sorrow or any experience that compels us to stop, that takes the work out of our hands for a little season, that empties our hearts of their thousand cares, and turns them toward God to be taught of Him.

But why should we wait for sickness or sorrow to *compel* into our lives these necessary quiet hours? Would it not be far better for us to train ourselves to go apart each day for a little season from the noisy, chilling world, to look into God's face and into our own hearts, to learn the things we need so much to learn, and to draw secret strength and life from the fountain of life in God? George Herbert's quaint lines contain wise counsel:

> By all means use sometimes to be alone;
>   Salute thyself, see what thy soul doth wear.
> Dare to look in thy closet—for 'tis thine own—
>   And tumble up and down what thou findest there.

With these sacred silent times in every day of toil and struggle, we shall be always strong, and "prepared unto every good work." Waiting thus upon God, we shall daily renew our wasted strength, and be able to run and not be weary, to walk and not be faint, and to mount up with wings as eagles in bold spiritual flights.

J. R. Miller, Silent Times, *1886*

FEBRUARY 25

In all thy ways acknowledge him . . . (Prov. 3:6).

A wise man has written, "The word 'Christian' means something . . . When a man calls himself a 'Christian,' he means that he admits Christ into every area of his life"—even into his recreation.

Jack Miner at Kingsville, Ontario had founded a bird sanctuary there in 1904, where he fed, protected, and cared for bird life, especially the wild ducks and geese. Then in 1909 he began "banding" them—placing a very light, numbered metal band around the leg of each bird. Later on, when one of them was shot down, or hurt, many miles away, the person who discovered the band would send it back to Jack Miner. Hundreds of these bands came back through the mail, and a vast fund of knowledge was obtained about the migration routes and habits of wild fowl. This was Jack Miner's recreation—he banded birds because he enjoyed it. Then in 1914 he had a brand new idea: "Early one morning, like a star shooting across the heavens, God's radio—or God's guidance, if you want to call it that—said to me, 'Stamp verses of Scripture on the blank side of your bird-bands.' From the very first time I stamped such a verse on a band, I felt the help of God, and knew I now had my tagging system complete."

So, the following spring, he began. A hunter, who had shot down a duck in the South, found the bird-band with Jack Miner's name and address and on the inside, "Mark 11:28"; and, looking it up in his New Testament, read, "Have faith in God." A man, serving time in prison in Arkansas, noticed the incident in a newspaper story, and thus started reading his Testament. Sportsmen, as the years went on, wrote Jack Miner that their lives had been changed by the Bible passages his bird-bands had directed them to. And a missionary deep in the Hudson Bay country came out, for the first time in twenty-six years, to tell Mr. Miner that these bird-bands had stirred up a new awakening of faith in the Indians and Eskimos who came in to have the missionary interpret the messages. Jack Miner commented, "My bird sanctuary would never have been what it is, nor have gained world recognition, had I not taken God into partnership, and given Him first place." He had let God into his recreation.

St. Stephen's Episcopal Church Bulletin

FEBRUARY 26 _____

Verily, verily, I say unto you, that ye shall weep and lament . . . and ye shall be sorrowful, but your sorrow shall be turned into joy (John 16:20).

Sorrows are too precious to be wasted. That great man of God in a past generation, Alexander MacLaren of Manchester, used to bring out this overlooked truth. He reminded God's people that sorrows will, if we let them, "blow us to His breast," as a strong wind might sweep a man into some refuge from itself. I am sure there are many who can thankfully attest that they were brought nearer to God by some short, sharp sorrow than by long days of prosperity. Take care that you do not waste your sorrows; that you do not let the precious gifts of disappointment, pain, loss, loneliness, ill health, or similar afflictions that come into your daily life mar you instead of mending you. See that they send you nearer to God, and not that they drive you further from Him."

Sorrows are God's winds, His contrary winds. Sometimes His strong winds. They are God's hurricanes. They take human life and lift it to higher levels and toward God's heavens. You have seen in the summertime, a day, when the atmosphere was oppressive. You could hardly breathe it was so unbearable. But when a cloud appeared on the horizon and grew larger and then threw out that blessing for the world, the storm rose, lightning flashed and thunder pealed. The storm covered the world and immediately the atmosphere was cleaned; new life was in the air and the world was changed. Human life is worked out according to exactly the same principle, and when the storm breaks the atmosphere is changed, clarified, filled with new life and a part of heaven is brought down to earth.   *Mrs. Charles E. Cowman*

I take this pain, Lord Jesus,
    From Thine own hand;
The strength to bear it bravely
    Thou wilt command.
I am too weak for effort,
    So let me rest
In hush of sweet submission
    On Thine own breast.

I take this pain, Lord Jesus,
    As proof indeed
That Thou art watching closely
    My truest need;
That Thou, my Good Physician,
    Art working still;
That all Thine own good pleasure
    Thou wilt fulfill.

'Tis Thy dear hand, O Saviour!
    That presseth sore;
The hand that bears the nail-prints
    Forevermore.
And now beneath its shadow,
    Hidden by Thee,
The pressure only tells me
    Thou lovest me.   *Anonymous,* At the Beautiful Gate, *1879*

FEBRUARY 27 ―――――――――――――――――――――――――――――

Great and marvellous are thy works, Lord God Almighty . . . (Rev. 15:3).

The heavens declare the glory of God; and the firmament sheweth His handywork (Ps. 19:1).

I will praise thee; for I am fearfully and wonderfully made: marvellous are thy works; and that my soul knoweth right well (Ps. 139:14).

God is great in great things, but *very* great in little things," says Henry Dyer. "A party stood on the Matterhorn admiring the sublimity of the scene, when a gentle man produced a pocket microscope, and having caught a fly, placed it under the glass. He reminded us that the legs of the household fly in England were naked, then called attention to the legs of this little fly, which were thickly covered with hair, thus showing that the same God who had made the lofty Swiss mountains had also attended to the comfort of His tiniest creatures, even producing *socks* and *mittens* for the little fly whose home these mountains were. This *God* is *our* God!"

> For the love of God is broader
> Than the measure of man's mind;
> And the heart of the Eternal
> Is most wonderfully kind.   *Frederick W. Faber*

All through the Bible there is a wonderful care of little things, God noticing them and bringing them to perfectness of meaning. "He putteth my tears in his bottle"; that is condescension. "None of his steps shall slide," as if He numbered step by step all the going of His people. One of those people said, "Thou knowest my downsitting and mine uprising," and "Thou hast beset me behind and before."   *Joseph Parker*

FEBRUARY 28 _____

For it became Him . . . to make the captain of their salvation perfect through suffering (Heb. 2:10).

The subject of human suffering is ever of the keenest interest to people generally, and questions regarding it are quite the order of the day. Its effects are so universal and results so often perplexing. Thankfully, we can turn to the Word for some light to aid in discovering at least partial explanation.

Three types of suffering appear to be quite clearly defined in the Scriptures: penal, disciplinary, and vicarious. Penal suffering is, of course, the result of evil or wrongdoing. Disciplinary suffering is usually the lot of the righteous and tends to temper and sweeten the soul. In Hebrews 12:5–11, the apostle refers to a chastening process obviously aimed at bringing us into line with the will of God.

Vicarious suffering doubtless lifts the soul to its highest plane of devotion. It is rare in comparison, but certainly not beyond human reach, or impossible to them that are willing and can be trusted with it. We have known husbands to suffer because of unsaved wives; wives for husbands; parents for children, and children for parents. It is not at all uncommon to learn of loved ones being drawn to Christ, or a more chastened Christian life because of the suffering of someone near and dear. Herein is revealed the suffering of our Lord as to its purpose and nature. How grateful we should be to discover someone cared enough to suffer.

Rev. H. L. Thatcher

FEBRUARY 29

Now when I am old and greyheaded, O God, forsake me not; until I have shewed thy strength unto this generation, and thy power to every one that is to come (Ps. 71:18).

In all walks of life are to be found the aged, who for positive achievement, or as conquerors over disability and circumstances, wear ever on their brows the laurel leaves of conquest. They are still men and women of affairs; they have not dropped out of the arena of active life, or, if so, yet wield influence that tells upon life, whether spiritual, moral, or mental. Here and there one thus stands out—a weather-beaten rock that has withstood the storms and ravages of time.

Whose life is thus fraught with usefulness and purpose, it can never be said to be lived in vain.

Emerson remarks, "We do not count a man's years until he has nothing else to count." Let us not live in past decades, but in an intense present, buying up the fast diminishing opportunities that yet remain to us for Christ-witness, holy living, privileged service, as this our attitude, "Lord use me, even me." Our life assets may only be five loaves and two small fishes, but in the Master's hands such things have ways of multiplying. And, in watering others, we are watered; in feeding others, we are fed; in blessing others, we are blessed; and in so doing we take fresh lease on life:

Because heaven is in us to bud and unfold,
We are younger for growing old.

Then—

Because of the beauty the years unfold,
We are cheerfully growing old.

Because of the glory the years unfold,
We are joyfully growing old.

Because of the peace the years unfold,
We are thankfully growing old.

Why give in to years while the springs of life are strong within us, and we are still capable of achievement?

Gertrude Cockerell, from the tract The Last Decade *1914*

MARCH 1

And he shall be as the light of the morning, when the sun riseth, even a morning without clouds (2 Sam. 23:4).

When the mists have rolled in splendor
  From the beauty of the hills,
And the sunlight falls in gladness
  On the river and the rills,
We recall our Father's promise
  In the rainbow of the spray:
We shall know each other better
  When the mists have rolled away.

We shall come with joy and gladness,
  We shall gather round the throne,
Face to face with those that love us
  We shall know as we are known:
And the song of our redemption
  Shall resound thro' endless day
When the shadows have departed
  And the mists have rolled away.   *Annie Herbert*

Fog in one's spiritual life need be no more lasting than that in nature. "It will burn off before long." How often weatherwise people say this when the gray mists of the seashore depress the hearts that were longing for a bright day; and so it proves. A glow of silver in the sky near the sun, a thinning out here and there of the vapory shroud; glimpses of blue, clean outlining and swift sailing away of the clouds, and the fine clear day is here long before noon. We might oftener save ourselves from heavy hearts and gloomy faces, when early morning shows gray in our lives or other lives about us. Mists are left over from a storm yesterday. The day closed on a misunderstanding. The morning is foggy and depressing. Why talk about it? Let the weather alone. Fog is shallow. It will burn off before long. There is a good warm sun of love at work, and the blue sky will soon be over us.

Maltbie Davenport Babcock
from Thoughts for Everyday Living

MARCH 2 ───────────────────────────

That ye study to be quiet . . . (1 Thess. 4:11).

Be silent . . . before the Lord (Zech. 2:13).

Have you not wondered, you who treasure the inspired verse and moving prose, from whence came these creations of hope, faith, love, courage, solace? J. R. Miller, a great man with an inspired pen, proclaims it is not an easy road. "It is only in the valley of silence with Christ that we can dream the dreams and see the visions which we desire to translate into actual life and character among men. There alone can we get the heavenly inspirations and impulses for holy earthly living. Only in the mount can we be shown the patterns of the sacred things which our hands should fashion in this world."

> In the hush of the valley of silence
>   I dream all the songs that I sing;
> And the music floats down the dim valley,
>   Till each finds a word for a wing,
> That to hearts, like the dove of the deluge,
>   A message of peace they may bring.
>
> But far on the deep there are billows
>   That never shall break on the beach;
> And I have heard songs in the silence
>   That never shall float into speech;
> And I have had dreams in the valley
>   Too lofty for language to reach.

And I have seen thoughts in the valley—
　　Ah me, how my spirit was stirred!
And they wear holy veils on their faces,
　　Their footsteps can scarcely be heard;
They pass through the valley like virgins,
　　Too pure for the touch of a word.

Do you ask me that place of the valley,
　　Ye hearts that are harrowed by care?
It lieth afar between mountains,
　　And God and His angels are there:
One is the dark mountain of sorrow,
　　And one the bright mountain of prayer.　　　*Unknown*

A converted slave trader, John Newton distilled his life's perfume into:

Amazing grace, how sweet the sound
That saved a wretch like me!

Pilgrim's Progress was not dashed off in a plush penthouse suite.

A broken heart guided Joseph Scriven's pen to exclaim:

What a friend we have in Jesus,
All our sins and griefs to bear!

That the Holy Spirit lives and breathes through the deep devotional writing of Oswald Chambers is no accident. His short forty-one years were spent in reckless abandonment to God; his stature of spiritual gianthood dearly bought.

God seems to exact as His price of "best-selling" writing success a diploma from His grueling school of experience. Courses are: discipline, suffering, faith, tests, and self-examination.　　*Selected*

Bruised, jostled, and mobbed, Charles Wesley sought refuge in a milkhouse and wrote:

Jesus, Lover of my soul,
Let me to Thy bosom fly,

Other refuge have I none,
　　Hangs my helpless soul on Thee.

67

I sought the Lord, and He heard me, and delivered me from all my fears (Ps. 34:4).

S ome naturalists were searching in the Alps for rare specimens of flowers. They saw an unusually interesting one a way down in a terrible precipitous canyon. It was on a little ledge of rocks very hard to get to. The only way was by means of a lifeline. They spied a shepherd boy over on the mountains. They called to him and held out some bright new coins and told the boy if he would allow them to put a lifeline about him and let him down to where he could reach and get the flower they would give him the coins.

He looked at those coins; oh, how he wanted them—then peered down into the deep cavern; then up into the strange faces. Then shook his head. It was a real struggle. He wanted the coins desperately. But the cliff was dangerous. The men were strangers. Again and again he took the full survey. The canyon, the coins, how his eyes did snap when he thought of having those coins as his very own; then up into the strange faces, only to again shake his head. All at once he had a thought. He ran across the mountainside and entered a mountain home. Soon he emerged with a great, strong, kindly man. Evidently it was his father. He had hold of his hand and was so eager for him to hasten that he almost dragged him along. Finally when almost at the edge of the cliff the boy ran up to the strangers and said, "You may tie the lifeline under my arms now. I will go down into the canyon—*if you let my father hold the rope.*"

Yes, yes!—down into the valley of sorrow if that must be; down into the gorge of pain; we can safely go anywhere if our loving Heavenly Father holds the rope.

No. 1436, Quests and Conquests

Prayer is the lifeline in God's blessed hands. "The Lord hath heard the voice of my weeping and has heard my supplication; the Lord will receive my prayer" (Ps. 6:8, 9).

He that dwelleth in the secret place of the most High shall abide under the shadow of the Almighty (Ps. 91:1).

A story appeared sometime ago in the *Congressional Record*. It suggests that "Whoso dwelleth under the defense of the Most High shall abide under the shadow of the Almighty." A nineteen-year-old G. I. who had been awarded a medal for bringing in a large group of Japanese prisoners, single-handed, during World War II tells his own story:

"I want someone to know that I don't deserve that medal. It happened this way. I was captured by the Japanese, with five of my pals. We were marched through the jungle with bayonets at our backs. I had to see my comrades one by one killed and mutilated. I said the 23rd Psalm. I said the Lord's Prayer. Die I must, but I determined not to let my captors see my fear. Trembling from head to foot, marching in mud up to my ankles, with a bayonet sticking in my back, I began to whistle the way I used to when I was a small boy, and had to go through a dark street. So I whistled, 'We gather together to ask the Lord's blessing; He chastens and hastens His will to make known; the wicked oppressing cease then from distressing, sing praises to His name, He forgets not His own.'

"Suddenly I became aware that someone had joined me in my whistling—it was my Japanese captor! He, too, was whistling the hymn. Soon I felt his gun fall back into place. He walked beside me then, and suddenly I jumped when, in perfect English, he said to me, 'I never cease to wonder at the magnificence of Christian hymns.' And a few minutes talk revealed that the Japanese soldier had learned English in a mission school to which I had contributed in my Sunday school days. The Japanese boy spoke of war and how the Japanese Christians hated it. We both agreed on the power of Christianity, and what would happen if people really dared to live it; and then we began to talk of our families and our homes. Finally, at the suggestion of the Japanese, we knelt in the mud and prayed for suffering humanity around the world, and for 'His peace that passeth understanding' among all men on earth.

"When we arose, he asked me if I could take him back as a prisoner to the American headquarters. He said that it was the only way that he could live up to his Christianity, and thus help Japan to become a Christian nation; and on the way back he found in various foxholes other Japanese Christians, and they too joined me. I shall never forget the hope and joy that came into their eyes as my friend unfolded to them, one by one, how we found each other, and why and where they were being taken. All the way back we talked of the Christian religion. When we neared camp, by mutual agreement they put on poker-faces and somber looks, and I, gun in hand, marched them into camp. So you see I don't deserve a medal for the most wonderful experience in my life."   *St. Stephen's Protestant Episcopal Church Bulletin*

MARCH 5

Thou hast put gladness in my heart (Ps. 4:7).

The glad heart maketh a cheerful countenance (Prov. 15:13).

> I had a friendly smile, I gave that smile away.
> The postman and the milkman seemed glad of it each day.
> I gave my smile away as happy as could be.
> And every time I gave it, my smile came back to me.

> Smile a smile!
> While you smile
> Another smiles,
> And soon there are miles
> And miles of smiles,
> And life's worthwhile
> If you but smile.   *Anon.*

It would be foolish to think that all who smile are happy.

There are "smiles" and "smiles"—smiles self-conscious, smiles self-complacent, smiles conceited, smiles sarcastic, smiles superficial, smiles satanic, smiles cynical, smiles critical, smiles occasional, smiles habitual, smiles spiritual. There are smiles good, smiles better, and smiles best. Each sort has its own peculiar value. It is the "best" sort of smiles we advocate. The "best" sort go deepest, last longest, and accomplish most good.

The best kind of smiles are not "put on." They "come out" because they are "in." They are the result of a satisfied, thankful, and glad heart. They are the exterior expression of an interior joy, which glows and grows as the days go by.

It is the satisfied and restful heart that makes a radiant face. When we are contented at the center, the countenance will be calmly cheerful. When the spirit is satisfied and glad, the glory is expressed in look and touch and tone.

Christ is the secret, the source, the substance, the center, and the circumference of all true and lasting gladness.

MARCH 6

. . . And her countenance was no more sad (1 Sam. 1:18).

They shall not sorrow any more at all (Jer. 31:12, 13).

To be "no more sad." Is this possible? If this be possible, then "Why art thou cast down, O my soul?" (Ps. 42:5). "Why?" It is good to get to the bottom of our troubles and our griefs. Get to the very bottom. To understand their cause is well on the way to their cure. We shall not reduce very much our sadness until we have discovered and dislodged its source.

The basic cause of our sadness is not in our circumstances. It is in ourselves. And there the remedy must be applied. We can receive much encouragement from this fact, for circumstances may be beyond our power to alter, but we may personally appropriate and apply a remedy to our "souls."

When the psalmist put the question to his soul, he discovered the cause for his deep grief. He found the trouble not so much in the severity of the conditions around him, as in the darkness that pervaded his own soul. He had lost sight of God. His heart was heavy and overcast by the "waves and billows" (Ps. 42:7), by "the oppression of the enemy" (v. 9), and by what people said (v. 10). Preoccupied with these, the vision and the experience of God's presence were obliterated. His "uplook" was obscured by his "outlook." He felt forsaken and undone and he was "sad."

O my soul, this too is the true cause of all thy grief and gloom. The sense of God's presence has been lost. The vision of Him has been obscured.

When God is introduced into the sorrow of our circumstances, and our eyes see Him, then sadness goes. "In His presence is the fulness of joy" (Ps. 16:11). "God is Light and in Him is no darkness at all" (1 John 1:5). It is when God is out of sight, and we are "out of touch" that the soul sinks into sadness, depression, and despair.

God is the universal dispeller of all gloom, and the glorious dispenser of all gladness in the soul.   *B. M'Call Barbour*

So mightily grew the word of God and prevailed (Acts 19:21).

It was an impressive city, standing proudly there on the Cayster River, back from the coast of the Icarian Sea, great-wharfed, geographically located to make it an emporium of Asia. Ephesus was the crossroads of commerce, the melting pot of mankind. Here milled the faces from a hundred lands. Here walked the magicians and the sorcerers who filled the people with awe. Big town, capital of Ionis, called "the first metropolis of Asia." Here in Ionic glory rose one of the seven wonders of the world, the temple of Diana, with its hundred marble monoliths, exhibiting the art of Phidias and Scopas and Apeles; and later there was the great theater that would seat nearly 25,000 people. Ephesus, city of wealth and culture and power; and into it came a disciple of Jesus on scuffed sandals, a man named Paul. He found a handful of Christians and he persuaded them to make a full surrender to the Holy Spirit, and to deepen their spiritual experiences. Out of this there came an awakening to truth that jarred the great city. Demetrius rose in defense of Diana, and the mobs cried out—but the gospel was planted securely in Ephesus!

Great was the history of Ephesus; countless nationalities walked through its streets; kings rode there and conquerors and merchant-chiefs and magic-makers; but nothing ever happened to it comparable to what happened when the gospel invaded it! Diana is gone, and the temples, and the commerce; the desert blankets the Ephesian glory; but the gospel that flowed forth from there still blesses the world! It's big news for any big town when Christ's Word comes in to stir it! *Lon Woodrum*

"For this cause also thank we God without ceasing, because, when ye received the word of God which ye heard of us, ye received it not as the word of men, but, as it is in truth, the word of God, which effectually worketh also in you that believe" (1 Thess. 2:13).

God was in Christ, reconciling the world unto Himself (2 Cor. 5:19).

There is on record a story of how a tribe of North American Indians who roamed in the neighborhood of Niagara offered year by year a young virgin as a sacrifice to the spirit of the mighty river.

She was called "the bride of the falls."

The lot fell one year on a beautiful girl who was the only daughter of an old chieftain. The news was carried to him while he was sitting in his tent; but on hearing it, the old man went on smoking his pipe, and said nothing of what he felt.

On the day fixed for the sacrifice a white canoe, full of ripe fruits, and decked with beautiful flowers, was ready, waiting to receive "the bride."

At the appointed hour she took her place in the frail bark, which was pushed out into midstream, where it would be carried swiftly toward the mighty cataract.

Then, to the amazement of the crowd which had assembled to watch the sacrifice, a second canoe was seen to dart out from the river's bank a little lower down the stream.

In it was seated the old chieftain.

With swift strokes he paddled toward the canoe in which was his beloved child, and, on reaching it, he gripped it firmly, and held it fast.

The eyes of both met in one last long look of love; and then, close together, father and daughter were carried by the racing current until they plunged over the thundering cataract and perished side by side.

In their death they were not divided.

The father was "in it" with his child!

"God was in Christ, reconciling the world unto Himself." He did not have to. Nobody forced Him. The only force behind that sacrifice was the force of His seeking love for His lost world.

Selected

Let us ponder, believe, and gladly follow, in His steps, into sacrificial service.

MARCH 9 ——————————————————————————

. . . For I know whom I have believed . . . (2 Tim. 1:12).

A most unusual incident occurred in colorful Mexico City a few years ago. A famous artist had painted a beautiful picture, and it was being displayed upon the walls of a new ultramodern hotel. The scene was of one of the charming beauty spots of the country landscape. It depicted with lucid clarity the rolling country landscape, quiet fields, purling streams, and a touch of virgin forest, carpeted with gorgeous flowers.

Across the top of the canvas four words were painted which stood out in bold outline. They were these: "God Does Not Exist." A strange bit of lettering to be found on such a famous work of art!

Spellbound visitors surged past the painting every day.

One evening a large group of young men entered the lobby of the hotel and made their way down the corridor to the room that housed the painting. They quietly and calmly removed paint cans and brushes from kits strapped to their shoulders and were soon busily at work. No one but those in the room could see what was going on; the air was freighted with suspense. Suddenly they stepped back and again the throng pressing against the doorway caught a glimpse of the masterpiece. At first they could see no change, but continued scrutiny revealed that three words in the caption had been brushed completely from the canvas—and what were the words? "Does Not Exist." One word remained—"God."

The group quietly, but with the stride of conquerors, left the hotel. The onlookers stared in awe. Under the soft lights which were thrown upon the picture, that one glorious word was emblazoned—it shone like a brilliant in a monarch's crown.

More than anything else that may be needed—more than changed conditions, more than release from pressure—is a vigorous faith in God: a rediscovery of Him who knows the paths of a hundred million stars and knows the way through every valley of difficulty and over every mountain of trial. Renew confidence in God; rediscover God, the mighty God—a match for mighty needs!

Mrs. Charles E. Cowman

MARCH 10 _____

The harvest truly is plenteous, but the laborers are few (Matt. 9:37).

Tragedy had struck at the very heart of the British Empire—one of her favorite sons lay still in death. The Duke of Wellington, once invincible in battle, now lay lifeless in the great hall, surrounded only by those vigilant sentries who maintained their final watch.

Dignitaries journeyed from every dominion and protectorate to pay tribute to their fallen hero and statesman, and a special section was established in the great cathedral for the chosen representative of every military unit of the vast colonial army—every regiment of every country flying the Union Jack would stand in final homage to their great leader.

One of the greatest imperatives of the gospel rings with undisguised urgency as it expresses the supreme wish of the Savior to be represented in His great kingdom by members of every tribe and nation. The Master gave vivid expression of the burning desire as He stood on the verdant mountain high above glimmering Galilee and spoke the words that have dominated Christian thought for centuries: "Go ye therefore, and teach all nations . . ."

A cry from the heart of black slaves reached the throne of God. Dark Africa stretched forth her dusky hands beseeching Him for help. God heard, but to answer their cry for help He needed a human voice. An angel could not carry to the black man the sweet story of the matchless love of God. A young Scotchman sat at his loom weaving when he heard a faint cry—a cry as of pain. He heard it in the stillness of the night; he heard it through the cacophonies of daytime city life. Should he leave home and friends to bury himself amid Africa's wilds? The whole wide world knows the answer, for David Livingstone gave of himself on Africa's soil. The harvest of his life may be seen in the countless multitude of Africa's sons and daughters who have been "transformed into His likeness."

The Lord of the harvest wanted to sow a great field with living seeds in age-old China. He needed a sower. One Sunday morning He found Hudson Taylor walking by the seashore. He spoke to him saying, "If you will let Me, I will walk all over China through you." On that day of days a grain of wheat fell into the ground and died. Multiplied thousands of living grains are the result.

Mrs. Charles E. Cowman

The things that are to us too hard,
The foes that are too strong,
Are just the very ones that may
Awake a triumph song.

J. H. S.

MARCH 11

Hence forth I call you not servants . . . but I have called you friends (John 15:15).

I would converse with Thee from day to day,
With heart intent on what Thou hast to say,
And through my pilgrim-walk, whate'er befall,
Consult with Thee, O Lord! about it all.
Since Thou art willing thus to condescend
To be my intimate, familiar friend,
Oh! let me to the great occasion rise,
And count Thy friendship life's most glorious prize!

In the New Testament the Christian's relation to Christ is represented as a personal acquaintance with Him. This acquaintance ripens into a close and tender friendship. A friendship such as this is our Lord's own ideal of discipleship. He invited men to come to Him. He asked them to break other ties and attach themselves personally to Him. Those invited were to leave all and go with Him. He must be first in the affections of His followers. He claimed full allegiance of their hearts and lives. He must be first in their obedience and in their service. Christ offered Himself to men, not only as a helper from without, not merely as one who would save them by taking their sins and dying for them, but as one who desired to form with them a close, intimate, and indissoluble friendship. It was not a tie of duty merely, or of obligation, or of doctrine, or of cause, by which He sought to bind His followers to Himself, but a tie of personal friendship.

J. R. Miller

MARCH 12

. . . and unto God would I commit my cause: which doeth great things and unsearchable; marvellous things without number (Job 5:8, 9).

76

God never gives all He has to give. The time never comes when He has nothing more to bestow. The child of God never reaches the best in divine blessings. There is always something better yet to come. Every door that opens into a treasury of love shows another door into another treasury beyond. Christian, never fear that you shall come to the end of God's goodness, or to any experience for which He will have no blessing ready.

God laid up goodness in the creation and preparation of the earth. Before man was made, God was fitting up this world to be his home, storing in mountain, hill, and plain, in water, air, and soil, and in all nature's treasuries, supplies for every human need. Think, for example, of the vast beds of coal laid up among earth's strata, ages and ages since, in order that our homes might be warmed and brightened in these later centuries; of the iron, silver, gold, and other metals secreted in the veins of the rocks; of the medicinal and healing virtues stored in leaf, root, fruit, bark, and mineral; and of all the latent forces and properties lodged in nature, to be called out from time to time to minister to human wants. It was divine forethought that laid up all this goodness for the welfare of God's children.

The same is true of spiritual provisions. In the covenant of the love of God, in the infinite ages of the past, He laid up goodness for men. Redemption was no afterthought; it was planned before the foundation of the world. We sometimes forget, while we pillow our heads on the promises of God, and rest secure in the atonement, and enjoy all the blessings of redemption and hopes of glory, what these things cost our Redeemer.

Human need is the key that unlocks the storehouses of God's provision for the children of men. *J. R. Miller*

MARCH 13 _____

. . . I will also glorify them, and they shall not be small (Jer. 30:19).

Do not be dazzled by the world's false judgments. The common soldier is often nobler than the general . . . nor is it otherwise on the battlefield of life. There is a yet harder and higher heroism—to live well in the quiet routine of life; to fill a little space because God wills it; to go on cheerfully with a petty round of little duties, little vocations; to accept unmurmuringly a low position; to smile for the joys of others when the heart is aching; to banish all ambition, all pride, and all restlessness, in a single regard to our Savior's work. To do this for a lifetime is a greater effort, and he who does this is a greater hero than he who for one hour stems a breach, or for one day rushes onward undaunted in the flaming front of shot and shell. His works will follow him. He may not be a hero to the world, but he is one of God's heroes, and though the builders of Nineveh and Babylon be forgotten and unknown, his memory shall live and shall be blessed.   *Fredric W. Farrar*

To be exultant, good, or strong,
When praised or flattered by the throng—
When circumstance and men conspire
To raise us to a level higher—
This was not hard: but if through long
Prosaic years we do not tire,
Can in small things be tried and yet true—
This is to live as heroes do.   *Joseph W. Sutphen*

Dream not of noble service elsewhere wrought,
   The simple duty that awaits thy hand
   Is God's voice uttering a divine command;
Life's common duties build what saints have thought.
                                    Minot J. Savage

MARCH 14

I am come that they might have life, and that they might have it more abundantly (John 10:10).

Life is back of love, back of believing, back of hoping, back of everything. Ezekiel in his vision of the "River of Life" understood life; he knew what it meant—at first a little stream to the ankles, then, as he went farther on, it came to the knees, and then to the loins, and finally a wide, mighty river. That is life. Do you know what life is? No; neither does anybody else. Life is indefinable; life is an ultimate; life is God; life is effectiveness; life is power. Adjustment to the things around you—correspondence to environment—that is life. The plodding man does not live. He goes out in the morning and hears the birds, the heralds of the spring, sweetly singing in the trees. The flowers are blooming in the fields, the whole world is full of music, it is everywhere; but the sweet primrose growing on the bank does not for him contain life and beauty and music—it remains a primrose still. Life is measured by the number of things you are alive to. The fullness of our life means what we are about to do. I must have a life that is more abundant than my own poor nature. I must take the power of Jesus and have inside fellowship with him.   *M. D. Babcock*

"All one's life is music if we touch the notes right and in time."
Ruskin

The life that counts must hopeful be,
In darkest night make melody,
Must wait the dawn on bended knee—
    This is the life that counts.

The life that counts is linked with God,
And turns not from the cross—the rod,
But walks with joy where Jesus trod—
    This is the life that counts.   *Pfc. Elbridge Walker*

MARCH 15

Heaven and earth shall pass away, but my words shall not pass away (Matt. 24:35).

Generations follow generations—yet it lives.
Nations rise and fall—yet it lives.
Kings, dictators, presidents come and go—yet it lives.
Torn, condemned, burned—yet it lives.
Hated, despised, cursed—yet it lives.
Doubted, suspected, criticized—yet it lives.
Damned by atheists—yet it lives.
Exaggerated by fanatics—yet it lives.
Misconstrued and mistated—yet it lives.
Ranted and raved about—yet it lives.
Its inspiration denied—yet it lives.
Yet it lives—as a lamp to our feet.
Yet it lives—as a light to our paths.
Yet it lives—as a standard for childhood.
Yet it lives—as a guide for youth.
Yet it lives—as an inspiration for the matured.
Yet it lives—as a comfort for the aged.
Yet it lives—as food for the hungry.

Yet it lives—as water for the thirsty.
Yet it lives—as rest for the weary.
Yet it lives—as light for the heathen.
Yet it lives—as salvation for the sinner.
Yet it lives—as grace for the Christian.
  To know it is to love it.
  To love it is to accept it.
  To accept it means Life eternal.   *Unknown*

A young man went home from a theological school to visit his aged grandmother. To have a bit of fun at her expense he said: "Grandmother, you know that the Bible you say you believe was written in Hebrew and Greek. It had to be translated by great scholars into our language. How do you know those who translated it got it right?" "Ah, Jamie, lad," she answered, "never mind the great men; I have translated a few of them promises myself."   *Selected*

MARCH 16

Give unto the Lord . . . (Ps. 29:1).

My son, give me thine heart . . . (Prov. 23:26).

Give, and it shall be given unto you; good measure, pressed down, and shaken together, and running over . . . (Luke 6:38).

Give of your best to the Master;
  Give Him first place in your heart;
Give Him first place in your service,
  Consecrate every part.
Give, and to you shall be given;
  God His beloved Son gave;
Gratefully seeking to serve Him,
  Give Him the best that you have.   *H. B. G.*

One morning a Hindu mother went out to the banks of the Ganges, leading by either hand her two children. A missionary saw her going to the banks of the river, and he knew why she was going there. He looked into her eyes with all the pleading of fatherhood and tried to persuade her not to do it—not to give up one of these little children. Then he looked at the faces of the two children. One of them was as perfect a baby as any mother ever held close to her heart in America or anywhere; the other was lame and blind. But he knew he could not persuade that woman to break from the thought of centuries in a single hour's pleading. He came back to the spot and saw the Hindu mother still standing by the river bank, her heart breaking! One child was missing. As the missionary drew near he discovered that the perfect child was gone; the mother had kept the little blind and lame one for herself. As he looked into the eyes of that mother, he said to her, "Woman, if you had to give one, why didn't you give this little lame and blind one and keep the perfect one for yourself?" She said, "O sir, I do not know what kind of God you have in America, but I know that out here in India our god expects us to give him our very best."

The greatest hero is perhaps the man who does his very best and fails, and yet is not embittered by his failure. *Unknown*

Not failure but low aim is the cause. *Unknown*

MARCH 17 _____

For thou wilt lighten my candle: the Lord my God will enlighten my darkness (Ps. 18:28).

> We would in Thee abide,
> In Thee be glorified,
> And shine as candles "lighted by the Lord." *Selected*

For long the wick of my lamp had served my purpose, silently ministering as I read beside it. I felt ashamed that I had not before noticed its unobtrusive ministry. I said to the wick:

"For the service of many months I thank thee."

"What have I done for thee?"

"Hast thou not given light upon my page?"

"Indeed, no; I have no light to give, in proof whereof take me from my bath of oil, and see how quickly I expire. Thou wilt soon turn me as a piece of smoking flax. It is not I that burns, but the *oil with which my texture is saturated*. It is this that lights thee. I simply mediate between the oil in the cistern and the fire on my edge. This blackened edge slowly decays, but the light continually burns."

"Dost thou not fear becoming exhausted? See how many

inches of coil remain! Wilt thou be able to give light till every inch of this is slowly charred and cut away?"

"I have no fear so long as the supply of oil does not fail, if only some kindly hand will remove from time to time the charred margin . . . exposing a fresh edge to the flame. This is my twofold need: *oil and trimming*. Give me these and I shall burn to the end."

You may seem altogether helpless and inadequate; but a living fountain of oil is prepared to furnish you with inexhaustible supplies: *Not by your might or power, but by His Spirit.* Hour after hour the oil climbs up the wick to the flame!

YOU CANNOT EXHAUST GOD

Let us not *flinch* when the snuffers are used; they only cut away the black charred debris. He thinks so much of His work that He uses *golden* snuffers! And the hand that holds the snuffers bears *the nailprint of Calvary!*   F. B. Meyer

MARCH 18

Ye are the light of the world (Matt. 5:14).

Let your light so shine before men . . . (Matt. 5:16).

Twenty-two planes from a naval air station were aloft at dusk participating in maneuvers when the fog swept in unexpectedly. Eight of them raced immediately to landing fields, but the others were caught in a swiftly forming impenetrable blanket. Four planes crashed, one of them bursting into flames, as twelve pilots dived blindly through the fog. Two hours later only two planes were aloft. Suddenly there went out over the radio this message, "All automobile owners go to the field outside the city. Two fliers are lost in the fog and you are going to help them land." Soon the roads approaching the field were crowded with cars creeping through the inky blackness, hardly able to see with their feeble lights. As the cars arrived the authorities lined them up with the cars facing inward around the field. More than twenty-five hundred completely surrounded the landing strip. The word was passed around, "All lights on!" The lights on no single car made much impression upon that night fog, but the lights of two-thousand five hundred of them lighted the field so brightly that a transport pilot could go aloft and guide the two aviators down to safety.

Neither your light nor mine is very bright, but if each and all would focus the light we have upon this world with its fog of sin and distress, then it would be so bright that our Master Pilot, Christ, could go aloft and bring every lost soul to a safe landing.

> Oh, let it not in any port be said
> By watchful pilots that some light of thine
> Failed on a certain stormy night to shine
> Beside the harbor head.
>
> Life's seamen, by whatever coast they fare,
> Call out to one another passing by;
> "Trim, firm the lamps, raise every beacon light.
> There are no lights to spare."   *Frank Walcott Hutt*

MARCH 19 _____

Look not every man on His own things, but every man also on the things of others (Phil. 2:4).

We once knew a poor old man who trudged miles to repair the country stiles that they might be a little easier for the aged and infirm. The people voted him mentally weak, but in the great day he will outshine Napoleon.

To take a stumbling block out of our brother's way, and to help the cripple over the stile, is to reveal the mind that was in Christ Jesus.

"Salute Apelles approved in Christ" (Rom. 16:10). Nothing more is known of Apelles than this. It is enough his was the ministry of the unnoticed—obscure, unseen, but approved. You pine for recognition, for publicity, for some great task which will bring great acclaim! Perhaps there is so much to be done around you of little significance that you shun the responsibility thinking one with less ambition will accomplish the mundane. Many little, unimportant responsibilities can add up to be greater than a few "illustrious" deeds. God is as concerned about the little tasks being accomplished as He is about the immense. Be an Apelles and be approved! So here you are in your little plot by the wayside, little known, and hardly noticed by the world at large; yet "the Lord hath commended you a task" and to that work you must bend your best talent and energy. Be an Apelles and be approved!

M. T.

> Let me be a little sweeter—
> Make my life a bit completer,
> By doing what I should do
> Every minute of the day.
> Let me toil without complaining,
> Not a humble task disdaining.
>
> *Unknown*

It is astounding that so much is actually accomplished in life when we reflect upon these age-old maxims:

> Moment by moment
> Step by step
> One by one
> Day by day
> Little by little.
>
> *M. Taylor*

MARCH 20

Now these are the commandments, the statutes, and the judgments . . . (Deut. 6:1).

The Bible is a beautiful palace, built up out of sixty-six blocks of marble—its separate books. In the first chapter of Genesis we enter the vestibule, which is filled with the mighty acts of creation. The vestibule gives access to the law courts, the five books of Moses. Passing through these we come to the picture gallery of the historical books. Here we find hung upon the walls scenes of battlefields, representations of heroic deeds, and portraits of eminent men belonging to the early days of the world's history. Beyond the picture gallery we find the philosopher's chamber, the Book of Job. Passing on we enter the music room, the Book of Psalms, where we listen to the grandest strains that ever fell on human ears. Then we come to the business office, the Book of Proverbs, where right in the center of the room stands facing us the motto: "Righteousness exalteth a nation; but sin is a reproach to any people." From the business office we pass into the chapel Ecclesiastes, or the preacher in his pulpit, and thence into the conservatory, the Song of Solomon, with the rose of Sharon, the lily of the valley, and all manner of fine perfumes, fruits, and flowers. Finally we reach the observatory, the prophets, with their telescopes fixed on near and distant stars, and all directed toward the bright and morning star that was soon to arise.

Crossing the court we come to the audience chamber of the King, the Gospels, where we find four lifelike portraits of the King Himself. Next we enter the workroom of the Holy Spirit, the Acts of the Apostles, and beyond that the correspondence room, the Epistles, where we see Paul and Peter and James and Jude busy at their desks. If you would know what they are writing about, their Epistles are open for all to study.

Before leaving we stand for a moment in the outside gallery, the Revelation, where we look upon some striking pictures of the judgment to come and the glories to be revealed, concluding with an awe-inspiring picture of the throne room of the King.

W. Duns

MARCH 21 _____

Fear ye not therefore, ye are of more value than many sparrows (Matt. 10:31)

I'm only a little sparrow,
    A bird of low degree;
My life is of little value,
    But the dear Lord cares for me.

I know there are many sparrows—
    All over the world they are found;
But our Heavenly Father knoweth
    When one of us falls to the ground.

Tho' small, we are never forgotten;
    Tho' weak, we are never afraid;
For we know that the dear Lord keepeth
    The life of the creatures He made.

I just fold my wings at nightfall,
    Wherever I happen to be;
For the Father is always watching,
    And no harm can happen to me.

I am only a little sparrow,
    A bird of low degree;

But I know that the Father loves me;
Doest thou know His love for thee?   *Unknown*

Not long ago I saw a little bird lying still and cold on the ground. I thought to myself, *I barely missed seeing God, for He has just been here to a funeral.* This was the bird that the Lord used as an illustration to impress His disciples with the precious lesson of trust. He told them that there was not a single sparrow which falls to the ground without being noticed by God the Father, and not one of them is forgotten by Him. Since the Heavenly Father cares so much for one of these little two-ounce sparrows, is it no wonder that we are of more value than many sparrows? Multiply the infinite care of the Creator of the universe by the word "many," and you have some idea of His care for you. Since He feeds them and clothes them with such warmth and attention, will He not much more feed and clothe you?   *M. T.*

MARCH 22

Know ye not, that to whom ye yield yourselves servants to obey, his servants ye are to whom ye obey; whether of sin unto death, or of obedience unto righteousness? (Rom. 6:16).

It was a dark and stormy night. Most of the sheep had come back to the fold, but three were missing. The faithful watchdog was lying in the corner in her kennel with her young and thought her toils were over for the day. Suddenly the shepherd called her, and pointing to the flock cried: "Three are missing, go." She gave a sad look at her little ones, and then a look of obedient love at her master, and off into the darkness she plunged. Back she came after an hour with two of the sheep. There was blood upon her and upon them. Hard she had fought for their lives with the thorns and torrents, but they were saved. With a grateful look she threw herself down in the kennel and gathered her brood to her bosom once more.

But once again the master called, with his stern but kind voice, and pointing to the wilderness, said: "One is still lost, go." She looked up in his face with a look of unutterable longing, but he still pointed to the wilderness, and if looks could speak, her glance entered one last farewell, and into the darkness she plunged once more. It was long ere she returned. Late in the night a feeble scratching was heard upon the door. The shepherd rose and opened it, and there she crouched half dead, and the poor wounded sheep trembling by her side. She had found the lost one but it was at the cost of her very life. One look she gave into his face, which seemed to say, "I have loved you better than my life," and then she crawled over into her kennel and lay down with her little ones and drew still in death. She had loved her master and had given her life for his lost ones.

If a dog could love like that, with no eternity to reward her, no heaven to await her, only the smile of her master's approval in the last instant of her life, what should He not expect from us for whom He has given His life already, and to whom He wants to give a recompense that can never fade away? Shall we catch His glance as He looks out into the darkness and cries, "A thousand millions are lost, go ye"?

MARCH 23 ———————————————————————————

. . . then had thy peace been as a river . . . (Isa. 48:18).

Someone once wrote that the man who can sing "It is well with my soul" at a time in his life when "Sorrows like sea billows roll," has learned the secret of the Lord, and can faithfully exclaim with Job, "Though He slay me, yet will I trust Him."·

Such a man was Horatio Spafford, a lawyer in Chicago. When the great fire swept the city in 1871, he lost all his material possessions. Two years later he sent his wife and four children to Europe, while he applied himself to retrieving his lost fortune.

They sailed on November 15, 1873, on the SS *Ville de Havre.*In midocean, one afternoon, six days after they had left New York, the ship collided with a sailing vessel.

Gathering her children on deck, immediately after the collision, Mrs. Spafford knelt in prayer, asking God to save them, or make them willing to die, if that were necessary. In fifteen minutes the boat sank! They were cast into the water and separated. She was taken out of the water, unconscious, by one of the oarsmen on duty in a lifeboat, but the children were lost.

Then days later Mrs. Spafford landed in Cardiff, Wales, and cabled to her husband: "Saved alone."

On receiving this terrible news Attorney Spafford exclaimed: "It is well, the will of the Lord be done!" And to give an expression to his faith he wrote the hymn which has blessed so many souls in deep trouble, "When peace, like a river, attendeth my way."

A wealthy man ruined in the panic of 1899, was giving himself up in despair, when a friend of his related to him the story of the writing of this hymn. Immediately he responded, "If Spafford could write such a beautiful resignation hymn, I will never complain again." And to thousands whose savings have vanished during the last few years, we commend Attorney Spafford's faith in One who understands and never fails.

The most tempestuous wind cannot disturb the quiet of the stars. *J. H. Jowett*

MARCH 24

. . . A time to keep silence . . . (Eccl. 3:7).

It is true that "there is no power given us by God which more evidently distinguishes us from the beast than the power of intelligent speech." But it is also true that the Christian who remains calm and without panic in the face of adversity and trial and refuses to speak critically and unkindly of any who have taken "the lower road" more nearly emulates the Spirit of Christ. . . . "And when he was accused of the chief priests and elders, *he answered nothing.* Then said Pilate unto him, hearest thou not how many things they witness against thee? And he answered him to *never a word*" (Matt. 27:12–14).

Here a master example was set for Christians of every age. The mighty, omnipotent Son of God at whose single word the universe emerged in all of its complex glory, chose to remain completely calm and utterly silent. How many of us in a like circumstance would have felt "called to preach," to justify, to take matters into our own hands and "set things straight."

Was it weakness that prompted Jesus to "answer nothing"? Was He a coward, fearful of the consequences of His actions or speech? Did the fact of His silence repudiate His previous pronouncements and decisions? Never! This is actually one of the most majestic pictures of divine strength in all of Scripture. To the spectators observing this drama it doubtless appeared that the presumptuous Galilean was being reduced to an insignificant cipher—completely defeated and discredited. You and I know that they were looking through the wrong end of the telescope for the centuries have reduced to dust and infamy the mob who murdered the Savior of mankind.

Our space age produces tension and stress, but this is not altogether a product of today. Remember, if you will, the very perilous condition and position of the Children of Israel as they perched precariously on the rim of the Red Sea with Pharaoh's mighty army thundering through a billowing dust cloud in hot pursuit. From a human point of view they had only two alternatives—be slaughtered in the desert or drown in the stifling waters of the Red Sea.

What did they do? They forgot God and discounted their faith and all that had gone on before. They murmured and complained and with vocalized bitterness expressed their desire to return to the slavery and misery of Egypt rather than take their chances with God. Moses' voice trumpeted through the camp with words that struck home and sobered the unruly mob—"The Lord shall fight for you, and *ye shall hold your peace.*"

The battles of life are not ours; they are the Lord's. We must learn to be quiet and calm. The psalmist said, "Be still, and know that I am God."

"Let me no wrong or idle word, unthinking say; Set Thou a seal upon my lips—Just for today."

MARCH 25 _____

. . . he that sent me is with me; the Father hath not left me alone; for I do always those things that please Him (John 8:29).

The Christian compulsion is threefold:

A sense of direction—to "do always those things that please him." Nothing can transcend the examples and practice of our Lord Jesus Christ. Among all treatises on personal relationship and conduct, there can be found no more reliable guide in matters of faith and conduct than that afforded in this simple and vital summary—that is, that we occupy ourselves with doing (not just contemplating) the things pleasing to Christ, "always."

A sense of mission. Christ, ever our example, recognized and accepted His Divine Mandate. With Him the task was not a self-appointed one, but rather He was conscious of Divine Compulsion. "He *sent* me." So it must be with all who bear His name.

A sense of companionship. Christ reiterates this fact of the Divine Presence. "He hath not left me alone." Supremely important is this reassurance. *Selected*

> The race of God's anointed priests shall never pass away;
> Before His glorious face they stand, and serve Him night
>   and day.
> Though reason raves and unbelief flows on, a mighty
>   flood,
> There are, and shall be till the end, the hidden priests
>   of God. *Unknown*

MARCH 26

Tell me, O thou whom my soul loveth, where thou makest thy flock to rest at noon . . . ? (Song of Sol. 1:7).

The art of "resting at noon" has been lost, and many are succumbing to the strain of life which is being lived in "high gear." Rest is not a sedative for the sick, but a tonic for the strong. It spells emancipation, illumination, transformation! It saves us from becoming slaves, even of good works.

"See that your clock does not run down!" is the timely admonition sung by the colored people of the South. In my possession is an eight-day clock. One night after an unusually strenuous day, when the physical was taxed to the uttermost, and we had forgotten the place where "the flocks rested at noon," we found ourselves carrying loads that belonged to the next day, the next month, the next year. Sleep wanted to take its departure— we listened to the slow and very feeble tick of this clock, and it seemed to say, "I am all run down and cannot go on much longer." It was growing fainter and fainter, and shortly would have stopped had not a voice from the adjoining room called out, "the clock is running down; someone had better get up and wind it before it stops." And, someone obeyed! After a few moments we listened, we heard again the strong, steady tick, tick, tick. The clock had been wound and this was the result. A still, small voice spoke to my inner heart, and the haunting refrain of the Negro spiritual, "See that your clock does not run down," hummed itself into the deepest recesses of my being.   *Mrs. Charles E. Cowman*

> Impatient hearts want action—now!
>   We fear God's time will be too late;
> How prone we are to rush ahead—
>   When God says, "Wait!"
>
> God's schedule always runs on time,
>   Though years seem days or days seem years;
> But happy he who moves God's pace
>   And has no fears.
>
> Not fast nor slow God's timepiece is,
>   So let us set our time with His.
>
> *Marjorie Allen Anderson*

MARCH 27

To every thing there is a season, and a time to every purpose under the heaven (Eccl. 3:1).

Tradition tells us that one day a hunter found the Apostle John seated on the ground playing with a tame quail. The hunter expressed his surprise that a man so earnest should be spending his time so profitlessly. John looked up and asked, "Why is the bow on your shoulder unstrung?" To this the hunter replied, "If kept always taut, it would lose its spring." The kindly apostle said with a smile, "For the same reason I play with this bird."

We must know how to put occupation aside. In an inaction which is meditative, the wrinkles of the soul are smoothed away.

It is not possible for many to have holidays and vacations at seashores or in mountain glens. We are a busy folk, and we must learn the blessed secret of resting just where we are.

Mrs. Charles E. Cowman

MARCH 28

Except a corn of wheat fall into the ground and die, it abideth alone: but if it die, it bringeth forth much fruit. He that loveth his life shall lose it; and he that hateth his life in this world shall keep it unto life eternal (John 12:24, 25).

According to the Master's teaching, one makes the most out of life if he is willing to lose it. His assignment is to lose one's life in servitude to Him, for losing it for His sake is saving it. Self must be cast aside—that is the lower self must be trampled under by the higher self. The alabaster jar must be broken, that the precious ointment of blessing may flow out to fill the house. Grapes must be crushed for there to be wine to drink. Wheat must be bruised in order for it to be made into bread to feed the hungry world.

The parable of life is the same. Unbroken and unbruised men are of little use. Life is one constant battle after another in which the good triumphs over the bad, the spirit over the flesh. We have not begun to live until we cease to live for self. True living is dying.

When the law of self-sacrifice has become the principle of the heart, then one's life becomes a rich full blessing to others. Until we have learned this lesson, we cannot be truly useful to those around us.

An illustration of usefulness out of uselessness is seen in the quarrying of granite and marble to build a house of worship. Just imagine the stones groaning and complaining as the quarrymen's drills bore deep into the solid walls. They suppose they are being destroyed as they are being torn out from the bedrock where they have been lying undisturbed for eons of time. After being cut into blocks and lifted out, and then chiseled and dressed into form, one realizes that they are being destroyed so that they might become of use. Think of it, to become hallowed stones in a place where their own Creator is honored and glorified, where the Word of God is preached, where the lost will find life and hope and a Savior, where the sorrowing will be comforted, the anxious find peace of heart! It is most natural then, that these cold gray stones should be torn away from their dark quarry walls, even amid agony, to become useful. They were saved from their uselessness by being destroyed.

Jesus put this law into a little parable to demonstrate how it applies to human life. He said that a seed must fall into the ground and die that it may bear fruit. Let us use His cross at Calvary to illustrate the truth. Some thought His precious life was wasted. Was it? Was it wasted when it was crucified?   *M. Taylor*

> For three and thirty years, a living seed,
>   A lonely germ, dropt on our waste world's side,
>   Thy death and rising, thou didst calmly bide;

Sore compassed by many a clinging weed
Sprung from the fallow soil of evil and need;
 Hither and thither tossed, by friends denied;
 Pitied of goodness dull, and scorned of pride;
Until at length was done the awful deed,
And thou didst lie outworn in stony bower—
 Three days asleep—oh, slumber godlike, brief,
 For Man of sorrows and acquaint with grief,
Heaven's seed, Thou diedst, that out of thee might tower
 Aloft, with rooted stem and shadowy leaf
Of all Humanity the crimson flower.

George MacDonald, from Making the Most of Life

MARCH 29

O thou afflicted, tossed with tempest, and not comforted, behold, I will lay thy stones with fair colors (Isa. 54:11).

I s there no end to trials? Is there no limit to affliction?" you ask. "Can there be assurance that God knows our every care, our every weakness? Will not the morning break with new hope and refreshing courage?" Yes, dear heart, there is hope, there is a limit. Did not our Lord Himself promise us that we would not have to suffer affliction beyond that which He had to endure? God sends affliction and He removes it. Quietly wait and patiently endure the will of the Lord till He comes. When His design in using the rod is fully served, He ends the trials and He limits the affliction. If the affliction is for a time of testing, that we might become as pure gold, that we might glorify God, it will end when the Lord has used us to bear witness to His grace and goodness. When we have given to Him all the honor which we can possibly render to Him, then we would wish the affliction to depart.

Today may be a day of quiet and serene calm. How can we tell but soon those raging billows will take the place of the sea of glass? Are you fitted with the "lifeline" of assurance and trust when that moment arrives? If so the griefs, the fears, the failures, and the mistakes can all be thrown overboard. The burdened cargo cast off then lightens the load and you can trust the "Helmsman" to bring you safely into port from the angry sea of life.

The hard things in life come for benefit later on. We must needs experience them to better endure the future where often lurks tribulations much greater than the present. Easy paths without sharp stones never fit the pilgrim for the steep, rough, exhausting climb up the "hill of difficulty."   *M. Taylor*

> I would not lose the hard things from my life—
>   The rocks o'er which I stumbled long ago,
> The griefs, the fears, the failures, the mistakes,
>   That tried and tested faith and patience so.
> I need them now; they make the deep-laid wall,
>   The firm foundation-stones on which I raise,
> To mount thereon from stair to stair,
>   The lofty towers of my House of Praise.
>
>   *Unknown*

MARCH 30

And the servant of the Lord must . . . be gentle unto all men (2 Tim. 2:24).

A beautiful legend says that one day the angel of the flowers— the angel whose charge it is to care for the adorning of the flowers—lay and slept beneath the shade of a rosebush. Awaking from his sleep refreshed, he whispered to the rose—

> "O fondest object of my care,
> Still fairest found where all are fair;
> For the sweet shade thou gavest me
> Ask what thou wilt, 'tis granted thee."

The rose requested that another grace might be given to it. The angel thought in silence what grace there was in all his gifts and adornments which the rose had not already. Then he threw a veil of moss over the queen of the flowers, and a mossrose hung its head before him, most beautiful of all roses. If any Christian, even the Christliest, would pray for a new charm, an added grace of character, it may well be for gentleness. This is the crown of all loveliness, the Christliest of all Christly qualities.

All human hearts hunger for tenderness. We are made for love—not only to love, but to be loved. Harshness pains us. Ungentleness touches our sensitive spirits as frost touches the flowers. It stunts the growth of all lovely things. Gentleness is like a genial summer to our life. Beneath its warm, nourishing influence beautiful things in us grow.

There are many people who have special need for tenderness. We cannot know what secret burdens many of those about us are carrying, what hidden griefs burn like fires in the hearts of those with whom we mingle in our common life. Not all grief wears the outward garb of mourning; sunny faces ofttimes veil heavy hearts. Many people who make no audible appeal for sympathy yet crave tenderness—they certainly need it, though they ask it not—as they bow beneath their burden. There is no weakness in such a yearning. We remember how our Master himself longed for expressions of love when He was passing through His deepest experiences of suffering, and how bitterly He was disappointed when His friends failed Him.

We can never do amiss in showing gentleness. There is no day when it will be untimely; there is no place where it will not find welcome. It will harm no one, and it may save some one from despair.   *J. R. Miller*

"Thy gentleness hath made me great" (Ps. 18:35).

MARCH 31 ⸻⸻⸻⸻⸻

Thou wilt keep him in perfect peace, whose mind is stayed on Thee, because he trusteth in Thee (Isa. 26:3).

Quiet tension is not trust. It is simply compressed anxiety.
                                       From Gospel Thumb Tack

Too often we think we are trusting when we are merely controlling our panic. True faith gives not only a calm exterior but a quiet heart.

Miss Amy Carmichael gives a beautiful illustration from nature of this kind of trust. The sun bird, one of the tiniest of birds, a native of India, builds a pendant nest, hanging it by four frail threads, generally from a spray of valaris. It is a delicate work of art, with its roof and tiny porch, which a splash of water or a child's touch might destroy. Miss Carmichael tells how she saw a little sun bird building such a nest just before the monsoon season, and felt that for once bird wisdom had failed; for how could such a delicate structure, in such an exposed situation, weather the winds and the torrential rains? The monsoon broke, and from her window she watched the nest swaying with the branches in the wind. Then she perceived that the nest had been so placed that the leaves immediately above it formed little gutters which carried the water away from the nest. There sat the sun bird, with its tiny head resting on her little porch, and whenever a drop of water fell on her long, curved beak, she sucked it in as if it were nectar. The storms raged furiously, but the sun bird sat, quiet and unafraid, hatching her tiny eggs.

We have a more substantial rest for head and heart than the sun bird's porch! We have the promises of God. They are enough, however terrifying the storm.   *J. C. Macaulay*

APRIL 1 _____

Let the redeemed of the Lord say so . . . (Ps. 107:2).

Pentecost gives utterance—'They all began to speak.' Testimony is an effectual way of spreading the Word of God."

The psalmist even encouraged men of his day, and down through the ages, to proclaim the almighty God and His wondrous works among the children of men.

We are in desperate need today for believers of this marvelous gospel to verbally share it with others; to proclaim its saving grace to those on buses, trains, in the office, at work, and on the street. We need an outspoken religion. "If you have gotten off the wreck in the midst of the breakers, why not tell of the crew and lifeboat that landed you? If you have a title clear to a mansion in the sky, why not tell your next-door neighbor about it so that he will know what to do to get one on the same street? So many Christians are paralyzed with timidity. They are dumb when they should be vocal, silent when they should be songful, fettered when they should be free.

"Witnessing is a means of grace for the soul. It is to the soul what a draft is to a stove. Shut the mouth, and the fire dies down; keep the mouth open, and the fire burns.

"If a man has religion, he must either give it up or give it away. Religion is not something merely to be enjoyed, it is to be shared; to corner it is to kill it." Have you ever considered how one generation carries the gospel of Christ to the next? Have you ever wondered what would happen to the gospel of Christ if one generation failed to pass it on?

Someone once told this story of Jesus: When He had finished His work here on earth, He was met by the angel Gabriel near the gate of heaven. Gabriel asked Jesus, "Have you seen to it that you left an organized group down on earth to carry on your work? Are you sure that there are some who will be diligent and faithful?" Jesus answered Gabriel, "I have left word with Peter, James, and John, and Mary and Martha. They are dependable. They will tell others and make my Word known to men. The work will go on." Gabriel, though an angel, knew the frailties of human nature. He pursued the issue further, "What if they forget? You should have made other plans." Jesus quietly replied, with a look of confidence on His face, "I made no other plans. I am counting on *them*." *M. Taylor*

The Savior's heart is yearning
  For the souls across the sea;
He loves them just as greatly
  As He cares for you and me;
The time is swiftly passing,
  His eye on you shall rest;
Oh, can you bear to face Him,
  If you have not done your best?
M. M., from Mrs. Carpenter's collection, typewritten, entitled The Macedonian Call

APRIL 2 _____

We are troubled on every side, yet not distressed; perplexed, but not in despair; persecuted, but not forsaken; cast down, but not destroyed (2 Cor. 4:8, 9).

George Matheson, the great Scottish preacher, who when he was told by a famous oculist that he was going blind, wrote these lovely words: "O love that will not let me go!—I rest my weary soul on thee." Also, "O joy that seekest me through pain, I cannot close my heart to Thee: I trace the rainbow through the rain";—listen to these lines from his pen:

"There are times when things look very dark to me—so dark that I have to wait even for *hope*. A long-deferred fulfillment carries its own pain, but to wait for hope, to see no glimmer of a prospect and yet refuse to despair; to have nothing but night before the casement and yet to keep the casement open for possible stars; to have a vacant place in my heart and yet to allow that place to be filled by no inferior presence—that is the grandest patience in the universe. It is Job in the tempest; it is Abraham on the road to Moriah; it is Moses in the desert of Midian; it is the Son of man in the Garden of Gethsemane."

It takes a real faith to trace the rainbow through the rain; but it takes the stormcloud to make the rainbow, and George Matheson learned to have a childlike trust, and his testimony has blessed millions throughout this generation.

> What then? Shall we sit idly down and say
> The night hath come; it is no longer day?
> Yet as the evening twilight fades away
> The sky is filled with stars, invisible to day.

Why art thou cast down? HOPE THOU IN GOD! for I shall yet praise Him.
Mrs. Charles E. Cowman

APRIL 3 _____

I will pour water on him that is thirsty, and floods upon the dry ground (Isa. 44:3).

> Oh, for the showers on the thirsty land!
> Oh, for a mighty revival!
> Oh, for a sanctified fearless band,
> Ready to hail its arrival.   *Selected*

Can we expect a revival ere the Lord's return? Is the world so war-minded that we need not pray for revival until conditions are better?

Charles G. Finney said, "Would you have an awakening in your community, your church, your own lives; then become the fuel, and a revival fire will be the result."

The cost is high. "Except a corn of wheat fall into the ground and die, it abideth alone, but if it die, it bringeth forth much fruit." Death to sin and self is the only roadway to power. Will we become God's fuel in bringing this to pass? Let us give the answer to God in some quiet place today as we covenant to wait upon Him until He has flooded our own souls with Himself.

Lord, send a revival! Begin it today!

Revive us, Lord! Is zeal abating
  While harvest fields are vast and white?
Revive us, Lord! The world is waiting;
  Equip Thy Church to send the Light.

When naught whereon to lean remaineth,
  When strongholds crumble to the dust,
When nothing's sure but that God reigneth,
  That, yes, that is the time to trust.   *Unknown*

Mrs. Charles E. Cowman

APRIL 4

His delight is in the law of the Lord; and in his law doth he meditate day and night (Ps. 1:2).

A man who loves the Word of God—a man who dwells upon what it says—a man who keeps a little text in his mind to think about as he is walking on his way, and who meditates upon it day and night— "whatsoever he doeth shall prosper." If you can find a man who carries out this direction and doesn't prosper, you can doubt the inspiration of the first Psalm; but find the man first.
                                                              J. H. T.

When John Wanamaker, the merchant prince, was eleven years old, he purchased a Bible. In later years he said of this purchase: "I have, of course, made large purchases of property in my time, involving millions of dollars, but it was as a boy in the country, at the age of eleven years, that I made my greatest purchase. In a little mission Sunday school I bought a small red leather Bible for $2.75, which I paid for in small installments. Looking back over my life, I see that that little red Book was the foundation on which my life has been built, and the thing which has made possible all that has counted in my life. I know now that it was the greatest investment and the most important and far-reaching purchase I have ever made.

Last eve I passed beside a blacksmith's door,
  And heard the anvil ring the vesper chime;
Then looking in, I saw upon the floor
  Old hammers, worn with beating years of time.

"How many anvils have you had," said I,
"To wear and batter all these hammers so?"
"Just one," said he, and then, with twinkling eye,
"The anvil wears the hammers out, you know."

And so, thought I, the anvil of God's Word,
For ages skeptic blows have beat upon;
Yet, though the noise of falling blows was heard,
The anvil is unharmed—the hammers gone.   *Unknown*

APRIL 5

. . . He had seen the Lord in the way . . . (Acts 9:27).

Having the Heavenly Father by our side does not keep the storms of life away; but He is with us in those storms. One who has put his trust in God very well knows he is safer in times of danger with Christ than in times of solace without Him. Only a foolish person would place his hopes in sinking sands. One's confidence is sure in the steadfast Rock of Ages.

Disciples of Christ must first come to their wits' end before they come to their journey's end. They must first experience the presence of their Lord along every step of the journey—His constantly abiding presence. Then why fear the tempest? Is it not under the controlling hand of the Heavenly Father?

In the time of deepest sorrow,
When life seems without a ray
And the wound is fresh and opened,
Can you see Him "in the way?"

When your plans and dearest projects
Shattered fell and broken lay,
And you vainly try to mend them,
Can you see Him "in the way?"

When your prayers remain unanswered
And you almost cease to pray,
Feeling that the heavens are brazen—
Can you see Him "in the way?"

When your dearest hope has vanished,
When your friends forsake, betray,

And all earthly props are broken—
Can you see Him "in the way?"

Broken rays become a rainbow;
Broken clods, a fruitful meadow;
Pruned vines bear richest clusters;
Cut and polished gems, rare lustres;
Harvests rise from buried grain;
Lives are born through grief and pain;—
God dwells in the broken clay.
He alone leads "in the way."

L. S. P.

APRIL 6

Thy kingdom is an everlasting kingdom, and thy dominion endureth throughout all generations (Ps. 145:13).

In the year 970 B.C., 480 years after the children of Israel had returned from the land of Egypt, Solomon, son of David, undertook to build the "house unto the name of the Lord." David, through wars and adverse conditions, had been unable to build the temple but Solomon was now given "rest on every side, so that there (was) neither adversary nor evil occurrent."

With the cooperation of Hiram, king of Tyre, a levy of builders was raised out of all of Israel, and the levy was thirty thousand men. In preparation for building, the materials were brought to Jerusalem. "And Hiram sent to Solomon, saying, I have considered the things which thou sentest to me for: and I will do all thy desire concerning timber of cedar and concerning timber of fir." While in Jerusalem ". . . the king commanded, and they brought great stones, costly stones, and hewed stones, to lay the foundations of the house." And the reports of the structure which followed are amazing to this day.

The size and structural beauty must have been inspiring to those peoples even more so than to us today. Even today after several destructions of the temple or rebuilding of others to take its place, parts of the original Temple of Solomon remain for all to see. Even now there is still upon the site, over Mt. Moriah, the Mosque of Omar, sometimes called the Dome of The Rock. It is here where Abraham was ready to sacrifice his son, Isaac, and which later became the resting place of the "Holy of Holies" (the ark of the Covenant). The temple area which, at the time of building, occupied one-fifth the area of the entire city, still covers approximately half a million square feet.   *From* Food for Tho't

> As o'er each continent and island
>   The dawn leads on another day,
> The voice of prayer is never silent,
>   Nor dies the strain of praise away.

APRIL 7

Jesus therefore, knowing all things that should come upon him, went forth . . . (John 18:4).

E aster is the most radiant day in the world, but the days before Easter do not lack in loveliness! Easter is a day of triumph, but the days that lead up to that triumph are fraught with deep meaning and deeper sentiment.

The days before Easter hold Christ's thrilling entry into Jerusalem, when the feet of His patient steed walked over a carpet of palms. They hold the Last Supper, when Christ—knowing that His life on earth was nearing its conclusion—broke bread with the ones He loved best. There is Holy Thursday when Christ prayed in the garden, and was kissed by a traitor and betrayed by a friend. There is Good Friday, that crowned the Supreme Sacrifice with thorns. There is the Saturday between Good Friday and Easter— a period of grief and patience and prayer. And then there are lily flowers in bloom and birds singing and the moment of resurrection.

The days before Easter teach us that applause must be accepted humbly; that it can swiftly fade into the twilight of forgetfulness. They teach us that we should be meek in our moments of triumph and that we should rely—not upon the fanfare of the crowd—but upon the unspoken praise of the Greatest Judge. They teach us tolerance—never the tolerance of a Pilate who washed his hands and let it go at that, but the sort of Christian tolerance that offers sympathy and help and refuses to take part in any wrongdoing. They teach us that God's will is not always our will, but that we must accept it. They teach us that life and love can survive even scorn and crucifixion.

Sometimes we know that there are barriers ahead and that pain will be a part of the future. Christ knew, all too well, that torture was His heritage—that, during Holy Week, He was rapidly approaching a moment of extreme grief. And yet the knowledge did not make Him a specter at the feast. He kept His appetite and His philosophy and His good cheer, and His trust in the Father . . . He was able, by so doing, to join in the festivity that filled the city!

Margaret Sangster, Christian Herald

APRIL 8

. . . for I called him alone, and blessed him . . . (Isa. 51:2).

Whenever God has required someone to do a big thing for Him, He has sent him to a "lonely furrow." He has called him to go alone.

What lonely men the great prophets of Israel were! John the Baptist stood alone from the crowd! Paul had to say, "all men forsook me." And who was ever more alone than the Lord Jesus?

Victory for God is never won by the multitude. The man who dares to go where others hold back will find himself alone, but he will see the glory of God. . . .

Gordon Watt

> There is a mystery in human hearts;
> And though we be encircled by a host
> Of those who love us well, and are beloved,
> To every one of us, from time to time,
> There comes a sense of utter loneliness:
> Our dearest friend is stranger to our joy,
> And cannot realize our bitterness.
> "There is not one who really understands,
> Not one to enter into all I feel."
> Such is the cry of each of us in turn;
> We wander in a "solitary way."
> No matter what or where our lot may be,
> Each heart, mysterious even to itself,
> Must live its inner life in solitude.
> And would you know the reason why this is?
> It is because the Lord desires our love;
> In every heart He wishes to be first.
> He therefore keeps the secret key Himself,
> To open all its chambers and to bless
> With perfect sympathy and holy peace,
> Each solitary soul that comes to Him.
> So when we feel this loneliness, it is

The voice of Jesus saying, "Come to Me";
And every time we are "not understood,"
It is a call to us to come again;
For Christ alone can satisfy the soul,
And those who walk with Him from day to day,
Can never have a "solitary way."   *Unknown*

APRIL 9

Sing unto the Lord a new song (Ps. 149:1).

Amid the springtime rejoicing we hear a new Easter anthem. It pours forth from the hearts of those to whom have been given a song in the night! A song taught to them by the Master Musician. It comes from crushed hearts that love Him supremely! Would we know that the major chords were sweet if there were no minor key?

When heartstrings have been stretched upon some cross of pain, and winds of sorrow and trial blow through them, then from the human aeolian harps we hear the very music of God! Tears are set to music, and a prayer arises from our hearts: "Help *me*, O Lord, to make all *my* sorrows and afflictions music for the world! Teach *me* to begin the music of heaven! Grant me grace to have many rehearsals of eternal hallelujahs, that I too may have a place in the heavenly chorus and to join with those who sing the "new song!"   *Mrs. Charles E. Cowman*

Lord, how trivial seems my Calvary
   When I consider Thine,
For only Simon helped Thee lift Thy cross,
   But many carry mine!
I am not scorned, nor scourged, nor ridiculed,
   And all along the way
Are many sweet unnamed Veronicas
   To wipe the tears away.
There are no cruel nail wounds in my hands,
   Nor thorns upon my brow,
And ministering angels walk with me
   To smooth the way. But Thou!
How dare I think it, call it Calvary—
   This sheltered life of mine—
O broken, beaten, bleeding Lord, my God,
   When I consider Thine.   *Vera Marie Tracy*

104

He is not here: for he is risen as he said (Matt. 28:6).

There is an Easter sunrise service every year at the famed Hollywood Bowl in Southern California. The Bowl is a natural outdoor amphitheater, which has a capacity for the seating of many thousands. There are people from all walks of life who come to this beautiful spot to acknowledge the resurrection of our Lord, and to receive a meaningful spiritual blessing. To this particular service there arrived a dear sister who was sorely bereaved. Long ere the dawn she came, and found that "He had risen as He said!"

"I was among the first to arrive," she related. "I meditated on the story of the first Easter, when they came and found the empty tomb, and I wondered how the women felt when they found the stone rolled away. That morning I had an awakening in my soul before the buglers on the hillside announced the arrival of the dawn! The sun did not shine, but the assurance of the resurrection of Jesus impressed me as never before! Suddenly the darkness within the shell on the stage turned to a white cross, and the children began to sing, "Christ is Risen!" Then something within me burst forth in praise, and for the first time of my entire lifetime I experienced the full significance of that revelation that came to the women on their first visit to the tomb! Then thousands of voices took up the song, "All Hail the Power of Jesus' Name!"—and I could understand why the women were perplexed on that first Easter morn—so overwhelming had been to them the demonstration of His power over death. I now know the power of the risen Lord! He lives! and they live whom I hold most dear! The dawn of Easter broke in my own soul! My night was gone!

> In all the world, there is no place
>   So dear to me,
> As in an empty tomb within
>   Gethsemane,
>
> Men sing the praises of the Cross,
>   And, rightly so,
> Yet, it is to the Empty Tomb
>   I love to go.

It's there with Paul, I daily die
  When sore oppressed,
It's there, where men are loathe to go
  I sweetly rest.

It's there, when heart ache's angry waves
  Envelop me,
In faith, I lift my mournful face
  My Lord to see.

There is no place so fraught with power
  Our souls to save,
As is our Lord's last resting place,
  His empty grave.

In darkest hours of grief, beside
  A new made mound,
I go again, the depths of God's
  Great love to sound.

And while I view the grave and clothes,
  The echoes ring:
"O, Grave, where is thy victory?
  O, Death, thy sting?"

As, one by one, the loved ones cross
  The threshold's gloom,
I fain believe, embrace, receive,
  The Empty Tomb.   *Mary D. Sammons*

APRIL 11

I count all things but loss for the excellency of the knowledge of Christ Jesus my Lord, for whom I have suffered the loss of all things . . . that I might win Christ (Phil. 3:8).

Jesus prayed in the garden that the cup might be taken away if it were the Father's will, but as He prayed He realized that it was *not* the Father's will, and He yielded to His choice.

Gethsemane is an eternal assurance that *it is not for lack of love that God permits suffering.*

How it would take the sting from many a severe blow and trial to see what Job saw in his hour of aggravated woe, when every earthly prop lay prostrate at his feet, no hand but the divine. He saw that hand in the awful silence of his rifled home, and his faith reached its climax when the once-powerful prince of the desert, seated on his bed of ashes, could say, "Though He slay me, yet will I trust Him!" "The Lord hath given; the Lord hath taken away; blessed be the Name of the Lord!"

There is a divine mystery in suffering! A strange and supernatural reason! There is no other way to reach these priceless blessings! They come via the hill called *Calvary.*

They tell me that I shall stand upon the peaks of Olivet, the heights of resurrection glory. But I want more, O Father! I want Calvary to lead up to it. I want to know that the shadows of this world are the shades of an avenue—the avenue to the house of my Father! Tell me I am only forced to climb because Thy house is on the hill! I shall receive *no* hurt from sorrow if I shall walk in the midst of the fire.

> He knelt alone with folded hands
>   In dim Gethsemane—
> He knelt beneath the shadow of
>   A spreading olive tree;
> And night-swept flowers hung their heads,
>   And night birds stilled their cry
> As, through the silence and the dusk,
>   The centuries swept by.
>
> His yesterdays were crowded with
>   Cruel treachery and sadness—
> The morrow would hold racking pain
>   And storm clouds and mob madness,
> And yet He knelt beneath a tree,
>   Calm to the very last—
> And murmured, "God—Thy will not mine!"
>   While time and space rushed past. . . .

Unknown

APRIL 12 _____

And very early in the morning the first day of the week, they came unto the sepulchre at the rising of the sun (Mark 16:12).

Mark tells us, "They came unto the sepulchre at the rising of the sun"—this little group of His devoted followers who had trudged along with the jeering, taunting mob up the steep hill to the place called Calvary. Just a few hours before had they seen

His enemies nail His precious body to an old wooden cross, and He had been left there to die on the hill lone and gray outside the city wall of old Jerusalem. How bleeding and broken were their hearts! How crushed their spirits! Suddenly all their lights had gone out and their future hopes had been snapped, as it were, in twain. When hope is gone, the last hope—desperate despair—invariably follows.

Had He not told them that He would rise again? Had He not said to Mary and Martha, "I am the Resurrection and the Life"? And had He not raised Lazarus after he had been dead four days! How easily His precious words are forgotten when we are plunged into a night of thick darkness, an hour of naked faith, and we cannot see our Father's hand or discern His presence! We fail to remember that "In the pitch-black night when there's no outer light, it is the time for faith to shine."

What wondrous surprises awaited these weary-hearted, bewildered followers! They were greeted by angels! They heard them make the announcement, and it was made exclusively to them: "He is not here: for He is risen as He said!" What rest is brought to them! It whispered peace! Sweet peace! Their bitter night of weeping now ended in a morning of joy! "Never the exquisite pain, then never the exquisite bliss." Oh, the gladness, the shouts of triumph on that first Easter morn! The morning time of all the ages! Christ's triumph over Satan! It reaches down the ages and touches our own hearts at this very hour. We triumph in His resurrection victory! Forever is Satan a defeated foe!

Mrs. Charles E. Cowman

APRIL 13 _____

He shewed himself alive after his passion by many infallible proofs, being seen of them forty days, and speaking of the things pertaining to the kingdom of God (Acts 1:3).

Easter season!—the lovely time of the year when we commemorate the glorious conquest of our *risen Lord!* How wonderously beautiful it is in each opening spring, after the bleak winter months, when the time of singing of birds is come and God's miracle touch is seen on every tree, leaf, and flower, and all things

108

are waking into new life—that we take into our hearts afresh the blessed fact of *our Lord's resurrection!*

What wondrous things occurred during the forty days, when to His own *He showed Himself alive!* How their hearts must have burned within them when He opened the Scriptures, and to them was given the revelation of the *living Christ!* How natural, how easy were His manifestations! How noiseless the footsteps of Omnipotence! He meets Mary in the early morning, just as of yore, and calls her by name. He greets those beloved fishermen, who had forsaken their nets to follow Him, and for these weary all-night toilers He prepares a simple meal on the shores of Tiberias. He joins the two downcast disciples on the Emmaus road on the Sabbath afternoon, and when He hears them saying, "We trusted that it had been He who would have redeemed Israel," He answers their doubts by a revelation of Himself! And that special revelation makes them "witnesses of these things." What definite testimonies they bore ever afterwards! Oh, the glory of His presence!

In every age a testimony has been left by people of every rank of having found themselves in awe and rapture in the radiant Presence! Abraham in the night, tending his altar fire, Moses on Sinai; Isaiah in the temple; Peter and James on the mount of transfiguration, and John on the isle called Patmos! We too may know the shining Presence. "The living God is *among you*" (Josh. 3:10). "Lo, I am *with* you alway, even to the close of the age!"

Oh, that our eyes were opened that we might behold the riches of the glory of our inheritance, and the exceeding greatness of His power, which was wrought in Christ when God raised Him from the dead!

APRIL 14 _____

And every branch that bringeth forth fruit, he purgeth it, that it may bring forth more fruit (John 15:2).

Every purpose regarding our lives will be fulfilled. Every flower will be crowned with blossom. Every vine will bear fruit. "His Calvary blossomed out into fertility." We shall have a calvary also, and it too shall blossom. There will be an abundant fruitage out of agony. There will be life out of death. This is the law of the universe.

Dr. Vincent relates an incident while viewing the luscious clusters of grapes hanging on the walls inside a great hothouse. The owner said, "When my new gardener came, he said he would have nothing to do with these vines unless he could cut them clear down to the stalk! And he did so, until there was seemingly nothing left! There were no grapes for two years, but *this* is the result!"

God has challenging futures for us, and will go miracle-lengths to get us to pay attention.

The pruning knife is clasped by the hand of love divine. At the most tender touch it cuts and breaks. Lives which have borne some fruit will now bear "much fruit." Those God wants to use to any significant degree will have to be pruned. Sorrow came more to Joseph than to his brethren, and the result was a great blessing to many nations. The Holy Spirit reported of him as "a fruitful bough . . . by a well; whose branches run over the wall" (Gen. 49:22). Human history projects the shadows of suffering in the *great* paintings, the *great* philosophies, and the *great* civilizations. They all have come into the light out of the shadows of torment. Do not fear the knife in the Pruner's hand.

> "Till He come!" Yes, He is coming—
> Coming midway first to air;
> Then, oh then, how blest the rapture
> Which His blood-bought saints shall share!
> In a brief—a twinkling moment—
> Loved ones, parted long, shall meet,
> In that sweet and blest re-union
> Round the dear Redeemer's feet!   *J. Danson Smith*

APRIL 15

I beheld, and lo, a great multitude which no man could number, of all nations, and kindreds, and peoples and tongues stood before the throne, and before the throne, and before the Lamb, clothed with white robes, and palms in their hands (Rev. 7:9).

> Hark! the sound of holy voices, chanting at the crystal
>   sea,
> Alleluia! Alleluia! Alleluia! Lord, to Thee.

110

Multitudes, which none can number, like the stars in
    glory stand,
Clothed in white apparel, holding palms of victory in
    their hand.

Patriarch, and holy Prophet, who prepared the way
    of Christ,
King, Apostle, Saint, Confessor, Martyr, and Evangelist,
Saintly Maiden, godly Matron, Widows who have watched
    to prayer,
Joined in holy concert, singing to the Lord of all—
    are there.

They have come from tribulation, they have washed their
    robes in Blood,
Washed them in the Blood of Jesus; tried they were, and
    firm they stood;
Mocked, imprisoned, stoned, tormented, sawn asunder,
    slain with sword,
They have conquered death and Satan by the might of
    Christ the Lord.

Marching with Thy Cross, their Banner, they have
    triumphed, following
Thee, the Captain of Salvation, Thee, their Saviour and
    their King;
Gladly, Lord, with Thee they suffered, gladly, Lord, with
    Thee they died;
And by death, to Life Immortal, they were born,
    and glorified.

Now they reign in Heavenly glory, now they walk in
    golden light,
Now they drink, as from a river, holy bliss and infinite;
Love and peace they taste for ever, and all truth and
    knowledge see
In the Beautific Vision of the Blessed Trinity.

God of God, the One-begotten, Light of Light, Emmanuel!
In Whose Body joined together, all the Saints for ever
    dwell;
Pour upon us of Thy fulness, that we may for evermore
God the Father, God the Son, and God the Holy Ghost,
    adore.
Amen.   *Bishop Christopher Wordsworth, 1862*

Wherefore God also hath highly exalted him, and given him a name which is above every name (Phil. 2:9).

To many, Jesus Christ is only a person subject for a painting, a heroic theme for a pen, a beautiful form for a statue and a thought for a song; but to those who have heard His voice, who have felt His pardon, who have received His benediction, He is music, warmth, light, joy, hope and salvation, a Friend who never forsakes, who lifts us when others try to push us down. We cannot wear Him out; we pile on Him all our griefs and troubles. He is always ready to lift us; He is always ready to help us; He addresses with the same love; He beams upon us with the same smile; He pities us with the same compassion. There is no name like His. It is more inspiring than Caesar's, more musical than Beethoven's, more conquering than Napoleon's, more eloquent than Demosthenes', more patient than Lincoln's. The name of Jesus throbs with all life, weeps with all pathos, groans with all pains, stoops with all love. Its breath is laden with perfume. Who like Jesus can pity a homeless orphan? Who like Jesus can welcome a prodigal back home? Who like Jesus can make a drunkard sober? Who like Jesus can illuminate a cemetery plowed with graves. Who like Jesus can make a queen unto God out of a woman of the street? Who like Jesus can catch the tears of human sorrow in His bowl? Who like Jesus can kiss away our sorrow?

I struggle for a metaphor with which to express Jesus. He is not like the bursting forth of an orchestra; that is too loud and it may be out of tune. He is not like the sea when lashed into a rage by a storm; that is too boisterous. He is not like a mountain wreathed in lightning, canopied with snow; that is too solitary and remote.

He is the lily of the valley, the rose of Sharon, a gale of spices from heaven. *Billy Sunday*

I am the Lord; that is my name; and my glory will I not give to another (Isa. 42:8).

There lives at this time in Judea a man of singular virtue, whose name is Jesus Christ, whom the barbarians esteem as a prophet, but His followers love and adore Him as the offspring of the immortal God. He calls back the dead from the graves and heals all sorts of diseases with a word or touch. He is a tall man, well shaped and of an amiable and reverend aspect; His hair of a color that can hardly be matched, falling into graceful curls, waving about and very agreeably couching His head, running as a stream to the front after the fashion of the Nazarites; His forehead high, large and imposing; His cheeks without spot or wrinkle, beautiful with a lovely red; His nose and mouth formed with exquisite symmetry; His beard, and of a color suitable to His hair, reaching below His chin and parted in the middle like a fork; His eyes bright blue, clear and serene, look innocent, dignified, manly, and mature. In proportion of body most perfect and captivating; His arms and hands delectable to behold. He rebukes with majesty, counsels with mildness, His whole address, whether in word or deed, being eloquent and grave. No man has seen Him laugh, yet His manners are exceedingly pleasant, but He has wept frequently in the presence of men. He is temperate, modest and wise. A man for His extraordinary beauty and divine perfection, surpassing the children of men in every sense.

Believed to have been written by Publius Lentulus,
President of Judea in the reign of Tiberius Casesar

". . . and, lo, the heavens were opened unto him, and he saw the Spirit of God descending like a dove, and lighting upon him: And lo a voice from heaven, saying, This is my beloved Son, in whom I am well pleased" (Matt. 3:16, 17).

APRIL 18 _____

But he was wounded for our transgressions, he was bruised for our iniquities . . . and with his stripes we are healed (Isa. 53:5).

Dr. Alexander Macleod had a friend who was teaching a school in Jamaica. This teacher had made a rule that everyone who told a lie in school should receive seven strokes on the palm with a strap. One day a little girl told a lie and was called before the school to receive her punishment. She was a sensitive little thing, and the teacher was very sorry to strike her, but he must carry out the rule of the school. Her cry of pain when she received the first stroke went to his heart; he could not go on with her punishment. Yet he could not pass by her sin, and this is what he did. He looked over to the boys and asked, "Is there any boy who will bear the rest of her punishment?" And as soon as the words were spoken, up started a little fellow called Jim, who said, "Please, sir, I will!" And Jim went to the desk and received, without a cry, the six remaining strokes.

Dr. Macleod tells the story, and adds: "And it was the vision of a heart gentler still than that of this brave boy, but gentle with the same kind of gentleness, which filled the master's eyes with tears that day and made him close his books, and bring his scholars round about his desk, and tell them of the Gentle One, who long ago bore the punishment of us all." The story he told them is ours today.

"Bear ye one another's burdens, and so fulfill the law of Christ" (Gal. 6:2).

No one is useless in the world who lightens the burden of it for anyone else.   *Charles Dickens*

> Wounded for me, wounded for me,
> There on the cross He was wounded for me;
> Gone my transgressions, and now I am free,
> All because Jesus was wounded for me.   *W. G. Ovens*

APRIL 19

I was in the Spirit on the Lord's day . . . (Rev. 1:10).

It was a day of God. The earth lay like one great emerald, ringed and roofed with sapphire; blue sea, blue mountain, blue sky overhead. There she lay, not sleeping, but basking in her quiet Sabbath joy, as though her two great sisters of the sea and air had washed her weary limbs with holy tears, and purged away the stains of last week's sin and toil, and cooled her hot, worn forehead with their pure incense-breath, and folded her within their azure robes, and brooded over her with smiles of pitying love, till she smiled back in answer, and took heart and hope for next week's weary work.   *Charles Kingsley, from* Daily Thoughts

114

Sunday to a Christian is the best day of all seven. True, a believer loves every day of the week, but he loves Sunday most of all because it is the day connected with his Lord's own hallowed name—"The Lord's Day." This day is a double memorial—a memorial of a finished creation (Gen. 2:3), and also a memorial of a finished redemption (Rom. 4:24, 25). It is thus a reminder of our happy position, that we are saved by a living, loving, victorious Savior.

What a gracious God-given provision it is that after six days of toil there should be a day different from the others—a day of rest.

Not only do our minds and bodies require this weekly recurring rest, but our souls also need the blessings of this hallowed day. When the holy day, the Christian's Sabbath of rest, comes round, the divine call to the pilgrim is: Turn aside from your ways and works and enter into the sanctuary of the Lord. "Ye shall keep My Sabbaths, and reverence My Sanctuary: I am the Lord" (Lev. 26:2).

When the Lord's day is spent in the Lord's presence in this way we come to learn more of Him and of His will concerning us. We join in worship, in praise, and in prayer, and gain a fresh vision of the Lord, the Altogether Lovely—our Savior—and in doing so our souls revive again. Like the Apostle John, we find ourselves rejoicing in the blessedness (i.e., the soul-happiness) of being found in the Spirit on the Lord's day.   *Selected*

APRIL 20 _____

Then shalt thou call, and the Lord shall answer; thou shalt cry, and he shall say, Here I am . . . (Isa. 58:9).

Then the fire of the Lord fell, and consumed the burnt sacrifice, and the wood, and the stones, and the dust, and licked up the water that was in the trench" (1 Kings 18:38).

He was a mighty man of prayer; and prayer is one of the most sacred and precious privileges vouchsafed to mortals. Here is a scene of this Elijah in prayer:

The summer of 1853 was unusually hot and dry, so that the pastures were scorched, and there seemed likely to be a total failure of the crops. Under these circumstances, the great congregation gathered one Sabbath in the church at Oberlin as usual, when, though the sky was clear, the burden of Finney's prayer was for rain. In his prayer he deepened the cry of distress which went up from every heart by mentioning in detail the prolonged drought, in about these words:

"We do not presume, O Lord, to dictate to Thee what is best for us; yet Thou dost invite us to come to Thee as children to an earthly father, and tell Thee all our wants. *We want rain.* Our pastures are dry. The earth is gaping open for rain. The cows are wandering about and lowing in search of water. Even the squirrels in the woods are suffering from thirst. Unless Thou givest us rain, our cattle will die and our harvests will come to naught. O Lord, send us rain, and send it now! Although, to us, there is no sign of it, it is an easy thing for Thee to do. Send it now, Lord, for Christ's sake. Amen."

He took a text and began to preach; but in a few moments he had to stop for the noise of the rattle and roar of the storm. He paused, and said, "We would better stop and thank God for the rain." *Excerpt from* The Life of Finney

Commit thy lot unto the Eternal, place in Him thy confidence and He will act. *Unknown*

Nothing with God can be accidental. *H. L. Longfellow*

APRIL 21 —————————————————————————————

Thanks be unto God which always causeth us to triumph in Christ, and maketh manifest the savour of his knowledge by us in every place (2 Cor. 2:14).

A young man went to an aged saint on one occasion and asked him to pray for him, saying, "I find myself giving way to impatience continually. Will you please pray for me that I may be more patient?" The old man agreed. They knelt together and the man of God began to pray: "Lord, send this young man tribulation in the morning, send this young man tribulation in the afternoon. . . ." The young man nudged him and said, "No, no not tribulation, *patience!*" "But," said the old saint, "it is tribulation that worketh patience! If you would know patience you must have the tribulation." If you would know victory, you must

116

have conflict; it is ridiculous for anybody to talk about having a victory when they have never been in a conflict. You must be prepared to enter into the arena with the Lord Jesus Christ Himself, and He will give you lessons day by day. But I warn you, you will have to be quite prepared to pay the price. No one can enjoy victory without paying a price, even in the ordinary realms of life.

It is only a crucified person that can have fellowship with a crucified Lord. It was via Calvary that the Lord Jesus Christ came into His wonderful victory. It is only via the cross that you and I can come into the experience of that triumph.

If you want patience, then it is tribulation—if you want victory, it must be conflict. *W. J. Brown*

Nay, in all these things we are more than conquerors through him that loved us. For I am persuaded, that neither death, nor life, nor angels, nor principalities, nor powers, nor things present, nor things to come; nor height, nor depth, nor any other creature, shall be able to separate us from the love of God, which is in Christ Jesus our Lord (Rom. 8:37–39).

"I can do all things through Christ which strengtheneth me" (Phil. 4:13).

APRIL 22

My voice shalt thou hear in the morning, O Lord; in the morning will I direct my prayer unto thee, and will look up (Ps. 5:3).

I will direct my prayer" as an arrow, and after that, "I will look up," to see if it has hit. When the prayer is directed in the morning, the "look up" lasts all day. *Dr. Charles Stanford*

There are many early risers mentioned in the Bible. These men of God found solutions to life's problems by directing their prayers to the One who would hear and assist them in their endeavors for the day. Before the day began they received the confidence necessary to shoulder responsibilities.

Abraham rose early in the morning to stand before the Lord (Gen. 19:27). Jacob rose early in the morning to worship the Lord (Gen. 28:18). Moses rose early to build an altar to God (Exod.

24:4) and to meet God at Sinai (Exod. 34:4). Hannah and Elkanah rose early to worship God (1 Sam. 1:19), Job rose early to offer sacrifices (Job 1:5), David awakened early for prayer (Ps. 119:147 and Ps. 57:8). Hezekiah rose up early and gathered the rulers of the city and went up to the house of the Lord (2 Chron. 29:20). The Son of God rose early to go to a solitary place to pray (Mark 1:35).

> Every morning lean thine arm awhile
> Upon the window sill of heaven
> And gaze upon thy God.
> Then will the vision in thy heart,
> Turn strong to meet the day.　　　　*Unknown*

> The camel kneels at break of day,
> 　To have his guide pack his load,
> Then rises up fresh to take
> 　The desert road.
> So thou should'st kneel at morning's dawn,
> 　That God may give thee daily care,
> Assured that He no load too great
> 　Will make thee bear.　　　　*Unknown*

APRIL 23

Bow down thine ear, O Lord, hear me: for I am poor and needy (Ps. 86:1).

Sometimes people wonder why prayers are not answered promptly, or why the reply is not what they expected. The following story will help them to understand:

Three large trees in a forest prayed that they might choose what they would be converted into when they were felled. One prayed to be made into a beautiful palace; the second, to be a large ship to sail the seven seas; the third to stay in the forest and always point toward God.

One day the woodman came and chopped down the first tree, but instead of a palace, it was made into a common stable, wherein was born the fairest Babe in all creation. The second tree was made into a small ship that was launched on the Sea of Galilee, on the deck of which stood a tall man who told the multitudes: "I am come that they might have life, and that they might have it more abundantly." The third tree was made into a cross, and to it men nailed that young man, the loveliest personality that ever walked the earth. Ever since then, that cross has been pointing men to God. And so each prayer was answered.

Unknown

Whate'er I ask I surely know
    And steadfastly believe
Thou wilt the thing desired bestow
    Or else a better give.

To Thee, I therefore, Lord, submit
    My every fond request
And own, adoring at Thy feet
    Thy will is always best.   *Wesley*

After looking at the earth for six days we need the Lord's day to look up.   *Unknown*

APRIL 24 _____

Ye observe days, and months, and times, and years (Gal. 4:10).

Order my steps in thy word (Ps. 119:133).

A little clock which had just been finished by the maker was put on a shelf in his wareroom between two older clocks who were busy ticking away the noisy seconds.

"Well," said one of the clocks to the newcomer. "So you've started on this task. I'm sorry for you. You're ticking bravely now, but you'll be tired enough before you get through thirty-three million ticks."

"Thirty-three million ticks!" said the frightened clock. "Why, I never could do that!" And it stood still instantly with despair.

"Why, you silly thing," said the other clock at this moment. "Why do you listen to such words? It's nothing of the kind. You've only got to make one tick this moment. There, now, isn't that easy? And now another, and that is just as easy, and so right along."

"Oh, if that's all," cried the new clock, "that's easily done, so here I go." And it started bravely on again, making a tick a moment and not counting the months and millions. But at the year's end, it had made 33,000,000 vibrations without knowing it.

Oh, if Christians would only live by the moment, not the year! "Day by day" is the limit of the Lord's Prayer. "Sufficient unto the day is the evil thereof," said the Lord. And "as thy days, so shall thy strength be" is the promise which four thousand years have not exhausted.

> I ask thee for a present mind,
>   By patient watching wise,
> A heart at leisure from itself
>   To soothe and sympathize.   *Unknown*

Christians have to be more than others and do more than others. Wild fruit, growing as it will, can never become like the fruit that is cultivated and watched.   *Spence*

APRIL 25 _____

By their fruits ye shall know them (Matt. 7:20).

> We shall do so much in the years to come,
> But what have we done today?
> We shall give our gold in a princely sum,
> But what did we give today?
> We shall lift the heart and shall dry the tear,
> We shall plant a hope in the place of fear,
> We shall speak the words of love and cheer;
> But what did we speak today?
>
> We shall be so kind in the afterwhile,
> But what have we done today?
> We shall bring to each lonely life a smile,
> But what have we brought today?
> We shall give the truth a far grander birth,
> And to steadfast faith a much deeper worth,
> We shall feed the hung'ring souls of earth;
> But whom have we fed today?
>
> We shall reap such joys in the by and by,
> But what have we sown today?
> We shall build us mansions up in the sky,
> But what have we built today?
> Oh, how sweet it is in fond dreams to bask,
> But right here and now we must do our task.
> Yes, this is the thing our souls must ask,
> "Just what have we done today?"   *Unknown*

If a person wishes to show that Confucius was wonderful, he quotes some of his words of wisdom. But when a Christian wants to show God's glory he does not quote from one of Jesus' sermons—he points to the cross and says, "God is like *that!*" Whatever Jesus said can be understood only in the light of God's willingness to suffer for men.

The hallmark of Christianity is *action,* not words. We comprehend God fully in what He has done rather than in what men say about Him.

Unknown

APRIL 26

They shall be abundantly satisfied with the fatness of thy house (Ps. 36:8).

Our world is one of vivid contrasts and fluent extremes. What a contrast there is between the arid, lifeless, barren desert and the luxuriant oasis with its waving palms and its glorious verdure; between gaunt and hungry flocks and the herd that lie down in green pastures and beside the restful waters; between the viewless monotony of the shimmering plains and the mountain heights, resplendent in magnificent beauty.

What a difference there is between the aridity of an artificial, stinted existence—a desert existence—and the almost overpowering fruitfulness of a rich fertile valley, washed by gentle rains and bathed in filtered sunlight—the abundant life!

This lesson of contrasts finds its daily counterpart in the lives and experience of Christian people. There are some who seem always to be kept alive on scant measure. Their spiritual garments are threadbare. Their existence is as barren and fruitless as the desert wastes. Life seems to have dried up, and purpose has so dehydrated that they wander aimlessly around the margins of life.

There are others who daily experience the inner peace and happiness that comes through a vigorous faith in the Savior—a practical day-by-day faith that ensures victory and "life more abundant." In a word, this is an experience that reaches out into the infinite as well as the eternal—sailing on the shoreless and fathomless seas of God and His unlimited grace. It is a life guaranteed to gratify the parched and arid soul.

"But ye shall *receive* power . . ." The word *receive* does not mean climbing up, but the coming down of something. This is not a thing to be wrought out of one by agony and effort, but something to be put into one like a seed in the earth. Receive, of course, one can receive. That needs no genius, no goodness, but only want. Any beggar can take a coin if it be given to him.

Mrs. Charles E. Cowman

APRIL 27

Brethren, if a man be overtaken in a fault, ye which are spiritual, restore such an one in the spirit of meekness; considering thyself, lest thou also be tempted. Bear ye one another's burdens, and so fulfill the law of Christ. For if a man think himself to be something, when he is nothing, he deceiveth himself. But let every man prove his own work, and then shall he have rejoicing in himself alone, and not in another (Gal. 6:1–4).

> A little seed lay in the ground
>   And soon began to sprout.
> "Now, which of all the flowers around,"
>   It mused, "shall I come out?"

Then the little seed said to itself: "I don't want to be a lily, for lilies are so cold and lofty. I don't want to be a rose, for the rose is rather loud in color, it dies quickly, its edges wilt and it isn't very practical. I don't want to be a violet, for the violet is too small, too dark, and grows too close to the ground."

The little seed was like some people we all know. It was critical. It was critical of everything around it. It found fault with its neighbors. It didn't like the colors of some, the perfume of others, the size and shape of others. It had nothing constructive to offer, even in its own behalf. The whole theme of its life was criticism.

> And so it criticized each flower,
>   This supercilious seed,
> Until it woke one summer hour
>   And found itself a weed!

There has been only one faultless Person in this world and He has promised to present all believers "faultless before the presence of His glory with exceeding joy" (Jude 24). Until then, let each believer be a *"flower"* rather than a *weed* in this scene of His rejection.

CMA Church Bulletin

O that thou wouldest hide me in the grave, that thou wouldest keep me secret . . . that thou wouldest appoint me a set time, and remember me (Job 14:13).

It must have been a wonderful day indeed, when almighty God spoke to His servant and said possibly something like this: "Bezaleel, I need you at just this particular time to do this particular piece of work for me." There could be no doubt left in the heart of the one addressed as to God's "blueprint" for his life at that time. To be sure, he was not being called to do some mighty work, such as Moses was chosen to perform as Israel's emancipator; but nevertheless God deemed it of enough importance to Himself to call Bezaleel to the task and not leave it to any lesser influence. What a confidence it must have given Bezaleel to know, as he labored day after day, that he was God-appointed to the work before him. No mere man, even Moses, had had anything to do with it. It must have given him courage and joy to continue the work until the last thing had been designed and finished for the tabernacle in which God was to dwell.   *Pameii*

There are men in ages past who have little more than their names recorded in the Holy Word. Yet they fulfilled a position at an appointed time for furthering the work of the Lord. Simeon, mentioned in Luke 2, was such a man. He waited his entire lifetime for just the one appointed task. He waited for the Messiah, and knew that he had not waited in vain.

Scientists tell us how the flowers of the Alps are buried for long months under the snow, yet all the time they are full of energy and expectation. No sooner does the sunshine labor a few hours melting the snow than they open into glorious bloom. So aged Simeon waited through a long life, waited as beneath cold snows, but at the first kiss of the Sun of Righteousness he broke into flower and was accepted for one glorious responsibility—that of prophesying the work of salvation through the Babe he blessed in his arms.   *Mrs. Charles E. Cowman*

. . . for I have learned, in whatsoever state I am, therewith to be content (Phil. 4:11).

The illness which culminated in an operation came upon me when I was not looking. It seemed that life stopped. Identity blurred. One hung up his personality with his clothes in a closet and became a case—the patient in Number 12. No longer quite a man, but a condition, a problem, stretched out there for daily examination, looked down upon, peered into, charted on paper with graphs like the rise and fall in the price of wheat. It was this indignity, even more than the pain and the weakness and the boredom, that made the experience difficult for me to bear. To be something, and then to be nothing! One is singled out for suffering. He goes alone; he takes no one with him.

While it was true that everything that had constituted a pleasant and satisfying life for me—my robust physical health, my habitual and interesting work, and all my books, my letters, my friends—while all these had been stripped away, I was still possessed of my own mind and my own thoughts. I had after all, my own inner life. I had my life! . . .

> Still to ourselves in every place consigned,
> Our own felicity we make or find.

. . . I began to reflect that so many men have owed their lasting contributions to the wealth of the race to some unhappy adventure of health or of fortune, some catastrophe of imprisonment or banishment wherein, having mastered their own spirits, they were, at length, able to live a complete life. I think it was in prison that Cervantes wrote *Don Quixote;* and Paul addressed some of the best of his letters from Roman jails.

The present moment, this burning instant of time, was all that I or any man could ever really possess or command—and I was allowing it to be ruined by anxieties of my own making. It came to me powerfully, that if I could be content at *this* moment, I could be content.   *Grayson, found clipped to pages of a Bible*

APRIL 30 —————————————————————————————

. . . *Be of good cheer: for I believe God . . . (Acts 27:25).*

A woman has no greater distress than to find that the color of some new material "runs" when it is washed. Most of our birds can boast of a plumage whose color is fast, but the poor luraco of Africa dashes from the treetops to the thickest foliage when the rains come to preserve what it can of the "running" crimson on the secondaries of its wings. The faith of some is like the crimson of the luracos. It is fair-weather faith, much in evidence in the sunny and bright day, but miserably "washed out" in the day of affliction.

The disciples were very confident until the squall hit their boat. Then they did what the storm could not do; they awoke the Lord with their panic-inspired question, "Master, carest thou not that we perish?" Of a different sort is the faith expressed in the forty-sixth Psalm: "God is our refuge and strength, a very present help in trouble. Therefore will not we fear, though the earth be removed, and though the mountains be carried into the midst of the sea; though the waters thereof roar and be troubled, the mountains shake with the swelling thereof."

John Newton has expressed the all-weather faith in one of his best hymns:

> Begone, unbelief, my Saviour is near,
> And for my relief will surely appear;
> By prayer let me wrestle, and He will perform;
> With Christ in the vessel, I smile at the storm.

Paul's was a faith which triumphed in all sorts of conditions. It was in the midst of a storm which threatened complete destruction that he stood up before all and said, "I believe God." How much rough weather can your faith stand?

Fair-weather faith contrasts with robust all-weather faith. There is also a counterfeit faith which stands over against true faith—a faith centering in self, not in God. The kind of faith I refer to is well exemplified in one of the saddest poems I know—a poem which has become popular in religious circles, now set to music and sung by outstanding artists, but which is totally the reverse of Christian sentiment. I refer to Henley's *Invictus*.

> Out of the night that covers me,
>   Black as the pit from pole to pole,
> I thank whatever God may be
>   For my unconquerable soul.
>
> It matters not how strait the gate,
>   How charged with punishment the scroll,

I am the Master of my fate,
I am the Captain of my soul.

MAY 1 _____

The flowers appear on the earth; the time of the singing of birds is come, and the voice of the turtle is heard in our land . . . (Song of Sol. 2:12).

Warped indeed must be the soul of the one who has no glad welcome for the magic month of May! What marvelous transformations a few warm days made! One day Mother Nature appears very unattractive in her shabby winter garb of dull browns and grays. But, behold! the soft southwest wind stirs through her rags; the sun gazes at her with fiery ardor one moment, and the dripping shower refreshes her the next; suddenly she comes before our wondering eyes robed in garments of tenderest green and filling the air with langorous blossom scents. Ever new, ever delightful, is the gracious beauty, the revivifying influence of the early spring. The Giver of all good has indeed placed us in a most beautiful world. But how many of us go on our way with unseeing eyes, shutting out all the sweet influences of this wonderful outer sanctuary, and never allowing ourselves to come near to the great throbbing heart of nature. We are too unready to learn the lessons spread on the open book of God's wide outdoors—lessons that only he who understands can interpret aright, so intangible are they, so elusive; but, when once comprehended, how sweet, how satisfying, how holy, is the communion with nature and nature's God!
Adelaide S. Seaverns,
from Thoughts for the Thoughtful, *1893*

MAY 2 _____

But he that is greatest among you, let him be as the younger; and he that is chief, as he that doth serve (Luke 22:26).

A kind word of praise, of sympathy, of encouragement; it would not cost you much, yet how often does pride or envy or indifference prevent you from speaking it? The cup of cold water, the barley loaves, the two farthings, how often are we too wretched and too self-absorbed to give even these! And are we

126

not to give them because we cannot endow hospitals or build cathedrals, or write epics? If we be in the least sincere, in the least earnest, let us be encouraged. The little gifts of our poverty, the small services of our insignificance, the barley loaves of the Galilean boy on the desert plain, the one talent of poor dull persons like ourselves, are despised by the world. But they are also dear. They are accepted. They will be infinitely rewarded by Him who gives the conies their homes in the rocks, who knows every sparrow's fall; who numbers the very hairs of our heads; who builds the vast continents by the toil of the coral insect, and by His grains of sand stays the raging of the sea.

Frederic W. Farrar, from Farrar's Year Book, *1895*

> It is so little I can do!
> It is so little I can say!
> Nay, but what God demands of you
> Is just that little: Hear—obey.   *J-L. M. W.*

The sweetest lives are those to duty wed, Whose deeds, both great and small, Are close-knit strands of an unbroken thread where love ennobles all. The world may sound no trumpets, ring no bells, The Book of Life the shining record tells.

From an old calendar

> The victories won by prayer,
> By prayer must still be held;
> The foe retreats . . . but only when
> By prayer he is compelled.   *Selected*

MAY 3 _____

She hath done what she could (Mark 14:8).

> Lord, let me do the little things
>   Which may fall to my lot;
> Those little inconspicuous ones
>   By others oft forgot.
>
> If, like the Master, I can give
>   Myself for those I love,
> Rich joy and peace shall come to me,
>   Sweet rest in heaven above.

I know not when the day shall close;
　But when life's curfew rings,
I want my Lord to find me then
　Still doing little things.   *Unknown*

I'm sure that those persons who are faithful in that which is least must wear very radiant crowns. They are the ones who tower above us when they are called upon to do the little tasks—never murmuring. They are meticulous in the furrowed roads of drudgery. They are the people who, when trudging up the "hill of difficulty," make it well. They are the folks who win the victories amid trivial irritations. They are as constant when they are wearing housedresses or overalls in their daily chores as when they are wearing royal purple and fine satin in the presence of the King. They complete the most obscure piece of work as though it were to be displayed before a great assembly who will pass judgment. Great are they who are faithful in little things.

Little hamlets act out their dramas in small events. Jesus lived most of His thirty years amid the insignificant incidents of the little village of Nazareth. He toiled faithfully as a carpenter in His father's little shop. He labored amid the humdrum, the petty cares, the trivial village gossip. Yet He was faithful in the little things— yes, even in the least! He wore His crown with dignity and honor. It was forever upon His brow!   *M. Taylor*

MAY 4 _____

Until the spirit be poured upon us from on high, and the wilderness be a fruitful field, and the fruitful field be counted for a forest (Isa. 32:15).

We are not apt enough to think of our daily work as the Good Shepherd's pasture field. We are too apt to give heed to a miserable distinction between the sacred and the secular, and to seek to get out from what we call the secular into what we call the sacred, that we may find spiritual pasture fields.

You and I know that the grand Martin, who dared to cease to be a monk and give himself to daily toil that had real meaning in it, was right. The most sacred service may sometimes consist as much in Paul's tentmaking as in Paul's preaching. This is sacred service, this is God's work: praying, communing, preaching, buying, selling, bricklaying, doing whatsoever things providence has thrust

into your hand to do—doing them for glory.
Wayland Hoyt, from Thoughts for the Thoughtful, *1893*

"Angel of the Springtime," said she,
  "Show me where to sow my grain.
Shall I plant it round my doorstep,
  Or afar upon the plain?"

"Fill the nearest spot with gladness.
  Fill thy home with goodness sweet;
Wider fields shall ask thy sowing,
  If thou first sow at thy feet!

"Thus for thee shall widening harvests
  Wave their manifolding grain,
Till the sixtyfold, the hundred,
  Gild the dooryard and the plain."

Mrs. Merrill E. Gates,
from Thoughts for the Thoughtful, *1893*

MAY 5

He sitteth alone and keepeth silence, because he hath born it upon him (Lam. 3:28).

For I called him alone, and blessed him, and increased him (Isa. 51:2).

There are a great many people in this world—hundreds of millions! Yet in a sense each one of us is the only one. Each individual life has relations of its own in which it must stand alone, and into which no other life can come. Companionships may be close, and they may give much comfort and inspiration, but in all the inner meaning of life each individual lives apart and alone. No one can live your life for you. No one but yourself can answer your questions, meet your responsibilities, make your decisions and choices. Your relations with God no one but yourself can fulfill. No one can believe for you. A thousand friends may encircle you and pray for your soul, but until you lift up your own heart in prayer no communication is established between you and God. No one can get your sins forgiven but yourself. No one can obey God for you. No other one can do your work for Christ, or render your account at the judgment seat.

This aloneness of life sometimes becomes very real in consciousness. All great souls experience it as they rise out of and above the common mass of men in their thoughts and hopes and aspirations, as the mountains rise from the level of the vale and little hills. All great leaders of men ofttimes must stand alone, as they move in advance of the ranks of their followers. The battles of truth and of progress have usually been fought by lonely souls. Elijah, for example, in a season of disheartenment and despondency, gave it as part of the exceptional burden of his life that he was the only one in the field of God. It is so in all great epochs; God calls one man to stand for Him.

But the experience is not that only of great souls; there come times in the lives of all who are living faithfully and worthily when they must stand alone for God, without companionship, perhaps without sympathy or encouragement.

J. R. Miller, from Making the Most of Life, *1891*

MAY 6 ─────────────────────────────

I was not disobedient unto the heavenly vision (Acts 26:19).

Though I speak concerning foreign missions with great eloquence, and have not vision, I am become as sounding brass, or a tinkling cymbal.

And though I spend long hours in study and reading missionary literature, and know much concerning the hardships and difficulties of a missionary's life, and have not vision, it profiteth me nothing.

A vision holdeth one steady before God; a vision enableth one to pray earnestly; a vision burdeneth, that others may have salvation.

Doth not exalt any but Christ, seeketh only the redemption of the lost, is given to those who earnestly seek for it, thinketh no price too great to pay.

Trieth not to discourage those who would be missionaries, but trieth to encourage them to answer the call of God.

Beareth another's burdens, believeth that God is willing to undertake, hopeth for the salvation of many, endureth seeming failure and disappointment.

A vision doth not soon fail; but where there be excitement aroused by hair-raising stories, it shall fail; where there be mere

130

tears at a missionary convention, they shall cease; where there be only interest, it shall vanish away.

For all Christians know in part, and all Christians see in part; but when they have a vision their lukewarmness and intermittent interest shall be done away.

Before I caught the vision, I spoke as one without a vision, I prayed as one without a vision; but when I caught the vision, I put away halfhearted things.

For now at least I have caught a faint glimpse of the need which Jesus alone can satisfy, but some day I shall realize it fully; now I know something of the price salvation cost, but then I shall see it clearly, even as also it hath been purchased for me.

And now to be a missionary Christian are necessary—a prayerful heart, a surrendered life, a vision; these three, with others, but one of the greatest of these is a vision.

Adapted from a clipping

MAY 7 _____

For our light affliction, which is but for a moment, worketh for us a far more exceeding and eternal weight of glory (2 Cor. 4:17).

Times of trial are often our times of greatest joy. It was when the apostles were turned out of Antioch by a mob of respectable men and honorable women, that the record was added, "The disciples were filled with joy, and with the Holy Ghost." It was when the fig tree refused to blossom, and the vines were stripped of their accustomed fruit, and nature was robed in a winding sheet of death, that Habakkuk's song rose to its highest notes of triumph, and he could say, "Yet I will rejoice in the Lord, I will joy in the God of my salvation."

If we would know the full comfort of the Holy Ghost, we must cooperate with Him, and rejoice by simple faith, often when our circumstances are all forbidding, and even when our very feelings give no response of sympathy or conscious joy. It is a great thing to learn to count it all joy. Counting is not the language of poetry or sentiment, but of cold, unerring calculation. It adds up the column thus: sorrow, temptation, difficulty, opposition, depression, desertion, danger, discouragement on every side, but at the bottom of the column God's presence, God's will, God's joy,

131

God's promise, God's recompense. How much does the column amount to? Lo, the sum of all the addition is *all joy,* for "the sufferings of this present time are not worthy to be compared with the glory which shall be revealed. . . ."

That is the way to count your joy. Singly, a given circumstance may not seem joyful, but counted in with God, and His presence and promise, it makes a glorious sum in the arithmetic of faith. We can rejoice in the Lord as an act of the will; and when we do, the Comforter will soon bring all our emotions into line, yea, and all our circumstances, too. They who went into battle with songs of praise in front soon had songs of praise in the rear, and an abundant, visible cause of thanksgiving. Therefore, let us say with the apostles, "I therein do rejoice, yea and will rejoice."

Selected from A Message From God,
edited by Heyman Wreford, 1884–1934, Exeter, England

MAY 8 _____

If we have forgotten the name of our God, or stretched out our hands to a strange god; Shall not God search this out? for he knoweth the secrets of the heart (Ps. 44:20, 21).

A missionary from India made the statement that if Christ had started out to preach the Gospel to every village of India, devoting but one day to each one *He would still be in India and would not yet be even nearly through.*

Today we face a task unfinished! But we can face it with the fullest assurance of faith, knowing it can be done! Millions of souls wait to be evangelized. Tolstoy said a few days before his death, and it seemed indeed like the word of a prophet, "The modern world has temporarily lost God, and without Him cannot live." Is not this the root cause of the suffering in our broken, bleeding world at this moment? A world that has lost God! Many are crying out with Job, "O that I knew where I might find Him!" (Job 23:3).

Mrs. Charles E. Cowman

Remember, men are still God's method for reaching men. Men who are utterly yielded to God, men like Gideon. Who was he? The Word says that "the Spirit of the Lord clothed [himself] with Gideon." "And Gideon was nothing in the fray, but just a suit of

132

working clothes the Spirit wore that day." God is today looking for people so small and insignificant that when God uses them people exclaim: "God is working through that man!" Used of God, ordinary instruments become extraordinary. Remember Abraham, Moses, Joseph, David! "The sword of the Lord and"—men! Think of Spurgeon, Moody, Luther, Wesley! Again, "the sword of the Lord and"—men! These were men for their generation and their hour. You can be the person for this hour—this portentous hour, this momentous hour before the return of our Lord Jesus Christ for His bride!

Christ alone can save this world, but Christ can't save this world alone!

MAY 9

She stretcheth out her hand to the poor, yea, she reacheth forth her hands to the needy. Strength and honor are her clothing; and she shall rejoice in time to come. She openeth her mouth with wisdom; and in her tongue is the law of kindness. She looketh well to the ways of her household, and eateth not the bread of idleness. Her children arise up, and call her blessed; her husband also, and he praiseth her. Many daughters have done worthily, but thou excellest all (Prov. 31:20, 25–29).

The young mother set her foot on the path of life. "Is the way long?" she asked.

And her Guide said: "Yes. And the way is hard. And you will be old before you reach the end of it. But the end will be better than the beginning."

But the young mother was happy, and she would not believe that anything could be better than these years. So she played with her children, and gathered flowers for them along the way, and bathed with them in the clear streams; and the sun shone on them and life was good, and the young mother cried, "Nothing will ever be lovelier than this."

Then night came, and storm, and the path was dark, and the children shook with fear and cold, and the mother drew them close and covered them with her mantle, and the children said, "Oh, Mother, we are not afraid, for you are near, and no harm can come," and the mother said, "This is better than the brightness of day, for I have taught my children courage."

And the morning came, and there was a hill ahead, and the

children climbed and grew weary, and the mother was weary, but at all times she said to the children, "A little patience and we are there." So the children climbed, and when they reached the top, they said, "We could not have done it without you, Mother." And the mother, when she lay down that night, looked at the stars and said: "This is a better day than the last, for my children have learned fortitude in the face of hardness. Yesterday I gave them courage, today I have given them strength."

And the next day came strange clouds which darkened the earth—clouds of war and hate and evil, and the children groped and stumbled, and the mother said: "Look up. Lift your eyes to the Light." And the children looked and saw above the clouds an Everlasting Glory, and it guided them and brought them beyond the darkness. And that night the mother said: "This is the best day of all, for I have shown my children God."

And the days went on, and the weeks and the months and the years, and the mother grew old, and she was little and bent. But her children were tall and strong, and walked with courage. And when the way was hard, they helped their mother, and when the way was rough, they lifted her, for she was as light as a feather; and at last they came to a hill, and beyond the hill they could see a shining road and golden gate flung wide.

And the mother said: "I have reached the end of my journey. And now I know that the end is better than the beginning for my children can walk alone, and their children after them."

And the children said: "You will always walk with us, Mother, even when you have gone through the gates."

And they stood and watched her as she went on alone, and the gates closed after her. And they said: "We cannot see her, but she is with us still. A mother like ours is more than a memory. She is a living presence."   *Temple Bailey, from* Food for Thought

---

MAY 10 _____

My times are in thy hand (Ps. 31:15).

It was more than seventy years ago that a memorable dinner was given in London. Christopher Neville gave this dinner in honor of some of the leaders of English thought. They were leaders in politics, art, literature, finance, and religion. For the after-dinner speeches Dean Stanley was asked to preside. No set address, and no topics were assigned. Upon arising the dean proposed for discussion the question, "Who will dominate the future?" The first speaker he called upon was Professor Huxley. After a little skirmishing, Huxley gave as his thought that the future will be dominated by the nation that sticks most closely to the facts. He left his audience profoundly impressed. The dean arose, after a moment of silence, and called upon an English writer, who was a member of Parliament as well as president of the Royal Commission of Education. Quietly he began by saying, "Gentlemen, I have been listening to the last speaker with profound interest and agree with him. I believe the future will belong to the nation that sticks to the facts. But I want to add one word—*all the facts,* not some of them, *all* of them. Now the greatest fact of history," he went on, "is God." God is the answer!

That dinner party in London is an event of the past, but the question, "Who shall dominate the future?" is still with us today in an aggravated form. The darkest days are just before the dawn.

Men see not the bright light that is in the clouds (Job 37:21).

Mrs. Charles E. Cowman

MAY 11 _____

He that is able to receive . . . let him receive . . . (Matt. 19:12).

It is not so hard to receive as it is to have to receive. To be obliged to take a gift makes us agree swiftly with the words of the Lord Jesus when He said, "It is more blessed to give than to receive." Then we see that it is harder to take gracefully the kindnesses of our friends, than even their buffetings for our faults. But when we must receive, then that is the will of God for us, and just then more beneficial to us than giving. We must be willing, not only to serve, but to be served; not only to bear others' burdens, but to let others bear ours; not only to minister to the sick, but to be simply and thankfully ministered unto; not only to give, but to receive. It is sometimes the will of God that we should let others do the will of God, and ourselves be the occasions instead of the authors of kindness. *Maltbie Davenport Babcock,*
from Thoughts for Every-Day Living, *1904*

How can there be any giving, any serving, if there be no receiving? Someone must receive if another is to give. We *give* joy to the giver when we become the *grateful* receiver. Thus, as paradoxical as it may seem, in receiving there is giving. The noble receiver is the noble giver.   *M. Taylor*

MAY 12

The Lord is good unto them that wait for Him, to the soul that seeketh Him. His compassions fail not (Lam. 3:25, 22).

The story is told of a shabby old gentleman who every day at twelve o'clock would enter the church, stay a few minutes, then leave. The caretaker was concerned for the valuable altar furnishings. Every day he watched to be sure nothing was taken, and every day just at twelve the shabby figure would arrive. One day the caretaker accosted him. "Look here, my friend, what are you up to, going into the church every day?"

"I go to pray," replied the old man politely.

"Now come," the cautious caretaker said, "you don't stay long enough to pray."

"True enough. I cannot pray a long prayer, but every day I just comes and says, 'Jesus, it's Jim.' Then I waits a minute, then comes away. I guess He hears me though it's but a little prayer."

One day Jim was knocked down crossing the street and was laid up in the hospital with a broken leg. The ward where Jim quite happily lay was a sore spot to the nurses on duty. Some of the men were cross and miserable, others did nothing but grumble from morning till night. Slowly but surely the men stopped their grumbling and were cheerful and contented.

One day as the nurse was walking through the ward she heard the men laughing. "What has happened to all of you? You are such a cheerful lot of patients lately."

"It's old Jim," they replied. "He's always cheerful, never complains, although he is uncomfortable and in pain."

The nurse walked over to Jim's bed where the silvery-haired Jim lay with an angelic look on his smiling face. "Well, Jim, these men say you are the cause for the change in this ward. They say you are always happy."

"Aye, that I am, nurse. I can't help it. You see, nurse, it's my visitor. He makes me happy."

"Visitor?" The nurse was indeed puzzled for she had never noticed any visitor by Jim's bed. The chair was always empty during visiting hours. "When does your visitor come?"

"Every day," replied Jim with the light in his eyes growing brighter. "Yup, every day at twelve o'clock He comes and stands at the foot of my bed. I see Him there, and He smiles at me and says, 'Jim, it's Jesus.' " *Adapted from* A Message from God
(a true story), Exeter, England

MAY 13 _____

Which of you by taking thought can add one cubit unto his stature? (Matt. 6:27).

So it is useless to worry. A short person cannot, by any amount of anxiety, make himself an inch taller. Why, therefore, should he waste his energy and fret his life away in wishing he wore an inch taller? One worries because he is too short, another because he is too tall; one because he has a lame foot, another because he has a mole on his face. No amount of fretting will change any of these things. People worry, too, over their circumstances. They are poor and have to work hard. They have troubles, losses, and disappointments which come through causes entirely beyond their own control. They find difficulties in their environment which they cannot surmount. There are hard conditions in their lot which they cannot change.

Now why should they worry about these things? Will worrying make matters any better? Will discontent cure the lame foot, or remove the ugly mole, or reduce corpulency, or put flesh on the thin body? Will chafing make the hard work lighter, or the burdens easier, or the troubles fewer? Will anxiety keep the winter away, or the storm from rising, or put coal in the cellar, or bread in the pantry, or get clothes for the children? Even wise philosophy shows the uselessness of worrying, since it helps nothing, and only wastes one's strength and unfits one for doing one's best. Then religion goes farther, and says that even the hard things and the obstacles are blessings, if we meet them in the right spirit— stepping stones lifting our feet upward, disciplinary experience in which we grow. So we learn that we should quietly and with faith accept life as it comes to us, fretting at nothing, changing hard conditions to easier if we can; if we cannot, then using them as means for growth and advancement.

J. R. Miller, D.D., from the book Come Ye Apart

MAY 14

Not by might, nor by power, but by my spirit, saith the Lord (Zech. 4:6).

I cannot always understand,
    The way God leadeth me,
The why, and when and wherefore
    Is oft a mystery.

But I can trust His wisdom,
    I know His way is best,
His heart knows no unkindness,
    And on His love I rest.   *Unknown*

Standing on a riverbank one day I noticed the swirling eddies next to the shore. The eddies made the water flow back upstream along the bank. At first it looked as though the river was going the wrong way, but when I looked out into the main stream of the channel I could see that the current was speeding on its way in the right direction toward the open sea.

God with power and might at His disposal yet works in this wise. His quiet performances are indirect, deep, serene, and seemingly slow, and have to be explored to be understood and appreciated. He quietly and confidently moves working wonders day after day. In everyday experiences, at work, in church, and in society, it sometimes appears as though God were being defeated, and the movements of His grace and providence were failures, and that all His plans were reversed flowing upstream in the opposite direction from the ocean of blessings. One has but to look up and cast his gaze out from the shore of frustrating encirclements of the present and consider the entire stream of God's purpose among His people in order to see that He is continually winning the battle in quiet circuitous ways.

God works through individuals, conquering some heart, and through that heart He pours His purpose like a mighty river. The Lord makes His conquests by keeping His saints in utter dependence upon Him making them live by faith. There is to be *none of self* in His program, but *all of Christ* instead. His children succeed in being what skeptics believe to be failures. They conquer their enemies by loving them and by quietly letting God do the rest. The Lord always comes out the victor. He continues to perform His wonders behind the scenes and beneath the surface of roaring waters.   *M. Taylor*

MAY 15 ───

Ye ought to say, If the Lord will . . . (James 4:15).

Thou, Lord, hast not forsaken them that seek Thee (Ps. 9:10).

They that most feel every word they speak, and every thought they think in prayer; they whose apprehensions of God are most overwhelming; whose affections to God are most spiritually passionate; whose prayers are most wrestling and graciously pressing; these are the men that pray best, and love God best.
                                                    Dr. Annesley

Though an archer shoot not so high as he aims, yet the higher he takes his aim, the higher he shoots.   *Archbishop Leighton*

There never was, and never will be a believing prayer unanswered.   *McCheyne*

One cold winter, many years ago, the people of a certain town were in great trouble. A hostile army was marching down upon them and they had little doubt the cruel soldiers would destroy their homes. In one family there was an aged grandmother. While the others were fearing and worrying, the grandmother was praying that God would protect them, and that He would build a wall of defense round about them.

During the night they heard the tramping of many feet, and other fearful sounds, but no harm came to them. In the morning they found that just beyond the house the drifted snow had built a wall that had kept the soldiers from coming to their home.

"See," said the grandmother, "God did build a wall around us."   *Selected*

I do not believe there is such a thing in the history of God's kingdom as a prayer, offered in the right spirit, that is forever left unanswered.   *T. L. Cuyler*

> To pray—is to desire; but it is to
>   desire what God would have us to desire.
> He who desires not from the bottom of his
>   heart, offers a deceitful prayer.
>   *Fenelon*

MAY 16

Whatsoever ye shall ask in my name, that will I do, that the Father may be glorified in the Son (John 14:13).

To pray in the name of Jesus is not only to use His name at the end of the prayer, but "it is to pray in the mind and spirit of Jesus, while we believe His promises, rely upon His grace, and work His works."

What is it to pray in Christ's name? There is nothing mystical or mysterious about this expression. If one will go through the Bible and examine all passages in which the expression "in My name" or "in His name" or synonymous expressions are used, he will find that it means just about what it does in modern usage. If I go to a bank and hand in a check with my name signed to it, I ask of that bank *in my own name.* If I have money deposited in that bank, the check will be cashed; if not, it will not be. If, however, I go to the bank with somebody else's name signed to the check, I am asking *in his name,* and it does not matter whether I have money in that bank or any other; if the person whose name is signed to the check has money there, the check will be cashed. . . . So it is when I go to the bank of heaven, when I go to God in prayer. I have nothing deposited there, I have absolutely no credit there, and if I go in my own name I will get absolutely nothing; but Jesus has unlimited credit in heaven, and He has granted to me the privilege of going to the bank with His name on my checks; and when I thus go, my prayers will be honored to any extent.   *R. A. Torrey*

> God can make good His promise when it seemeth to be
>   broken;
> Can find out means when all men's inventions fail.
> He doeth more than we can challenge when He seemeth

To do less than He hath promised: And sometimes
openly,
Sometimes secretly, but always most certainly,
He is as good as His Word.   *Unknown*

MAY 17

Let him trust in the name of the Lord, and stay upon his God (Isa. 50:10).

Man's relationship to his God should not be shaken by the fact
that he does not understand God's providence. Quite the
contrary, when the climb is difficult and rugged and the way is
dark, he must desperately cling even more to his faith. For it is the
only thing this side of heaven that can give strength and courage to
face the obstacles of life's journey.

Alexander Duff was on his way to India to give himself to service
for Christ. He was to devote his life teaching the children of that
sad land the glorious gospel. But before reaching his destination
he was subjected to hardships severe enough to discourage one
unless he had a faith in God such as Alexander Duff.

His boat went down on the rocks near the Cape of Good Hope.
Fortunately Duff and the others were saved, but everything else
was lost. Duff found he had nothing, no clothes, no trunks. And
his fine library of eight hundred books, which he had brought with
him, had been swept to sea!

Duff stood on the bleak shore of that desolate country, looking
out over the waves. He hoped he might see something which
could be salvaged. Then he did see a small object tossing up and
down on the water. Nearer and nearer it floated. "Nothing was
worth bothering about," said Duff. It was a book, one from his
library. When a huge wave washed it up on the sand, Duff picked
it up. The book was his own Bible, out of which he read every
day!

Silently Duff gave thanks to God that of those eight hundred
books, the single one that was saved should be his Bible. He called
his friends about him. Opening it, he read to them the beautiful
psalm: "They that go down to the sea in ships, that do business in
great waters, these see the works of the Lord, and His wonders in
the deep. . . ."

Again on their way to India they once more suffered disaster. A

141

terrible storm broke out when their ship was on the very shores of India. The ship was dashed on the beach only a few miles from where Duff was to be stationed. With no other shelter at hand, he spent the night in a heathen temple . . . and the next day began his ministry to those people he was called to serve.　　*Selected*

When Jesus then lifted up his eyes, and saw a great company come unto him, he saith unto Philip, Whence shall we buy bread that these may eat? And this he said to prove him; for he himself knew what he would do (John 6:5, 6).

In this instance referred to there is a most interesting sidelight on our Lord's training of the disciples. He was not only giving them instruction constantly regarding the spiritual laws of the kingdom, but also He was seeking to have them put into practice the lessons they were learning so slowly. Philip failed his Lord in this test. He saw only the inadequacy of their own small resources. The disciples had seen the miracles of the turning of water into wine, the healing of the sick, the casting out of demons, and the stilling of the tempest, but like ourselves, they were prone to forget that the Lord of creation—the Maker of heaven and earth—was in their midst and could abundantly supply the need.

We are faced constantly with circumstances in our own lives that place us in jeopardy, and with situations in the work of the Lord which we are utterly unable to meet; but if they are rightly interpreted, they constitute a call to enter into a larger life of faith. If we place ourselves and the little we possess in His hands, we shall find that by His blessing and supernatural touch every need will be met.

Christ is ready to honor the largest demand we may make upon Him for His resources are inexhaustible, and He would have us ask largely that our joy might be full. If our hearts are kept filled with His love, and we are seeking the blessing of others and the glory of God, it is our privilege to so trust Him that we shall experience answers to our prayers continually. The difficulties that confront us are not intended to discourage us, but to teach us new lessons in the life of faith, and to prove us to see whether we will depend upon the natural, or trust Him to perform the impossible.

Clipping from unknown periodical

MAY 19

. . . searcheth all things, yea, the deep things of God (1 Cor. 2:10).

Dwell deep . . . (Jer. 49:8).

Geologists assure us that there still exist in the deep sea living species of animals which, in former geologic periods dwelt in coastal districts of the ocean. Here they seemed to have found an asylum from the dangers which seemed to threaten their existence.

Just as the safety of these animals depended upon their abiding in the deep sea, even so our own safety as believers on the Lord Jesus Christ depends altogether in our abiding in the secret place of the Most High. No matter how unsafe the surroundings, no matter how disagreeable the circumstances, no matter how unhealthy the climate, just as long as the child of God has learned the secret of dwelling deep in the refuge that has been provided for the child of God, there is no danger of his being swamped by anything that may come his way.

The psalmist undoubtedly realized this or he would not have been so faithful in boasting of his safe hiding place, his eternal refuge. Child of God, get away from the surface dwelling. Plunge into the ocean of God's love. Dwell deep! There are surface dwellers who come in contact with every storm that crosses their ocean. There are others who plunge for God. They are so far out in the ocean, so far away from the surface, so deep in the waters, underneath the waves, that no matter what comes their way, they remain unmoved, untouched, unharmed. Thank God for those that dwell deep. They will be kept safe.

Selected from an unknown periodical

Dwell deep, my soul! Forbid thou shouldst stay shallow!
  Dwell deep in thought, in purpose, wish, and will!
Dwell deep in God—let His own presence hallow;
  Thy inner being let His presence fill.

Dwell deep, my soul! The Master's glad returning
  May hindered be, through those who shallow stay;

143

The luke-warm hearts, who know no holy burning,
May hinder much that coming welcome Day!

J. Danson Smith, *from* Daily Meditations,
Thou Remainest, *published in London*

MAY 20

Be subject one to another, and be clothed with humility: for God resisteth the proud, and giveth grace to the humble (1 Peter 5:5).

The world, I thought, belonged to me—
Goods, gold and people, land and sea—
Where'er I walked beneath God's sky
In those old days my word was "I."

Years passed; there flashed my pathway near
The fragment of a vision dear;
My former word no more sufficed,
And what I said was—"I and Christ."

But, O, the more I looked on Him,
His glory grew, while mine grew dim,
I shrank so small, He towered so high,
All I dared say was—"Christ and I."

Years more the vision held its place
And looked me steadily in the face;
I speak now in humbler tone,
And what I say is—"Christ alone."   *Unknown*

Humility is perfect quietness of heart. It is to have no trouble. It is never to be fretted or vexed, or irritated, or sore, or disappointed; it is to expect nothing, to wonder at nothing that is done to me, to feel nothing done against me. It is to be at rest when I am blamed and despised. It is to have a blessed home in the Lord where I can go in and shut the door and kneel to my Father in secret, and be at peace, as in a deep sea of calmness when all around and above is trouble.   *From an old bookmark*

We tread life's upper road when we walk humbly with our God.

144

We grope for the wall like the blind; and we grope as if we had no eyes; we stumble in noon day as in the night; we are in desolate places as dead men (Isa. 59:10).

What graphic words! What a perfect word picture of the bewildered world in which we live today. In every land and in every walk of life, among Christians and unbelievers alike, there is the universal realization of one fact: our world is face to face with some great cataclysmic change. The heart of every Christian thrills with expectation, for the Spirit of God whispers to every born-again soul: "It must be the breaking of the day." But to spiritually blind leaders of spiritually blind men and nations each passing day brings an ever increasing fear of some nameless, indefinable force which is slowly but irresistibly gripping the hearts of affairs of the human race.

A little mother, leading a baby girl about four years of age, boarded a streetcar . . . She sat down and took her daughter upon her lap. Beside her sat a woman who held a lovely bouquet of roses; and attracted by the sweet face of the child with the big blue eyes, the woman took one flower from the bouquet and offered it to the little tot. "Here is a rose for you, darling," she said.

The child looked strangely at her and then drew back. Puzzled, the woman repeated her offer, and this time touched the child's hand with the petals of the rose. The child seemed frightened, for in confusion she quickly reached up and touched her mother's face to attract her attention. The mother turned to the kindly woman beside her and spoke just four words. Upon her careworn face there was a sweetly sad little smile that told the eloquently tragic tale of a mother heart. "My darling is blind."

Blind! Oh yes, physical blindness arouses the emotion of pity in the hearts of all of us, but how much more tragic is the plight of countless thousands of men and women whose *spiritual* eyes are blind. Oh that men might see and admire the beauties of the lovely rose of Sharon. *First Mate Bob, used by permission*

Fight the good fight of faith . . . (1 Tim. 6:12).

This is the victory that hath overcome the world, even our faith (1 John 5:4).

N apoleon quickly observed where the strategic position for a battlefield lay. He would then thrust all his forces and resources into conquering and keeping that position, no matter what the sacrifice to his troops.

To claim spiritual conquests, soldiers in the army of God must be prepared and alert to do the same. Gordon B. Watt once said: "The point of obstruction must be found out, and prayer focused upon it. The mind must be convicted. The will must be stirred into right action. On the obstruction, whatever it may be, as it is revealed through waiting upon God, prayer must be concentrated.

Oh, the wonders of prayer! "Abraham's servant prays . . . Rebekah appears. Jacob wrestles and prays and prevails with Christ . . . Esau's mind is wonderfully turned from the revengeful purpose he has harbored for twenty years. Moses cries to God . . . the sea divides. Moses prays . . . Amalek is discomfited. Joshua prays . . . Achan is discovered. Hannah prays . . . Samuel is born. David prays . . . Ahithophel hangs himself. Asa prays . . . a victory is gained. Jehoshaphat cries to God . . . God turns away his foes. Isaiah prays . . . the dream is revealed. Daniel prays . . . the lions are muzzled. Daniel prays . . . the seventy weeks are revealed. Ezra prays at Ahava . . . God answers. Nehemiah starts a prayer . . . the king's heart is softened in a minute. Elijah prays . . . a drought of three years succeeds. Elijah prays . . . rain descends apace. Elisha prays . . . Jordan is divided. The church prays ardently . . . Peter is delivered by an angel."

The weapon of prayer against the forces of evil prevails. It brings power. It brings fire. It brings rain. It brings life. It brings God! There is no power like that of prevailing prayer. Dare to be definite with God; dare to lay hold of the promises and to wait in faith until the answer comes. Victory is through Calvary!   *Unknown*

MAY 23 _____

According to my earnest expectation and my hope (Phil. 1:20).

A mbition is a word which has been so much soiled with ignoble use that it seems at first sight out of place in Christian

146

thought. Yet the word is used by the great Apostle, once and again. *Philotimia,* "love and honor," that is to say, ambition is Saint Paul's chosen word. For example, in 2 Corinthians 5:9 it reads, "We labour that . . . we may be accepted of him." But the Greek is, literally, "We are ambitious to be accepted." "Honor" may be "loved" with widely different motives. It may be sought on grounds merely selfish. It may be sought, on the other hand, on grounds which are pure and unselfish. Look at the ardent student at the university, striving for intellectual distinction that he may lay his honors at the feet of parent or of schoolmaster. Look at the soldier in the field, resolved to "distinguish himself," so that his admired commander may win another victory with his aid.

The believer may "seek honor," the honor which cometh ultimately from God only, "the praise of the glory of His grace," with the pure desire that fresh laurels may be added to the wreath of his victorious Lord. If so, he is called to be ambitious.

The above verse from the Philippian Epistle is exactly in point. "The Apostle discloses to us his ambition. It is, 'that *Christ should be magnified* in my body, whether it be by life or by death.' He is ambitious—for his Lord." He wants the world to see that Christ is glorious. In order to do this, he desires *himself* to live and die in no common way. He is ambitious. But it is for his Christ.

> *Handley C. G. Moule, Bishop of Durham,*
> from Thoughts for the Sundays of the Year, *London 1906*

Make me Thy labourer,
Let me not dream of ever looking back.
Let not my knees be feeble, hands be slack,
O make me strong to labour, strong to bear,
From the rising of the morning till the stars appear.

Selected from unknown periodical

MAY 24

Thy way is in the sea, and thy path in the great waters, and thy footsteps are not known (Ps. 77:19).

And the sea appears to be the most trackless of worlds! The sea is the very symbol of mystery, the grim dwelling-house of innumerable things that have been lost. But God's way moves here and there across this trackless wild. God is never lost among our mysteries. He knows His way about. When we are bewildered He sees the road, and He sees the end even from the beginning. Even the sea, in every part of it, is the Lord's highway. When His way is in the sea we cannot trace it. Mystery is part of our appointed discipline. Uncertainty is to prepare us for a deeper assurance. The spirit of questioning is one of the ordained means of growth. And so the bewildering sea is our friend, as some day we shall understand. We love to "lie down in green pastures," and to be led "beside the still waters," and God gives us our share of this nourishing rest. But we need the mysterious sea, the overwhelming experience, the floods of sorrow which we cannot explain. If we had no sea we should never become robust. We should remain weaklings to the end of our days.

God takes us out into the deeps. But His way is in the sea. He knows the haven, He knows the track, and we shall arrive!

J. H. Jowett, from My Daily Meditation, *1914*

In his early days of learning the ways of the sea an old seaman tells this story on himself. When out in a boat by himself, he got lost several times. He was told to use his compass. Out into the water he went again. He soon got lost and lay overnight as usual. Upon being found he was asked why he did not use his compass. He said he did not dare to. He wished to go north, and he "Tried hard to make the thing go north, but it wasn't any use; 'twould shake, shake, right around, and point southeast every time." Many people fail to go the right direction on the sea of life for the very same reason of the mishap which befell our seaman—they are afraid to take the Captain at His Word and follow the direction in which He points.   *M. Taylor*

MAY 25 _____

. . . the whole creation groaneth and travaileth in pain together until now. And not only they, but ourselves also, which have the firstfruits of the Spirit, even we ourselves groan within ourselves, waiting for the adoption, to wit, the redemption of our body (Rom. 8:22–23).

In one of Ralph Connor's books he tells a story of Gwen. Gwen was a wild, willful lassie and one who had always been accustomed to having her own way. Then one day she met a terrible accident which crippled her for life. She became very

148

rebellious, and in the murmuring state she was visited by the "sky pilot," as the missionary among the mountaineers was termed.

He told her the parable of the canyon: At first there were no canyons, but only the broad, open prairie. One day the Master of the prairie, walking over His great lawns where were only grasses, asked the prairie, "Where are your flowers?" and the prairie said, "Master, I have no seeds."

Then He spoke to the birds, and they carried seeds of every kind of flower and strewed them far and wide, and soon the prairie bloomed with crocuses and roses and buffalo beans and the yellow crowfoot and the wild sunflowers and the red lilies all summer long. Then the Master came and was well pleased; but He missed the flowers He loved best of all, and He said to the Prairie: "Where are the clematis and the columbine, the sweet violets and the windflowers, and all the ferns and flowering shrubs?"

And again He spoke to the birds, and again they carried all the seeds and scattered them far and wide. But, again, when the Master came He could not find the flowers He loved best of all, and He said, "Where are those, my sweetest flowers?"

And the prairie cried sorrowfully, "Oh, Master, I cannot keep the flowers, for the winds sweep fiercely, and the sun beats upon my breast, and they wither up and fly away."

Then the Master spoke to the lightning, and with one swift blow the lightning cleft the prairie to the heart. And the prairie rocked and groaned in agony, and for many a day moaned bitterly over the black, jagged, gaping wound.

But the river poured its waters through the cleft, and carried down deep black mold, and once more the birds carried seeds and strewed them in the canyon. After a long time the rough rocks were decked out with soft mosses and trailing vines, and all the nooks were hung with clematis and columbine, and great elms lifted their huge tops high up into the sunlight, and down about their feet clustered the low cedars and balsams, and everywhere the violets and windflowers, and maidenhair grew and bloomed, till the canyon became the Master's favorite place for rest and peace and joy.

Then the "sky pilot" read to her: "The fruit—I'll read 'flowers'—of the Spirit are love, joy, peace, longsuffering, gentleness—and some of these grow only in the canyon."

"Which are the canyon flowers?" asked Gwen softly, and the pilot answered: "Gentleness, meekness, longsuffering; but though the others—love, joy, peace—bloom in the open, yet never with so rich a bloom and so sweet a perfume as in the canyon."

For a long time Gwen lay quiet, and then said wistfully, while her lips trembled: "There are no flowers in my canyon, but only ragged rocks."

"Someday they will bloom, Gwen dear; the Master will find them, and we, too, shall see them."

Beloved, when you come to your canyon, remember!

From Mountain Trailways

MAY 26

My presence shall go with thee . . . (Exod. 33:14).

Christ's presence does not keep the storms away; but He is with us in the storms. We are safer in danger with Christ than in quietness without Him. We do not place our hopes in the sinking sands of time, rather is our confidence in the steadfast Rock of Ages. But we must be like our Master; it is the spirit of sacrifice and yielding to the cross that invests our lives with value . . . Amid the wildest tumult, Christ was never too weary to listen to the cry of human distress. Then why fear the tempest, when it is under the control of our Heavenly Father? He was never so engrossed in one case of need that He could not stop to give attention to another. The restoration of a sick child to her parents represents how He will restore friend to friend. Some who most needed His help took no notice of His desire to help them, like drowning men, amazed at the beauty of the lifeboat, might stay in the waves to perish. The waves that seemed to take their Lord away from the disciples really brought Him nearer to the boat. The fishermen had come to their wits' end before they came to their journey's end. How often has the Savior intervened when the strength of man is exhausted!

G. G. Cawston, from Living Waters *leaflet printed by Christian Progress Scripture Union, London*

MAY 27

When the poor and needy seek water and there is none, and their tongue faileth for thirst, I the Lord will hear them. . . . I will open rivers in high places and fountains in the midst of the valleys. I will make the dry land springs of water (Isa. 41:17–21).

To the heart that is hungering and thirsting after God and His fullness—for a drink from the living springs, the promise will be found literally true. Come thirsty one, bring your cup of need to God's measureless supply. Come and drink. Yes, drink abundantly.

> Though millions their thirst now are slaking,
> It never runs dry:
> And millions may still come partaking,
> It never runs dry.

An eastern caravan was overtaken once in the desert with a failure of the water supply. The accustomed fountains were all dried; the oasis was a desert. They stopped an hour before sunset to find, after a day of scorching heat, that they were perishing for want of water. Vainly they explored the usual wells, but they were all dry. Dismay was upon all faces; despair was in all hearts. Suddenly an old man approached the sheik and advised him to unloose the two beautiful deer that he was taking home as a present to his bride. Surely the sensitive nostrils of the deer would detect the presence of water if any was to be found. Their tongues were protruding with thirst, their bosoms heaved with distress, but as they were led out to the borders of the camp, they lifted their heads and sniffed the air. Then, with unerring instinct, with a course as straight as an arrow and speed as swift as the wind, they darted off across the desert. Swift horsemen followed close behind, and an hour or two later hastened back with the good news that water had been found. The camp moved with shouts of rejoicing to the newly discovered fountains.

Mrs. Charles E. Cowman

MAY 28

The dogs eat of the crumbs which fall from their masters' table (Matt. 15:27).

While Jesus was ministering in Tyre and Sidon a woman came to Him asking that He heal her daughter. According to His wisdom He hesitated until her persistent pleading drew from Him these words: "It is not meet to take the children's bread, and to cast it to dogs."

Both the humility and the quick, eager faith of this woman appear in her response. "Truth, Lord: yet the dogs eat of the crumbs which fall from their masters' table." She was not offended by the figure our Lord had used. She was willing to be as a little dog under the Master's table. The children were first served, and then the pieces they let fall belonged to the dogs. All she asked was the portion that ordinarily went to the dogs. And even the crumbs from that table were enough for her, more than the richest dainties from any other table.

Thus both humility and faith were shown in her answer; and in both she is an example to us. We should come to Christ with a deep sense of our unworthiness, ready to take the lowest place. It is such a precious thing to be permitted to take even the crumbs from the Master's table, that we should exult in the privilege. The crumbs of His grace and love are better than the richest feasts of this world.

> Not worthy, Lord, to gather up the crumbs
>   With trembling hand that from Thy table fall,
> A weary, heavy-laden sinner comes
>   To plead Thy promise and obey Thy call.

Yet we are not fed with crumbs; we are seated at the full table, with the richest provisions before us. The prodigal, returning, asked only to be made a servant, as he felt unworthy to be restored to a son's place. But father-love knew no such halfway restoration as that. The white robe, the ring, the shoes, were given to him, insignia of sonship. God puts the lowliest and unworthiest at once into the children's place, and feeds them abundantly.

J. R. Miller, from Come Ye Apart

MAY 29

Thus saith the Lord, In an acceptable time have I heard thee, and in a day of salvation have I helped thee: and I will preserve thee (Isa. 49:8).

> Oh, it is hard to work for God,
>   To rise and take His part
> Upon this battle-field of earth,
>   And not sometimes lose heart!

He hides Himself so wondrously,
  As though there were no God;
He is least seen when all the powers
  Of ill are most abroad.

Or He deserts us at the hour
  The fight is all but lost;
And seems to leave us to ourselves
  Just when we need Him most.

Ill masters good, good seems to change
  To ill with greatest ease;
And, worst of all, the good with good
  Is at cross purposes.

Ah! God is other than we think;
  His ways are far above,
Far beyond reason's height, and reached
  Only by childlike love.

Workman of God! oh, lose not heart,
  But learn what God is like;
And in the darkest battle-field
  Thou shalt know where to strike.

Thrice blest is he to whom is given
  The instinct that can tell
That God is on the field when He
  Is most invisible.

Blest, too, is he who can divine
  Where real right doth lie,
And dares to take the side that seems
  Wrong to man's blindfold eye.

For right is right, since God is God;
  And right the day must win;
To doubt would be disloyalty,
  To falter would be sin.

F. W. Faber, from Quiet Hours, *1874*

"O the depth of the riches both of the wisdom and knowledge of God! how unsearchable are his judgments, and his ways past finding out! For who hath known the mind of the Lord? or who hath been his counsellor?" (Rom. 11:33–34).

_____

She goeth unto the grave to weep there (John 11:31).

The Jews thought Mary was going to weep at the sepulchre, and so she did; but she heard that the Master had come, and she went *first to Him* and *He went with her to the grave.* He went with her first to weep and then to turn her mourning into joy with life from the dead. Ah! my friend, whatever we mean to do, let us go to Jesus first.

Mary wept for her brother and she had the sympathy of Him whom it is our blessed privilege to claim as our Elder Brother; but the widow weeping over the grave of him who was the bosom companion of her life, until it pleased God to receive his spirit sanctified through Christ, may appeal to the Mediator's heart by a yet dearer name; for whom the Lord would show how tenderly and faithfully He "nourisheth and cherisheth His Church" (Eph. 5:29). He calls Himself her husband, her precious, holy, affectionate "husband." "Thy Maker is thine Husband" (Isa. 54:5).

So, heartstricken mourner, He knows the grief and anguish you feel; He knows the desolations of your spirit and its yearnings after a solace the world cannot give!

Go to the grave of your beloved one; but as you go let not your tears so blind you, neither so hang down your head that you may not see that Jesus has come to sustain you. Hear His gracious voice from beside the tomb, *"I am the Resurrection and the life."*

Your beloved is not dead. His believing soul that lived with Christ here, now lives with Christ in heaven; and his Christian dust is sleeping sweetly until He shall rise, immortal, glorious, and incorruptible at the resurrection of the last day. All your love, and watching, and anxious nursing could not save him from suffering and sickness and the tomb; but the love of Jesus has delivered him from all, and taken him up to that sinless, sorrowless home where there "shall be no more death, neither sorrow or crying, neither shall there be any more pain; for the former things have passed away."

Here you were united in a better than an earthly love, the love of Christ, and in that love you are and shall be united forever. Look, then, beyond the scene of your mortal grief, to the home of your perpetual bliss. Christ has lain in the tomb and sweetened it for the sleep of His beloved and yours; but as you stoop to see within the sepulchre see you not that it is broken, and that the uprising Master has opened a way through it, up through the rent veil, up through the everlasting doors, to the paradise of God? There seek to follow; and when you draw near the celestial band you will find waiting to welcome you one more radiant than an angel, in whose transfigured countenance you will recognize him you have not lost, but who has gone before to our Father's house.

> If I should die and leave you here awhile,
> Be not like others, sore undone, who keep
> Long vigils by the silent dust, and weep:
> For my sake turn again to life, and smile,
> Nerving thy heart and trembling hand to do
> Something to comfort weaker hearts than thine;
> Complete these dear unfinished tasks of mine,
> And I, perchance, may therein comfort you.

Selected from Consolation

MAY 31

Whosoever is angry with his brother without a cause shall be in danger of judgment (Matt. 5:22).

Our Lord always leads us to the secret innermost roots of things. He does not concern Himself with symptoms, but with causes. He does not begin with the molten lava flowing down the fair mountain slope and destroying the vineyards. He begins with the central fires in which the lava is born. He does not begin with uncleanness. He begins with the thoughts which produce it. He does not begin with murder, but with the anger which causes it. "He that hateth his brother is a murderer," does not mean that hatred is as great a crime as murder, but that it grows from the same root and is of the same nature. Murder is only anger full-grown.

And there is anger which is like a smoky bonfire, and it pollutes while it destroys. It is the unclean anger which is of sin. It seeks revenge, not righteousness. It seeks "to get its own back," not to get the wrongdoer back to God. It follows wrong with further wrong. It spreads the devil's fire. The way to keep out such feelings is to yield to every gentle and loving impulse of the Spirit—to "overcome evil with good."

Now all anger is not of sin. The Apostle Paul enjoins his readers to "be angry, and sin not." To be altogether incapable of anger would be to offer no antagonism to the wrongs and oppressions of the world. "Who is made to stumble, and I burn not?" cries the apostle. If wrong stalked abroad with heedless feet he burned with holy passion. There is anger which is like clean flame, clear and pure, as "the sea of glass mingled with fire."

John Henry Jowett, from My Daily Meditation, *1914*

Speak not in anger with one another.
  There is no cause to hate a brother.
Overcome those thoughts with good today
  And help thy brother on his way.

God is concerned with heart's intent,
  Not what is said, but what is meant.
Your heart, thought, and tongue possessed
  By Him will every day be blessed.

Marie Taylor

JUNE 1

. . . that ye might be filled with all the fullness of God (Eph. 3:19).

. . . yet not I, but Christ liveth in me . . . (Gal. 2:20).

Christ within makes an inner joy that all the darkness of earth's trials cannot quench. There are great diversities of experience in sorrow. Some when this world's lights are quenched are left in utter gloom, like a house without lamp or candle or flickering firelight when the sun goes down. Others, in similar darkness, stand radiant in the deep shadows: They have bright light within themselves. Christ dwells in them, and the beams from His blessed life turn night into day.

It is in sorrow-darkened hearts that Christ truly dwells. The light streaming from Him who is the Light of the World, in whom is no darkness, illumines all the gloom of grief. Indeed, when Christ dwells in the heart, sorrow is a blessing, because it reveals beauties and joys which could not have been seen in the earthly light. It is one of the blessings of night, that without it we could never see the stars; it is one of the blessings of trial, that without it we could never see the precious comforts of God.

156

Were there no night, we could not read the stars,
　The heavens would turn into a blinding glare;
Freedom is best seen through prison bars,
　And rough seas make the haven passing fair;
We cannot measure joys but by their loss;
　When blessings fade away, we see them then;
Our richest clusters grow around the cross,
　And in the night-time angels sing to men.

When Christ is within us, sorrow is a time of revelation. It is like the cloud that crowned the summit of the holy mountain into which Moses climbed, and by which he was hidden so long from the eyes of the people. While folded in the clouds, he was looking upon God's face. Sorrow's cloud hides the world, and wraps the wondering one in thick darkness; but in the darkness, Christ Himself unveils the splendor and glory of His face. There are many who never saw the beauty of Christ, and never knew Him in the intimacy of a personal friendship, till they saw Him, and learned to talk with Him as Friend with friend, in the hour of sorrow's darkness. When the lamps of earth went out, Christ's face appeared.　　　　　　　　　*J. R. Miller, from* Silent Times, *1886*

JUNE 2 ────────────────────────────────────

And they departed into a desert place by ship privately (Mark 6:32).

If you have a desert place in your heart to which you must sometimes go, you should depart to it in a "ship privately." No man should make a thoroughfare of his desert. Keep your grief for the private ship. Never go into company with an abstracted mind; that is to display your desert. You have sometimes refrained from God's table of communion because your thoughts were away. You did well. Man's table of communion has the same need. If you are bidden to a feast when you are troubled in your mind, try first whether you can carry your burden privately away. Let thy heart be reconciled to thy Father, and then come to the world and offer thy gift.

O Thou that hast hid Thy thorn beneath a rose, steer the ship in which I conceal my burden! Thou hast gone to the feast of Cana from the fast in the wilderness; where hast Thou hid the print of the nails? In love. Steer me to that burying-ground! Let the ship,

157

on its way to my desert, touch for an hour at the desert of my brother! Let me feel the fellowship of grief, the community of sorrow, the kindredness of pain! Let me hear the voices from other wildernesses, the sighs from other souls, the groans from other graves! And, when I come to my own landing-place and put down my hand to lift up my burden, I shall meet a wondrous surprise. It will be there, but it will be there half-sized. Its heaviness will be gone, its impossibility will have vanished. I shall lift it easily; I shall carry it lightly; I shall bury it swiftly. I shall be ready for Cana in an hour, ready for Calvary in a few moments. I shall go back to enter into the struggle of the multitude; and the multitude will say, "There is no desert with *him*."

George Matheson, from Leaves For Quiet Hours, *1904*

JUNE 3 _____

I am the vine, ye are the branches: He that abideth in me, and I in him, the same bringeth forth much fruit: for without me ye can do nothing (John 15:7).

> O, struggle not to abide
>   Nor labor to bring forth fruit,
> But let Jesus unite thee to Himself
>   As the Vine-branch to the root.
>
> So simple, so deep, so strong
>   That union with Him shall be;
> HIS life shall ever replace thine own
>   And His love shall flow thru thee.
>
> *Found written in Charles E. Cowman's Bible*

Fruit comes from living in God. It is the result of His life flowing in us, of our yielding to His power; not of our trying and struggling to be good. In the Waldensian Valleys in Italy some of the vines are grown on huge wooden crosses—and in September they are a beautiful sight, laden with grapes. The branches are stretched out on the cross, and so get every drop of rain, every ray of sun. I do not suppose these branches are conscious of the cross, as much as they are of the warmth, and life, and joy of fruit-bearing, and is not that a parable of the Christian life? It explains the joy and peace of the early church, even in persecution. They had utterly given themselves to Another; self was crucified with Christ,

158

and joy and fruitfulness were the result, as it will be with us today, if our lives are hid with Christ in God.   *S. T. Fraser*

Unconditional yielding to the Lord brings us into full unity with Christ to abide in Him, and He in us, and causes us to walk humbly with Him among our fellow men. It places us in sweet fellowship with Him and His. While waiting for His glorious return we are privileged to live on His life, nourished, fed, strengthened, and constantly filled with His Spirit and presence. Our part is just to give ourselves to Him, fully recognizing our own worthlessness, and ever abide in Him.   *Selected*

> Here I bring within my trembling hands,
> This will of mine, a thing that seemeth small,
> Yet Thou alone, O Lord, canst understand
> How when I yield Thee this, I yield mine all.
>
>   *Unknown*

JUNE 4

Before I was afflicted I went astray, but now have I kept thy word (Ps. 119:67).

A master of metaphor has made the complaining wax speak thus:

"Unaccountable, this!" said the wax, as from the flame it dropped melting upon the paper beneath.

"Do not grieve," said the paper, "I am sure it is all right!"

"I was never in such agony!" exclaimed the wax, still dropping.

"It is not without a good design, and will end well," replied the paper.

The wax was unable to reply at once, and when it again looked up it bore a beautiful impression, the counterpart of the seal which had been applied to it.

"Ah, I understand now!" said the wax, no longer in suffering. "I was softened in order to receive this lovely durable impress."

> It's not a bit of good to grumble and complain;
>   It's just as cheap and easy to rejoice;
> When God sorts out the weather and sends rain,
>   Why—rain's my choice.   *Unknown*

159

God has made affliction as a shower to the green grass.

Unknown

We must needs go to glory by the way of the weeping cross; and as we were never promised that we should ride to heaven in a feather bed, we must not be disappointed when we see the road to be rough, as our fathers found it before us. *C. H. Spurgeon*

I used to think that God's gifts were on the shelves one above the other; and that the taller we grew in Christian character the easier we could reach them. I now find that God's gifts are on shelves one beneath the other; and that it is not a question of growing taller but of stooping lower, and that we have to go down always to get His best gift. *F. B. Meyer*

JUNE 5 _____

Speaking to yourselves in psalms and hymns and spiritual songs, singing and making melody in your heart to the Lord (Eph. 5:19).

O ne lovely June morning I went out to work in the yard just at the break of day when the sun began to rise. A little mountain canary lighted on a branch of the tree next to where I was standing and began his morning song of praise. At first I was so intent upon the work before me, and quite accustomed to the sounds of the mountain folk both day and night, that I hardly noticed his singing. Determined that there was to be an appreciative audience for his melodious performance, he hopped down to a branch within arm's reach and warbled more resoundingly. This time I stopped, gazed and listened. The little yellow creature put his whole soul into his ethereal song; and I sensed deep within me that he was a choralist sent from God to brighten my whole day with his aria.

Someone has said that a song at the right time and in the right place will outlive any sermon. Perhaps it may be that a song really comes from the melody in the heart. Down through the ages singing has been the mode of expression of all people. Song has immortalized national events, has cemented relationships, has endeared experiences. To those who are parted, a certain song can fuse their breach.

That feathered messenger caused me to avow that I was to keep

160

the spirit of song in my life; to be useful to others, and become an inspiration to those within the sound of my voice. The beloved psalmist sings, "Awake up, my glory . . . I will sing unto the Lord as long as I live; I will sing praises unto thee among the nations." Let us sing together our song for today: "For the Lord is good; His mercy is everlasting."   *M. Taylor*

JUNE 6

He shall break in pieces mighty men without number . . . (Job 34:24).

A shattered and broken personality releases the fragrance of Christ. Jacob was broken at Peniel when he wrestled with God. Mary was broken at Bethany when Lazarus was taken from her.

Why must it be a broken personality? Is it not wholeness of character that we have always heard about that gives off the perfume of holiness? The word wholeness is connected with holiness and health—spiritual health. We know that wholeness without God means danger and finally failure.

Charles Fox knew what it was to be broken. He wrote during a time of mending,

Dark waters blossom white in breaking,
High souls are made in the unmaking.

The dark waters in breaking have united with the unseen oxygen; that is why they can reflect the glory of the light.

Another illustration is given regarding broken personality. James McConkey purposed to be a lawyer, and spent years training for the bar. Family bereavement led him to combine his study with his business. It was too much for him. Though he reached his desired goal, he broke under the strain. In his breaking God brought him into the life of full surrender, reflecting the glory of God. He had written many meditations and thoughts for those who needed encouragement and strength. In his *God Planned Life* he uses this illustration: A beautiful, very beautiful stained-glass window in a cathedral was the object of attraction to many tourists. One night an awful storm raged; the whole window frame blew in, and the glass smashed in atoms on the floor. The sorrowful people of the city gathered up the fragments, placed them in a box and removed them to the crypt. One day a stranger came, and asked permission to see them and if he might take them away. "Yes," they said, "we have no use for them." Later came a mysterious invitation to some of those city authorities from a well-known artist in stained glass. A curtain was removed in his studio, and there was their beautiful window, only more, *much more beautiful* than before— a gift from the artist to take home.   *Mrs. Charles E. Cowman*

JUNE 7

. . . and many others which ministered unto Him of their substance (Luke 8:3).

There is a legend which says that long ago there dwelt in a royal palace three fair maids. While they were in the wonderful garden one morning with its strong streams and blushing roses, there arose the question as to which of them had the most beautiful hands. Eleanor, who had tinted her white fingers while gathering the luscious strawberries, thought hers the most beautiful. Antoinette had been among the fragrant roses and her hands had partaken of their dewy sweetness. To her they were the loveliest. Joan had dipped her dainty fingers in the lucid stream and as the clear diamond drops sparkled on her tapered fingers she thought her hands the most beautiful. Just then there came a beggar girl who asked for alms, but the royal maidens drew aside their rich robes and turned away. The beggar passed on to a cottage nearby and a woman with sunburned face and toil-stained hands gave her bread. The beggar, so the legend runs, was immediately transformed into an angel and appeared at the garden gate saying, "The most beautiful hands are those which are found ready to bless and help their fellowmen."   *Selected*

The Lord looked down from the heavenly place,
   And searched the whole world through
For those who were working in love for Him,
   And He found but very few.
Said the Lord: "They shall labor not in vain
   Though the earth is dark with woe;
I will strengthen the hands of them that toil,
   I will bless the fields they sow.

Bertha D. Martin,
from the Log of the Good Ship Grace

Take my hands and let them move at the impulse of Thy love.

Frances R. Havergal

JUNE 8

Praying always with all prayer and supplication in the Spirit, and watching thereunto with all perseverance . . . (Eph. 6:18).

To be permitted to go "behind the scenes" is ever a fascinating experience. It is a great privilege to have access to a studio where the famous artist is at work. It is surpassingly interesting to be informed of some great scholar's method of study, to be allowed to open his notebook and observe his mode of approach. The mind of every divinity student becomes peculiarly vigilant and absorbed when he is admitted into some great preacher's workshop, and sees his tools, and, better still, hears him tell how he sets about to use them. But surely, the supreme privilege is to obtain entry, by a private door, into the life of some radiant saint, and to watch with what kind of grasp he lays hold of the unseen, and how he sets about to pray, and what is the character of his supplication. Well, now, here is a great expert in the devout life, the Apostle Paul, and in the Epistle to the Ephesians he takes us into his innermost room, and tells us what he thinks about prayer, and he permits us to hear him engaged in its sacred exercise. I propose that we should accept the privilege, and use it for the instruction of our own souls.

How ought this great business of prayer to be done? First replies this expert apostle, *"in the spirit."* That distinguishes true prayer from all professed prayer which takes its rise upon the doorstep of the lips. Again, it is to be done *"always,"* says the expert. Prayer to him was not the exercise of an hour, but the mood of a life. And what other implication is in the great apostle's conception of prayer? *"And watching thereunto in all perseverance."* It is surely reasonable, when we have fired a projectile, to watch if it has hit the mark. It is surely reasonable, when we pray for illumination of China, to keep vigilant eyes perseveringly looking for the morning, and, when any consecrated scout comes home, to question him and say, "Watchman, what of the night?"

Dr. J. H. Jowett, in The Illustrated Missionary News, *1911*

163

If thou canst believe, all things are possible to him that believeth (Mark 9:23).

What should be the attitude of a Christian when placed in a difficult and trying situation—a place of severe testing? There can be but one attitude! A simple and unwavering trust in God! A refusal to look *at* the difficult circumstance, but *above* it. The only sure way to do this is to live very close to God. As the turbo-supercharger enables an airplane to maintain full power at an altitude of thirty thousand feet, where an ordinary plane has lost four-fifths of its power, so the Christian who walks with his God, listening and obeying, keeps strong at the toughest heights of life. The fact is that God is stronger than any temptation and danger; and the person who has God in his heart is unconquerable.

It is true that God often seems to place His children in positions of profound difficulty, leading them into a tight corner—from which there is no way of escape—contriving a situation which no human judgment would have permitted.

During such periods, the words of Jesus quoted above take on added significance. It should be clearly understood that this kind of faith in God is the most practical approach to the problems and testings of life—it is not sense, or sight, or reason, but taking God at His Word. Experience reveals that such a faith will not make the sun rise sooner, but it will make the night seem shorter.

A story is told by Francis Browne of a little pilgrim band sitting by the seashore recounting their losses, while one tells of a ship that went down with all his household, and another, the sweet memories of a lost youth, and others of vanished gold, of proud honors gone, and of faithless friends: "a stranger seeming from all sorrow free," said:

> Sad losses have ye met,
> But mine is heavier yet:
> For a believing heart hath gone from me.

"Alas!" said the pilgrims. "Thine, stranger, is life's last and heaviest loss."

Life's greatest loss is the loss of faith. "Christ's anxiety to retain Peter's faith," says one writer, "can only be explained one way.

He did not interfere between him and failure, but He did interfere between him and the loss of faith. A man is lost when honor, truth, and character are gone; but when faith has gone, he has suffered the greatest loss.   *Mrs. Charles E. Cowman*

JUNE 10 _____

. . . because the love of God is shed abroad in our hearts (Rom. 5:5).

It is interesting to think of the new era of love which Jesus opened. Of course there was gentleness in the world before He came. There was mother-love. There was friendship, deep, true, and tender. There were lovers who were bound together with most sacred ties. There were hearts even among heathen people in which there was gentleness almost beautiful enough for heaven. There were holy places where affection ministered with angel tenderness.

Yet the world at large was full of cruelty. The rich oppressed the poor. The strong crushed the weak. Women were slaves and men were tyrants. There was no hand of love reached out to help the sick, the lame, the blind, the old, the deformed, the insane, nor any to care for the widow, the orphan, the homeless.

Then Jesus came; and for three and thirty years He went about among men, doing kindly things. He had a gentle heart, and gentleness flowed out in His speech. He spoke words which throbbed with tenderness. Mr. Longfellow said that there was no sermon to him, however eloquent or learned or beautiful, in which he could not hear the heartbeat. There was never any uncertainty about the heartbeat in the words which fell from the lips of Jesus. They throbbed with sympathy and tenderness.

The people knew always that Jesus was their friend. His life was full of rich helpfulness. No wrong or cruelty ever made Him ungentle. He scattered kindness wherever He moved.

> The best of men
> That e'er wore earth about him was a sufferer,
> A soft, meek, patient, humble, tranquil spirit,
> The first true gentleman that ever breathed.

One day they nailed those gentle hands upon a cross. After that the people missed Him, for He came no more to their homes. It

165

was a sore loss to the poor and the sad, and there must have been grief in many a household. But while the personal ministry of Jesus was ended by His death, the influence of His life went on. He had set the world a new example of love. He had taught lessons of patience and meekness which no other teacher has ever given. He had imparted new meaning to human affection. He made love the law of His kingdom.

As one might drop a handful of spices into the brackish sea, and therewith sweeten its waters, so these teachings of Jesus fell into the world's unloving, unkindly life, and at once began to change it into gentleness. Wherever the gospel has gone these sayings of the great Teacher have been carried, and have fallen into people's hearts, leaving there their blessings of gentleness.

J. R. Miller, from A Gentle Heart, *1904*

O the love that drew salvation's plan!
O the grace that bro't it down to man!
O the mighty gulf that God did span
　At Calvary!

Wm. R. Newell

JUNE 11 ───────────────────────────

If we suffer, we shall also reign with him (2 Tim. 2:12).

One does not travel very far in the pathway of life without encountering what we call trouble. Trouble is a relative term in that it does not mean the same thing to all people. Some of the human experiences we are accustomed to call "trouble" have to do with bodily affliction, to another it may be a great sorrow brought about by the death of a loved one or a friend. To another it may take the form of failure or disappointment.

Some folk seem to think that the best way to deal with trouble is simply to laugh it off—"Keep smiling"—"Chins up!" etc. That philosophy is good as far as it goes; but how inadequate is this advice of laughing off one's trouble when we have to deal with stark reality. The really decisive question is not what happens to us, but what happens *in* us. Not what kind of troubles come to us; but *our attitude* toward them that counts most. Self-pity and resentment is all wrong and un-Christian. So many interpret trouble and sorrow in this manner. God so often enables us to triumph over our troubles. This is always true when we let Him have His way with us.

The Christian way is to transform our troubles into triumph. Just as the oyster must put up with the irritable grain of sand and suffer the long process of spinning a gummy substance around the trouble spot to produce a pearl, our suffering can be transformed into a blessing. The liability can be changed into an asset. The adversity and disappointment can beget victory. Shall we not try hard to transform our troubles into triumph?   *Selected*

> For every hill I've had to climb,
> For every stone that bruised my feet,
> For all the blood and sweat and grime,
> For blinding storms and burning heat,
> My heart sings but a grateful song—
> These were the things that made me strong.
>
> For all the heartaches and the tears,
> For all the anguish and the pain,
> For gloomy days and fruitless years,
> And for the hopes that lived in vain,
> I do give thanks, for now I know
> These were the things that helped me grow!   *Unknown*

JUNE 12

The Lord preserveth all them that love him (Ps. 145:20).

How great are his signs! and how mighty are his wonders! His kingdom is an everlasting kingdom, and his dominion is from generation to generation (Dan. 4:3).

Mrs. Starr Stuart revealed the following adventure illustrating the above Scripture selections at a morning worship service during World War II. She was one of the many victims of German brutality on the high seas and had been on board the SS *Rangitane* when it was shelled and sunk on the Pacific, in November, 1940, while traveling from the Friendly Islands to British Guiana. After their capture, they all were put ashore on the cannibal island of Emirau—a beautiful but malaria-haunted islet—where it was the intention of their captors all should perish.

167

Judge Stuart, having experience with the Polynesians of the Friendly Islands, and knowing, too, from personal acquaintance in South Africa of the wonderful influence of the missionaries on the savage races, proposed to visit the native village and see what the prospects were for obtaining food. Knowing the danger they faced, he and his wife set out. They cautiously made their way so as not to alarm the natives unaccustomed to the sight of white people. The picturesque village hidden beneath dense tropical vegetation was quiet, empty, and deserted. Drawing near they heard the sound of a voice singing in the English tongue: "Jesus loves me, this I know, for the Bible tells me so." How reassuring were the words. They entered the hut unafraid. It was the village church. A tall, fine-looking Solomon Islander with hawk-like features was conducting the service. They were put up for the night in a little hut in the village. As they lay in an uneasy sleep on the floor they heard rustling out in the brush. Their hearts skipped. The natives! Were they hostile or friendly? In the dim light they saw a pair of black arms lift up on to the verandah a tray of food and water. A voice said the words for "Food. Eat." At the dawn, when the meal was over, they went to call on the missionary.

He was the son of cannibal parents of the Solomon Islands, but, coming under the influence of the Wesleyan missionaries, had become a Christian and been sent to Fiji to be educated as a catechumen. When his training was completed, his desire had been to go to Emirau, which no missionary had yet visited, and where the people were savage cannibals. Many had become Christian and been baptized during his ministry. "I t'nk none cannibal now. I t'nk all friendly." With these words he took up his guitar, twanged the strings and sang sweetfully and tunefully the beautiful chorus: "I will make you fishers of men if you follow Me." *Adapted from the story told by Lettice M. Rae,* Messenger from God, *Exeter, England*

JUNE 13 _____

. . . a faithful man who can find? (Prov. 20:6).

. . . for the faithful fail from among the children of men (Ps. 12:1).

It was a glorious night of midsummer—a moon at full and a host of stars. The old bee-garden was bathed in soft crystal-line light—and ever so light a breeze lisped in the treetops. At the door of one of the hives we came to a halt. There arose from the hive a sibilant sound . . . persistent . . . not unlike the sound of sea waves . . . advancing . . . retreating.

"They are fanner-bees," whispered the old beekeeper. "It's their job to keep the hive sweet and fresh. They're standing with their heads lowered, turned toward the center of the hive. Their wings are moving so rapidly that if you saw them you would think you were looking at a gray mist. They are drawing the bad air through one side of the entrance, whilst the pure air is sucked in on the other side."

Standing there close to nature, listening to the bee fanners, I felt close to one of nature's wonders, the mystery of the hive life. Presently the old beekeeper stooped to the hive, holding a lighted candle in his hand. Instantly the light was extinguished by a strong air current, those infinitesimal bee wings, moving in unison, were making a draft so strong that the candlelight was instantly quenched.

As we stood there in the starlit garden, the old preacher said, "The fanners are drawing out the bad air, letting in the fresh. Isn't that how people who call themselves Christians ought to act?" If we had enough fanners, if they were as keen on their jobs as those bees were on theirs, wouldn't the great hive of the world grow sweet and fresh?

The church is filled with willing people—some willing to work and others willing to let them.   *Unknown*

All that is necessary for the triumph of evil is that good men do nothing.   *Edmund Burke*

JUNE 14 ─────────────────────────────────────

Your rod (to protect) and Your staff (to guide), they comfort me (Ps. 23:4 AMPLIFIED).

The shepherds of Palestine will tell you the purpose for their staff. One such shepherd was asked in what sense the staff could be said to be a comfort for his sheep. The experienced leader of his flock proceeded to explain that in daylight he always carried the staff across his shoulder, and when the sheep saw it, it spoke of the presence of the shepherd (to guide), and thus it was a means of comfort. On the other hand, if night overtook him with the sheep on the mountainside, or if they were caught in a heavy mountain mist so that the sheep could no longer see the staff, then he would lower it, and as he walked he would tap with it on the ground, so that by hearing if not by sight the staff (to guide) comforted the sheep by speaking the presence of the shepherd. If wild animals would prey upon his flock, he could use the rod (to protect) and ward them off. On occasion the lambs would fall into ravines and among brambles. The shepherd would use the crook on the end of the staff for lifting the fallen one to safety. The person who is carrying the rod is the leader or ruler of his flock. The sheep know their shepherd by his rod and they follow him— not any other person who may pass by, or attempt to lead them astray.

David remembered these things and said in effect to himself, "It would be unreasonable to suppose that God has less care for me than I had for the sheep!"

"Yea, though I walk through the valley of the shadow of death, I will fear no evil; for thou art with me; thy rod and thy staff they comfort me." *King James Version*

We are Thine—do Thou befriend us, Be the Guardian of our way; Keep Thy flock, from sin defend us, Seek us when we go astray. *Dorothy A. Thrupp*

JUNE 15 ───────────────────────────

Go forth, and stand upon the mount before the Lord (1 Kings 19:11).

A rebuke is often a blessing in disguise. Elijah needed this form of address in order to arouse him to an understanding of his causeless fear. Such an one as he has no right to be fitful and repining. If he will "go forth and stand upon the mount before the Lord," instead of hiding himself away in a cave, he will find new inspiration in a new vision of His power. And so it ever is. When we are living on earth's low levels, we fail to catch the inspiring visions of God which are the true support of the prophetic life. We must come out into the sunshine and make the ascent of the mountain, if we would discern those evidences of God's power which are always available for the recreation of faith and courage.

Selected

Make me Thy mountaineer; I would not linger on the
    lower slope.
Fill me afresh with hope, O God of hope, That undefeated
I may climb the hill
As seeing Him who is invisible.

Make me to be Thy happy mountaineer, O God most high;
My climbing soul would welcome the austere; Lord, crucify
On rock or scree, ice-cliff or field of snow,
The softness that would sink to things below.

Thou art my Guide; where Thy sure feet have trod Shall
    mine be set;
Thy lightest word my law of life, O God; Lest I forget,
And slip and fall, teach me to do Thy will,
Thy mountaineer upon Thy holy hill.

Amy Wilson Carmichael, from Mountain Trailways

I would not have my life go on A level stretch, from sun
    to sun,
And miss the glorious sights I get From Calvary
    and Olivet.
These rugged paths that wound my feet, These tribulations
    that I meet
Are stepping-stones, by which I climb To glories endless
    and sublime!

Unknown,
from At the Beautiful Gate, 1879

JUNE 16

The Lord is thy shade upon thy right hand (Ps. 121:5).

There are ferns in the garden of the soul, as well as flowers. The flowers grow best in the sunshine; and the ferns grow best in the shade.

There is the fern of patience, and the fern of long-suffering, and the fern of meekness. And the great Gardener of the soul delights in the ferns, and purposes to save them from destruction by the garish day.

And so He takes us into the shade—the shade of disappointment, or the shade of sorrow, or the shade of sickness and pain. But it is a very blessed shadow, for it is the "Shadow of the Almighty." And here the ferns flourish and the cloudy day makes the garden beautiful.   *J. H. Jowett*

There cannot be shade without sunshine. There is no night without day. There are clear skies above the clouds. Only he who has rested in the shade, kept vigil through the night, or walked under the clouds can light the path for others.   *M. T.*

God is above the clouds!—the darkest; most depressing;
The clouds of disappointment, burden, anguish, pain;
The clouds of long suspense;—of tidings most distressing;
God is above the clouds!—and skies will smile again.
J. Danson Smith, from Thou Remainest, *London, England*

JUNE 17 _____

True worshippers shall worship the Father in spirit and in truth (John 4:23).

To worship God in spirit and in truth means to offer to Him the worship that we owe. God is Spirit; therefore we must worship Him in Spirit and in truth—that is to say, by presenting to Him a true and humble spiritual worship in the very depth of our being. God alone can see this worship, which, offered unceasingly, will in the end become as it were natural, and as if He were one with our soul, and our soul one with Him: practice will make this clear.

To worship God in truth is to acknowledge Him to be what He is, and ourselves as what in very fact we are. To worship Him in truth is to acknowledge with heartfelt sincerity what God in truth is—that is to say, infinitely perfect, worthy of infinite adoration, infinitely removed from sin, and so of all the divine attributes. That man is little guided by reason, who does not employ all his powers to render to this great God the worship that is His due.

To worship God in truth is to confess that we live our lives entirely contrary to His will, and contrary to our knowledge that,

172

were we but willing, He would fain make us conformable to Him. Who will be guilty of such foolishness as to withhold even for a moment the reverence and the love, the service and the unceasing worship that we owe to Him.

From *Spiritual Maxims of Brother Lawrence*

O worship the King, all glorious above,
And gratefully sing His pow'r and His love;
Our Shield and Defender, the Ancient of days,
Pavilioned in splendor and girded with praise.

Robert Grant

JUNE 18 _____

How precious also are thy thoughts unto me, O God, how great is the sum of them! If I should count them, they are more in number than the sand (Ps. 139:17, 18).

During a hillside vesper service, the message brought by His messenger was on "The Signs of the Times and World Conditions." Many were assembled there, a large group of believers, facing the future—so unseen, so unknown!—facing facts and grim realities. The question uppermost in all hearts was: "How are God's children to meet the testings that are certain to be theirs in the months ahead?" Believers cannot be as ostriches, burying their heads in the sand in a refusal to see things as they are. They must be prepared to face the issues! But how is this to be done? God prepares His own for the awful days and makes them *overcomers!*

He said not:
    Thou shalt not be Tempested;
    Thou shalt not be Travailed;
    Thou shalt not be Afflicted:
But He said:
    Thou shalt not be Overcome!

But when a Christian loses heart, he loses everything! To keep one's heart in the midst of life's stream and to maintain a front that knows no defeat in the face of its difficulties, is not an achievement that springs from anything that a laboratory can demonstrate, or that logic can affirm. It is an achievement of faith! If you lose your sky, you will soon lose your earth!

173

We quote a few helpful excerpts from a message given by a minister in Scotland: "Nothing is more beautiful than our Lord's forethought! He was always thinking ahead of the disciples. When He sent them to prepare the Passover there was found an upper room furnished and prepared. His plans were not only for *that* day. He was always in advance of time! When the disciples came back from fishing, Jesus was on the seashore with a fire of coals and fish laid thereon. In the morning He thinks of the day before you are astir! He is waiting long before you are awake. His anticipations are along all the way of life before you!

After the resurrection, the disciples were bewildered and the way looked black! But the angel said, "Behold, He goeth before you into Galilee"; He is always thinking ahead! preparing ahead!

"Let not your heart be troubled, neither let it be afraid."

"I go to prepare a place for you!"

You will discover His insight! His over-sight! and His foresight! You may not always see Him, but you can walk by faith in the dark if you know that He sees you; and can sing as you journey, even through the night.   *Mrs. Charles E. Cowman*

> Let shadows come, let shadows go,
> Let life be bright or dark with woe,
> I am content, for this I know,
> Thou thinkest, Lord, of me.
>   *Selected*

JUNE 19

A son honoureth his father . . . if then I be a father, where is mine honour? (Mal. 1:6).

It is not surprising that there are many more references in the Word of God to "father" and "Father" than there are to "mothers" when one takes into account how important it is for an individual to understand the Heavenly Father. It is impossible for one to comprehend fully the "Father image" of God without experiencing an earthly father.

There are some who may disagree as to which one is the more influential in the life of a child, the mother or the father. The mother is the one who guides the child to his immediate goals in daily living, whereas generally speaking, the father is the one who establishes the long-range ambitions—those ideals for which to strive in order to make a success in life.

It is extremely difficult for a person to establish right relationship with the Heavenly Father without having first established a healthy and loving relationship with his earthly father. How does one experience God as Father if he has never known a father's love, or concern, his support and protection, his sharing and understanding, discipline, wisdom, or even his firm warm hand?

A child deems what is important to his father as being paramount to him. As God's child one wants to please Him because he knows it pleases Him. What is important to God is significant to His child.

"Father knows best," is an old maxim, but sometimes the child must experience his own choices in order to appreciate more the wisdom of his father. The Heavenly Father allows His children to do their own bidding in order to more fully appreciate God's will.

Fathers many times think they are needed only for special favors desired by the son or daughter. The Father in heaven is noted for granting special favors to His own.

A child revels in his times of fun and fellowship with his father. How it thrills the child of God to have those moments of sweet communion with his Father above.

A father labors day after day to be a provider for his family. One of God's attributes is that of being the Provider of all our needs.

The father takes time to hear and understand the difficulties of his child. Father God knows all about our troubles. He hears, He understands and promises to lighten our burdens.

Is it not therefore a responsibility, a challenge of utmost importance for a father to be really a "father" to his children? The father who knows God the Father will be the most complete father, the most honored father. He cannot risk being less.

Marie Taylor

JUNE 20 ———————————————————————

Thou shalt teach them diligently unto thy children, and shalt talk of them when thou sittest in thy house, and when thou walkest by the way; and when thou liest down and riseth up (Deut. 6:7).

Only take heed to thyself and keep thy soul diligently, lest thou forget the things which thine eyes have seen, and they depart thine heart all the days of thy life; but teach them to thy sons, and thy son's sons (Deut. 4:9).

In the *Log of the Good Ship Grace*, First Mate Bob retells Dr. Joplin's version of the parable of the prodigal son which is apropos to the Father's Day theme. It requires the admonition concerning God's laws which are given to fathers in Deuteronomy, and is quoted in the Scripture selection above.

A certain man had two sons and the younger of them said to his father, "Father, give me the portion of thy time and thy attention and thy companionship and thy counsel and guidance which falleth to me." And he divided unto him his living, in that he paid his boy's bills and sent him to a select preparatory school and to dancing school and to college, and tried to believe that he was doing his full duty to his son.

And not many days after, the father gathered all his interests and aspirations and ambitions and took his journey into a far country, into a land of stocks, bonds, securities and other things which do not interest a boy, and there he wasted his precious opportunity of being a chum to his son. And when he had spent the very best of his life and had gained money but had failed to find any satisfaction, there arose a mighty famine in his heart and he began to be in want of sympathy and real companionship.

And he went and joined himself to one of the clubs of that country, and they elected him chairman of the house committee and president of the club and they sent him to the legislature. And he fain would have satisfied himself with the husks that other men did eat, and no man gave him any real friendship.

But when he came to himself, he said, "How many men of my acquaintance have boys whom they understand and who understand them, who talk about their boys and associate with their boys and seem perfectly happy in the comradeship of their sons, while I perish here with heart hunger? I will arise and go to my son and will say unto him, "Son, I have sinned against heaven and in thy sight, and I am no more worthy to be called thy father. Make me as one of thy acquaintances." And he arose and came to his son.

But while he was yet afar off, his son saw him and was moved with astonishment, and instead of running and falling on his neck, he drew back and was ill at ease. And the father said unto him,

176

"Son, I have sinned against heaven and in thy sight. I have not been a father to you and I am no more worthy to be called thy father. Forgive me now, and let me be thy chum."

But the son said, "Not so, for it is too late. There was a time when I wanted your companionship, your advice and counsel, but you were too busy. I got the information and the companionship I needed, but I got the wrong kind, and now, alas, I am wretched in soul and body. It is too late—too late—too late!"

JUNE 21

But if we hope for that we see not, then do we with patience wait for it (Rom. 8:25).

It is a wonderful thing to be "alive unto God," and I believe it is the only way to be kept alive to every good thing that is worth anything. We can so live in God that we are in touch with the past, the present, the future. The most interesting things are those we haven't seen. The most of life is before us, because life is not extension, it is satisfaction. We have never seen His face yet; we have never seen our dear ones in their new bodies; and we are yet to see the coming of Christ; we are to see Him take to Himself His great power, and reign from the rivers to the ends of the earth. All this is before us.

"If the Father deigns to touch with divine power the cold pulseless heart of the buried acorn and to make it burst forth from its prison walls," wrote William Jennings Bryan, "will He leave neglected in the earth the soul of man made in the image of the Creator? If He stops to give the rosebush, whose withered blossoms float upon the summer breezes, the sweet assurance of another springtime, will He refuse the words of hope to the sons of men when the frosts of winter come?

"If matter, mute and inanimate, though changed by the forces of nature into the multitude of forms, can never die, will the spirit of man suffer annihilation when it has paid a brief visit like a royal guest to this tenement of clay? No! I am sure that there is another life as that I live today."

We share a gem from the heart of Dr. Hinson. While speaking from the pulpit about a year after the commencement of the disease from which he ultimately died, Dr. Hinson said: "I remember a year ago when a man in this city said, 'You are a dying man.' I walked the five miles from his office out to my home—I looked across toward that majestic mountain that I love and I looked at the river in which I rejoice, and I looked at the stately trees that are always God's own poetry to my soul. Then in the evening, I looked up into the great sky when God was lighting His lamps, and I said, 'I may not see you many more times, but mountain, I shall be alive when you are gone; and river, I shall be alive when you cease running toward the sea; and stars, I shall be alive when you have fallen from your sockets in the great down-pulling of the universe.' "

JUNE 22

Hide thyself as it were for a little moment . . . (Isa. 26:20).

In the Talmud there is a story of a peasant worker who fell in love with the daughter of his wealthy employer. She returned his love and, despite her father's violent objections, married him. Aware of her husband's ardent love for learning, she insisted that he go to the great rabbinical academy at Jerusalem to slake his intellectual thirst. He studied for twelve years while she, disowned by her family, suffered in poverty and loneliness. Though still eager for advanced studies, he returned home. When he reached the door of his house, he overheard his wife saying to a neighbor that even though the pain of separation seemed more than she could bear, she hoped and prayed that he would return to the academy for further study.

Without a word to anyone, he went back to the school for twelve years more of study. Once again he turned determined footsteps toward his native village, but this time all Palestine was singing his praises as the most brilliant and scholarly mind of his generation. As he entered the marketplace, he was caught in the crowd of a reception committee that had gathered to honor their native son. While people were pressing about him, he saw a woman—her body bent, her face wrinkled—desperately trying to break through to reach him. Suddenly he realized that this prematurely old woman, whom the milling crowd ignored and pushed back, was his beloved wife.

"Let her through," he shouted. "Let her through. It is she, not I, whom you should honor—she who sacrificed while I studied. Had it not been for her willingness to work and wait, to serve and suffer, I would be today a peasant laborer and not Rabbi Akeba."

Today we find ourselves conditioned only for the spectacular. We scan our newspaper only for momentous news—our admiration is so linked with the glamorous that we have almost forgotten the usual everyday activities of the average person. We have been so busy acclaiming and applauding the amazing exploits of our military technicians, the extraordinary maneuvers of national and world statesmen as they direct the destinies of great masses of people, and the miraculous discoveries and contributions of scientific geniuses and industrial giants that we have failed to appreciate those individuals and accomplishments which have played and presented their vital roles in the drama of life—toiling quietly but effectively behind the scenes, performing only so-called minor parts. *Mrs. Charles E. Cowman*

Sometimes we find within the heart
    Of those whom other folks pass by
A strong desire to do their part,
    To bless the world before they die.

I mean to breathe an earnest prayer
    From day to day as moments fly.
And have within my heart a care
    For those whom other folks pass by.
                    Unknown, taken from flyleaf of book, handwritten

JUNE 23 _____

He endured, as seeing him who is invisible (Heb. 11:27).

Safety first has no place in God's missionary program. We are called upon to live dangerously." These are the words of the late Mrs. Charles E. Cowman who had spent many years serving her Lord on foreign soil. Oft in the silence of the night we seem to hear voices calling to us out from the past, voices of martyrs who loved not their lives unto death, martyrs who went joyfully to the stake singing His praises as the flames leaped about them; voices of those who laid down their lives during their servitude; voices of the pilgrims of the night, who with faces upturned toward the light which streamed down upon them from the pearly white city as they marched bravely up the steep mountainsides to the place of death. "How long, O Lord," cry the martyrs who wait under the altar!

> They climbed the steep ascent to heaven,
>   Through peril, toil or pain,
> Oh God, to us may grace be given
>   To follow in their train!

They "endured, as seeing Him who is invisible." What a challenge! Whose name will appear on the next roll of martyrs? "Let us exhort one another . . . as ye see the day approaching." "Seeing we also are compassed about with so great a cloud of witnesses, let us run with patience the race that is set before us, looking unto Jesus."

They are peering over the battlements on high, watching us as we run. Are they wondering if we are going to faint and fall out by the way—faint in this day of adversity? They have fought the good fight, kept the faith, and are wearing victors' crowns. They are looking into the face of Him whose visage was marred more than any man's. They followed Him up Calvary's hill, and now, He is looking upon them with love and is seeing of the travail of His soul, and is satisfied.

JUNE 24

You show and make obvious that you are a letter from Christ delivered by us, not written with ink but with [the Spirit] of [the] living God, not on tablets of stone but on tablets of human hearts (2 Cor. 3:3 AMPLIFIED).

We long to leave something behind us which shall last, some influence of good which shall be transmitted through our children, some impress of character or action which shall endure and perpetuate itself. There is only one way in which we can do this, only one way in which our lives can receive any lasting beauty and dignity; and that is by being taken up into *the great plan of God*. Then the fragments of broken glass glow with an immortal meaning in the design of His grand mosaic. Our work is then established, because it becomes a part of His work.

Henry Van Dyke, from The Friendly Year, *1907*

The influence of the Master was love, kindness, meekness, gentleness, patience, long-suffering. Though He had extreme devotion to the cause of His Father, He did not play a fanatic, vehement role. The Master was not a zealot! Violence is not strength, noisiness is not earnestness. Noise is a sign of want of faith, and violence is a sign of weakness.

By using a quiet, modest, silent, private influence we shall win. "Neither strive nor cry nor let your voice be heard in the streets," was good advice for ages past and it still is for the present day. Many movements have succeeded by this motto. Many have tried the other method of striving and crying and making a noise in the streets, but never succeeded thereby, and never shall. They burst into blaze and the flames roar with a sudden blast of enthusiasm, but soon die and smolder into forgotten embers which flicker with interest occasionally until they completely die out and become a cold bed of cinders. A zealot never won a battle!   *Marie Taylor*

> This I learned from the shadow of a tree,
> That to and fro did sway upon a wall;
> My shadow self, my influence may fall
> Where I can never be.   *Dwight M. Kitch*

JUNE 25

Hitherto have ye asked nothing in My name: ask, and ye shall receive, that your joy may be full (John 16:24).

Beware in your prayers of limiting God, not only by unbelief, but by fancying that you know what He can do. Expect things above all that you ask or think. "The Lord is able to give thee much more than this" (2 Chron. 25:9).

Ask largely, and thy God will be a kingly giver unto thee.

God gives His children the liberty to ask whatever they will because through growth in Christ they have reached a position of intelligent responsibility in His kingdom. He recognizes the fact that one attains this wisdom and He honors the asking aright. "You may ask what you will, and it shall be done unto you" (John 15:7).

Alexander the Great had a famous, but indigent, philosopher in his court. The adept man of science was once particularly hard-up financially. To whom alone should he apply but to his patron, the conqueror of the world? His request was no sooner made than granted. Alexander gave him a commission to receive of his treasury whatever he wanted. He immediately demanded in his sovereign's name ten thousand pounds. The treasurer, surprised at so large a demand, refused to comply, but waited upon the king and represented to him the affair, adding withal how unreasonable he thought the petition and how exorbitant the sum. Alexander listened with patience, but as soon as he heard the remonstrance replied, "Let the money be instantly paid. I am delighted with this philosopher's way of thinking; he has done me a singular honor: by the largeness of his request he shows the high idea he has conceived, both of my superior wealth and my royal munificence."

Thus let us honor what the inspired writer expresses as the marvelous loving-kindness of Jehovah: "He that spared not His own Son, but delivered Him up for us all, how shall He not with Him freely give us all things?"

> Prayer is the door to God's treasury.
> Faith is the key which opens it.

"Ask, and it shall be given you; seek, and ye shall find; knock, and it shall be opened unto you" (Luke 11:9).

JUNE 26

For this day is holy unto our Lord: neither be ye sorry; for the joy of the Lord is your strength (Neh. 8:10).

C hrist is not a friend for sorrow alone. We do not have to wait till trial comes to enjoy His love, and be blessed by His indwelling. His light shines in many places where the brightness of other lamps still beams. Yet, even there, it does not shine in vain. Christ within has a deep meaning to the joyous as well as to the sad. All blessings are richer, all gladness is sweeter, all love is purer, because we have Christ. Peace in the heart makes every earthly beauty lovelier. Indeed, all human gladness is but a vanishing picture, a passing illusion, unless the joy of the Lord be its spring and source.

What confidence it gives to us in our enjoyment of the transient and uncertain things of earth, to know that these are not our only possessions; that if we lose them, we shall still be rich and secure, because we shall still have Christ. All day the stars are in the sky. We cannot see them in the glare of the sunshine; but it is something, surely, to know that they are there, and that, when it grows dark, they will shine out. So, amid abounding human joy, it is a precious confidence to know that there are divine comforts veiled, invisible to our eyes in the sunshine about us, which will flash out the moment the earthly joy is darkened.

> I wonder if the world is full
> Of other secrets beautiful,
> As little guessed, as hard to see,
> As this sweet, starry mystery?
> Do angels veil themselves in space,
> And make the sun their hiding-place?
> Do white wings flash as spirits go
> On heavenly errands to and fro
> While we, down-looking, never guess
> How near our lives they crowd and press?
> If so, at life's set we may see
> Into the dusk steal noiselessly
> Sweet faces that we used to know,
> Dear eyes like stars that softly glow,
> Dear hands stretched out to point the way—
> And deem the night more fair than day.

To the happiest heart that really makes room for Christ within, there is always the assurance of a world of spiritual blessings, hopes, and joys, lying concealed in the lustre of human gladness, like stars in the noonday sky, but ready to pour their brightness upon us the moment the night falls with its shadows. Whether, therefore, the earthly light be bright or dark, Christ in the heart gives great blessedness and peace.

J. R. Miller, from Silent Times, *1886*

JUNE 27 _____

Exalt ye the Lord our God, and worship at his footstool; for he is holy (Ps. 99:5).

A DECALOGUE OF WORSHIP

If Thou wouldst make the hour of worship more rich and meaningful, these things observe and do:

I. Thou shalt arise early on the Lord's day and prepare to worship God in the sanctuary, saying to thyself after this manner, "This is the day that the Lord hath made; I will rejoice and be glad in it."

II. Thou shalt expect to meet God in the temple of worship, calling to remembrance the words of Jesus: "Where two or three are gathered in my name, there will I be in the midst of them."

III. Verily, thou shalt be on time and no laggard be, as if reluctantly thou turnest thy feet toward the altar of God.

IV. When thou arrivest at the appointed place, thou shalt pray— for thyself, those who minister, and those who worship beside thee—knowing that so the "whole world round is bound by gold chains about the feet of God."

V. If thou hast aught against anyone thou shalt forgive him, even as God for Christ's sake hath forgiven you. "This do and thou shalt live."

VI. Thou shalt draw as nigh unto the altar as the ushers may lead thee, calling to mind that which is written: "Draw nigh unto me, and I will draw nigh unto thee."

VII. Moreover, thou shalt sing with joy in thy heart, such songs and hymns as may be suggested, "making melody in thy heart unto the Lord."

VIII. Yea, verily, thou shalt fully share in all the service, "worshipping God with all thy heart, mind and strength."

IX. Thou shalt receive the spoken word as from the Lord, with all openness of mind, and then "search the Scriptures earnestly to see if those things be true."

X. Amen. Amen. Thou shalt, withal, reverent and quiet be, waiting on the Lord. "Wait, I say, on the Lord, and thou shalt see what wonderous things he shall do for thee."

E. R. McWilliams, in the Log of Good Ship Grace

He "walked with God!" Could grander words be written?
Not much of what he thought or said is told:
Not where or what he wrought is even mentioned;
He "walked with God"—brief words of fadeless gold!

How many souls were succoured on his journey—
Helped by his words, or prayers, we may not know;
Still, this we read—words of excelling grandeur—
He "walked with God," while yet he walked below.

J. Danson Smith, from the booklet Thou Remainest

JUNE 28

Surely goodness and mercy shall follow me all the days of my life (Ps. 23:6).

J. Hudson Taylor once said: "The Lord *is* my Shepherd; *is* on Sunday, *is* on Monday, and *is* through *every* day of the week; *is* in January, *is* in December, and *every* month of the year. *Is* at home, and *is* in China; *is* in peace, and *is* in war; in abundance, and in penury!"

At another time he wrote: "All God's dealings are full of blessing: He is good, and doeth good, good only, and continually. The believer who has taken the Lord as his shepherd can assuredly say in the words of the psalmist: "Surely goodness and mercy shall follow me all the days of my life." Hence we may be sure that the days of adversity, as well as days of prosperity, are full of blessing. The believer does not need to wait until he sees the reason of God's afflictive dealings with him ere he is satisfied; he *knows* "that all things work together for good to them that love God."

The shepherd is responsible for the sheep; not the sheep for the shepherd! The worst of it is that we sometimes think we are both the shepherd and the sheep, and that we have both to guide and follow! Happy are we when we realize that He is responsible; that He goes before; and goodness and mercy shall follow us!

This devotional thought may be read by someone who is being severly tested almost to the breaking point! Someone wondering about the tomorrows! He knows all about *your* tomorrows, and is thinking in advance for *you!* Yes, *for you!* For *you* He careth! Hide away in your heart the gracious promise: "How precious are thy thoughts unto me, O God!"   *Mrs. Charles E. Cowman*

Let shadows come, let shadows go,
Let life be bright or dark with woe,

I am content, for this I know,
Thou thinkest, Lord of me.

Selected

JUNE 29

Why art thou cast down, O my soul? and why art thou disquieted in me?
hope thou in God: (Ps. 42:5).

The longest lane
  must have a turning;
The darkest night
  gives place to day,
Somewhere bright stars
  are always burning,
Hope's rainbow
  spans the future way;
The fiercest storm
  has soonest ending,
The dreariest winter
  heralds spring,
With sunshine, blossom,
  fragrance, blending—
To bring new joy to everything.

Selected

C. H. Spurgeon once wrote: "The path of the Christian is not
always bright with sunshine; he has his seasons of darkness and of
storm." True, it is written in God's Word, "Her ways are ways of
pleasantness, and all her paths are peace"; and it is a great truth,
that religion is calculated to give a man happiness below as well as
bliss above. But experience tells us that if the course of the just be
"as the shining light, that shineth more and more unto the perfect
day," yet sometimes that light is eclipsed. At certain periods,
clouds cover the believer's sun, and he walks in darkness and sees
no light.

There are many who have rejoiced in the presence of God for a
season; they have basked in the sunshine in the earlier stages of
their Christian career; they have walked along the "green
pastures," by the side of the "still waters," but suddenly they find
the glorious sky is clouded; instead of the land of Goshen, they
have to tread the sandy desert; and they say, "Surely, if I were a
child of God, this would not happen."

Oh, say not so! The best of God's saints must drink the

wormwood; the dearest of His children must bear the cross. Perhaps the Lord allotted you at first a smooth and unclouded path, because you were weak and timid; but now that you are stronger in the spiritual life, you must enter upon the riper and rougher experience of God's fullgrown children. We need winds and tempests to exercise our faith, to tear off the rotten bough of self-dependence, and to root us more firmly in Christ. The day of evil reveals to us the value of our glorious hope.

Hope sings to me a cheerful song—
The way may seem both dark and long,
But days are passing one by one,
And all is glory farther on.

And HOPE has wings as well as song,
And when she spreads her pinions strong,
My thoughts soar up and dwell upon
The heavenly glory farther on.

And HOPE has eyes that pierce the gloom;
She looks beyond death and the tomb,
And thrills as though already shone
The deathless glory farther on.

Hope, blessed hope, abide with me,
Still sing thy cheerful melody,
Till, clouds and tears for ever gone,
I reach the glory farther on.

J. T. Mawson

JUNE 30

Who for the joy that was set before him endured the cross, despising the shame . . . (Heb. 12:2).

If we will but catch a glimpse of the glory awaiting us in yonder city, new strength will be given us. Our Forerunner "for the joy that was set before Him endured the cross, despising the shame."

The fight in this eleventh hour is not with flesh and blood—it is a fight of faith. With an anointed vision we discern the trend of the time in which we live and our call is renewed to "earnestly contend for the faith which was once delivered to the saints." Are we guarding the faith as a sacred treasure? "When the Son of man cometh, shall He find faith on the earth?" Searching question! Can we sing from the depths of our hearts:

Faith of our fathers! living still,
In spite of dungeon, fire, and sword;
O how our hearts beat high with joy
Whene'er we hear that glorious word:

Our fathers' chained in prisons dark,
Were still in heart and conscience free;
How sweet would be their children's fate,
If they, like them, should die for Thee!

Faith of our fathers! we will strive
To win all nations unto Thee;
And through the truth that comes from God,
Mankind shall then indeed be free.

Faith of our fathers, holy faith
We will be true to Thee till death.
                                        Frederick W. Faber

                                        Mrs. Charles E. Cowman

JULY 1

Why art thou cast down, O my soul? and why art thou disquieted within me? hope thou in God: for I shall praise him (Ps. 42:5).

Hope—what a precious word! David's question to himself is answered by a "Hope thou!" How often have the Lord's dear children turned to the Psalms when perplexed and heavily laden and found just the right word to give strength, heartease and encouragement!

Commentators and reporters today have recently been giving to the nation some alarming facts of the present-day world conditions. Through the medium of television one catches a glimpse of world leaders sitting in their peace conferences and at the United Nations seeking some satisfactory way out of the chaotic and hopeless condition. What is to be gained by crying "Peace! Peace!" when there is no peace? Mankind already exists amid the ruins of a world full of broken homes, broken hopes, and broken hearts. One wonders no longer how true is the statement, "The world has gone to pieces." Man and all his wisdom, devices, and schemes will not solve the present-day problems. Look up, dear heart. There is a way out—but *one* way—and that way is God's way!

The wonderful apostle of faith, George Mueller, has left this testimony: "There is never a time when we may not *hope in God!* Whatever the necessities, however great our difficulties, and though to all appearances help is impossible, yet our business is to *hope in God,* and it will be found that it is not in vain."

A dear old gentleman, who evidently experienced a close walk with his God, trudging in from a long arduous day in the fields was heard giving words of encouragement to his fellow laborer. "An' when He hears yo' sing, He bends down wid a smile on His kin' face and listens mighty keerful, an' He says, 'Sing on, chile, I hears, an' I's comin' down to deliber yo': I'll tote dat load fer yo'! Jes lean hawd on Me and de road will get smoother bime by.' "

. . . and he shall give you another Comforter, that He may abide with you and for ever (John 14:16).

JULY 2 _____

Let us hold fast the profession of our faith without wavering; for he is faithful that promised (Heb. 10:23).

God's children often find themselves in positions of profound difficulty. He leads them into tight corners. From here there seems to be no way of escape. No human judgment would have permitted such predicaments had they been previously consulted.

What are the attitudes of His children when they are placed in circumstances such as these? There is but one! A steadfast and sure trust in God! Refusing to look at circumstances. Look above them. Both light and darkness are alike to the *One* who dwells in them. Our loving Heavenly Father seeks the highest good for each of His own. We are in the school of faith, and there are lessons to be learned. Even God's severe dealings are dealings in love. He "scourgeth every son whom He receiveth!"

It is the supernatural with which faith deals—from things seen to the unseen, which are eternal. Faith cannot rest in things seen. If birds would fly, they have to leave their lofty branches and flutter into space. If one is going to swim, he has to leave the shore and plunge out into the depth. There is nothing for faith to rest upon but God's inviolable Word! When one takes the leap into the seeming void, he finds beneath him solid ground.

Where can one find faith? In some hour of desperate need it will be born within just when we are "at the end of the rope." A precious experience given to a child of God is knowing no helper but God Himself. "When He hath tried us we shall come forth as gold."

From the Bible one learns the secret of victorious living. The Old Testament saints picture how God triumphantly brought them through impossible situations. Their examples encourage us. Read the story of the Red Sea and its marvelous deliverance! (Exod. 14 and 15). Study the prayers of Jehoshaphat and Asa in the Book of Chronicles, when they cried out, "We know not what to do, But our eyes are upon thee!" And Hezekiah, in his great distress, with his face turned to the wall. When these saints were sore-pressed and knew not what to do, *they looked to their never-failing refuge!* Daniel in the den of lions, and the three Hebrew children in the midst of the fiery furnace have ever been a challenge to our faith! Take courage, tested and tried one, and you too shall come forth with a shout of triumph and will be able to say with the psalmist, "We went through fire and through water, but thou broughtest us out into a wealthy place."

JULY 3

The memory of the just is blessed (Prov. 10:7).

A pear tree was overheard in my garden sighing to itself, shuddering in the cold November wind at the time for the season's first snowfall. "To what end is summer, if it must go away so soon? Why have I basked in the blessed sunshine, and drunk the evening dews, if now I am to be left by them both to the bitterness of this wintry desolation?" And it writhed and moaned in the agony of the storm. An ancient apple tree nearby replied, "You have forgotten that you have helped beautify the garden with the luxuriance of your foliage; that you have sweetened the air with the odor of your blossoms; that you have gladdened the household by the lusciousness of your fruits; that children have played under your shade; and, more than all, that you have grown, and that you still retain the gift of the summer in full six inches of length of bough, by which amount you are nearer the sky, stronger to bear the storm, readier to meet the coming of another spring, and fitter to enter on your new career with advantage."

Dear ones may be gone, but "the influence of the summer of their lives" is left upon us. Our hearts are warmer blessed and of use to others because of the benefits received from them. We can rest in their shadow and be the "better fitted for spring of immortality, where the sun shall never go down."

What a comforting promise was bestowed by Jesus when He left the fellowship of friends and loved ones of this earth. "I go to prepare a place for you." He was speaking to His followers of all generations and wanted them to be content that it was He who prepared it. Therefore, the fettered imagination can only anticipate what that place will be like. A writer aptly expressed his thinking when he said: "Its glory will surprise the rising of the sun, when the orb comes up with trembling shafts of light, through filmy curtains of clouds, and fills the eastern sky with opalescent splendors."

JULY 4

Let us rise up and build (Neh. 2:18).

B uilding is the noblest occupation of the race, whether it be the building of a cabin in the wilderness, a mansion in a city, a railroad across a river or a canal across an isthmus. Builders are always dreamers and dreamers have lifted the world from "null and void" to form and order.

Nehemiah was a dreamer as well as a patriot. He was a Jew, born in exile, who grieved because the city that held his forefathers' graves lay in ruins. His king gave him permission to go over to Jerusalem with a company of people and restore it. Reaching it to his heart's great relief, he went out one night and surveyed the ruins. Then, calling the poor Jews together who still clung to the old ruins, he said, "Come, let us rebuild the walls of Jerusalem." The people, as though aroused from sleep, replied: "Let us rise up and build." And so with rekindled hearts they went to work.

Our Lord said of His body: "Destroy this temple and in three days I will raise it up again" (John 2:19).

If Nehemiah had not rebuilt Jerusalem, it would not have changed the history of the world very much; someone else would likely have done it later. But if Jesus Christ had not rebuilt that wilted, shrunken, bloodless body of His, what a difference that would have made! There would be no Christian churches anywhere, for they were built on the resurrected Christ. That was the greatest boast of the early Christians. That is what then made Christianity different from all other religions and still does.

Matthew, who wrote his gospel some years after the event, said: "This saying is commonly reported among the Jews until this day." It was a matter of common knowledge and no one questioned the resurrection. Why should any man question it now? We have no more right to question it now than we have to question the signing of the Declaration of Independence. That only happened once, too, and because it was common knowledge, we accept it today. Furthermore, we have fifty states to prove it. They are the results of that document. So are the Churches the result of the resurrection of Christ."

Adapted, from a radio sermon
by J. B. Baker, D.D., York, Pa., 1946

JULY 5

It was hard for me until . . . (Ps. 73:16).

In strange places and in unexpected ways God meets His own. Many times to one in deep soul distress there is a fresh revelation of the divine presence. He brings the balm of healing. If one accepts the nail-pierced hand, or a word from Him who whispers peace, all will be changed.

Two men were startled on the Emmaus Road when the Savior overtook them. They were grieving because of His death. The crucifixion had been a tragic experience, too painful for them to bear. He stole softly to their side as they walked and talked. At His appearing the heavy weight was lifted from their troubled hearts.

The disciples were on their way back to their nets, to take up their old occupation which was their livelihood three years before. At the dawn of day, after a night of despairing toil, they found a meal prepared for them by One who stood on the shore. The Lord

Jesus Christ, with this tender touch, made Himself a living bright reality to them.

He still meets His own today in their hours of bitter disappointment; and such was the experience of one whose heartstrings have been torn from the very roots. Bereavement had broken a loving home and life was like a tree that had been uprooted by a terrific tempest. While walking along the streets of a British city on the way to a Sunday service, a beautiful stone church was passed. On the bulletin board near the entrance were these words, "All ye who are weary, enter the sanctuary for quietness and prayer." The silent invitation was accepted. On one of the walls in the foyer of this great church something was written in mosaic. It was a miniature sermon in varicolored stones: "It was too hard for me until I went into the sanctuary of God: then understood I" (Ps. 73:16, 17).

That blessed morn in the lovely shrine of quietness, Gethsemane opened its secrets. The saddened heart beheld One who took the cup—alone. Everything was changed from that moment. The long wearisome road with its sunless canyons, high hills, and steep slopes suddenly lost its dread as He whispered, "Come share the road with Me, My own, we will climb the slopes together—aye, together." The hard road offers sweet fellowship with a loving Companion. The fragrant memory of that revelation of the risen Christ lingers on.

JULY 6 _____

Flee as a bird to your mountain (Ps. 11:1).

People who study and understand birds know they fly much higher when migrating than when in local flight. They concluded that migrating birds take wing higher than the others for three reasons: They get a boundless view and more easily find their points of direction; they are out of the flight path of birds of prey and clear of obstacles; and their flight is accelerated due to the greater depuration of the atmosphere. The higher the child of God soars the more clearly discernible is God's flight plan.

The soul cannot find escape from the attacks of satanic forces in "Doubting Castle." Neither does it find refuge by prostrating itself face downward. Depressing thoughts give no relief to the mind, nor does doubting God's love when the storm clouds envelop. It is true that one defeated, cast-down person can innoculate a whole group at work, at school, in the community, with the gloom of despair. Attitudes are catching!

The sweetest songs of David were born in the storms of his life. This shepherd boy was ordained of God to wear the badge of honor as "earth's greatest songster." He found himself one day listening to the voice of the tempter and the Master Musician had positioned him in the heart of a storm to teach him how to sing. But instead the psalmist only muttered this moaning cry: "Oh, that I had the wings of a dove I would fly away and be at rest; I would make my escape from this windy tempest!" Out from the fury of the storm rose loud notes of praise to his God on high. The result is two beautiful and melodious Psalms—23 and 91. These Psalms have comforted people of all generations. What would David have done with doves' wings? How far from the tempest would those frail pinions have carried him? How much the world would have lost without those comforting words from the struggling heart of "earth's greatest songster."

Be watchful of your pleas to the throne of heaven when you are walking through storm clouds of testing and physical exhaustion.

JULY 7

Let patience have her perfect work, that ye may be perfect and entire, wanting nothing (James 1:4).

There are times of testing for everyone. When there are, *wait!* Use all the forces of faith and put patience into practice. God's timing is never late. Deliverance is at hand! For He "standeth in the shadows keeping watch above His own."

In living the life of faith we come to learn that God's thoughts are not our thoughts, nor His ways our ways. Great pressure means great power in both the physical and spiritual realm. Some circumstances may bring us into difficult times. But these need not spell discouragement for "our times are in His hands." If we trust in the Lord and wait patiently for Him to perform, that simply provides the opportunity for Him to display His almighty power. Even Pharaoh's host is on Israel's heels. A path through the waters will be suddenly opened. And when the bed of the brook is dry, Elijah shall hear the guiding voice, "Wait!" "Remember His marvelous works that He has done: His wonders, and the judgments of his mouth" (Ps. 105:5).

> Do you remember how your way was blocked,
> And coming to a gate you knocked and knocked?
> Till God's time came and then He opened wide
> A way thine eyes ne'er saw, thy foot ne'er tried.   *Selected*

"For we would not, brethren, have you ignorant of our trouble which came to us in Asia, that we were pressed out of measure, above strength, insomuch that we despaired even of life: But we had the sentence of death in ourselves, that we should not trust in ourselves, but in God which raiseth the dead: Who delivered us from so great a death, and doth deliver: in whom we trust that he will yet deliver us" (2 Cor. 1:8).

Our Master said, "Have faith in God!" (Mark 11:22). The faith of God is in-wrought within our hearts by the Holy Ghost! And that is the faith which will say to the mountains, "Be removed!"— and they will melt like wax at His spoken Word through us.

JULY 8 _____

. . . but be ye transformed by the renewing of your mind . . . (Rom. 12:2).

In the ditch there grows a briar, scratching, tearing. It sighs within itself and says, "Ah me, I cannot think what I was made for. I have no beauty and no worth. If only I were a bunch of violets on the bank, I might make somebody happy—but a briar! If I were but the oak tree whose branches come out so far and whose leaves make such sweet music as they rustle under the prodding of gentle breezes—then I would be of some good."

But now, here comes the gardener and digs up the briar by the roots and plants it in his garden. The briar is heard to mutter, "He doesn't know me or he wouldn't waste his time like this. He will never get any good out of me—a wretched briar covered with prickers!" But the gardener just laughs and says, "If I cannot get any good out of you, maybe I can put some good into you. We shall see."

Now, however, the briar was sadder than before. "It was bad enough living in the ditch, but to be among all of the sweet and dainty flowers and still be just a briar is just terrible. I knew I could never amount to anything!"

One day the gardener came and made a little slit, put a tiny bud in it, and fastened it there. After a few weeks the little briar rose was aflame with color, and its fragrance was most exquisite. What a transformation! There was now little resemblance to the scraggly, bedraggled briar whose first home was in the ditch.

Our Heavenly Father is the husbandman. He understands the rough stock of our humanity. He knows its evil nature and its little worth, but He also knows how to put within it a new nature. Not of our struggling or strife does it come, for it is not from within that this grace must spring, but by our surrender to the divine Gardener—letting Him have His way perfectly with us in everything. If we will but permit Him to put into us what He desires, He can get out of us what He wills. Receiving is more than asking—it is claiming and taking. The manifestation of His indwelling may be as gradual as the development of the bud in the briar, but be assured that it will be there.

Mrs. Charles E. Cowman

JULY 9

Be still and know that I am God (Ps. 46:10).

In this modern day everything is performed with urgency. Efficiency experts are called in to perfect operations so the result will be speedier production. If a business does not have the latest technological apparatus, it is in danger of being "lost in the dust" of advancement.

Speed also has its disadvantages. The world seems smaller and less spectacular when you realize how few hours it takes to span the oceans and circle the globe. The wonder at the beauty along the wayside is transferred to the awesomeness at the genius of man to create the marvelous machines which whirl us past at enormous speeds. Can you wonder that modern life today is such a strain? Do you ever reflect upon the quietness in nature? Off into the hills, away from the busy thoroughfares of life, there is a stillness that is pulsating with growing things. The forests and fields are with quiet patience absorbing the warmth of sun and drops of rain.

Have you ever thought how pleasant is the voice of God? It is to be compared with the refreshing sound of running water in a pebbly brook—musical, delightfully gentle, humble. His command of "stand still" is to slow us down to a more moderate pace. We can then see His signs along the way.

Dr. Griffiths has written, "Quietness is not only the opposite of noise. It is the absence of excitement, haste, and consequent confusion. These dissipate strength, while calmness and deliberateness conserve it. The world's mighty men have grown in solitude. The prince of lawgivers and leader of Israel spent forty years in the wilderness and obscurity of Midian; the forerunner and pathmaker of our Lord found the flame of his forgiveness upon his lips and a "Here am I, Lord." Christ Himself faced the great questions involved in His ministry in quiet solitude. The zeal of Saint Paul sprang from the silence of Arabia. The vision of John was born in banishment. Peter, the hermit, aroused Europe to undertake in the Crusades. Luther, the retiring monk, turned the current of history into a new civilization. Lincoln, the emancipator, came out of quiet mountains in Kentucky and vast forests in Illinois. Solitude—periods of quietness gave these heroes a chance to know self, nature, and God, and fitted them for their great service.

The silence beckons us. Learn the "art of stillness." It is safety, solace, strength. With this armament we overcome the noisesome pestilence.

JULY 10 _____

Who is among you that feareth the Lord, that obeyeth the voice of his servant, that walketh in darkness, and hast no light? let him trust in the name of the Lord, and stay upon his God (Isa. 50:10).

The following words were brushed on a lovely handpainted scroll: "Trust in the dark brings triumph at the dawn!" These words bring to mind the years of testing for Moses—his dark years—out in the waste places of the arid Sinai Desert. It was *faith in the dark*. Luxurious surroundings had been Moses' environment for forty years. Now he was to spend that same length of time in absence from those comforts. Humanly speaking it would be almost impossible to bear the strain. He had a secret Resource. "He endured as seeing Him who is invisible." *God* was by his side in the desolate waste, and out there he found "what manner of man" God was, and experienced His lovingkindness. Moses knew his God as "a Rock in a weary land," and when the enduring was near breaking, he found himself hidden beneath its Shadow. "He drank from the desert streams and thirsted not."

The day of the great revelation finally came to Moses. It was at the burning bush he learned of his great commission. He accepted, though reluctantly. He still was obedient at any cost. As time passed we see him as a God-trained leader standing on the shores of a seemingly impossible situation with his trusting throng. With no visible way before them God commands them go forward. "By faith" Moses obeys. "By faith" Moses takes his flock through the Red Sea. His obedience gave birth to the faith that caused the Almighty Arm to stretch forth across the sea and make dry land. What an Omnipotent God! What a joyous experience! Oh, believer, give God the chance to perform an answer to your prayer of faith!

"Imagine, Oh child of God, if you can," said a noted writer, "that triumphal march!—The excited children restrained from ejaculations of wonder by the perpetual hush of their parents—the almost uncontrollable excitement of the women!—but as they found themselves suddenly saved from a fate worse than death, while the men followed, or accompanied them—ashamed or confounded that they had ever mistrusted God, or murmured against Moses; and as you see those mighty walls of water piled by the outstretched hand of the Eternal, in response to *the faith of a single man,* learn what God will do for His own! Above the voices of many waters, the mighty breakers of the sea, the Lord sitteth King forever!

Confusion is not the walk of faith. When other lights are going out, the lamps of faith are brightly burning.

JULY 11 —————————————————————————

Hold up my goings in thy paths, that my footsteps slip not (Ps. 17:5).

I walk down the Valley of Silence—
  Down the dim, voiceless valley—alone!
And I hear not the fall of a footstep
  Around me, save God's and my own;
And the hush of my heart is as holy
  As hovers when angels have flown!   *Unknown*

A woman dreamed a dream that she says dominated her life and turned all its bitter channels into sweetness. She dreamed that, one of a crowd, she stood in an open green, young, joyous. As she looked forth she beheld a way narrow, steep, rugged, hemmed in like a canyon. It led always uphill and was carpeted thick with Scotch thistles and the needles of the thorn tree. A voice full of imperativeness said to her, "Yon is your way of life. Walk in it." She cowered and shrank and refused. She said, "No human feet could tread those thistles and not bleed. No human strength can always climb a rugged, thorny path—I should faint and bleed and die." Sternly the voice said, "It is the path marked out for *you*. Go in it." So she went and in a few paces were the stones and briers. But, behold, when she put out her foot, a little boy, like an angel, stepped in before her and began to clear away space for one foot, then for another foot, and so on—never more than one step at a time. At last she turned to see how far she had gone, and there, standing at the beginning of the path, was the Saviour, and she saw Him pointing to the boy just where to brush away for her foot.

  Union Signal, from Thoughts for the Thoughtful, *1893*

JULY 12 _____

I had fainted, unless I had believed to see the goodness of the Lord in the land of the living (Ps. 27:13).

This encouraging testimony was written for us by the psalmist, David, after he had gone through some shadowing experiences of severe trial and testing. More than once he was willing to give up in despair; to lie down and die. Not a few of his Psalms quake with his mournful dirges; and we come upon the man crying out in agony for a way to be rid of the violent storms of life. The sweet psalmist of Israel reveals the secret which kept his soul from fainting in Psalm 27. He "believed to see the goodness of the

Lord in the land of the living." That means in the present life, not in the life hereafter.

> Wrestling prayer can wonders do,
>   Bring relief in deepest straits;
> Prayer can force a passage through
>   Iron bars and brazen gates.

A supernatural deliverance was given to one who feared God. The heartening account is recorded in 2 Kings 4:4. A minister of God had died and left his widow with two sons in dire straits. She could not shoulder the responsibilities and soon the creditors came to take her two sons who were her only means of support. The little mother in desperation took her sons and behind the closed doors of her humble cottage raised the heart cry of a widow to the One who "hears the prayers of little children and widows."

Pay a visit to this widow's cottage. It will stimulate your faith to learn from her what God did on her behalf. When every prop is gone—all else but God—then He knows your heart cry is one of utter dependence upon Him. You can also experience the "hardest place in life" as being the sweetest. It is there one makes a fresh discovery of God.

JULY 13 _____

I know that this shall turn to my salvation through your prayer and the supply of the Spirit of Jesus Christ (Phil. 1:19).

What an opportunity to be able to look into a strong man's life and examine his resources. That is our privilege with Saint Paul the apostle, the greatest itinerant missionary. He found a gracious part of his resources in the prayers of others. Thus, we see that a person with one talent can be the invisible helpmeet of the man with ten.

What was the occasion that so desperately required the faithful to be in prayer? Paul was in bonds! He had covered vast areas on enterprising ventures for the cause of the kingdom of God. He had passed through Asia Minor, remote lands, icy-cold mountains, fever-haunted plains. Genial fires had been kindled by God's torchbearer for the "kingdom of light." Now the great missionary Paul was a captive. His torch seemingly was to be blown out. Not

Paul! To such as he "the imprisonment of the body is not the paralysis of the soul." A cell can become the genesis of heavenly springs of blessings. His chain was proof of his faith—a witness of a nobler freedom. Now was the time for another to battle for him and reap a conquest. How? By putting to use the greatest force in the known world. By prayer the powers of great men and women can be liberated and make them mighty masters of difficult circumstances.

One can travel through foreign fields with missionaries and can help them to be lighthearted in the midst of appalling tasks. The preacher needs a companion when he stands in the pulpit. His resources need to be multiplied when he proclaims the Word of Life. Yes, there are many who can make conquests in the league of prayer. In this way Onesimus was a part of Paul. Aquila was a part of Apollos. And any Christian can be a part of any great "kingdom" warrior in the field of life.

Prayer by those at home-base is the appointed means by which God's arm of love reaches out to the crying needs of His servants. Therefore, vital prayer is not just a word—it is an act!

> The weary one had rest, the sad had joy that day,
>   And wondered how?
> A ploughman singing at his work had prayed
>   "Lord, help them now."

JULY 14

Remember all thy offerings, and accept thy burnt sacrifice (Ps. 20:3).

While I was visiting the lovely redwoods of California, one grand old sequoia brought a new revelation into my heart. This was the place where live the giants—some over three hundred feet in height. Imagine what it would be like to actually see something living today that was alive when our Lord walked the earth! Walking among these trees you can gaze upon and even touch those who shared the age of Abraham! Astounding as it is, this was not the revelation.

One day a thoughtless person had dropped a lighted match near the foot of an ancient sentinel. There it had stood for centuries guarding the forest, deepening its roots, expanding its height, and as a tree it filled its place. A slow steady fire continued for three long years until gradually it burned the heart out leaving but a reddish-brown wrinkled shell. To passersby it appeared as any of the other gigantic redwoods. But one can enter its base and look up clear through the top and view the starry heavens. Amazing, but this was not the secret revealed.

What was the result of its devastation? The heart's ashes had become the impregnator for seven new young giants to sprout around that old dead base. Many are the hard cold winters of snow and wind on these mountains. (The tallest mountain peak in the continental United States is here.) Storms have sought to uproot them, but "the wind that blows can never kill the tree God plants."

That morning we found a secret sanctuary, and turning to God's Word we read in Psalm 20:3, margin, these words: "Turn to ashes my burnt offering." Life comes out of death! This was the revelation! If there is no death, there is no resurrection!

Is the price for fruitage too great?

> Oh, not for Thee, my fading fires
> But the ashes of my heart!

Many there are who travel the Calvary Road; therefore, may the old redwood's experience bring consolation.

JULY 15

The Lord hath His way in the storm (Nah. 1:3).

> God of the gallant trees
>   Give to us fortitude;
> Give as Thou givest to these
>   Valorous hardihood.
> We are the trees of Thy planting, O God,
>   We are the trees of Thy wood.
>
> Now let the life-sap run
>   Clean through our every vein,
> Perfect what Thou hast begun,
>   God of the sun and rain,
> Thou who dost measure the weight of the wind,
>   Fit us for stress and strain.   *Selected*

A Frenchman has painted a picture of universal genius. There stand orators, philosophers, and martyrs, all who have achieved preeminence in any phase of life. The remarkable fact about the picture is this: every man who is preeminent for his ability was first preeminent for suffering. In the foreground was a man denied the Promised Land, Moses; beside him is another, feeling his way— blind Homer; Milton is there, blind, heartbroken. Were each to give his testimony, he would say this: "I glory in tribulation." "In all these things we are more than conquerors through Him that loved us." God takes the things that are against us and the very enemies that would fight us and the forces arrayed against us to lift us up to the heights.

You may be one of those whom He has "chosen to suffer." You may be one who feels himself like a tree on the mountain height alone in the wind of God. Take courage, dear one! "God's eye is upon His child in the heart of the storm. The winds may seem to be uprooting your trees, but fastened to the Rock of Ages, you shall not be moved." Join in the army of saints who have sung in the storm, and though it may continue to rage, you will see your springtime and you will come out with glorious new song:

> And I know not any trouble
> For I have the tempest's King
> To change my winter's fury
> To the gladness of His spring.   *Selected*

JULY 16

. . . a sacrifice acceptable, well-pleasing to God (Phil. 4:17).

For me to live is Christ, and to die is gain (Phil. 1:21).

An event during the war between the states bears retelling to illustrate the truth that to die is to live, to lose your life is to save it. Self placed on the altar of sacrifice to be consumed by the fire of love will glorify God and do good to men.

It was at Fredericksburg, after a bloody battle. Hundreds of Union soldiers lay wounded on the field. All night and all the next day the space was swept by artillery from both armies, and no one could venture to the sufferers' relief. Agonizing cries for water were going up from where the wounded lay, but there was no response save the roar of the guns. One brave fellow behind the ramparts, a southern soldier, felt that he could endure these piteous cries no longer. His compassion rose superior to his love of life.

"General," said Richard Kirkland to his commander, "I can't stand this. Those poor souls out there have been praying for water all night, and all day, and it is more than I can bear. I ask permission to carry them water."

The general assured him that it would be instant death for him to appear upon the field, but he begged so earnestly that the officer, admiring his noble devotion to humanity, could not refuse his request. Provided with a supply of water, the brave soldier stepped over the wall and went on his Christlike errand. From both sides wondering eyes looked on as he knelt by the nearest sufferer, and gently raising his head, held the cooling cup to his parched lips. At once the Union soldiers understood what the soldier in gray was doing for their own wounded comrades, and not a shot was fired. For an hour and a half he continued his work, giving drink to the thirsty, straightening cramped and mangled limbs, pillowing men's heads on their knapsacks, and spreading blankets and army coats over them, tenderly as a mother would cover her child; and all the while, until this angel-ministry was finished, the fusillade of death was hushed.

Again we must admire the heroism that led this brave solider in gray so utterly to forget himself for the sake of doing a deed of mercy to his enemies. There is more grandeur in five minutes of such self-renunciation than in a whole lifetime of self-interest and self-seeking. There is something Christly in it. How poor, paltry, and mean, alongside the records of such deeds, appear men's selfish strivings, self-interest, boldest venturings!

J. R. Miller, in Making the Most of Life

JULY 17 _____

For it is God which worketh in you both to will and to do of His good pleasure (Phil. 2:13).

We are told that the shivering weeds of the Arctic regions are nothing less than our forest trees—the stately oak and the sturdy elm. The very grasses and ferns of the temperate climate become trees in the tropics.

Who knows of what development we are capable when we find ourselves lifted from the dreary realm of our coldness and doubt to dwell in the summer of God's presence? How often have men and women without special genius or great gifts risen up into resistless power for God by the indwelling might of His Spirit! It is not only the reception of a germ of new life that is promised; it is a change of soil, of atmosphere, of condition.

If God can paint the blush on the bud which hangs from the limb of the rose, and make the dew-drops of morning tremble like molten diamonds on the virgin-white lip of the lily; if He can plant the rivers in lines of rippling silver, and can cover His valley floor with carpets of softest green, tacked down with lovely daisies and laughing daffodils; if He can scoop out the basin of the seven seas and pile up the rugged granite of the mountains until they pierce the turquoise skies; if He can send a Niagara thundering on a mighty and majestic minstrelsy from century to century; if He can fuel and refuel the red-throated furnace of a million suns to blaze His universe with light; if on the lovely looms of heaven, He can weave the delicate tapestry of a rainbow, and at eventide fashion a fleece of crimson to curtain the couch of the dying sun, and across the black bosom of the night that follows bind a glittering girdle spangled with ten thousand stellar jewels; then we cannot doubt His willingness to provide for us, His children, fathomless oceans of spiritual power which are ours "to receive" as we walk daily in glad obedience to His voice. The power of God through His Spirit will work within us to the degree that we permit it.

The choice is ours.   *Mrs. Charles E. Cowman*

JULY 18 _____

One day is with the Lord as a thousand years (2 Peter 3:8).

Peter has learned the use of the microscope since he was a youth in Galilee. He was then all for the telescope—for bringing big things near. He saw the opposite hills across the seas so near that he thought he could reach them at a bound. To plant his feet upon the wave, to build his tabernacle upon the mountain, were his first ideals of glory. The aim of his youth was to diminish great things—to see a thousand years as one day. But with age there has come to him the other side of the picture—the magnifying of little things. The microscope takes the place of the telescope. He had begun by seeing big things as trifles; he ends by seeing trifles as big things. To the eye of his youth a thousand years were as one day; to the eye of his age one day is a thousand years.

I should like my latest experience to be that of Peter—the experience of God's microscope. I need it in old age more than in youth. In age I have the sense of wasted years and little time to retrieve them. How can the short time at my command outweigh the long years I have squandered! How grateful is the answer of God's microscope—"One day is as a thousand years!" Thy Father says to thy soul: "I measure not thy path by length of time. One day in My courts can retrace the steps of a thousand days outside My courts. Hast thou pondered the meaning of the eleventh hour! Hast thou considered the promise to the penitent, "Today shalt thou be with Me in Paradise!" Thinkest thou he got too generous measure! He did not. There was nothing pretermitted from his disciple; it was only compressed. He saw the kingdoms of the world in a moment of time—not in their glory but in their unrighteousness. There are for him and for thee moments of acceleration—times when I bind together yesterday and today and tomorrow. Say not it is too late to retrace so long a journey! My Spirit has wings. One day in My chariot can bring thee home—home to thy first purity. . . ."

George Matheson, from Leaves for Quiet Hours

JULY 19 _____

. . . be ye steadfast, unmoveable, always abounding in the work of the Lord . . . (1 Cor. 15:58).

The business of a river is to flow. Its banks may be beautiful or unpleasing; its current strong or sluggish; its skies blue or clouded; its waters may mirror flowers in spring and ferns in summer; may float the dead leaves of fall, or be hemmed in and pressed by the ice in winter—it must flow on. A noisy brook in its youth, a noble river at last, so deep that men say, "There go the ships," majestically entering the ocean; but from its birth to its bourne its business is to flow. Here eddies may seem to be turning it back, there the current may be checked by a resisting arm of land, but the central stream moves steadily onward as though led by the hand of destiny.

Is not this steadfastness to mark, to make, the character of your lives? Is it not God's will that we should press steadily on to our goal in obedience to Him, in channels of His choosing, whether in sunshine or shadow, in the cheer of spring or in the chill of winter, neither detained by pleasure nor deterred by pain?

The hosannas of the children rang about Jesus and gladdened His heart, the palm branches were strewn in His path and gave Him joy, but He would not build a tabernacle of the branches, good as it was to be there. The agony of Gethsemane confronted Jesus.

His life moved unfalteringly onward, neither beguiled by pleasures nor daunted by perils. He felt both, but would not let them determine anything for Him. They must be incidental; to please His Father was fundamental. "It is enough for the disciple that he be as his Master, and the servant as his lord."

Remember, then, amid the joys of life, the glad but steadfast face of our Lord. How strong, how peaceful, how deeply joyful our lives may be, if they are sacramental, lived in memory of Jesus, the central stream of their deep determination, like His—doing the will of the Father.

Maltbie Davenport Babcock,
from Thoughts for Everyday Living

JULY 20 _____

He did not need anyone to tell Him what people were like: He understood human nature (John 2:25 PHILLIPS).

The author of the Book of Hebrews (a letter to Jewish Christians) tells us how Jesus shares a common humanity with us, to the point of not being ashamed to call us His brothers and sisters. The author continues to emphasize how God joined us in our human predicament for a number of reasons. One stands out: to make it possible for Him to be compassionate and to be able to help us in our time of need by His *understanding* of our needs. In other words, God wants to fully understand what is involved in our human situation. This is the reason for His identifying Himself with us, to the point of "being in our shoes."

The American Indian has been quoted as believing that he should not criticize others until after he has "walked in their moccasins for two moons."

God, in His attempt to be fair with us, and to understand our deepest feelings, essentially releases us to become real persons. Modern psychology tells us that in order to mature to psychological manhood we need the understanding of someone important to us, who loves us. So, in one way, God's loving us means that He has taken the trouble to understand us by carefully *listening* to our human experience through a man like us—our Lord Jesus.

Those who practice listening find it to be one of the most powerful and influential factors in human relations. It is a magnetic and creative force. In fact, those who listen to us are the very ones toward whom we move. Listening to us creates us, unfolds and expands us. Ideas begin to grow and come to life within us. The same happens when we listen to others with an attentive, uncritical ear. Listening recharges us so that we never get tired of each other. We are recreated.

Listening is one way to better fulfull the whole law toward others as summed by Paul using the command, "Thou shalt love thy neighbor as thyself." We may love our neighbor better by listening affectionately and attentively with those who talk with us. That is, the attitude "tell me more." By listening to others in order to understand them, we are doing God's work with a form of God's love. So, to identify ourselves with others is to listen, and to listen lovingly is to understand. To understand is to forgive, making us less ashamed to call others *our* brothers. And, according to our Lord, to forgive is to be forgiven.

Thus, let us be creative and listen as Jesus did; listen to God, to others, to ourselves.   *Kelly Bennett*

JULY 21 ─────────────────────────────────────

As well the singers as the players on instruments shall be there; all my springs are in Thee (Ps. 87:7).

The time will come when the musicians will sit down among the saints because all our springs are religious springs. No music, no painting, no sculpture, no poetry, will any more be deemed secular. They will all be recognized as an inspiration of God. And are they not so! Is not the source of art the same as the source of religion! Do not both spring from the one feeling—the wish for something better! The saint and the artist both picture another world because to both the present is unsatisfactory. Each conceives a higher beauty. Each imagines a fairer sky, a purer air, a lovelier life. Each matures from a sense of want, of dissatisfaction with things below. Each strives to erase the blots in the present system. Each aims at the building of a palace which will supply the omissions of the human architect. Each has one and the same motto, "We seek a better country."

Why do I fancy other scenes than these before me? Why do I depict more perfect forms than life has yielded? Why do I sing more melodious songs than the brook, more stirring anthems than the sea? It is because I am not satisfied. It is because my heart cries out for more than nature—for Thee. I should have no art if I had no religion. I consider the lily of the field, but it does not content me. I consider the song of the brook, but it does not fill me. I consider the joys of life, but they do not come up to me; I was made for *Thee*. Therefore I paint other fields, I weave other songs, I fancy other joys; and all the time I am in search of Thee. Thou art my picture, my poem, my song; my dream of beauty is a dream of Thee. It is because I have seen Thy face that I seek a new heaven and a new earth; it is because I have heard Thy voice that I aspire to richer than nature's music. "All my springs are in Thee."

George Matheson, from Leaves for Quiet Hours

JULY 22 _____

Their soul shall be as a watered garden; and they shall not sorrow any more at all (Jer. 31:12).

Down through the annals of time poets have compared rain to tears. They say "the heavens are weeping" when it rains. Jeremiah, one of the great Old Testament poets, compares the joyful soul to a watered garden. Being one of the most eloquent and wise among the many scribes he expressed his innermost feelings in his description of the watered garden of the soul. It is like a garden on which there is falling an abundance of rain. Every plant stands erect with shining dignity. Each leaf glistens with fresh reviving. Each fragrant blossom displays its brightest hue. How lucid was Jeremiah. Rain does not shed tears, but pours forth resplendent beauty.

One poet recognized the shimmering splendor of the gentle rain as a most welcome blessing.

> Art thou weary, tender heart?
>   Be glad of pain!
> In sorrow sweetest things will grow,
>   As flowers in rain.
> God watches; thou wilt have the sun,
> When clouds their perfect work have done.
>> *Adelaide Procter, from flyleaf of Bible*

Sometimes it is hard to be joyous over rain. Is one glad for pain? Both can be sad disturbances in life. We often rebel within because of both. Who is the one who does not desire cloudless skies and painless bodies? The people who live in places of constant sunshine long for a few cloudy days. The joys of heaven will be magnified because of the memory of our clouded overcast days here on earth.

In a life where perpetual springtime reigns there will be a watered garden of the soul—though it ofttimes is watered by tears. It is the life closest to the "Man of Sorrows" who was Himself acquainted with grief that can bring blossoms of joy and peace. If His joy is in us, our joy is made full.

JULY 23

And when they had sung an hymn, they went out into the mount of Olives (Matt. 26:30).

There were any number of occasions when our Lord might have sung, but the only time there is a record of His singing is in the darkest night of His life on earth. It was just at the beginning of His trek to Gethsemane. He sang not alone, for His disciples were with Him. He could have sung on the Mount of Transfiguration, or on the day He entered Jerusalem amid the shouts of hosannas, or at the wedding feast in Cana. But it was a "song in the night."

The joy that broke forth in His hymn of praise was the joy that was set before Him to endure the cross, despising the shame. The joy of doing His Father's will was cause for joy in His heart. He was to face the agony of shame and mockery. He had to look into the black shadows He was about to enter in order to prepare the way for saving lost souls. There was gladness in that heart buried beneath all His griefs and sorrows. In His God-heart was great love for mankind.

> The song I sing is faint and sad,
> Yet 'tis of love I'm singing;
> And soon it shall be strong and glad
> Through realms of glory ringing.
>
> A song of love and sighs today,
> Of love and joy tomorrow,
> To Him Who poured His life away
> Upon the tree of sorrow.   *Anonymous*

Must Jesus bear the burden alone? Must He sing forever "songs in the night"? Is not there a lesson for us, too? Have you, dear Christian, had your turn of singing? We must learn to sing—to sing as we enter the valleys of shadow. We sing as we work. We sing as we rejoice. Can we sing as we suffer? How difficult it is to sing when you cannot see beyond affliction. But the secret is to look beyond the immediate circumstance and behold the reward in glory. Christ saw that reward—the redemptive work accomplished.

JULY 24 _____

If there be any virtue, and if there by any praise, think on these things (Phil. 4:8).

It is not what one does, nor is it what one says, but it is what one thinks that makes the man. What one thinks determines what he will say and do. A person may try to make his words and actions to be much different than he actually thinks, but it will be all in vain. For it is still the thoughts that manage to break through the actions and the words regardless how closely they are guarded. Others can always see the soul when it is off guard.

Paul knew the human mind and character very well. He suggests that we are to think on all things that are true, honorable, just, pure, lovely, and well esteemed, all virtue, all things praiseworthy; and as these are allowed to dwell in our thoughts, they cannot help but transform us into their likeness. Paul's thought was put to verse by F. G. Burroughs:

Think noble thoughts if you would noble be;
Pure thoughts will make a heart of purity;
Kind thoughts will make you good, and glad thoughts gay,
For like your thoughts your life will be alway.

Whate'er is true and reverend and just,
Think o'er these things, and be like them you must;
Of good report, of lovely things and pure,
Think, and your mind such nectar shall secure.

Think much of God and you shall like Him be,
In words of faith and hope and charity;
Protect His image from all foul abuse,
And keep the temple holy for His use.

Do not weary of the training that is in store for you. To be the person you most desire will take a very large part of your Christian life. Do not tire of trying the good thoughts, putting aside the bad. When you are about to give up in despair, the Holy Spirit is willing to live those thoughts through you. Give Him the opportunity to do the work which He was placed in your life to do.

JULY 25

For, behold, I am for you, and I will turn unto you, and ye shall be tilled and sown (Ezek. 36:9).

God does not use the plough and harrow without intention! Where God ploughs He intends to sow! His ploughing is proof He is for, and not against us! The husbandman is never so near the land as when he is ploughing it: the very time when we are tempted to think that He hath forsaken us!

The ploughman is a proof that he thinks you of value and worth cultivating—and He does not waste His ploughing on the barren sand. He will not plough continually, but only for a time, and for a definite purpose. Soon He will close that process. "Doth the ploughman plough continually to sow? Doth he continually open and break up the clods of his ground?" (Isa. 28:24 RV). Verily, no! Soon, aye soon, we shall, through these painful processes, and by His gentle showers of grace, become His fruitful land. "The

desolate land shall be tilled . . . and they shall say, This land that
was desolate is become like the garden of Eden" (Ezek. 36:34,
35). And thus shall we be a praise unto Him.

"Someone must go through sore travail of soul before a life
movement, outwardly visible, can be born," said Josephine
Butler. The one who seeks release from the process of fruitage
would expel the furrows from the face of Lincoln, and make Saint
Paul a mere aesthetic—would rob the Divine Sufferer of His
sanctity. We cannot have the result of the harvest without the
process! The price must be paid.

> O God, wert Thou ploughing
>   Thy profitless earth
> With the brave plough of Love,
> And the sharp plough of Pain?
>   But hark to the mirth
> Of wheat-field in harvest!
>   Dear Plougher, well worth
> That ploughing, this yellow-gold grain.   *Unknown*

Mrs. Charles E. Cowman

JULY 26 _____

*. . . when ye shall have done all those things which are commanded you
. . . (Luke 17:10).*

If Christ were here, we say, we would do many things for Him.
The women who love Him would gladly minister to Him as
did the women who followed Him in Galilee. The men who are
His friends would work to help Him in any ways He might direct.
We all say we would be delighted to serve Him if only He would
come again to our world and visit our homes. But we can do
things for Him just as really as if He were here again in human
form.

Nothing pleases Him so well as our obedience. It is told of a
great philosopher that a friend called one day to see him, and was
entertained by the philosopher's little daughter until her father
came in. The friend supposed that the child of so wise a man
would be learning something very deep. So he asked her, "What
is your father teaching you?" The little maid looked up into his
face with her clear eyes and said, "Obedience." That is the one

great lesson our Lord is teaching us. He wants us to learn obedience. If we obey Him always we shall always be doing things for Him.

We do things for Christ which we do through love to Him. Even obedience without love does not please Him. But the smallest services we can render, if love inspire them, He accepts. Thus we can make the commonest tasks of our lives holy ministries, as sacred as what the angels do.

J. R. Miller, from Making the Most of Life

We can best minister to Him by helping them
Who dare not touch His hallowed garment's hem;
Their lives are even as ours—one piece, one plan.
Him know we not, Him shall we never know.
Till we behold Him in the least of these
Who suffer or who sin. In sick souls He
Lies bound and sighing, asks our sympathies;
Their grateful eyes thy benison bestow,
Brother and Lord—"Ye did it unto Me."

Lucy Larcom, from Making the Most of Life

JULY 27

The steps of a good man are ordered by the Lord (Ps. 37:23).

We have the fullest assurance that our God can and does guide His children in all things. He can signify His mind to us as to this or that particular act or movement. If not, where are we? How are we to get on? How are we to regulate our movements? Are we to be drifted hither and thither by the tide of circumstances? Are we left to blind chance, or to the mere impulse of our own will?

We thank God it is not so. He can, in His own perfect way, give us the certainty of His mind in any given case; and, without that certainty, we should never move. Our Lord Jesus Christ (all homage to His peerless name!) can intimate His mind to His servant as to where He would have him go, and what He would have him to do; and no true servant will ever think of moving or acting without such intimation. We should never move in uncertainty. If we are not sure, let us be quiet and wait! Very often it happens that we harass and fret ourselves about movements that

God would not have us make at all. A person once said to a friend, "I am quite at a loss to know which way to turn." "Then don't turn at all," was the friend's wise reply. . . . But it is the meek He will guide in judgment and teach His way! We must never forget this.

C. H. Mackintosh, from typewritten copy

Years ago a circuit minister made a call on one of his churches out in the backwoods. He found that he had to return by dark. A member of his flock, accustomed to living in the woods and having to walk by night, gave him a pitch-pine wood torch. The minister was sure that it would blow out. "It will give you light all the way home," confidently declared the woodsman. "But the wind will blow it out," insistently came the minister's reply. "It will light you home," again came the answer. "But what if it should rain?" "It will light you home!" It did. The woodsman had walked by that light before and knew it was dependable. God is our light. Those who have experienced that light know that it will light us to our destination.

JULY 28 _____

As thou goest step by step, the way shall open up before thee (Prov. 4:12 HEBREW VERSION).

And the Lord shall guide thee continually (Isa. 58:11).

A father and his son were camped in a wooded area a little ways from the nearest village. The father had a letter which needed mailing and asked his son to take it to the post office in the village. The father took his son to the edge of camp and showed him the trail which led to the village. "But Father," said the little boy, "I don't see how that path will ever reach town." The father took his hand in his and pointed, explaining, "See down the trail to that big tree where the trail seems to come to an end?" "Oh, yes, sir, I see that the path goes that far; but the village is not there!" "Well, when you get to that big tree, you will see farther on around the bend and down the trail. Just go to the tree and then follow the trail until you come to the next corner, then look ahead and follow it some more until you see some houses. When

215

you come to the houses, you will see the post office. There you can mail my letter!"

> I know not when or where I go from this familiar scene;
> But He is here and He is there, and all the way between.
> And when I pass from all I know, to that dim, vast
>   unknown,
> Though late I stay or soon I go, I shall not go alone.
>
> *Selected*

The love of God quite as often withholds the view of the entire distance of the winding path through life. He reveals it to us step by step and from corner to corner. Hence it is necessary to trust Him to lead, for He can see around the bend in the road. He knows what lies ahead, and whether we can cope with the situation now or later. He consults our wants, not our wishes, like a wise and loving Father. His corners are not the end of the way. Corners discipline faith, teach us patience to walk step by step, and fit us for blessing. Because our vision is limited, it causes us to continually seek His guidance.

JULY 29

Wait on the Lord: be of good courage, and He shall strengthen thine heart (Ps. 27:14).

An old prayer book says it this way, "O, tarry thou the Lord's leisure." "This modern life of ours, with its hurry and its bustle, is fatal, unless we exercise watchfulness to all deep and noble things. Most of us spend our lives as some amateur photographers do their days, in taking snapshots; and the mystery, and the beauty, and the secret, and the power escape us. Let the loveliness soak into you, if you want to understand the fairest scenes of nature. Sit down in front of Jesus Christ and take your time; and, as you look, you will learn that which no hasty glance, no couple of minutes in the morning, no still more abbreviated and drowsy moments at night, will ever reveal to you.

Maclaren, from typewritten copy

I heard a Quaker lady who had to spend half an hour every day sitting quiet and doing nothing calling it her *still lesson.* I wish we could enjoy such a half-hour daily in God's presence; our *still lesson* would be one of the most useful lessons of the day. "Be still and know that I am God."

In times of difficulty be still! Thine enemies are plotting thine overthrow! They laugh at thy strong confidence! But hast thou not heard His voice saying: "This is the way, walk ye in it"? Then leave Him to deal with thy foes from whatever quarter they come. He is thy rock, and rocks do not shake. He is thy high tower, and a high tower cannot be flooded. Thou needest mercy, and to Him belongeth mercy. Do not run hither and thither in panic! Just quietly wait, hushing thy soul, as He did the fears of His friends on the eve of Gethsemane and Calvary. "Rest in the Lord, wait patiently for Him." "Be still, for He will not rest, until He hath finished the thing this day."

One hour of real communion with God is worth more than a lifetime of everything else.   *Waterbury*

JULY 30 ───────────────────────────────────────

It is like the precious ointment upon the head . . . (Ps. 133:2).

. . . for she hath wrought a good work upon me (Matt. 26:7).

Though we may not be important to the affairs of state, and though we work only in the most obscure of places where we will never hear a praising word from human voice, there is still a record of our deeds. Some "golden daybreak" a rich and grand reward will await us. God's praise is far better than man's stuttering words of appreciation.

> Ungathered beauties of bounteous earth,
>   Wild flowers which grow on mountain-paths untrod
>   White water-lilies looking up to God
> From solitary tarns—and human worth
> Doing meek duty that no glory gains.
>   Heroic souls in secret places sown.
>   To live, to suffer, and to die unknown—
> Are not that loveliness and all these pains
> Wasted? Alas, then does it not suffice
>   That God is on the mountain, by the lake,
>   And in each simple duty, for whose sake
> His children give their very blood as price?

The Father sees. If this does not repay,
What else? For plucked flowers fade and praises slay.
George MacDonald, from Making the Most of Life

It is true that Mary's ointment was wasted when she broke the alabaster box and poured it upon her Christ. Suppose she did not break the container nor pour out the ointment? Could there have been a remembrance of her act of love? It surely would not have been recorded within the gospel story. Surely her deed would have then been told over the whole world. She broke the vase and poured it out. She lost it, all of it. It was her sacrifice. Now the perfume from the precious ointment fills all of the earth.

"Our lives must be kept, carefully preserved from waste," say those who are not close enough to their Lord to stoop down and anoint His feet. Little they know that the reward will not be theirs to claim. They will not have honor to cherish. Only if life is poured out in loving service will it be a blessing to the world. Then and only then will there be reward. God will remember such a giver forever.

JULY 31

And why take ye thought for raiment? Consider the lilies of the field, how they grow; they toil not, neither do they spin: And yet I say unto you, That even Solomon in all his glory was not arrayed like one of these (Matt. 6:28, 29).

Standing searching for life, one at first glance would hardly find it on the hillside in the heat of midsummer. The blistering winds from the burning desert daily pass over it, and the freshness in the spring beauty of the poppy and lupin, daisy and buttercup, has faded. One views nothing but the mellow golden-brown of the dried grass, broken by the dusty gray-green sage, and here and there a deep dead umber of dried-up shrubs.

Contrary to what one beholds in the panoramic scene before him life is there. Life is reigning, not death. It is there in infinitely greater abundance than when the field was bathed in emerald green. There is life sufficient to dress a score of hills next spring.

Bend down and peer into that parched grass, and an entire new creation of God's handiwork will come into perspective within the withered tangle. For of all the plant life out here, the seed vessels are among the most wonderful. Even the little unpretentious weeds that would scarcely capture your glance when in bloom, develop forms of quaint beauty as the capsules ripen. And now that their task for the season is completed, they lie stored with vitality in the midst of their arid surroundings.

Unfold the parable step by step. Go back to the sunburst days of early spring. The annuals that carpeted the slope in the riot of color had each but one life then; a perishing survival, though it appeared so vibrant in its brief existence. Left alone, it stood "condemned already." *Marie Taylor*

AUGUST 1

For all things are yours . . . and ye are Christ's; and Christ is God's (1 Cor. 3:21–23).

"All things are yours!"
  Do you believe it?
"All things are yours!"
  Can you receive it?
The sea, the sky, the air;
The beauties everywhere:
  God's wonderful "out-of-doors"—
    . . . All yours.

"All things are yours"—
  You're rich beyond all measure!
Not here alone,
  But with eternal treasure.
Yet here also, and now,
For every waving bough
  And lovely flower,
  And gentle shower:
God's wonderful "out-of-doors"—
    . . . All yours.

And as the sun
Tells that the day is done,
  And shadows fall
  Upon us all,
You whisper low—
For Him to know—
  "Saviour Divine,

And I am Thine! Thine!!"
Jean Newberry, from a card printed in England, 1925

Lord, give me eyes that I may see, lest I as people will,
Should pass someone's Calvary and think it just a hill.
Unknown

AUGUST 2 _____

For we are laborers together with God (1 Cor. 3:9).

One morning long before the Carpenter was to appear in His shop, the Carpenter's tools decided that they needed to have a conference to settle some of the problems which were steadily arising in their work. The first tool called to take the chair was Brother Hammer. The meeting informed him that he was to leave because he was too noisy with his work. "But," he said, "if I am to leave this carpenter shop, Brother Gimlet must go too; he is so insignificant that he makes very little impression."

Little Brother Gimlet rose to his feet and said, "All right, but Brother Screw must go also; you have to turn him around and around again and again to get him anywhere."

Brother Screw then said, "If you wish, I will go, but Brother Plane must leave as well; all his work is on the surface; there is no depth to it!"

To this, Brother Plane replied, "Well, Brother Rule will have to withdraw, if I do, for he is always measuring other folks as though he were the only one who is right!"

Brother Rule then complained against Brother Sandpaper, and said, "I just don't care, he is rougher than he ought to be, and he is always rubbing people the wrong way!"

In the midst of this discussion, the Carpenter of Nazareth walked in—earlier than they expected. He had come to perform His day's work. He first put on His apron and then went over to the bench to make a pulpit. He employed the screw, the gimlet, the sandpaper, the saw, the hammer, the plane, and all the other tools. After the day's work was over and the pulpit was finished, Brother Saw arose and said, "Brethren, I perceive that all of us are laborers together with God!"

Do there happen to be any people within your circle of acquaintances who do not perform their duties just the way you think they should? Perhaps it would be well to think twice before making any criticism or finding any fault with any one of God's instruments of service who is furthering His kingdom here on earth. If a selfish judgment were made against one of God's necessary tools and that tool was removed from his work, who would be the one causing God's work to be delayed?

AUGUST 3 _____

He hath sent me to bind up the brokenhearted, to proclaim liberty to the captives, and the opening of the prison to them that are bound . . . to comfort all that mourn (Isa. 61:1, 2).

Have ye looked for My sheep in the desert,
  For those who have missed the way?
Have ye been in the wild, waste places,
  Where the lost and wandering stray?
Have ye trodden the lonely highway,
  The foul and darksome street?
It may be you'd see in the gloaming
  The print of My wounded feet.

Have ye carried the living water
  To the parched and thirsty soul?
Have ye said to the sick and wounded,
  "Christ Jesus can make thee whole"?
Have ye told My fainting children
  Of the strength of the Father's hand?
Have ye guided the tottering footsteps
  To the shore of the Golden Land?

Have ye stood by the sad and weary,
  To soothe the pillow of death,
To comfort the sorrow-stricken,
  And strengthen the feeble faith?
And have ye felt, when the glory
  Has streamed through the open door,
And flitted across the shadows,
  That there I have been before?

Have ye wept with the broken-hearted
  In their agony of woe?
Ye might hear Me whispering beside you,
  "'Tis the pathway I often go!"

Selected

God does not comfort us to make us comfortable, but to make us comforters. *J. H. Jowett*

AUGUST 4

And as thy days, so shall thy strength be (Deut. 33:25).

It is not the great achievement of the Red Sea crossing by Moses and the Israelites that is so stupendous and miraculous. The awesomeness of the wilderness journey is the fact that approximately three million people were sustained for forty years in a small, dry, fruitless desert. Have you thought of what it must have been like to merely exist from *day to day* with every human means of survival out of reach? Let us look at a few facts to see how impossible it would have been for Moses and his people to rely upon their own means of subsistence: "To get through the Red Sea in one night they had to have a space at least three miles wide, so they could walk 5,000 abreast. If they walked doublefile, it would have been 800 miles long, and it would have taken them 35 days and nights to get through. At the end of each day of the journey they would have needed space two-thirds of the size of the state of Rhode Island for them to camp. This would have been a total of 750 square miles. The amount of food for consumption alone is absolutely astounding when you consider the fact that they were traveling in a country where there was no abundance of natural food to be found. Just the amount needed to keep from starving would have added up to 1,500 tons a day. But to feed them the way we would eat, it would take at least 4,000 tons. Just to haul it would take two freight trains, each one a mile long. At today's prices it would cost $4 million a day! Then consider the amount of water required for barest necessities of drinking and washing dishes each day. It has been calculated that they would have to have 11 million gallons every single day. Think of the gigantic task of hauling water. It would have taken a freight train with tank cars, 1,800 miles long!

Now Moses may or may not have had to do the figuring for managing the survival of his people, but God surely knew the cost! It may be more easily understood why Moses hesitated to be the great emancipator of God's enslaved people if he had had any inkling as to what an immense chore there was before him. We do know for a surety that he knew the land, its seasons and size. But God was the Provider, not Moses. The requirement for him and the multitude was to proceed day by day. God supplied for just one day at a time. To think that they did not even have to transport their food and water. God took care of them—and for 14,600 days!

AUGUST 5

The unsearchable riches of Christ (Eph. 3:8).

My Master has riches beyond the count of arithmetic, the measurement of reason, the dream of imagination, or the eloquence of words. They are *unsearchable!* You may look, and study, and weigh, but Jesus is a greater Savior than you think Him to be when your thoughts are at the greatest. My Lord is more ready to pardon than you are to sin, more able to forgive than you to transgress. My Master is more willing to supply your wants than you are to confess them. Never tolerate low thoughts of my Lord Jesus. When you put the crown on His head, you will only crown Him with silver when He deserves gold. *My Master has riches of happiness to bestow upon you now.* He can make you to lie down in green pastures, and lead you beside still waters. There is no music like the music of His pipe, when He is the Shepherd and you are the sheep, and you lie down at His feet. There is no love like His, neither earth nor heaven can match it. To know Christ and to be found in Him—oh! this is life, this is joy, this is marrow and fatness, wine on the lees well refined. My Master does not treat His servants churlishly; He gives to them as a king giveth to a king; He gives them two heavens—a heaven below in serving Him here, and a heaven above in delighting in Him forever. *His unsearchable riches will be best known in eternity.* He will give you on the way to heaven all you need; your place of defense shall be the munitions of rocks, your bread shall be given you, and your waters shall be sure; but it is there, THERE, where you shall hear the song of them that triumph, the shout of them that feast, and shall have a face-to-face view of the glorious and beloved One. The unsearchable riches of Christ! This is the tune for the minstrels of earth, and the song for the harpers of heaven. Lord, teach us more and more of Jesus, and we will tell out the good news to others.

C. H. Spurgeon, from Spurgeon's Morning and Evening

AUGUST 6

A little one shall become a thousand, and a small one a strong nation (Isa. 60:22).

We remember Moses, the great emancipator, lawgiver, prophet, and leader; we forget Aaron, his brother, who served as his spokesman before Pharaoh. We remember Joseph, the fair-haired dreamer who rose to fame and fortune on Pharaoh's throne and brought deliverance to his famine-ridden family; we forget Reuben and Judah and the other brothers who watched over their father and the entire household of Israel and brought them safely to Egypt. We remember Abraham, the courageous founder of a new faith; we forget his wife, Sarah, who as his companion and co-worker also sacrificed and suffered. We remember Ruth; we forget Naomi. We remember David; we forget Jonathan.

Some years ago a lady approached me at the close of a meeting with the following words: "I wish that God had called me to the mission field! I live such a useless, monotonous life, just spending my days in humdrum work that seemingly amounts to so little." Further conversation brought to light the fact that she was a faithful worker in her church, and her influence in the community had inspired many to abundant living and fruitful service.

A life need not be great to be beautiful. There may be as much beauty in a tiny flower as in a majestic tree, in a little gem as in a great jewel. A life may be very lovely and yet be insignificant in the world's eyes. A beautiful life is one that fulfills its mission in this world, that is what God made it to be, and does what God made it to do. Those with only commonplace gifts are in danger of thinking that they cannot live a beautiful life—cannot be a blessing in this world. But the smallest life that fills its place well is far lovelier in God's sight than the largest and most splendidly gifted—yet fails in its divine mission.

> Far better in its place the lowliest bird
> Should sing aright to Him the lowliest song,

Than that a seraph strayed should take the word
And sing His glory wrong.   *Selected*

Mrs. Charles E. Cowman

AUGUST 7 _____

The grass withereth, the flower fadeth: but the word of our God shall stand forever (Isa. 40:8).

> Century follows century—there it stands.
> Dynasty succeeds dynasty—there it stands.
> Empires rise and fall and are forgotten—there it stands.
> Kings are crowned and uncrowned—there it stands.
> Storms of hate swirl about it—there it stands.
> Atheists rail against it—there it stands.
> Profane, prayerless punsters caricature it—there it stands.
> Unbelief abandons it—there it stands.
> Thunderbolts of wrath smite it—there it stands.
> The flames are kindled about it—there it stands. *Unknown*

The Bible is a great treasury of reserved blessing. There has not been a chapter, a line, a word, added to it since the pen of inspiration wrote the final Amen; yet every new generation finds new things in this Holy Book. How true it is in every individual experience. As younger people we study the Bible, but many of the precious verses have little or no meaning for us. The light, the comfort, the help are all there, but we do not see it. We cannot see it until we have a fuller sense of need. The rich truths seem to be hiding away, refusing to disclose their meaning. When we begin to experience the struggles, trials, and conflicts of real life, then the new senses begin to reveal themselves in the old familiar sentences. Promises that seemed as if they were written in invisible ink now begin to glow with rich meaning, flash out like newly lighted lamps, and pour bright beams upon the path of life. The light is not new. It had shone there all the while, but could not be seen until now because other lights were shining about obscuring this one.

Daniel Webster once said that he "believed that the Bible is to be believed and understood in the plain and obvious meaning of its passages; for I cannot persuade myself that a book intended for the instruction and conversion of the whole world should cover its true meaning in any such mystery and doubt that none but critics and philosophers can discover it.

AUGUST 8

I am with thee to deliver thee, saith the Lord (Jer. 1:8).

. . . I will be with thee: I will not fail thee, nor forsake thee (Josh. 1:5).

Come my heart, be calm and hopeful today. Clouds may gather, but the Lord can blow them away. Since God will not fail me, my faith shall not fail; and, as He will not forsake me, neither will I forsake Him. Oh! for a restful faith!   *C. H. Spurgeon*

God does not grant the necessary grace before the trial. He builds the bridge when we reach the river. We often fear that we shall sink under the fiery trials that we see others endure. We see in the distance and are afraid of the mystery and anguish of what is to befall us; but we have not yet reached the crises, and grace is not vouchsafed before it is needed. "Jesus comes with our distress."   *Mrs. Charles E. Cowman*

The chains which bound Peter when he was in prison were struck off. He followed the angel sent to help him. On the way out of the prison they came to an impossible barrier, the iron gate leading into the city. But that "opened to them of his own accord" (Acts 12:10). "If you will do all the possible things, God will take care of the impossible." God did nothing for Peter that night, that Peter could do for himself. If the iron gate is locked and barred and staring you in the face, God's call is to do for yourself whatever He has asked you to do, and trust Him to do the rest.

The Lord in that great Sermon on the Mount said, "Be not therefore anxious for the morrow; for the morrow will be anxious for itself. Sufficient unto the day is the evil thereof."

While we let ourselves worry, we are not trusting. But still it is a habit of ours to worry. Bishop Quayle had a sense of humor concerning himself. So he tells humorously of a time when he sat in his study worrying over many things. He relates that finally the Lord came to him and said, "Quayle, you go to bed; I'll sit up the rest of the night."

He . . . hangeth the earth upon nothing (Job 26:7).

R est upon God to do for you more than you can understand. In looking to God for deliverance of any kind, we are prone to try to discover what material He has on hand to work on in coming to our relief. It is so human to look and crave for something in sight that will help the Lord in supplying our needs. In time of desperation, if we can only find a little something for God to begin on, we seem so much better satisfied. To need a sum of money and not to be able to think of a friend, a man, or a monied institution from which it might be obtained, gives a dark background to the scene. The outlook is all liabilities, with no resources to help out.

To God's child, what is the real situation? Is there nothing but liabilities? Are there no resources? Yea, thousands, millions, billions, trillions! Where are they? Above you, below you, around you. Earth and air are full of wealth untold. Keep your eye on Him. It is not necessary for us to see any help in sight, nor is it really necessary for God to have any relief on hand. He does not need anything to begin on. "In the beginning God created the heavens and the earth." What did He make them out of? Nothing. Pretty satisfactory earth to be made of nothing. Remember, not a scrap of anything was used to make it. "He . . . hangeth the earth upon nothing." It hangs all right. A God who can make an earth, a sun, a moon, and stars out of nothing, and keep them hanging on nothing, can supply all your needs, whether He has anything to begin work with or not. Trust Him and He will see you through, though He has to make your supplies out of nothing.

Adapted from a tract

Ere thou sleepest, gently lay
Every troubled thought away;
Put off worry and distress
As thou puttest off thy dress.
Drop thy burden and thy care
In the quiet arms of prayer. . . .

Henry Van Dyke

He giveth power to the faint; and to them that have no might He increaseth strength (Isa. 40:29).

How well does the Lord Jesus know our tendency to faint and be discouraged when the enemy presses us sore, when the darkness thickens around us, and when the stormy winds blow down upon and around us, and especially when our prayers do not seem to prevail. "He remembereth that we are dust," and in His great love He has given a parable on purpose for just such troubling times as these. Instead of fainting we are to pray, and to keep on praying until He sees fit to send to us the deliverance He thinks is best for us. How true it is that God is not unwilling to answer our requests, as was the unjust judge the poor widow. Sad to say, only some know Him well enough to know that we do not trouble Him by our importunity, nor do we weary Him by our continual coming to Him. Someone once said, "Don't be afraid to go to God. He will never say, 'Come back when I'm not so busy.'" But deferred hope makes for discouraged hearts. Sometimes we are ready to faint and give up in despair of ever receiving deliverance. How necessary it is to be reminded of the importunate widow who obtained all her petition at last because she refused to give up hope.

God does not want us to faint. He will not let us faint. He has given us a precious remedy against fainting. "They that wait upon the Lord shall renew their strength . . . they shall walk and not faint" (Isa. 40:31). "What things soever ye desire, when ye pray, believe that ye receive them and ye shall have them" (Mark 11:24). We only have but to praise Him, and wait for the fulfillment of His promises in our lives. The patience of faith is that which awaits to see what we have already trusted for, and there is no need for fainting now. King David, who experienced instances of near fainting said, "I had fainted unless I had believed to see the goodness of the Lord in the land of the living." The One that "fainteth not, neither is weary," is the everlasting Helper and Comforter. "He giveth power to the faint; and to them that have no might He increaseth strength."

For the Son of man shall come in the glory of His Father with his angels; and then he shall reward every man according to his works (Matt. 16:27).

The story is told of a soldier in the Crimean War. He had received a medal with Inkerman upon it—for that was his battle; but he said the most touching part of it all was the experience of a friend of his who fought at his side. A cannon ball took off one of his legs, but the brave fellow sprang up immediately and, taking hold of a tree, drew his sword, and was ready to fight even to death. Immediately another cannon ball came crashing past and took off the other leg. They carried him, wounded, bleeding, and, as they supposed, dying, to the hospital. Strangely enough, he came back to life again, and when the day came for the awarding of medals they carried him upon his stretcher before her majesty, the queen. To the other soldiers she had simply given the medals by the hands of her secretary, but when she saw this man carried in on a stretcher, his face so thin and pale, she rose from her throne, stooped down by his side, and pinned with her own hands the medal upon his breast, while the tears fell like rain upon the face of the brave soldier.

Thus I trust it will be with many of us. We shall come into His presence, stand face to face with Him, and He will rise from His throne, coming forward to receive us, and as we look up into His face, thrones will vanish away and crowns will be nothing, for to see Him with all His beauty will be the full reward.

J. Wilbur Chapman, from Thoughts for the Thoughtful

> A man may go to heaven
>   Without health,
>   Without honors.
>   Without learning,
>   Without friends;
>   But
> He can never get to heaven
>   Without Christ.   *Selected*

. . . they which have believed in God might be careful to maintain good works (Titus 3:8).

Moreover it is required in stewards, that a man be found faithful (1 Cor. 4:2).

Men said the old smith was foolishly careful as he wrought on the great chain he was making in his dingy shop in the heart of the great city. But he heeded not their words and only wrought with greater painstaking. Link after link he fashioned, and at last the chain was finished and carried away. In time it lay coiled on the deck of a great ship which sped back and forth on the ocean. There seemed no use for it, for the great anchor was never needed and the chain lay there uncoiled. So years passed. But one night there was a terrible storm, and the ship was in sore peril of being hurled upon the rocks. Anchor after anchor was dropped, but none of them availed. The chains were broken like threads. At last the mighty sheet anchor was cast into the sea, and the old chain was quickly uncoiled and run out until it grew taut. All watched to see if it would bear the awful strain. It sang in the wild storm as the vessel's weight surged upon it. It was a moment of intense anxiety. The ship, with its cargo of a thousand lives, depended upon this one chain. What now if the old smith had wrought carelessly even on one link of his chain! But he had put honesty and truth and invincible strength into every part of it, and it stood the test, holding the ship in safety until the storm was over and the morning came.
                    J. R. Miller, from Thoughts for the Thoughtful

> Full many forms the "chain" may take:
>   Perchance 'tis some infirmity
> That doth for thee thy fetter make;
>   Or duty-call; or poverty;
>
> If thou art His—then this thy rest—
>   If in His will disposed to be—
> The "chain" may be a thing most blest,
>   Though, meantimes, it so fetters thee.
>
> And at the End it may be seen,
>   When things, now dark, are all made clear,
> The "chain" God's method kind hath been
>   To hold us safe—to keep us near.
>   *J. Danson Smith, from* Thou Remainest

230

And being fully persuaded that, what he had promised, he was able also to perform (Rom. 4:21).

I am not able" (Num. 11:14). These are the words which the great leader of Israel uttered when he was at the point of absolute despair. If any man had a burden of responsibility, it was he. The people of Israel whom he was leading under God through the wilderness came to him with all their troubles and complaints. They were filled with murmuring and always poured it into his ear. No matter what sacrifice he made for them, or how much God did for them, they were swift to find fault. They were easily elated and easily discouraged. To have the care of one family, one shop, one office, one school, one church, is more than enough for the average person; but here is a man who had the personal supervision of three million or more souls, most of whom were inconsiderate and often unreasonable. One day the pressure was so intense that he felt he could stand it no longer, and cried out, "I am not able."

"But God is able" (2 Cor. 9:8). The difficulty with Moses was the same as with many of us—we take responsibility which belongs to God, and which He has promised to bear. Although Moses was a wonderfully devout and disciplined man, he had not yet reached the point of committing all responsibility and anxious moments of care to God. He evidently had some confidence in his own ability to do what God wanted him to do. This crisis served to teach him his inability. It is necessary to learn the absolute inability of ourselves to do anything spiritual and to see that all resource and responsibility for Christian life and service belong to, and are inherent in, God alone and that nothing is "too hard" for Him. No necessity, no exigency, no difficulty ever surprises Him. "He is able." He worketh both the willing and the doing. May He give us the vision of His ability! *C. H. P., from a tract*

Stormy wind fulfilling his word (Ps. 148:8).

There are some natures that only a tempest can bring out. I recollect being strongly impressed on reading the account of an old castle in Germany with two towers that stood upright and far apart, between which an old baron stretched large wires, thus making an aeolian harp. There were the wires suspended, and the summer breezes played through them, but there was no vibration. Common winds, not having power enough to move them, split and went through them without a whistle. But when there came along great tempest winds, and the heaven was black, and the air resounded, then these winds, with giant touch, swept through the wires, which began to sing and roar, and pour out sublime melodies. So God stretches the chords in the human soul which under ordinary influences do not vibrate; but now and then great tempests sweep them through, and men are conscious that tones are produced in them which could not have been produced except by some such storm-handling.   *From* A Message from God

All day the wind, with bitter breath, had with the trees
      been plying;
Had rocked and tossed them to and fro, and filled the air
      with sighing.
The pallid earth was cold and still, the heavens were gray
      and lowering;
Between, a shifting veil of snow, in fleecy softness
      showering.

It was a day that seemed to moan of earth's dull weight
      of anguish,
Of joys that die, and love that pales, and hopes that
      slowly languish;
Of all that carries jarring notes, where should be sweetest
      singing;
Of discords in the music that the hand of God set ringing.

But as the hidden sun went down the snowflakes ceased
      descending,
And golden beams like lances flashed, the clouds in
      shivers rending.
While through the rifts a flood of light burst on the
      treetops hoary,
And set the white earth in a blaze of radiant sunset-glory.

Then in the golden sheen, the load of weary thoughts
      was lightened—
The Hand is one that sent earth's pain, and darkest storm
      clouds brightened.
He lets the mists obscure His sun, and lives bedimmed

> with sadness,
> But in His own mysterious way doth crown the end with
> gladness.   *Anonymous, from* At the Beautiful Gate

AUGUST 15

Commit thy way unto the Lord; trust also in Him; and He shall bring it to pass (Ps. 37:5).

Faith is a condition of salvation and being a condition it must be our act. Saving faith is a volition and we are responsible not only for our actual volitions, but for those we might and ought to have put forth. Many people pray for faith and quote Ephesians 2:8, "By *grace* are ye saved through faith; and that not of yourselves, *it* is the gift of God," and conclude that faith is the gift of God. Instead of asking God for faith, it is their duty to believe. When people say they cannot believe they utter a libel against God. A man in an enquiry room said to D. L. Moody, "I have no faith, I can't believe." Mr. Moody said to him, *"Who* can't you believe?" The man replied several times that he couldn't believe, Mr. Moody each time, asking, "Who?" Finally the man replied, "I can't believe myself." "Well," said Mr. Moody, "I don't want you to. Make yourself out a liar, but make God true."

Believe then for all God has promised. We cannot well go outside the promises. Prayer is pleading the promises. Faith is claiming them. There must be a "Thus saith the Lord," either expressed or implied for all we ask, and everything that God has promised is His will for us.

When you retire at night, you do not worry all night lest the bed break down. Neither do you hold on to something for fear of falling. Very little rest would you find in that way. No! you simply trust yourself to the bed and just rest. Thus we should trust ourselves wholly to Jesus, and "Cease from our own works as God did from His" (Heb. 4:10). "We that believe do enter into rest." Why? Because someone else is going to do for us. God requires us to yield and trust in Him and His Word. Trust for *all* you need. Trust with *all* your heart. Trust *all* the time. *From a tract*

Commit! and then committed, trust His Word!

_____

The righteous shall flourish like the palm tree . . . (Ps. 92:12).

How meaningless this statement is by the psalmist, unless you are acquainted with palm trees. People who live in tropical and semitropical areas are so familiar with their graceful towering beauty, they are a very common tree to them. But I am sure that few realize what meanings the characteristics of this stately tree have. The first simile is life. The life of the tree comes through its center or heart. Just as all the other trees, it draws its moisture up through its roots from the earth. But instead of the sap going up on the outside between the bark and the wood of the tree, and so on up into the branches and twigs, as is true in most other trees, in the palm tree the sap goes up the very heart of the tree. Most trees can be killed by simply severing the bark completely around the tree about an inch or two. The life of the palm however, does not lie so close under the surface, and is not affected by surface injury. It must be completely cut off to be killed.

The same applies to "palm-tree Christians." The Word of God states this so aptly in Romans 10:10, "For with the heart man believeth unto righteousness." A "palm-tree Christian" is not affected by outward environment, but draws his life and strength through the heart.

The palm tree is perennially green. Life flows within its being continually. Those who are considered "palm-tree Christians" never change. They are the same vibrant witnesses of God's grace day in and day out, because Jesus Christ Himself is "the same yesterday, today, and forever."

It is impossible to graft a palm tree into another palm tree. It will die. This is a unique characteristic for "palm-tree Christians" as well. "No man can serve two masters" (Matt. 6:24). There is but one God and Him only shalt thou serve.

_____

A sacrifice acceptable, well pleasing to God (Phil. 4:18).

The living sacrifice is "acceptable to God." It ought to be a wondrous inspiration to know this, that even the lowliest things we do for Christ are pleasing to Him. We ought to be able to do better, truer work, when we think of His gracious acceptance of it. It is told of Leonardo da Vinci, that while still a pupil, before his genius burst into brilliancy, he received a special inspiration in this way: His old and famous master, because of his growing infirmities of age, felt obliged to give up his own work, and one day bade da Vinci finish for him a picture which he had begun. The young man had such a reverence for his master's skill that he shrank from the task. The old artist, however, would not accept any excuse, but persisted in his command, saying simply, "Do your best."

Da Vinci at last tremblingly seized the brush and kneeling before the easel prayed: "It is for the sake of my beloved master that I implore skill and power for this undertaking." As he proceeded, his hand grew steady, his eye awoke with slumbering genius. He forgot himself and was filled with enthusiasm for his work. When the painting was finished, the old master was carried into the studio to pass judgment on the result. His eye rested on a triumph of art. Throwing his arms about the young artist, he exclaimed, "My son, I paint no more!"

There are some who shrink from undertaking the work which the Master gives them to do. They are not worthy; they have no skill or power for the delicate duty. But to all their timid shrinking and withdrawing, the Master's gentle yet urgent word is, "Do your best." They have only to kneel in lowly reverence and pray, for the beloved Master's sake, for skill and strength for the task assigned, and they will be inspired and helped to do it well. The power of Christ will rest upon them and the love of Christ will be in their heart. And all work done under this blessed inspiration will be acceptable unto God. We have but truly to lay the living sacrifice on the altar; then God will send fire.

J. R. Miller, from Making the Most of Life

AUGUST 18 _____

Why art thou cast down, O my soul? and why art thou disquieted within me? Hope thou in God (Ps. 42:11).

George Muller, the great man of prayer and faith, had placed his hope and trust in God for sixty-eight years when he made the declaration that he had read considerably more than one hundred times through the whole of the Old and New Testaments, with prayer and meditation. Through faith and prayer, Mr. Muller provided and cared for 10,000 orphans, at Ashley Down, Bristol, England. He was once asked how he could manage this. He replied with great confidence, "I hope in God!"

What is hope? Webster says, "Hope is desire, accompanied by expectation." The Apostle Paul says, "Hope that is seen is not hope; for what a man seeth why doth he yet hope for?" (Rom. 8:24). George Muller said that whatever our necessities, however great our difficulties, and even though to all appearances help is impossible, it is still our business to hope in God. "There is never a time when we may not hope in God." Hope placed in men and conditions may be thwarted or disappointing, but hope placed in God will never be disappointing. God has never let one down who hopes in Him. In the Lord's own time help does come! "Oh, the hundreds, yea the thousands of times that I have found it thus within the past seventy years and four months!" testifies George Muller. "When it seemed impossible that help could come, help did come from God and His own resources may be counted by hundreds, by thousands. He is not confined to this thing or that thing, or to twenty things; in ten thousand different ways, and at ten thousand different times, God may help us."

"Assured hope keeps the heart young," someone said. "Life is ever at the dawn. Life is continuously at a beginning. It is always morn. Morning is the daughter of night. One cannot be discouraged no matter how long, or hard, or wearisome the way; one keeps right on climbing—for he knows the path leads not only somewhere, but to the *Everywhere*. He knows he shall arrive."

Selected

AUGUST 19

Let not your heart be troubled; ye believe in God, believe also in Me. Let not your heart be troubled, neither let it be afraid (John 14:1, 27).

A soldier had returned home from the war and was telling about the grace of God which was with him:

A short time before I was wounded, I was invited by the officers of the regiment to a supper given in honor of a soldier who had been through all the war, and had done many brave deeds, but had received no reward for them. After the supper was over, one of the officers said to him, "You have been through a lot, and you have not told us a single incident. Now tell us what you consider the most wonderful thing you have experienced in it." He waited a moment, then replied, "I was walking near my trench one day, when I saw a young soldier lying on the ground intently reading a book. I went up to him and asked him what he was reading. He told me it was the Bible. Now I had read the Bible for many years and it never did me any good. But this soldier said to me, 'Listen to what I'm reading, "Let not your heart be troubled . . . In my Father's house are many mansions . . . I go to prepare a place for you.' " He read on to the end of the chapter. 'Oh, I have read that chapter many times! It never did me any good; give it up, man, give it up.' He looked up at me and said, 'If you knew what the Bible is to me, you'd never ask me to give it up,' and, as he spoke, the light on his face was so bright, I never saw anything like it—it fairly dazzled me. I could not look at it, so I turned and walked away.

"Soon after a bomb fell near the place where we had been and when the dust had cleared away I thought I'd go and see if that young soldier was safe. I found him fatally wounded, but I saw his Bible sticking out of his breast pocket, 'and here it is,' he said, holding it up. I say the most wonderful thing I have experienced during the war was the light on that young soldier's face, and more than that, I can now say that his Savior is my Savior too!"

AUGUST 20 —————————————————————————

. . . a workman that needeth not to be ashamed . . . (2 Tim. 2:15).

E very child of God is a new creation in Christ Jesus, and God has a plan for every life. It is a very reasonable plan. Shall the architect draw the plans for his stately palace? Shall the artist sketch the outlines of his masterpiece? Shall the shipbuilder lay down the lines for his colossal ship? And yet shall God have no plan for the immortal soul which He brings into being and puts "in Christ Jesus"? Surely He has. Yea, for every cloud that floats across the summer sky: for every blade of grass that points its tiny spear heavenward: for every dewdrop that gleams in the morning sun: for every beam of light that shoots across the limitless space from sun to earth, God has a purpose and a plan. How much more then, for you who are His own, in Christ Jesus, does God have a perfect before-prepared life plan.

And not only so, but God has a plan for your life which no other man can fulfill. "In all the ages of the ages there never has been, and never will be a man, or woman, just like me. I am unique. I have no double." That is true. No two leaves, no two jewels, no two stars, no two lives—alike. Every life is a fresh thought from God to the world. There is no man in all the world who can do your work as well as you. And if you do not find, and enter into God's purpose for your life, there will be something missing from the glory that would otherwise have been there. Every jewel gleams with its own radiance. Every flower distills its own fragrance. Every Christian has his own particular bit of Christ's radiance and Christ's fragrance which God would pass through him to others. God has given you a particular kind of personality. He has also created a particular circle of individuals who can be reached and touched by that personality as by none other in the world. And then He shapes and orders your life so as to bring you into contact with that very circle. Just a hair's breadth of shift in the focus of the telescope, and some man sees a vision of beauty which before had been all confused and befogged. So, too, just that grain of individual and personal variation in your life from every other man's and someone sees Jesus Christ with a clearness and beauty he would discern nowhere else. What a privilege to have one's own Christ indwelt personality, however humble! What a joy to know that God will use it, as He uses no other for certain individuals susceptible to it as to no other! In you there is just a bit of change in the angle of the jewel—and lo, some man sees the light! In you there is just a trifle of variation in the mingling of the spices—and, behold, someone becomes conscious of the fragrance of Christ.   *James H. McConkey*

AUGUST 21

Now God anointed Jesus of Nazareth with the Holy Spirit and power, who went about doing good, and healing all that were oppressed of the devil; for God was with Him (Acts 10:38).

One day, a long, long time ago, a Carpenter laid aside His tools, walked forth from His shop, kissed His mother farewell, walked seventy miles to the Jordan River, and was baptized by His cousin John. That baptism was marked by three memorable events: The heavens were opened; the Spirit as a dove descended upon Him; the voice of God was heard saying, "This is my beloved Son; in whom I am well pleased." In this high and holy hour Jesus was consecrated to His public ministry by this threefold evidence of open sky, descending Spirit, and approving voice. Into the wilderness went Jesus to meet and master the prince of this world. Forty days later He emerged victor—coming forth in the power of the Spirit; took for His motto these words, "Who went about doing good"; took for His mission, making things beautiful.

Two times the word "God" appears in the verse above. It stands at the beginning and at the end of the verse, like two sentinel mountains, between which lie the fertile fields and fragrant flowers of the work of Him who "went about doing good." The original text, in the Greek language, may be read thus, "Who went about making things beautiful." God is the God of beauty; His fingerprints of beauty are on all the face of nature. Jesus, the virgin born Son, walked in the footsteps of His Father—God. He also went about making things exquisitely and immortally beautiful! He did not go about making beautiful things. No, that is to miss the thought. He took things existing and fashioned them into enduring beauty. He took things as they were and made them the things they ought to be; for in a world of finished beauty there would be no room for creative beauty. He remade the world He found, contented to work on what was at hand. He asked for nothing more than to transform what He found into divine beauty.

He was willing to live in a little provincial, despised, uncouth village of three thousand souls, which bore the scorn of men, as they sneeringly asked, "Can any good thing come out of Nazareth?" But from this despised town of Palestine, He walked forth, and with this motto for His life word and work, "He went about doing good." He made that town the city of all time.

It was the anointing of the Spirit which gave Jesus the power to go about doing good. We have everything but spiritual power—those radiant spiritual personalities that battle for God, defeat the devil, rescue the people and beautify their lives with the beauty of God. Under this anointing men ruled in kingship, with sceptre and crown. Under this Spirit anointing, men spoke for God; gave His message of love and life and beauty to men in power. Under this anointing, the priest went into God, and came forth with blessing and benediction in uplifted hands.

This anointing of the Spirit will give the kingship of spiritual power; the message of God, the power to bring benefits to the world.   *Adapted from a radio message by Dr. John Matthews*

AUGUST 22

Incline your ear . . . hear, and your soul shall live . . . (Isa. 55:3).

At a wayside shack just off a highway where we stopped to inquire directions, recalls Carrie Jacobs Bond (who wrote those beautiful words, *The End of a Perfect Day*), a wistful-looking woman, drawn into conversation, said, "We don't have any music, we haven't a radio, and we don't get to town. I wish I was you-all." . . . Behind the shack there was a little pond where, in the shade of overhanging willows, some ducks drifted lazily. "Have you any frogs in your pond?" I inquired, and she said indifferently, "Yes, and they croak every night!"

In my hillside garden the frogs have a choral which I would not exchange for any other. When twilight comes the big basso tunes up, directs and leads, and soon the woodland music of a score of lusty throats take up the symphony, deep and tuneful, in a manner peculiar to frogs. To me this is one of the night's loveliest sounds. Often we silence the radio, which we enjoy in its way, to get the quivering chorus of the little brown and green choristers of the pool. There is no other music like it. At dawning the twittering and calling of the birds awakens the sleeper. During the day the gladsome note of feathered songsters is heard over the garden.

This poor "deaf" woman had her ears tuned to the horizon, and never knew that she was missing the wonderful harmonies of nature. Just as so often we fix our eyes on the "apples on the other side of the wall."   *From an old clipping*

AUGUST 23

And ye shall know the truth, and the truth shall make you free (John 8:32).

Plato . . . compares men who have never tried to face the truth to prisoners in a deep underground cavern, who have been so chained . . . that they cannot turn their heads. In front of them is the rocky wall of their prisonhouse. Behind them and above them is a causeway, on which fires are burning, and along this causeway pass wayfarers singing and conversing and bearing burdens, whose shadows are thrown by the firelight on the cavern wall, and whose voices are reflected back from it. The imprisoned denizens of the dark cave, seeing only these flickering shadows, take them for substance and realities; and hearing only these vague echoes, take them for songs and voices. . . .

Imprisoned in self-chosen darkness, steeped in emptinesses, how few among living men even care for that wisdom which consists in seeing the things that are, and seeing them as they are! Let a man but once catch a glimpse of the true light and he learns utterly to despise the dim rushlight of this world's tinseled stage. Let one ray out of eternity shine down upon him, and for him the world and the things of the world shrivel into insignificance.

AUGUST 24

Therefore with joy shall ye draw water out of the wells of salvation (Isa. 12:3).

> Oh blessed day when first I found,
>   The stream that for my healing flowed;
> I stooped and drank, and then, unbound,
>   My soul on Jesus praise bestowed.
>
> No shore, no bottom then I found;
>   I swam, I drank, until a well
> Where life's pure waters did abound
>   Within my soul with joy did swell.
>
> Without, within, the waters rolled,
>   And every wave with life was fraught;
> And blessings more than can be told
>   To me this matchless river brought.
>   *Abbie Mills, from* Quiet Hallelujahs

The wells of the Lord are to be found where most I need them. The Lord of the way knows the pilgrim life, and the wells have been unsealed just where the soul is prone to become dry and faint. At the foot of the hill difficulty was found a spring! Yes, these health-springs are lifting their crystal flood in the cheerless wastes of evil antagonisms and exhausting grief.

Sometimes I am foolish, and in my need I assume that the well is far away. I knew of a farmer who for a generation had carried every pail of water from a distant well to meet the needs of his homestead. And one day he sank a shaft by his own house door, and to his great joy he found that the water was waiting at his own gate! My soul, thy well is near, even here! Go not in search of Him! Thy pilgrimage is ended, the waters are at thy feet!

But I must "*draw* the water out of the wells of salvation." The hand of faith must lift the gracious gift to the parched lips, and so refresh the panting soul. "I will *take* the cup of salvation." Stretch out thy "lame hand of faith," and take the holy, hallowing energy offered by the Lord. *J. H. Jowett, from* My Daily Meditation

AUGUST 25 _____

. . . that in me ye might have peace (John 16:33).

All is allowed to drive us closer to Him. Someone has recently said: "I never see a crowded assembly of men and women but I think of the privations and disappointments, the unsatisfied hungers and unalleviated sorrows which make up their lot. How much they have suffered, how much they have lost, how frequent have been their sicknesses and bereavements, how humbling have been their defeats, how searching have been their mortifications and betrayals, how full of anxiety their outlook on life! I never sit and speak with an older person who opens out the story of his long life, but I realize again how closely sealed the Book of Life is to a man himself. The story told is one of hope unfulfilled, work unfinished, love baffled, trial upon trial, sorrow upon sorrow, death upon death, impoverishing and shadowing life all the way through.

The sharp blasts are to cause us to rely more upon Him—to drive us nearer. Many things, which we thought we could ill spare, may have been uprooted in the storm of life, but His love abides as warm and unchanging as ever, and He desires our dependence upon Him so that He can give us peace.

I have been through the valley of weeping,
   The valley of sorrow and pain;
But the "God of all comfort" was with me,
   At hand to uphold and sustain.

As the earth needs the clouds and the sunshine,
   Our souls need both sorrow and joy;
So He places us oft in the furnace,
   The dross from the gold to destroy.

So we'll follow wherever He leadeth,
   Let the path be dreary or bright;
For we've proved that our God can give comfort,
   Our God can give songs in the night.

Selected from Consolation

AUGUST 26

Let the heavens rejoice, and let the earth be glad; let the sea roar, and the fulness thereof. Let the field be joyful, and all that is therein: then shall all the trees of the wood rejoice (Ps. 96:11, 12).

I've traced His footsteps in the wood,
   His handiwork in moss and bud:
   To soothe my heart, just where I stood,
He tuned for me Heaven's symphony,
   A consonance of harmony,
   The rustling breeze among the trees;
A sound as of a myriad wings,
   The river, babbling, murmuring,
   And feathered songsters of the spring.
Laughter of children at their play,
   A girlish voice in simple lay,
   Assured me, God had passed that way.   *M. Hamilton*

There is a story of the highlander of Scotland who every morning went out to a certain viewpoint near his cottage and stood with uncovered head. Asked if he prayed there, he said, "I come here every morning that I may take off my hat to the beauty of the world."

Of nature one has written, "God is speaking to us in the shimmering lake and placid river, in the mighty oak and tiny flower, in the lift of the mountain and in the surge of the sea. The

243

world of nature, to the observing, responsive, and appreciative soul, is ever the garment of the Eternal."

Surely if the unbelieving astronomer is mad, so also must he be who sees the order, the service, and the beauty of the garden, the field, the valley, and the mountain, and the river, but has found no God back of it all.

We believe not only that the rain "hath a father" but so also hath the rest of this blessed cosmos.

> Full many a gem of purest ray serene,
> The dark unfathomed caves of ocean bear;
> Full many a flower is born to blush unseen,
> And waste its sweetness on the desert air.   *Gray's Elegy*

AUGUST 27 _____

Thou wilt keep him in perfect peace, whose mind is stayed on thee (Isa. 26:3).

A happy life is not built up of tours abroad and pleasant holidays, but of little clumps of violets noticed by the roadside, hidden away almost so that only those can see them who have God's peace and love in their hearts; in one long continuous chain of little joys, little whispers from the spiritual world, little gleams of sunshine on our daily walk.
Edward Wilson of the Antarctic

It has been related that when the ground in London was cleared of the old buildings to make way for the new Kingsway, it lay for several seasons without use exposed to the rain and sunshine. After a while naturalists were coming to view the cleared land. A strange thing had happened and they wanted to observe. In spots it is certain that the soil had not felt the touch of spring since the days when the Romans sailed up the Thames—perhaps even before then. When the blessed air and light had drenched the uncovered soil, a host of wild plants and flowers sprang up to be kissed by the sun. Some of these flowers were never seen in England before. But they were blooming in the Mediterranean countries at that very same time of year. These many years they seemingly were dead, buried beneath the mass of rocks, bricks, and mortar lying dormant season after season. But they were merely obeying the laws of life under these new conditions and were blossoming into new beauty.

There is a simile here. Every life, no matter how crushed and bruised by the cares and sorrows of circumstances, needs only to be laid bare to the sunshine of God's love, and the healing touch of His grace. Then a new life with new possibilities and new beauties will blossom forth in abundance, no matter how desolate the surroundings may appear.

> Thus ever on through life we find
> To trust, O Lord, is best,
> Who serve Thee with a quiet mind
> Find in Thy service rest.
>
> Their outward troubles may not cease,
> But this their joy will be—
> "Thou wilt keep him in perfect peace
> Whose mind is stayed on Thee."
>
> *Unknown*

AUGUST 28

If any man thirst, let him come unto me, and drink (John 7:37).

> Men wondered why, in August heat,
> The little brook with music sweet
> Could glide along the dusty way,
> When all else parched and silent lay.
>
> Few stopped to think how, every morn,
> The sparkling stream anew was born
> In some moss-circled, mountain pool.
> Forever sweet and clear and cool.
>
> A life that, ever calm and glad,
> One melody and message had.
> "How keeps it so," men asked, "when I
> Must change with every changing sky?"
>
> Ah! if men knew the secret power
> That gladdens every day and hour,
> Would they not change to song life's care,
> By drinking they find Jesus there?
>
> *James Buckham, from* Thoughts for the Thoughtful

Merely going to the spring and looking at its sparkling waters will never quench anyone's thirst; we must drink of the waters. So, looking at Christ is not enough to bless us; we must take Him into our life and let His Spirit fill our hearts. Christ is presented as a great well in the desert. The water gushes from a cleft in the rock. We understand the meaning of the cleft—Jesus died that there might be water for our soul's thirst.

J.R. Miller, from Come Ye Apart

AUGUST 29

I know that the way of man is not in himself; it is not in man that walketh to direct his steps (Jer. 10:23).

There are a number of circumstances which cause a person to fail in following God's chosen way of his life. Some of these are his own choosing—then again, some are caused by others interfering in his life.

"Among the curiosities of a little fishing village on the great lakes where we were summering," James McConkey tells the story, "there was a pair of captive eagles. They had been captured when but two weeks old, and confined in a large roomlike cage. Year after year the eaglets grew, until they were magnificent specimens of their kind, stretching six feet from tip to tip of wings. One summer when we came back for our usual vacation the eagles were missing. Inquiring of the owner as to their disappearance this story came to us. The owner had left the village for a prolonged fishing trip out in the lake. While he was absent some mischievous boys opened the door of the cage, and gave the great birds their liberty. At once they endeavored to escape. But kept in captivity from their earliest eaglet days, they had never learned to fly. They seemed to realize that God had meant them to be more than mere earthlings. After all these weary years the instinct for the sky and the heavens still smoldered in their hearts. And most desperately did they strive to exercise it. They floundered about upon the village green. They struggled, and fell, and beat their wings in piteous efforts to rise into the airy freedom of their God-appointed destiny. But all in vain. One of them, essaying to fly across a small stream, fell helpless into the water and had to be rescued from drowning. The other, after a succession of desperate and humiliating failures managed to attain to the lowermost limb of a nearby tree. Thence he was shot to death by the hand of a cruel boy. His mate soon shared the same hapless fate. And the simple tragedy of their hampered lives came to an end."

Often since has come to us the tragic life lesson of the imprisoned eagles. God had designed for these kingly birds a noble inheritance of freedom. It was theirs to pierce in royal flights the very eye of the midday sun. It was theirs to nest in lofty crags where never foot of man had trod. It was theirs to breast with unwearying pinion the storms and tempests of midheaven. A princely inheritance indeed was theirs. But the cruelty of man had hopelessly shut them out from it. And instead of the limitless liberty planned for them had come captivity, helplessness, humiliation, and death. Even these birds of the air missed God's great plan for their lives. Much more may the sons of men.   *From a tract*

AUGUST 30

. . . for thy love is better than wine (Song of Sol. 1:2).

Once when Charles Garret was preaching to a large congregation about the mysterious troubles that often come to the Christian, he was saying that "we are not exempt from trouble; whom the Lord loveth He chasteneth, and some converted men had more trouble after their conversion than before. He had known Christians who were steeped in trouble—surrounded by it; trouble to the right, trouble to the left, trouble in front, trouble behind. Then an old man in the gallery, who had served God for seventy years, shouted, 'Glory be to God, it's always open at the top.'"

"I love the knowledge that has come through sorrows and trials and pardoned sins"; wrote one, "of a love that has never wearied towards me, and is fresher than the freshest dew of youth, and mellower than the ripest tenderness of age."

It may be in the hour of some sorrow, it may be of human forsaking, or of hope deferred which makes the heart sick, that the love visits us and seems to borrow sweetness from the very pangs it seeks to assuage. In such an hour use these blessed words of hope: "Herein is love, not that we loved God, but that He loves us." In an hour of disappointment which left the heart questioning there came to one the words: "Thy love is better than wine." They were dropped into the heart from the very throne of light, and distilled an infinite peace. Instantly the whole outlook, and every feeling within and every aspect around was changed. Wine stands for the symbol of earthly joy, of whatever kind; yet there is something *better,* and if the earthly joy is denied or removed there is this "something better" to fill its place, if only we will accept it. Do not stop short of a blessed experience! Even if your most cherished object has been removed, and the light of your life seems to have gone out, if disappointment seems to dog your steps, your schemes to fail, and your labors to bring no reward, learn to bow your head and say, "*Thy* love is better than wine."

Russell Elliot, from a tract printed in London, England

AUGUST 31

Jonathan stripped himself of the robe that was upon him, and gave it to David, and his apparel, even to his sword, and to his bow, and to his girdle (1 Sam. 18:4).

Jonathan is one of the few Bible characters regarding whom that honest and outspoken book records no fault whatsoever. He was one of the noblest men that ever lived, and perhaps the finest element in his character was his unselfishness. Though he was a prince, the heir apparent to his father's throne, and though David was only a shepherd boy, yet so deep was Jonathan's love for David that he was ready to give him all he had. Jonathan fully expected that David would some day be king instead of himself; but nevertheless he felt no twinge of jealousy, and rejoiced in every step of David's advancement. To do this indicated a wonderfully sweet nature, completely attuned to the will of God.

A poet pictures this spirit in moving lines:

> I will try to find contentment in the paths that I must tread;
> I will cease to have resentment when another
>   moves ahead.
> I will not be swayed by envy when my rival's strength
>   is shown;
> I will not deny her merit, but I'll strive to prove my own.

Envy is one of the most weakening and debasing of all flaws in one's character. It poisons all one's life. It takes the joy out of every experience. It makes a foe out of every one that surpasses us. We are intended to find a large part of our pleasure in the joys and successes of others, and envy transforms all this possible pleasure into wretchedness.

Amos Wells, from Think On These Things

SEPTEMBER 1 _____

. . . *Who for the joy that was set before him endured the cross (Heb. 12:2).*

A soldier can never fight successfully in another man's armor.
A. W. Tourgee

Taking up one's cross means simply that you are to go to the road which you see to be the straight one; carrying whatever you find is given you to carry, as well and stoutly as you can; without making faces, or calling people to come and look at you. Above all, you are neither to load or unload yourself, nor cut your cross to your own liking. Some people think it would be better for them to have it large; and many, that they could carry it much faster if it were small; and even those who like it largest are usually very particular about its being ornamental, and made of the best ebony. But all that you have really to do is to keep your back straight as you can, and not think about what is upon it—above all, not to boast of what is upon it.

John Ruskin, from Thoughts for the Thoughtful

It is not His cross that is heavy;
It is those that our hands have made
That hinder us on our journey,
On our aching shoulders laid;
There is strength for the load He gives us
And balm for the thorn He sends,
But none for the needless burdens,
And none for our selfish ends.

For His yoke is easy to carry
And His burden is light in weight;
He will do His share of the labor,
For He is a true yoke-mate.
Are we weary and heavy-laden?
Are we anxious and full of care?

That is not the cross of His giving
But the one we make and bear.   *Unknown*

SEPTEMBER 2

If God so loved us, we ought also to love one another (1 John 4:11).

The great business of a true Christian life is to learn to love. Mr. Browning, in his *Death in the Desert,* puts into the mouth of the dying Saint John these words:

> For life, with all it yields of joy or woe,
> And hope and fear—believe the aged friend—
> Is just our chance o' the prize of learning love,
> How love might be, hath been indeed, and is;
> And that we hold thenceforth to the uttermost
> Such prize despite the envy of the world.

Life with all its experiences is just our chance of learning love. The lesson is set for us—"Thou shalt love"; "As I have loved you, that ye also love one another." Our one thing is to master this lesson. We are not in this world to get rich, to gain power, to become learned in the arts and sciences, to build up a great business, or to do large things in any line. We are not here to get along in our daily work, in our shops, or schools, or homes, or on our farms. We are not here to preach the gospel, to comfort sorrow, to visit the sick, and perform deeds of charity. All of these, or any of these, may be among our duties, and they may fill our hands; but in all our occupations the real business of life, that which we are always to strive to do, the work which must go in all our experiences, if we grasp life's true meaning at all, is *to learn to love, and to grow loving in disposition and character.*

We may learn the finest arts of life—music, painting, sculpture, poetry, or may master the noblest sciences, or by means of reading, study, travel, and converse with refined people, may attain the best culture; but if in all this we do not learn love, and become more gentle in spirit and act, we have missed the prize of living. If in the midst of all our duties, care, trials, joys, sorrows, we are not day by day growing in sweetness, in gentleness, in unselfishness, in thoughtfulness, and in all the branches of love, we are not learning the great lesson set for us by our Master in this school of life.   *J. R. Miller*

250

Consider Him . . . lest ye be wearied and faint in your minds (Heb. 12:3).

What a strange cure for mental weariness! There is prescribed an increase of thought *"consider* Him." I should have expected an invitation to mental *rest.* When a man's *body* is weary, we send him to sleep. When a man's mind is weary, why do we not also prescribe repose? Because the weariness of the mind needs an opposite cure from the weariness of the body. The weariness of the body is cured by slumber; but the weariness of the mind can be cured only by stimulus. The cry to a languid body is, "Sleep on now, and take your rest"; the cry to a languid mind is, "Awake, thou that sleepest, and arise from the dead." To all who labor in *spirit,* Christ says, "Come unto me." He prescribes not a sedative, but an irritant; not more sleep, but more waking. To the man of the weary *hand* He says, "Cast *your* cares upon *Me";* but to the man of the weary heart he cried, "Take *My* yoke upon you."

Lord, it is *wings* I need for my weariness—love's wings. That which ties my heart is not its toil, but its inaction. It will never cease to be tired until it can soar—soar to Thee. The burden and heat of my spiritual day is not its work, but its aimlessness; give me an aim, O Lord! Sometimes even the entrance of an earthly friend transforms my soul from languor into light; much more shalt *Thou* if Thou wilt enter in. I want a new interest to heal my heart's weariness—some one to live for, some one to work for, some one to wait for, some one to long for. It is my want of longing that makes my want of strength; it is my listlessness that brings my languidness. Create a new heart within me—an eager, beating, bounding heart, a heart vibrating in response to Thy love! Let me feel the passion and the pathos of life, of Thy life! Let me be taken captive by Thy bounty! Let me catch the spell of Thy loveliness! Let me be thrilled at the sound of Thy footsteps! Let me learn the rapture of hearing Thy name! Let me experience the glow of excitement when the murmur runs round, "Jesus of Nazareth passeth by!" Then shall the weariness of the heart vanish, then shall the languor of the spirit cease; for the liberty of flight is the Sabbath of the soul. Then as eagles, we shall not faint nor be weary. *George Matheson*

Christ is all and in all (Col. 3:11).

> He came and took me by the hand
>   Up to a red rose tree;
> He kept His meaning to Himself,
>   But gave a rose to me.
> I did not pray Him to lay bare
>   The mystery to me;
> Enough the rose was Heaven to smell,
>   And His own face to see.   *Unknown*

Because there are millions of roses we do not thank God for them, and yet the glory of creation is but as one rose flung down from the summer affluence of God. And as though this wealth of creation, as though this magnificence around us were too little, God gives, even to the poorest and least instructed of us, art, science, literature, appealing not only to the senses but to the soul. By the aid of those teachers of mankind we may, if we choose, build such houses and palaces within us as shall be proof against adversity—bright fancies, glad memories, noble histories, faithful sayings, treasure-houses of perfect and restful thoughts, which care cannot disturb, nor pain make gloomy, nor poetry take away from us. These He gives us as the foretastes of the many mansions which He has for us in His home above.

> There's not a single happy hour—
>   An hour that's ever worth the living—
> But holds the truth within its power,
>   That happiness is God's own giving;
>
> That He in whom all fulness dwells,
>   Who gives to each of His good pleasure,
> Reserves a bliss that far excels
>   The compass of our finite measure.
>
> My pleasant draught but makes me bold
>   To taste a drop of Heaven's sweetness,
> And find the tiniest flower doth hold
>   An atom of the Lord's completeness.
>   *A. W. A., from* Farrar's Year Book

Behold, the Lord's hand is not shortened . . . (Isa. 59:1).

. . . the hand of God hath touched me (Job 19:21).

Yes, God can reach His hand down from the heavens and touch a life. He can with His arm span the distance of space and encircle the tired and weary to His loving breast. His arm of love is not shortened that He cannot bless the lost and hopeless. He uses those who are the nearest by to lend a helping hand, to comfort, to lift from despair, to stroke the fevered brow of discontent. For how can that discouraged and fretful soul experience the love of God except through the love of one who is beside him ready to love. How can that disheartened and downcast soul feel the touch of encouragement and peace except by the touch of the closest hand reaching out in tender concern. It may be a friend or a stranger, but God uses hands which are consecrated to Him for touching lives. You may say that it is only another human being. But what is meant by God if it is not love? God also speaks to us through other human voices.

Let me tell you of a dear friend in distress and loneliness of soul. She felt God no longer near. She had prayed and beseeched Him for a touch of His hand once more in her life. "How can He leave me?" she queried. Her friend leaned near and whispered, "Just pray to Him and ask Him to touch you. He'll put His hand on you."

In anguish of soul she began to pray once more. Suddenly she felt the hand of her Heavenly Father touching her and she cried out in exaltation, "He has touched me! What joy fills my soul again! What warmth floods over me! But you know, it felt just like it was your hand." "It was my hand," replied her friend. A look of complete dismay and disappointment rushed across her face, "*Your* hand?" "Of course, do you actually think there'd be a real live hand reaching down through the ceiling to touch you? God just used the hand that was closest!"

. . . [Nothing] shall be able to separate us from the love of God, which is in Christ Jesus our Lord (Rom. 8:39).

253

Such wondrous love!

What is there about the cross of Christ that gives it such great power and unwaning glory? From earliest history the cross has been known as the "accursed tree"—an instrument of torture, a place of punishment for the most hardened and wicked criminals—a mark of deepest shame and disgrace. But since the time of Christ, the cross adorns great cathedrals and beautiful altars. Throughout Christendom it is the symbol of all that is true and holy, all that is noble and merciful and loving. If we understand this, we know why the cross "towers o'er the wrecks of time."

The cross symbolizes God's great love for us. It is not an accident or a tragedy, but the universal sign of God's love for sinful man. The cross is the only adequate explanation of John 3:16. Our Father was not compelled to permit the cross; His love for us constrained Him. Willingly Christ gave His life because He loved us and desired us to live with Him in His eternal kingdom. "Greater love hath no man than this that a man lay down his life for his friends."

"Out from the ivory palaces into the world of woe" came the One who was sent—the One who delighted in doing His Father's will. They called His name Jesus.

> Under an Eastern sky
> Amid the rabble cry,
> A man went forth to die
> For me!
>
> Thorn-crowned His blessed head,
> Blood-stained His every tread.
> To Calvary He was led
> For me!
>
> Did e'er such love and sorrow meet,
> Or thorns compose so rich a crown?

Love led Him to Calvary. Love costs!

SEPTEMBER 7

Faultless . . . with exceeding joy (Jude 24).

When I was a young girl an intense passion for music was awakened within my soul. Father brought great joy into my life by presenting me with a beautiful organ. It would thrill me to the very fiber of my being as the day slipped by to be able to draw forth such wonderful harmony from my beloved instrument.

I used to sit at the organ in the early morning hours, just as the birds began to awaken, and through the open windows listen to their sweet little bird notes as they mingled with the melody of the organ, like a paean of praise to our Creator!

Then, one morning, quite suddenly, and at a time when I was preparing with girlish enthusiasm for my first concert appearance, one of the notes became faulty. How the discordant sound grated upon my sensitive ear! Father, sensing my grief said: "Never mind, daughter, I will have the tuner come." Long hours the tuner worked on that faulty note before it again rang out all sweet and true with the others. And the concert was a success *because the tuner was successful!* Mrs. Charles Cowman

> Good Tuner, why
>   This ruthless, slow examination?
> Why, on that one poor note,
> Expend such careful concentration?
> Just pass it by.
> Now I will let my soul respond to Thee!
>   And see.
>
> Then, as the haloed glories of the sunset
>   flamed and gleamed,
> Swift through the storied windows long
>   shafts of crimson streamed:
>
> And we poor whispering wayfarers heard,
>   round about and o'er us,
> The throbbing, thundering triumphs of the
>   Hallelujah Chorus! *Fay Inchfawn,*
> *from* Mountain Trailways

SEPTEMBER 8

Behold, what manner of love the Father hath bestowed upon us . . .
(1 John 3:1).

From somewhere out of the past came the greatest story ever told of the greatest life ever lived. From whence came the

Book of all books, the Lamp of our feet, the light of our path as we travel along earth's dark roads? How did it reach you—reach me?

God's will and His plan was made known to those who were willing to lose their lives that the story of Calvary love might reach every creature. He found those to whom He could commit sacred costs—men who were willing to be hidden away in underground dungeons, lay their heads upon martyr's blocks, and die for the cause. Because they were not disobedient to the heavenly vision, God's precious Word has been printed in more than a thousand languages. Today, faithful servants of His are busily engaged in the translation of other thousands of tribal tongues. What a debt of gratitude we owe to these honored heroes of the cross.

It costs to carry the message. "Except a corn of wheat fall into the ground and die, it abideth alone," were the words spoken by the Holy Spirit to a humble servant of His who had, after a day of heavy toil, gone aside into a quiet room to spend a night in prayer. What followed that trysting time with his Master during the brief hours of that night? What had happened that so completely changed his life thereafter? He had met Someone! To the one known throughout missionary circles as "the Missionary Warrior"—Charles E. Cowman—had come a revelation of God's will that every home in an entire nation was to receive a portion of the sacred Scriptures, that a personal invitation was to be given to everyone living within that nation. That the time for such a crusade was now. When God says "today" He does not mean "tomorrow."

The challenge was accepted and in the name of the God of the impossible, action began—for action ever follows vision. During the following five years the greatest gospel distribution crusade since Pentecost was launched when 10,320,000 homes in the mikado's empire were visited personally and given portions of the precious old Book we so love. Thousands destroyed their idols and accepted the invitation of the One who said, "Come unto Me."

SEPTEMBER 9 _____

. . . let him labour, working with his hands the thing which is good, that he may have to give to him that needeth (Eph. 4:28).

Few are needed to do the out-of-the-way tasks which startle the world, and one may be most useful just doing commonplace duties, and leaving the issue with God. And when it is all over, and our feet will run no more, and our hands are helpless, and we have scarcely strength to murmur a last prayer, then we shall see that, instead of needing a larger field, we have left untilled many corners of our single acre, and that none of it is fit for our Master's eye were it not for the softening shadow of the cross.

George MacDonald

When the wheat is carried home,
And the threshing time is come,
  Close the door.
When the flail is lifted high,
Like the chaff I would not fly;
At His feet O let me lie
  On the floor!

All the cares that o'er me steal,
All the sorrows that I feel
  Like a dart,
When my enemies prevail,
When my strength begins to fail—
'Tis the beating of the flail
  On my heart.

It becomes me to be still,
Though I cannot all His will
  Understand.
I would be the purest wheat,
Lying humbly at His feet,
Kissing oft the rod that beat
  In His hand.

By and by I shall be stored
In the garner of the Lord
  Like a prize;
Thanking Him for every blow
That in sorrow laid me low,
But in beating made me grow
  For the skies.

Anonymous

He brought us out . . . that He might bring us in (Deut. 6:23).

Out of the distance and darkness so deep,
Out of the settled and perilous sleep,
Out of the region and shadow of death,
Out of its foul and pestilent breath,
Out of the bondage and weary chains,
Out of companionship ever with stains:
  Into the light and glory of God,
  Into the holiest, made clean by blood,
  Into His arms, the embrace and the kiss,
  Into the scene of ineffable bliss,
  Into the quiet and infinite calm,
  Into the place of the song and the psalm.
Wonderful love, that has wrought all for me!
Wonderful work, that has thus set me free!
Wonderful ground, upon which I have come!
Wonderful tenderness, welcoming home!

Out of disaster and ruin complete,
Out of the struggle and dreary defeat,
Out of my sorrow, and bondage, and shame,
Out of the evils too tearful to name,
Out of my guilt and criminal's doom,
Out of the dreading, and terror, and gloom:
  Into the sense of forgiveness and rest,
  Into inheritance with all the blest,
  Into a righteous and permanent peace,
  Into the grandest and fullest release,
  Into the comfort without an alloy,
  Into a perfect and confident joy.
Wonderful holiness, bringing to light!
Wonderful grace, putting all out of sight!
Wonderful lowliness, draining my cup!
Wonderful purpose, that ne'er gave me up!

Out of the horror of being alone,
Out and forever of being my own,
Out of the bitterness, madness, and strife,
Out of myself and all I called life,
Out of the hardness of heart and of will,
Out of the longings that nothing could fill:
  Into communion with Father and Son,
  Into the sharing of all that Christ won,

Into the ecstasies full to the brim,
Into the bearing of all things with Him,
Into Christ Jesus, there ever to dwell,
Into more blessings than words can e'er tell.
Wonderful Person, whose face I'll behold
Wonderful story, there all to be told
Wonderful, all the dread way that He trod!
Wonderful end, that He brought me to God!

Anonymous, from At the Beautiful Gate

SEPTEMBER 11

The eternal God is thy refuge . . . (Deut. 33:27).

One night during a terrific storm a man walked along the shore of the sea. The clouds hung low overhead. The wind howled. Thunders roared. Lightning flashed and the rain poured down in torrents. The man pulled his overcoat closer around him, bent his body to the wind and hurried home. A little bird lost in the storm sought shelter under his coat; he took it in his hand, carried it home, placed it in a warm cage. The next morning after the storm had subsided, and the clouds had cleared away, he took the little bird to the door. It paused on his hand for a moment; then lifting its tiny wings, it hurried back to its forest home. Then it was that Charles Wesley caught the vision, and going back to his room he wrote the words to a song that is loved around the world today and will live on in time:

Jesus, Lover of my soul
  Let me to thy bosom fly,
While the nearer waters roll,
  While the tempest still is high:

Hide me, O my Saviour, hide,
  Till the storm of life be past;
Safe into the haven guide,
  O receive my soul at last!

Other refuge have I none,
  Hangs my helpless soul on thee;
Leave, ah! leave me not alone,
  Still support and comfort me.

I have surely seen the affliction of my people . . . come now, therefore, I will send thee (Exod. 3:7, 10).

Does that seem a weak ending to a powerful beginning? The Lord God looks upon terrible affliction and He sends a weak man to deal with it. Could He not have sent fire from heaven? Could He not have rent the heavens and sent His ministers of calamity and disasters? Why choose a man when the archangel Gabriel stands ready at obedience?

This is the way of the Lord. He uses human means to divine ends. He works through man to the emancipation of men. He pours His strength into a worm, and it becomes "an instrument with teeth." He stiffens a frail reed and it becomes as an iron pillar.

> Lead on, O King Eternal, The day of march has come—
> Henceforth in fields of conquest Thy tents shall be our home:
> Thro' days of preparation Thy grace has made us strong,
> And now, O King Eternal, we lift our battle song.
>
> *Ernest Shurtleff*

And this mighty God will use thee and me. On every side there are Egypts where affliction abounds, there are homes where ignorance breeds, there are workshops where tyranny reigns, there are lands where oppression is rampant. "Come now, therefore, I will send thee." Thus saith the Lord, and He who gives the command will also give the equipment.

J. H. Jowett, from My Daily Meditation

Wait on the Lord: be strong, and let thine heart take courage; Yea, wait thou on the Lord! (Ps. 27:14 RV).

The psalmist had just said, "I had fainted unless I had believed to see the goodness of the Lord in the land of the living." If it had not been for his faith in God, his heart had fainted. But in the confident assurance in God which faith gives, he urges himself and us to remember one thing above all—to wait upon God.

One of the chief needs in our waiting upon God, one of the

deepest secrets of its blessedness and blessing, is a quiet, confident persuasion that it is not in vain; courage to believe that God will hear and help; we are waiting on a God who never could disappoint His people.

"Be strong and of good courage." These words are frequently found in connection with some great and difficult enterprise, in prospect of the combat with the power of strong enemies, and the utter insufficiency of all human strength. Is waiting on God a work so difficult, that, for that, too, such words are needed, "Be strong, and let your heart take courage"? Yes, indeed. The deliverance for which we often have to wait is from enemies, in the presence of whom we are impotent. The blessings for which we plead are spiritual and all unseen; things impossible with me; heavenly, supernatural, divine realities. Our hearts may well faint and fail. Our souls are so little accustomed to hold fellowship with God, the God on whom we wait so often *appears* to hide Himself. We who have to wait are often tempted to fear that we do not wait aright, that our faith is too feeble, that our desire is not as upright or as earnest as it should be, that our surrender is not complete. Amid all these causes of fear or doubt, how blessed to hear the voice of God, "Wait on the Lord! Be strong and let thine heart take courage! Yea, wait thou on the Lord!" Let nothing in heaven or earth or hell—let nothing keep thee from waiting on thy God in full assurance that it cannot be in vain.

Andrew Murray, from Living Waters

SEPTEMBER 14 —————————————————

This poor man cried, and the Lord heard him, and saved him out of all his troubles (Ps. 34:6).

Many years ago, there was a little boy on a trundle bed, having just retired for the night. Before going to sleep, he turned in the direction of the large bed on which his father lay, and said, "Father, are you there?" and the answer came back, "Yes, my son." That boy turned over and went to sleep without a thought of harm. Tonight that little boy is an old man of seventy, and every night before going to sleep he looks up into the face of his Heavenly Father, and says, "Father, are you there?" and the answer comes back, "Yes, My son." And then he asks in childish faith, "Will You take care of me tonight?" and the answer comes back, clear and strong, "Yes, My son, I will never leave thee, nor forsake thee." Whom need we fear, if God our Father is with us?

From a tract

Thy prayer is heard, O gracious word from Heaven!
Thy burning prayer of passionate appeal;
The Father's ear has caught thine earnest pleading—
The Father who can all our sorrows feel.

Thy prayer is heard, tho long thy heart's petition
Has mounted to the Father's throne on high;
Tho years have passed since first that prayer you uttered,
E'en from the first He heard thy bitter cry.

Thy prayer is heard, fear not! look up and praise Him,
The God whose tender love remembered thee;
Rejoice! be glad, and rest upon His promise,
His word is sure, it cannot broken be!

Thy prayer is heard, then let us all take courage;
Press on and on, till night is done;
And in the golden glow of early Morning,
We'll sing His praise before the glory throne.   *Anonymous*

SEPTEMBER 15 _____

Men ought always to pray, and not to faint (Luke 18:1).

A sign on a church bulletin board in Los Angeles read, "When your knees knock, kneel on them." How true it is that the knees of the world are knocking today. Our adversary, the devil, is seeing to it that even the knees of the Christian are almost constantly knocking. Can Satan cause one's knees to fold up from under him because of the weakness in his faith due to knocking knees?

Spend an hour upon the knees and let God put strength into them. The hard task and the difficulties you may have to face, the unpleasant circumstances, the disappointments which rend the heart, the hopes which are crushed, the sorrows that seem to be constantly abiding, all can be lifted if God is given some of the time He requires of thee on thy knees.

The essence of praying is to get out of ourselves so that God can get in.

If we are thinking so much about our own problems, we may not hear His knock on the door.

The victories won by prayer must still be held;
The foe retreats, but only when by prayer he is compelled!

Have you ever toyed with the key of a telegraph instrument while the circuit was closed? On that key you may write a complete message from address to signature. Upon it every telegraphic character may be perfectly formed; every condition of expert operating may be fulfilled. But it matters not how skillful an operator you are, so long as the electric circuit is closed, all your efforts are simply sounding brass and clattering platinum. Not a single spark of electric life do you transmit; not a single message of good or ill, of bane or blessing is conveyed to the waiting listener at the other end of the line. Why? Because the battery is not working. And all your working is effort without result, activity without power. Open the little brass lever which connects your key to the battery hidden beneath the table. Immediately every letter you form thrills with life, every word you write flashes a living message into the mind and heart of the faraway receiver. Through your work, dead and mechanical in itself, the electric battery is now pouring forth its vital stream, flooding with life and power every deft motion of your flying fingers.

The lesson is plain. It is in spiritual telegraphy as in material. If the battery is not working the message is mere clatter. We may do, but if God is not doing through us then all our doing is naught. Prayer connects us with the divine battery of life and power. Prayer puts you "in the Spirit," and "it is the Spirit that quickeneth."

J. H. McConkey, from the booklet Prayer

SEPTEMBER 16 _____

Whom the Lord loveth He chasteneth (Heb. 12:6).

C hastening is God's "child-training." This is the meaning of the word. It is built upon the Greek word "child." It means "to deal with as a child," to "child-train." God's "child-training" is not a kind of parental revenge for childish wrongdoing on our part. It is far from the truth even though we may think so at times. "For they [our earthly parents] verily for few days child-trained us after their own pleasure, but He for our profit, that we might be partakers of His holiness" (Heb. 12:10). God's one supreme purpose in child-training us is purification. He is seeking to purge from us all that mars the likeness of Jesus Christ within us. It is His own holiness that He is seeking to perfect within us.

A visitor was watching a silversmith heating the silver in his crucible. Hotter and hotter grew the fires. All the while the smith was closely scanning the crucible. Presently the visitor said: "Why do you watch the silver so closely? What are you looking for?" "I am looking for my face," was the answer. "When I see my own image in the silver, then I stop. The work is done." Why did the silversmith light the fires under the silver? To purify and perfect it. Is God's child-training an executioner visiting upon us the wrath of God? Nay, it is rather a cleansing angel pouring forth upon us the love of God. The furnace, the suffering, the agony of child-training, what do they mean? God is looking for a face! It is the face of His Son. "For he hath fore-ordained us to be conformed to the image of his son." And He is purging from us all that dims that image. Like all true parents, God has a model, a pattern to which He is fashioning the lives of His children. That pattern is Jesus Christ. And God's great purpose is that Christ should be "formed in us."
James McConkey, from Chastening

SEPTEMBER 17 _____

. . . The effectual fervent prayer of a righteous man availeth much (James 5:16).

David Brainerd was a man of great spiritual power. The work which he accomplished by prayer was simply marvelous. Dr. A. J. Gordon, in giving a sketch of Brainerd's experience says of him:

In the depths of these forests alone, he was unable to speak the language of the Indians, but he spent whole days literally in prayer. What was he praying for? He knew that he could not reach these savages. He did not understand their language. If he wanted to speak at all, he must find somebody who could vaguely interpret his thoughts; therefore he knew that anything he could do must be absolutely dependent upon the power of God. So he spent whole days in prayer simply that the power of the Holy Ghost might come upon him so unmistakably that these people should not be able to stand before him. What was his answer? Once he preached through a drunken interpreter, a man so intoxicated that he could hardly stand up. That was the best he could do. Yet scores were converted through that sermon. We account for it only in that it was the tremendous power of God behind him.

William Carey read of his life, and he was so moved by it that he went to India. Henry Martyn read of his life, and by its impulse, he went to India. Payson read it, as a young man of twenty, and he said he had never been so impressed by anything in his life as by the story. Murray McCheyne read it, and was powerfully impressed by it. The prayer and consecration of that one man, David Brainerd, did more for the great missionary revival of the nineteeth century than did any other single force.

The hidden life, a life whose days are spent in communion with God in trying to reach the Source of power, is the life that moves the world.

Prayer without faith is but husk; with faith it contains the seed-corn of a million harvests.

When we depend upon organizations, we get what organizations can do, when we depend upon education, we get what education can do; when we depend upon man, we get what man can do; but when we depend upon prayer, we get what God can do! *A. C. Dixon*

SEPTEMBER 18 ⸻

Now no chastening for the present seemeth to be joyous, but grievous: nevertheless afterward it yieldeth the peaceable fruit of righteousness . . . (Heb. 12:11).

The late summer showers are falling. The poet stands by the window watching them. They are beating and buffeting the earth with their fierce downpour. But the poet sees in his imaginings more than the showers which are falling before his eyes. He sees myriads of lovely flowers which shall soon be breaking forth from the watered earth, filling it with matchless beauty and fragrance. And so he sings:

It isn't raining rain for me, its raining daffodils;
In every dimpling drop I see wild flowers upon the hills.
A cloud of gray engulfs the day, and overwhelms the town;
It isn't raining rain for me; it's raining roses down.

Perchance some one of God's chastened children is even now saying: "O God, it is raining hard for me tonight. Testings are raining upon me which seem beyond my power to endure. Disappointments are raining fast, to the utter defeat of all my chosen plans. Bereavements are raining into my life which are making my shrinking heart quiver in its intensity of suffering. The rain of affliction is surely beating down upon my soul these days." Withal, friend, you are mistaken. It isn't raining rain for you. It's raining blessing. For if you will but believe your Father's Word, under that beating rain are springing up spiritual flowers of such fragrance and beauty as never before grew in that stormless, unchastened life of yours. You indeed see the rain. But, do you see, also, the flowers? It isn't raining afflictions for you. It is raining tenderness, love, compassion, patience and a thousand other flowers and fruits of the blessed Spirit which are bringing into your life such a spiritual enrichment as all the fullness of worldly prosperity and ease was never able to beget in your innermost soul. *Selected from McConkey's* Chastening

SEPTEMBER 19 _____

The living God is among you (Josh. 3:10).

It is strange we go on living our everyday lives—
So carelessly, stumbling, dully we plod
Our commonplace paths, and forget that we walk
Every day, every hour, in the presence of God.
Martha Snell Nicholson

From the first page of the Bible to the last, as well as in other books, men of every rank and every age have left testimony of having found themselves with awe and rapture in the radiant Presence. A few of this great host are Abraham in the night tending his altar fire; Moses on Sinai (it was six days on the mount before the Lord revealed himself); Isaiah in the temple; the three apostles at the transfiguration; Paul at Damascus; and John on Patmos. In each instance some great task confronted them and offered a chance to be a fellow worker with God. No excuse was adequate. Their reply was like that of Mary: "Behold, the handmaid of the Lord," or that of Paul, "I was not disobedient unto the heavenly vision."

Like Isaiah in the temple, we, too, when we face the shining Presence, must be ready to reply: "Here am I; send me."

Selected

God often visits us, but most of the time we are not at home.

No enemy can come so near that God is not nearer.

> Near to Thy heart, O Christ Divine, leaning like John on
>   Thy breast—
> Till with Thy glory I will shine, near to Thy heart I'd rest.
>
> Near to Thy heart O may I be, hearing Thy sweet words
>   of love,
> Learning Thy precious will for me, seeking those things
>   above.
>
> Near to Thy heart where all is peace, lost in the light of
>   Thy face,
> There will my faith and trust increase, there will I grow
>   in grace.
>
> *John W. Peterson, copyright 1956 by Singspiration, Inc.,*
> *and used by permission, Crowning Glory Hymnal*

SEPTEMBER 20

The weapons of our warfare are . . . mighty to the pulling down of strongholds (2 Cor. 10:4).

In the Great War in France a strong position had to be taken. The enemy's lines were so defended by trenches, parapets and barbed wire, that any assault, however determined, by whatever number of men, must have failed. However brave the attackers might have been, not a man would have reached the enemy's trenches alive. It was, in fact, quite impossible for the place to be taken by infantry assault. But the attacking general had collected large numbers of the most powerful artillery, firing the most powerfully explosive shells. With this excessive strength of massed artillery a continuous fire was kept up for over five hours on the one objective till trenches were blown in, palisades thrown down, and wire entanglements blown to pieces.

Then, when the artillery had done its work, the waiting troops were at last able to go up "every man straight before him," and, with comparatively little loss, to capture the position. What had been absolutely impossible to them before had been made possible by the sustained fire of the artillery.

I believe this is a most accurate and instructive picture of spiritual warfare. There are positions of the adversary that cannot be stormed or starved. There are defenses that are impregnable. There are obstructions which effectually bar the progress of the most devoted members of God's great missionary army. Before such can possibly succeed there is necessary the sustained and continuous fire of the artillery of prayer. Nothing else will take its place. Nothing will avail until it has done its work.

Too often, in the absence of prevailing prayer, the assault has to be made without, and precious lives are sacrificed, time is lost, and all efforts are in vain; not because God is unfaithful, or the servant is not devoted, but because the artillery of prayer has been lacking, and no breach has been made in the enemy's defenses.

Northcote Deck

SEPTEMBER 21

Commit . . . trust . . . rest . . . and wait patiently for him (Ps. 37:5, 7).

Prayer may be as simple as a baby's cry; as eloquent as a tear; as secret as a heart-pang; as swift as the lightning; as mighty as the tornado; as sweet as May blossoms; as deep as hell; as high as heaven; as strong as love; and as divinely human as the Christ of God. Prayer is only real prayer when inspired by Him and His Spirit. *Unknown*

> Pray!
> When life flows like a placid river,
> On thru verdant fields, 'neath smiling sun:

Pray!—
>   When darkness lowers and tempest gathers,
>   Day is past and sorrow's night begun.
>   Pierce the envolving gloom with earnest PRAYER,
>   God still reigns on yonder throne of light!
>   In the Name He holdeth—aye, so dear,
>   He will bare for thee His arm of might!   *Anonymous*

A young man had been struggling for months over yielding himself to God. At almost every service, when the invitation for seekers was given, he went to the altar to seek. The more he tried the more he seemed to fail. Finally he wondered if the blessing of yielding was to be his. However, he kept on attending the services. One night the preacher said, "If there are souls here who are struggling, I would advise them to stop this moment, and let God." This idea appealed to the young man. Upon going home, he cut the letters, L-E-T G-O-D, and pinned them to the wall of his room. Then he tried to let God. He walked back and forth still trying, but he seemingly could get no farther than the idea. Finally he went out. Returning some time later he was greeted, as he opened the door, with the words, "LET GO." The D in the sentence LET GOD had dropped to the floor, and by what had appeared an accident, the truth was made clear to the young man. Let God! Let Go! When we really commit ourselves to God, we are "letting God" by "letting go."   *Selected*

SEPTEMBER 22 _____

Though he were a Son, yet learned he obedience by the things which he suffered (Heb. 5:8).

We recall a striking story," says James H. McConkey, "from the lips of a friend. A lady was summering in Switzerland. One day she started out for a stroll. Presently, as she climbed the mountainside, she came to a shepherd's fold. She walked to the door and looked in. There sat the shepherd. Around him lay his flock. Near at hand, on a pile of straw, lay a single sheep. It seemed to be in suffering. Scanning it closely, the lady saw that its leg was broken. At once her sympathy went out to the suffering lamb. She looked inquiringly to the shepherd. 'How did it happen?' she said. To her amazement, the shepherd answered:

'Madam, I broke that sheep's leg.' A look of pain swept over the visitor's face. Seeing it, the shepherd went on: 'Madam, of all the sheep in my flock, this one was the most wayward. It never would obey my voice. It never would follow in the pathway in which I was leading the flock. It wandered to the verge of many a perilous cliff and dizzy abyss. And not only was it disobedient itself, but it was ever leading the other sheep of my flock astray. I had before had experience with sheep of this kind. So I broke its leg. The first day I went to it with food, it tried to bite me. I let it lie alone for a couple of days. Then, I went back to it. Now, it not only took the food, but licked my hand, and showed every sign of submission and even affection. And now let me tell you something. When this sheep is well, as it soon will be, it will be the model sheep of my flock. No sheep will hear my voice so quickly. None will follow so closely at my side. Instead of leading its mates astray, it will now be an example and a guide for the wayward ones, leading them, with itself, in the path of obedience to my call. In short, a complete transformation will have come into the life of this wayward sheep. It has learned obedience through its suffering.' "

The chamber of suffering—is it not the birthplace of obedience?

Very often a complete submission to the will of God—in a fiery furnace if needs be!—is the quickest way to deliverance.

SEPTEMBER 23 _____

The Lord hath his way in the whirlwind and storm (Nah. 1:3).

The fiercest wind that may blow on me is held in the hollow of His hand. Behind what seems cruel chance, there is the love so wise and wisdom so loving of our God.

> If God can send a storm through space;
>   And dot with trees the mountain's face,
> If He the sparrow's course can trace,
>   What can He do for you?
>
> If God can hang the stars on high,
>   Can paint the clouds that drift on by,
> Can send the sun across the sky,
>   What can He do for you?

If God can send us sunny days,
    And nature from her slumber raise
Till song birds lift their notes of praise,
    What can He do for you?

If God can do these many things,
    Can count each little bird that sings,
Control the universe that swings,
    What can He do for you?

If God can bring sweet peace to me
    And to my soul bring liberty.
By Christ who hung upon the tree,
    This He can do for you.
        G. E. Wagoner, from the Log of the Good Ship Grace

God's eye has never yet become dimmed with age; His ear has never yet become dulled with the years; His arms have never yet been wanting in strength, nor have His footsteps ever faltered. He is not changed; He is still the same immortal, immutable, invincible God, from all the ages. He makes a commitment of Himself to me. What a gift, what an offering, what a measureless, boundless condescension of the infinite God to give Himself.   *Unknown*

SEPTEMBER 24 _____

He came and dwelt in a city called Nazareth (Matt. 2:23).

In that little village, until ready for His public ministry, Jesus made His home. It is a sweet thought that the Son of God dwelt for so many years in a home on earth. His pure and sinless life opened out there as a bud opens into a lovely rose, pouring fragrance over all the lowly place.

The study of the childhood and the youth of Jesus, even from the few fragmentary glimpses of those years given us in the gospel, ought to prove an inspiration to every child and young person. No doubt, we wish that we could know more of that sweet and blessed home-life; but the little we are told about it is enough, or God's Spirit would have given us more of the story. We know there was no sin in Jesus, and we can think of His gentleness, His obedience, His love, His unselfishness, and of all His other graces and beauties of character. He was a natural child, glad, joyous, interested in beautiful things, studious, earnest without being

271

precocious or morbidly religious. He was such a boy as God loves, and as He would have every other boy strive to be. We have one glimpse of Him at twelve, when He began to think of His relation to the Heavenly Father; yet we must note the fact that He went back to Nazareth and resumed His place of filial duty, staying there for eighteen years longer. The Father's business on which He entered at twelve was not preaching and working miracles and going about doing good in a public manner, but for the time remaining at home, a dutiful child, a glad, helpful youth, and an industrious, growing man.

Some young men chafe under the providence that keeps them so many years in a quiet, obscure home, where they can do only plain, common duty. But if Jesus found His Nazareth home a wide enough sphere for His blessed life, surely we should not think any home too narrow for our little lives to grow in.

J. R. Miller, in Come Ye Apart

SEPTEMBER 25 _____

. . . denying ungodliness and worldly lusts, we should live soberly, righteously, and godly, in this present world (Titus 2:12).

Prophylaxis may be a technical term, but it stands for practical truth. To guard against perils is better than subsequent attempts at remedy or consequent pains of remorse. God told His people of old that when they build their flat-roofed houses, on which many an hour would be spent, they must build a battlement. If they did not, and anyone fell off, his blood would be on the owner's head.

Ought we not put guards at points of peril in our lives—not for others alone, but for our own exceptional moments? We are not always at our best. We are not always safe where ordinarily we move without peril. Every deepened conviction, every outward commitment, every vow and pledge and new act of consecration is putting a guard at the point of possible personal danger. Should we not learn the lesson, too, in our city life, that railings are better than ambulances, and building parapets than setting bones? Looking for the springs of evil is better investment of time than groaning at the muddy mouth of the river; and preventing the sowing of seeds of sin, than taking care of harvests of shame. How much better to guard lives with new hopes and opportunities, new interests and outlooks, to fortify them in advance against danger, than to attempt the restoration and reformation of lives that have suffered remediless!

And who shall dare refuse, though he be strong and steady, to build battlements at dangerous edges of his life, lest a weaker brother may fall where he stood safe? Can any pleasure of "uncharted freedom," any pride of personal self-indulgence, justify the moral catastrophe which our self-confidence may provoke, our example encourage? Better any barrier of loving self-denial than another's blood through our loveless self-assertion. Let the brotherhood of Jesus Christ remember the weak brother, and interpret Christian liberty in the light of Christian love.

Maltbie Davenport Babcock,
from Thoughts for Every-Day Living

SEPTEMBER 26

Blessed are the poor in spirit (Matt. 5:3).

Our Lord called the twelve disciples; but what about all those other disciples of His who were not specially called? The twelve were for a special purpose; but there were hundreds who followed Jesus and were sincere believers in Him who were unnoticed. We are apt to have a disproportionate view of a Christian because we look only at the exceptions. The exceptions stand out as exceptions. Not one in a million has an experience such as the Apostle Paul had. The majority of us are unnoticed and unnoticeable people. If we take the extraordinary experiences as a model for the Christian life, we erect a wrong standard without knowing it, and in passing of time we produce that worst abortion, an intolerant unlikeness to Jesus Christ.

"Blessed are the poor in spirit" literally means, "Blessed are the paupers in spirit." A pauper is exceedingly commonplace! At the basis of our Lord's kingdom is the unaffected loveliness of the commonplace. The average type of preaching emphasizes strength of will, beauty of character—the things that can be easily noticed. If I know I have no strength of will, no nobility of disposition, then says Jesus, "Blessed are you," because it is through that poverty that I enter into the kingdom of heaven. I cannot enter as a good man or woman; I can only enter heaven as a complete pauper.

"As the lily among thorns, so is my love among the daughters" (Song of Sol. 2:2). The lily Solomon refers to is as common as our daisy, but a perfume pervades it. The illustration in this verse is as if a traveler were passing a field and suddenly a fragrant aroma was wafted to him from a bush; marveling at the sweetness, he looked into the bush and found a lily growing in its bosom. People come to a good, but worldly home, and they say—"What beautiful influence comes from that home!" But begin to draw aside the ordinary commonplace things of that home, and you discover that tucked away somewhere there is a mother or a daughter who is really a "lily" of the Lord.

Or take it with regard to individual lives. We may see a man who is generally disadvantaged in appearance or in education, a thoroughly commonplace man, yet a marvelous influence radiates from him. The true character of the loveliness that tells for God is always unconscious. When we begin to wonder whether we are of any use, we instantly lose the bloom of the touch of the Lord. Jesus says—"He that believeth in Me, out of him shall flow rivers of living water." If we begin to examine the outflow, we lose touch with the Source. We have to pay attention to the Source and God will look after the outflow.

Oswald Chambers, from The Ministry of the Unnoticed

SEPTEMBER 27

Lord, thou hast been our dwelling place in all generations (Ps. 90:1).

You cannot detain the eagle in the forest. You may gather around him a chorus of the choicest birds; you may give him a perch on the goodliest pine; you may charge winged messengers to bring him choicest dainties; but he will spurn them all. Spreading his lordly wings, and with his eye on the alpine cliff, he will soar away to his own ancestral halls amid the munitions of rocks and the wild music of tempest and waterfall.

> I cannot find Thee! Still on restless pinion
> My spirit beats the void where Thou dost dwell;
> I wander lost through all Thy vast dominion,
> And shrink beneath Thy Light ineffable.

I cannot know Thee! Even when most adoring
Before Thy shrine I bend in lowliest prayer;
Beyond these bounds of thought, my thought upsoaring,
From furthest quest comes back; Thou art not there.

Yet high above the limits of my seeing,
And folded far within the inmost heart,
And deep below the deeps of conscious being,
Thy splendor shineth; there, O God, Thou art.

I cannot lose Thee! Still in Thee abiding
The End is clear, how wide soe'er I roam;
The Law that holds the worlds my steps is guiding,
And I must rest at last in Thee, my home.

Eliza Scudder, from Quiet Hours

SEPTEMBER 28

I know also my God that thou triest the heart and hast pleasure in uprightness. As for me in the uprightness of my heart I have willingly offered all these things (1 Chron. 29:17).

That is, the Lord has pleasure in willing offerings. He is watching for willing offerings that He may find pleasure therein, and so He tries our wills by placing us in circumstances where our gifts cost so as to hurt. He watches then to see whether we give grudgingly or of necessity, or whether by reliance on His indwelling presence we still offer willingly unto the Lord. He tests our wills in order that He may see His own life in us and thus rejoice over us with great joy.

Pressed out of measure, and pressed to all length,
Pressed so intensely it seems beyond strength;
Pressed in the body and pressed in the soul,
Pressed in the mind till the dark surges roll;
Pressed by foes and a pressure by friends,
Pressure on pressure till life nearly ends.   *Unknown*

Close the door upon your treasures of love and fortune—they leak through and are gone. If you would keep and increase them, share generously.

They may be charmed into entering a door set ever so slightly at the crack, but they cannot be kept in the tight-shut dungeon of the closed mind. . . .

Bless your one loaf and pass it out to the multitude and it will feed them and return you seven basketfuls. Hoard it and guard it and it will shrivel down to a mildewed crust.   *Unknown*

SEPTEMBER 29 _____

He hath given meat unto them that fear him: he will ever be mindful of his covenant (Ps. 111:5).

> Bear not a single care thyself, one is too much for thee;
> The work is mine, yea, mine alone; thy work is—Rest in Me.

Selected

A missionary found herself without means, among a heathen people, far from any source of supplies. In her distress she claimed the promise of God that He would supply her need. She was also in poor health. From a businessman in another part of the country came several large boxes of Scotch oatmeal. She already had several cans of condensed milk, so with these two commodities she was obliged to sustain life for four long weeks. As time went on, it seemed to agree with her better; and by the time the four weeks had passed, she felt in excellent health. In relating the experience some time later to a company of people, which included a physician, she was asked more particularly of the nature of her former illness. The physician said, "The Lord heard your prayer and supplied your need more truly than you realize. For the sickness from which you were suffering, we physicians prescribe a four weeks' diet of nothing but oatmeal gruel for our patients. The Lord prescribed it for you, and saw to it that that was all you took. It was the proper remedy."   *Selected*

> "Be all at rest"—so shalt thou be an answer,
> To those who question "Who is God and where?"
> For God is REST, and where He dwells is stillness,
> And they who dwell in Him that rest shall share.

Freda H. Allen

SEPTEMBER 30 _____

For I reckon the sufferings of this present time are not worthy to be compared with the glory which shall be revealed in us (Rom. 8:18).

276

Methought I saw two gems of clearest ray,
  Alike in colour, purity and weight;
Yet when athwart them shone the light of day,
  Not the same lustre did they radiate.
I marvelled, why?—The one in facets few
  Eight times by graver's art had chiselled been;
The other, so resplendent in its hue,
  Ten times as oft; hence came its dazzling sheen;
And now the long, keen work of fashioning o'er,
  Far brighter doth it shine for evermore.

Learn, then, sad heart, a lesson from a gem:
  The King of glory, passing by this way,
Doth seek bright jewels for His diadem.
  Wouldst thou for such high honour say Him nay?
Lord, if Thy chastening thus can make us shine,
  Take Thine own way, enough that it is Thine.   *J. H. S.*

Several years ago there was found in an African mine the most magnificent diamond in the world's history. It was presented to the king of England to blaze in his crown of state. The king sent it to Amsterdam to be cut. It was put in the hands of an expert lapidary. And what do you suppose he did with it? He took this gem of priceless value. He cut a notch in it. Then he struck it a hard blow with his instrument and lo! the superb jewel lay in his hand, cleft in twain. What recklessness! what wastefulness! what criminal carelessness! Not so. For days and weeks that blow had been studied and planned. Drawings and models had been made of the gem! Its quality, its defects, its lines of cleavage had all been studied with minutest care. The man to whom it was committed was one of the most skillful lapidaries in the world. Do you say that blow was a mistake! Nay. It was the climax of the lapidary's skill. When he struck that blow, he did the one thing which would bring that gem to its most perfect shapliness, radiance, and jeweled splendor. That blow which seemed to ruin the superb precious stone was in fact its perfect redemption. For, from these two halves were wrought the two magnificent gems which the skilled eye of the lapidary saw hidden in the rough, uncut stone as it came from the mines.

So, sometimes, God lets a stinging blow fall upon your life. The nerves wince. The soul cries out in an agony of wondering protest. The blow seems to you an appalling mistake. But it is not, for you are the most priceless jewel in the world to God. And He is the most skilled lapidary in the universe. Some day you are to blaze in the diadem of the King of Kings. As you lie in His hand now He *knows* just how to deal with you. Not a blow will be permitted to fall upon your shrinking soul but that the love of God permits it, and works out from its depths of blessing and spiritual enrichment unseen, and unthought of by you.

J. H. McConkey, from Chastening

OCTOBER 1

Let him that thinketh he standeth take heed lest he fall (1 Cor. 10:12).

A ngels fell in heaven, Adam in paradise, Peter in Christ's presence. *Theophilus Polwheile*

If you ask the way to the crown—'tis by the cross; to the mountain—'tis by the valley; to exaltation—'tis he that humbleth himself. *J. H. Evans*

Between the great things we cannot do and the small things we will not do, the danger is that we shall do nothing. *Monod*

While it takes every one of the three hundred and sixty degrees to complete a cricle; while ninety cents won't make a dollar; while a wheel is made up of many spokes; there are no small things.

While ten cents will buy the news of the world; while a minute will catch an important train; while a fingermark will discover a criminal; while a five-cent postage stamp will take a letter to thousands of miles away; there are no little things.

While a battle may be lost for a moment's delay; while a man may starve for a morsel of food, or famish for a glass of water, there are no small things.

If you say, "I am hedged about, I can do nothing, and fain would help, but cannot," your very longing is help. It is never true that we are not helpers; where the fervent heart is, there is the servant of God, and unto him comes ever with work the reward. *Robert Collyer*

It is when we are in the way of duty that we find giants. It was when Israel was going forward that the giants appeared. When they turned back into the wilderness they found none. *Selected*

It is most needful for all servants of Christ to remember that whenever the Lord places a man in a position of responsibility, He will both fit him for it and maintain him in it.

It is, of course, another thing altogether if a man will rush unsent into any field of work, or any post of difficulty or danger. In such a case we may assuredly look for a thorough breakdown, sooner or later. But when God calls a man to a certain position, He will endow him with the needed grace to occupy it.

This holds good in every case. We can never fail if we only cling to the living God. We can never run dry if we are drawing from the fountain. Our tiny springs will soon dry up; but our Lord Jesus Christ declares, "He that believeth in me, as the Scripture hath said, out of his belly shall flow rivers of living water."   *C. H. M.*

OCTOBER 2

But without faith it is impossible to please Him: for he that cometh to God must believe that He is, and that He is a rewarder of them that diligently seek Him (Heb. 11:6).

Faith is a wonderful key to every situation where we come to God in prayer. Faith is a wonderful key that opens God's storehouse. God's storehouse is filled, shelf after shelf, clear to the top, with the good things that men and women need.

On the shelves of God's storehouse there is salvation—a born-again experience, victory over the world, the flesh and the devil. On the shelf of God's storehouse there is divine healing, there is blessing, there is deliverance for your body as well as your soul and your spirit. On God's shelves is a rich spiritual experience; there is joy unspeakable and full of glory, hope, peace, blessing, and answer to prayer.

Every man, woman and child may have the key of faith to God's storehouse put in his hand that he may turn the lock of prayer and swing wide the portals.

Faith moves mountains. Have you a mountain to move? Have you a mountain of heartache, despair, discontent, discouragement? Faith in Jesus Christ as the Son of God can move it. Faith in the precious blood that flowed from the wounded side of Immanuel can cleanse the heart and make it whiter than the driven snow.

There is a mountain of unbelief. The Lord can move that mountain. You cannot move it with all the power of your reasoning, not even with your vain imaginations. What you need is just a little spark of faith down in your heart and it will move the mountain.

The Lord does answer prayer. Use the key He has placed in your hand. Have faith in God! You can look upon those shelves in the storehouse and claim any number of the fruits He has stored thereon. *From a newspaper clipping*

OCTOBER 3

Lord, increase our faith (Luke 17:5).

Faith is not clinging—it is letting go.

Somewhere we have read a story that goes like this: "A traveler upon a lonely road was set upon by bandits who robbed him of all he had. They then led him into the depths of the forest. There in the darkness they tied a rope to the limb of a great tree, and bade him catch hold of the end of it. Swinging him out into the blackness of surrounding space, they told him he was hanging over the brink of a giddy precipice. The moment he let go he would be dashed to pieces on the rocks below. And then they left him. His soul was filled with horror at the awful doom impending. He clutched despairingly the end of the swaying rope. But each dreadful moment only made his fate more sure. His strength steadily failed. At last he could hold on no longer. The end had come. His clenched fingers relaxed their convulsive grip. He fell—six inches, to the the solid earth at his feet! It was only a ruse of the robbers to gain time in escaping. And when he let go it was not to death, but to the safety which had been waiting him through all his time of terror.

Clutching will not save anyone from his hopelessness. It is only Satan's trick to keep you from being afforded security and peace in the solid promises of God. And all the while you are swinging over the supposed precipice of fear and mistrust. Let go! It is God's plan that you fall—not to defeat, but into His arms, the solid Rock. As soon as you recognize your sheer helplessness and your failing strength, you let go; and falling upon Him, your fear goes, your mistrust goes, and the blessed assurance comes forever. For *He*—not your clinging but—"*He* shall save *his* people from their sins."

. . . and gave us rain from heaven, and fruitful seasons, filling our hearts with food and gladness (Acts 14:17).

We thank Thee, gracious Lord of the seasons that Thou hast planned the kaleidoscope we call the year; that the earth in its journey makes the one cycle a perpetual delight, Thy calendar, one of accomplished loveliness, beautiful beyond man's dream.

> All good gifts around us
> Are sent from heaven above;
> Then thank the Lord, O thank the Lord
> For all His love.

Who with the least bit of love of nature in his disposition has not gone out of his way to see the hills covered and the vales filled with the glory and the splendor of falling leaves? Did you take notice of the color of the maple leaves that bear the mark of the Master Painter's unrivaled pencil?

To Turner, the great artist, a lady remarked, "I cannot see in nature what you put in your pictures." "Don't you wish you could, Madam?" was the artist's reply. Oh for opened eyes!

We pray for bounteous harvests on the plowed lands of the soul. We have grown shrubs where we should have grown trees. Some years ago, when a new railway cutting was made in East Norfolk, you could trace it through the next summer, winding like a blood-red river through the green fields. Poppy seeds, that must have lain buried for generations, had suddenly been upturned and had germinated by the thousand: The same thing happened a while back in the Canadian woods. A fir forest was cut down, and the next spring the ground was covered with seedling oaks, though not an oak tree was in sight; unnumbered years before there must have been a struggle between the two trees, in which the firs gained the day, but the acorns had kept their latent spark of life underground, and it broke out at the first chance.

Who can tell what harvest after harvest may be waiting in the eternal years, after the summer of earth has faded into the far past?   *I. Lilias Trotter*

OCTOBER 5

. . . he is gone forth from this place to make thy land desolate . . . (Jer. 4:7).

He hath made everything beautiful in his time . . . (Eccl. 3:11).

> On the maple trees
> The scarlet leaves hang shining in the breeze;
> And the brown stubble fields are crisp and sere,
> Touched by the hoarfrost of the waning year.

The frost's frigid breath has swept across the more delicate garden blossoms, leaving blackness and blight; but the chilling nights only bring into brighter bloom many hardier flowers, and set the forest trees burning with transient gold-and-scarlet loveliness. "A melancholy month," urges a plaintive voice. Yes; perhaps so—to some. But the blessed harvest season, the fruition period, can never be wholly sad, wholly desolate. Pain, gloom, and sorrow should not be permitted to cloud these rarely beautiful, twilight-clipped autumn days.

> Rather let our spirits borrow
> Gladness from the rich libation,
> Nectar-brimmed at coronation
> Of this loveliest month of all,
> Diamond-threaded, of the fall.

And remember, "when the leaves are gone, we see more of the blue." Ah, yes! There are always compensations. So be thou hopeful, O tried and despondent soul, even though the branches of thy life are swept bare by the bitter wind of sorrow or adversity! Look always up into the unfathomable depths of the Father's love. He "knoweth"; He "remembereth." This somber period in your experience, when everything desirable seems taken from you, is necessary for your future growth in spiritual life. Can you not already see "more of the blue"?

Adelaide S. Seaverns, from Thoughts for the Thoughtful

. . . the Father of lights, with whom is no variableness, neither shadow of turning (James 1:17).

What the sun in the heavens is to the earth, that the Father is to us. Was there ever an act of unenlightened worship more dignified and exalted than his who, from his silent hilltop, watched the flushing east, and bowed before the great day-bringing, life-giving sun? How fine, how true the apostle's comparison! What light that brightens a human face or lightens a page or a pathway but springs from the sun! The blaze of a pine knot, the shining lamp, the glowing of coals or their reduction and refinement in jets of light, all are only the release of imprisoned sunshine. The gentle beauty of the rainbow, the blue of sky and sea, the endless joy of the flowers, the witchery of spring, the luxury of summer, the wealth of autumn, the flashing splendor of a snowy field, all bless the sun for their being.

Now past the figure of speech, we have reached the glorious matter of fact: that God is the true Father of lights; the Author of every good and perfect gift. But pride awakens and airs itself and says, "Should I thank God for the health and wealth, the education, the social position, the political influence, which by my care and skill, by my judgment and perseverance and pluck I possess today? Why should I not put the crown on my own head when I dug the gold and cut and fitted the jewels? It is mine."

Oh, be careful, child of God, listen: A voice is sounding across the years and over the graves of a hundred generations. "Beware that thou forget not the Lord thy God . . . and say in thine heart, my power and the might of mine hand hath gotten me this wealth. But thou shalt remember the Lord thy God: for it is He that giveth thee power to get wealth."

If we owed everything to ourselves, no one could live with us. Dependence upon God means association with God, and that is life's supreme opportunity and noblest hope. Every gift is from above to take our thoughts and thanks above. God's gifts are to lift up our faces to His, to awaken us to love Him. Every bad and imperfect thing drags us down to darkness; every good and perfect gift woos us into the light. The birds and flowers are His appeal to trust; the stately order of the heavens, to symmetry and steadiness; the beauty of nature, to the beauty of holiness; the affections of earth, to the perfect love of which they are but dear fragments. And God be thanked for His supreme appeal—that good and perfect Gift, the Gift unspeakable: His life, His love, His very Self in Jesus Christ. *Maltbie Davenport Babcock*

OCTOBER 7

. . . and the love of every one of you all toward each other aboundeth (2 Thess. 1:3).

It is the abounding love toward others that stands up under the test of gossip, envy, jealousy and suspicion. To abound it has to be a higher love, a deeper love, a broader love than any of these petty, hurtful characteristics that may crop up in your closest relationships with loved ones, friends and acquaintances. The abounding love is able to overwhelm and even conquer them. However, there are some individuals with "turned around" personalities who actually find excitement and change from boredom by welcoming these contemptible attacks upon others. To tell them of their plight—that they are emptied of love would but anger them and thus give them more fuel to cast upon the fire they must keep burning.

The inspired writer of the beautiful love chapter said, "Love believeth all things"—that are good about others. Actually he implies that love refuses to believe anything that is evil, degrading, belittling, harmful, hurtful. Many are those who have been rescued from these evils by simply refusing to let love think evil.

If some bit of gossip come,
  File the thing away:
If a scandalous, spicy crumb,
  File the thing away;
If suspicion comes to you
That your neighbor is not true,
Let me tell you what to do—
  File the thing away.

Do this for a little while,
Then go out and burn the file. *Anonymous*

Instead of the thorn shall come up the fir tree, and instead of the brier shall come up the myrtle tree: and it shall be to the Lord for a name, for an everlasting sign that shall not be cut off (Isa. 55:13).

Strange gift indeed!—a thorn to prick—
  To pierce into the very quick;
To cause perpetual sense of pain;
  Strange gift! And yet, 'twas given for gain.

Unwelcome—yet it came to stay;
  Nor could it e'en be prayed away.
It came to fill its God-planned place—
  A life-enriching means of grace.

And he who bore it, day by day,
  Found Christ his power, his strength, his stay;
In weakness gloried, since thereby
  The power of Christ might on him lie.

Oh much-tired saint, with fainting heart,
  The thorn with its perpetual smart,
With all its wearing ceaseless pain
  Can be thy means of priceless gain.

God's grace-thorns—ah, what forms they take!
  What piercing, smarting pain they make!
And yet, each one in love is sent,
  And always just for blessing meant.

And so, whate'er thy thorn may be,
  From God accept it willingly;
But reckon Christ—His life—the power
  To keep, in thy most trying hour.

And sure—thy life will richer grow;
  He grace sufficient will bestow:
And in Heav'n's morn thy joy 'twill be
That, by His thorn, He strengthened thee.   *J. Danson Smith*

Pray without ceasing (1 Thess. 5:17).

A number of ministers was assembled for the discussion of difficult questions. Among others, it was asked how the command to "pray without ceasing" could be complied with. Various suppositions were started, and at length one of the number was appointed to write an essay on it to be read at the next monthly meeting. This being overheard by a servant exclaimed, "What, a whole month to tell the meaning of that verse? It is one of the easiest and best texts in the Bible." "Well, well, Mary," said an old minister, "what can you say about it? Let us know how you understand it. Can you pray all the time?" "Oh, yes, sir." "What, when you have so many things to do?" "Why, sir, the more I have to do the more I can pray." "Indeed. Well, Mary, do let us know how it is. Most of us think otherwise."

"Well, sir," said the girl, "when I first open my eyes in the morning I pray, 'Lord, open the eyes of my understanding'; and while I am dressing I pray that I may be clothed with the robe of righteousness; when I wash I ask for the washing of regeneration; as I work I pray that I may have strength equal to my day; when I begin to kindle the fire I pray that God's work may revive my soul; as I sweep out the house I pray that my heart may be cleansed from all its impurities; while preparing and partaking of breakfast I pray to be fed with the hidden manna and sincere milk of the Word; as I am busy with the little children I look up to God as my Father and pray for the spirit of adoption, that I may be His obedient child—and so on all day. Everything I do furnishes me with a thought for prayer."

"Enough! Enough!" cried the minister. "These things are revealed to babes and hid from the wise and prudent. Go on, Mary," said he. "Pray without ceasing. And as for us, my brethren, let us bless the Lord for this exposition, and remember that He said, 'The meek will He guide in judgment; and the meek will He teach His way' " (Ps. 25:9).   *From a tract*

"Watch ye and pray always" (Luke 21:36).

OCTOBER 10 _____

I will yet for this be enquired of by the house of Israel, to do it for them (Ezek. 36:37).

286

For thou, O Lord of Hosts, God of Israel, hast revealed to thy servant, saying, I will build thee an house: therefore hath thy servant found in his heart to pray this prayer unto thee (2 Sam. 7:27).

> What comes from heaven in a promise
> Should be sent back to heaven in a prayer.

A well-known and dearly loved Bible teacher in Seattle, Washington, Dr. Arthur Petrie, wrote: "God in heaven is looking for those on earth in whose hearts He can put prayer for the performance of His promises. If He does not find your heart open for His prayer, He will find other hearts that are, and you will surely miss something.

"There is a beautiful illustration of this in the story of Queen Esther. Her people, according to the law of the Medes and Persians, which altereth not, were doomed to destruction. The great Mordecai knew the Word of God. He knew the promises of God in the books of the prophets concerning his people, the Jews. He knew from those promises that the Jews as a people were indestructible. He knew that Haman's plot could not succeed. He knew that there was yet a glorious future for the Jews in the land of Israel. But he knew that something must be done. He therefore charged Esther 'to make supplication unto the king,' and to 'make request before him for her people' (Esther 4:8). But Mordecai knew that if Esther failed to pray and supplicate, some others would. He said: 'For if thou altogether holdest thy peace at this time, then shall there enlargement and deliverance arise to the Jews from another place: but thou and thy father's house shall be destroyed: and who knoweth whether thou art come to the kingdom for such a time as this!' (Esther 4:14).

"God's promises cannot fail. He has appointed prayer to bring them to pass. Some will pray them into performances. If you do not, God will seek out others that will.

" 'For the eyes of the Lord run to and fro throughout the whole earth, to show himself strong in the behalf of them whose heart is perfect toward him' (2 Chron. 16:9). And into such hearts, the Spirit of God will put the prayer of God, for 'Prayer is nothing but the breathing that out before the Lord, that was first breathed into us by the Spirit of the Lord.' The teaching that promise and prayer must go together and be used together is one of the primal laws of the spiritual world."
Dr. Arthur Petrie

For we are . . . God's building (1 Cor. 3:9).

With such skill and grace does the architect plan and build. Have you ever watched the creator of a building in the throes of conceiving a plan, his blueprint for a grand edifice? Step by step he proceeds from foundation to spire. To the very last nail driven securely in its place he watches and schemes and brings his masterpiece to its completion. With pride he avails it for occupancy.

What matchless precision the Infinite Artisan applied to His great construction project—that of building a spacious and endless universe! It is unparalleled in majesty.

Then, dear despaired one, let your spirits rise in gratitude for the very fact this Master Tactician and Strategist had sketched your life upon His celestial drawing board ere He erected it upon earth. From the instant He designed the first stroke of His imagination until He breathed into you the breath of life, you were of great consequence to Him. What glorious comprehension! What splendid persistency! What unequalled prevision! What endless patience! One's mind is astounded as it seeks to follow this vast undertaking.

Can the Creator of the universe have an interest in our finite affairs, the trifling details of our petty worries, the trivial fears and hopes? Consider how precisely He maneuvers season upon season; how He causes the day to consistently chase the night; how skillfully He correctly places the blossom on its stem; how faithfully He brings them to fruitage. He tends His garden with sunshine and showers. He never perfumes a violet with the fragrance of the rose. If He makes His creation His concern, then how much more does He plan for us. Think of it—He made us for Himself! He has formed us in His own image! We are His temples. He built us for His occupancy.   *Marie Taylor*

Holding the mystery of faith . . . (1 Tim. 3:9).

> She asked for a faith strong yet simple:
> He permitted the dark clouds to come,

And she staggered by faith through the darkness,
For the storm had quite obscured the sun.   *Unknown*

Faith is vision plus valor.

Faith is the eye by which we look to Jesus. A dim-sighted eye is still an eye; a weeping eye is still an eye.

Faith is the hand with which we lay hold of Jesus. A trembling hand is still a hand. And he is a believer whose heart within him trembles when he touches the hem of the Savior's garment, that he may be healed.

Faith is the tongue by which we taste how good the Lord is. A feverish tongue is nevertheless a tongue. And even then we may believe when we are without the smallest portion of comfort; for our faith is founded not upon feelings but upon the promises of God.

Faith is the foot by which we go to Jesus. A lame foot is still a foot. He who comes slowly nevertheless comes.   *George Mueller*

Habakkuk shouted God's praises when he beheld the vines without fruit, the fields burned and bare, the stalls without herds. He rejoiced because he had faith in God. It was his audacious certitude of faith that made him the prophet of the ages.

Abraham believed God when everything witnessed to the contrary, and "under hopeless circumstances, hopefully believed." And we are called to set our feet in the footprints of the giants of faith, and follow them as they followed their Lord.

A staunch soldier of the cross said that he loved to sit at the feet of the old heroes of faith in Hebrews the eleventh chapter, hear them relate their experiences, tell of the darkness of their night, the humanly impossible extremities and situations in which they so often found themselves. It was in those dark places that they were taught the strength of omnipotence.

OCTOBER 13 _____

Who is among you that feareth the Lord . . . that walketh in darkness, and hath no light? Let him trust in the name of the Lord, and stay upon his God (Isa. 50:10).

In fierce storms," said an old seaman, "we can do but one thing, there is only one way; we must put the ship in a certain position and keep her there."

This, Christian, is what you must do. Sometimes, like Paul, you can see neither sun nor stars, and no small tempest lies on you; and then you can do but one thing; there is only one way. Reason cannot help you. Past experiences give you no light. Even prayer fetches no consolation. Only a single course is left. You must put your soul in one position and keep it there. You must stay upon the Lord; and, come what may—winds, waves, cross seas, thunder, lightning, frowning rocks, roaring breakers—no matter what, you must lash yourself to the helm, and hold fast your confidence in God's faithfulness, His covenant engagement, His everlasting love in Christ Jesus.

Richard Fuller, from Thoughts for the Quiet Hour

What matter how the winds may blow
    Or blow they east, or blow they west
What reck I how the tides may flow,
    Since ebb or flood alike is best.
No summer calm, no winter gale,
    Impedes or drives me from my way;
I steadfast toward the Haven sail
    That lies, perhaps, not far away.

I mind the weary days of old,
    When motionless I seemed to lie;
The nights when fierce the billows rolled,
    And changed my course, I knew not why.
I feared the calm, I feared the gale,
    Foreboding danger and delay,
Forgetting I was thus to sail
    To reach what seemed so far away.

I measure not the loss and fret
    Which through those years of doubt I bore;
I keep the memory fresh, and yet
    Would hold God's patient mercy more.
What wrecks have passed me in the gale,
    What ships gone down on summer-day;
While I, with furled or spreading sail,
    Stood for the Haven far away.

Anonymous, from At the Beautiful Gate

. . . but it shall be given to them for whom it is prepared of my Father (Matt. 20:23).

When James and John asked Jesus for the best places in His kingdom, they were told in His gentle, gracious way that the main point was not wanting the best places but being worth them. It is a question of preparation—"For whom they are prepared" is only another way of saying for those who are prepared.

We are so used to favoritism in public life that we turn every way for enough influence to get ourselves appointed. But perfect governments are officered, not by official favorites, but by qualified men. "God is no respecter of persons." He does not look twice at a man's petition and signatures. It is wholly a question of personal fitness. Let us put the emphasis of our life, then, in the right place. It is not wanting something, but being worth something. God has plenty of time in which to make discoveries, but we have none too much time in which to become worth discovering. We should care, not so much about being recognized as about being worth recognition. The real values of life are spiritual and eternal, and the fit man will someday succeed the favorite.

Maltbie Davenport Babcock,
from Thoughts for Every-Day Living

God wants our best, He in the far-off ages
Once claimed the firstling of the flock, the finest of
    the wheat;
And still He asks His own, with gentlest pleading,
To lay their highest hopes and brightest talents at
    His feet.
He'll not forget the feeblest service, humblest love;
He only asks that of our store we give to Him the best
    that we have!   *Unknown*

Heaven and earth shall pass away, but my words shall not pass away (Matt. 24:35).

Oh, wonderful, wonderful Word of the Lord!
   The hope of our friends in the past:
Its truth where so firmly they anchored their trust,

Through ages eternal shall last.
Oh, wonderful, wonderful Word of the Lord!
Unchanging, abiding and sure;
For we know that when time and the world pass away,
God's Word shall forever endure.   *Julia Sterling*

You never get to the end of the words of our Lord. They pass into proverbs, they pass into laws, they pass into doctrines, they pass into consolations, they pass into hymns, they pass into poems, but they never pass away, and after all the use that is made of them they are still as fresh and inexhaustible as ever.
F. E. W.

Priscilla Howe once described the Word of God as the Book that contains the mind of God, the state of man, the way of salvation, the doom of sinners, and the happiness of believers. Its doctrines are holy, its precepts are binding, its histories are true, and its decisions are immutable. Therefore, how can it ever fade from the grasp of man? Read it to be wise, believe it to be safe, and practice it to be holy.

It contains light to direct you, food to support you, and comfort to cheer you. It is the traveler's map, the pilgrim's staff, the soldier's sword, and the Christian's charter. Here paradise is restored, heaven opened, and the gates of hell disclosed.

Christ is its grand object, our good its design, and the glory of God its end. It should fill the memory, rule the heart, and guide the feet. Read it slowly, frequently, and prayerfully. It is a mine of wealth, a paradise of glory, and a river of pleasure.

It is given you in life, will be opened in the judgment, and be remembered forever. It involves the highest responsibility, will reward the greatest labor, and will condemn all who trifle with its sacred content.

OCTOBER 16 ⸻⸻⸻⸻⸻⸻⸻

I sought the Lord, and he heard me, and delivered me from all my fears (Ps. 34:4).

I once heard the famous Scottish preacher, John McNeil, relate this personal incident. During his boyhood in Scotland, he worked a long distance from home. The walk home took him through a dense forest and across a wide ravine. The ravine was known to house such nefarious tenants as wild animals and robber gangs. Darkness would often gather before he got to the woods, and he said, "How I dreaded to make the last part of the trip! I never went through those woods without trembling with fear.

"One night it was especially dark, but I was aware that something or someone was moving stealthily toward me. I was sure it was a robber. A voice called out, and its eerie tone struck my heart cold with fear. I thought I was finished. Then came a second call, and this time I could hear the voice saying, 'John, is that you?' It was my father's voice. He had known my fear of the ravine and the darkness of the forest, and he had come out to meet me. My father took hold of my hand and put his arm around me; I never had a sweeter walk in my life. His coming changed the whole trip."

That is God's relationship to you and me! He is your Father and my Father. Through the darkness and mist we hear His voice— He has come to meet us. Just at the time we need Him, He will be there. Through the darkest moment of life our Heavenly Father says, "Fear not! Here is My hand! I will walk the rest of the way with you."   *Mrs. Charles E. Cowman*

> Nor will I rebel if the Master
> Sees fit in His plan divine,
> To lead me through darkest of valleys,
> Without e'en a ray of light,
> Where loneliness wrappeth around me
> The awesomeness of the night.
> I will not, I dare not to falter—
> And He who is wise and true
> Has promised Himself to be with me
> Until I am safely through.   *J. Danson Smith*

OCTOBER 17

He leadeth me (Ps. 23:3).

A s the traveler journeys through a strange country he finds it is covered with a network of byways. Some skirt the banks of swift-flowing streams; others plunge into the great forest and are soon lost in its depths. Some make their way up the steep mountainside until they reach its lofty summit; others pierce great landed estates, and meander through lawn, field, and woodland copse. All these are byways, and most of them private ways. In them you and I would be trespassers for they are not meant for us. But in addition to these byways the same country will be overrun with broad highways. Stretching from town to town and city to city run these great highways of shining sand, or rich red clay, or gray macadam. And they are the ways of the people. They are free to all who will walk therein. Rich and poor, bond and free, high and low, alike may enter upon and use these great arteries of commerce and travel.

Even so is it in the Christian life. Men say, "God has never revealed to me any individual plan for my life. I have never found His byway of guidance for me." And that may be true. Perchance you have never seen God's byway for your life. But here is a greater truth. For running all the way through this Book of God, and blazoned upon every page of it is a great highway. It is the highway of consecration. It is for all believers. No man who walks in this highway need ever fear missing God's byway. And the reason most men are missing the particular call of God to their own personal life-work is because they have never obeyed the general call of God to all believers to enter upon this highway of dedication to Him. "If any man will to do My will he shall know the teaching," is an absolute promise of guidance to the child of God who yields his own will to do the will of God.

James H. McConkey

OCTOBER 18 _____

I must work the works of him that sent me, while it is day; the night cometh when no man can work (John 9:4).

We must solemnly devote each day and all its actions to the glory of God.

They say the world has an eagle eye for anything inconsistent, an eye sharp to discover the vagaries and inconsistencies in the defaulty and the unworthy. It has an eagle eye; but the eagle winks before the sun, and the burning iris of its eye shrinks abashed before the unsullied purity of noon. Let your light so shine before men, that others, awed and charmed by the consistency of your

godly life day by day, may come to enquire, and to say you have
been with Jesus.   *Punshon, from* Thoughts for the Quiet Hour

> Each day is like an angel, which with wings,
> Comes from, and goes to Heaven: but empty never
> Comes or returns, but some occasion brings;
> Then hastens back to Heaven, its tale to bear
> Of evil, or fresh good to harbour there.
>   *Isaac Williams, from* Thoughts for Glad Days

I expect to pass through this world but once—therefore, if there
be any kindness I can show or any good thing I can do to any
fellow human being, let me do it today; let me not defer or neglect
it, for I shall not pass this way again.   *Marcus Aurelius*

Every day is a little life; and our whole life is but a day repeated:
whence it is that old Jacob numbers his life by days; and Moses
desires to be taught this point of holy arithmetic—to number not
his years, but his days. Those, therefore, that dare lose a day, are
dangerously prodigal; those that dare misspend it desperate.
                                    Bishop Hall

"So teach us to number our days, that we may apply our hearts
unto wisdom" (Ps. 90:12).

OCTOBER 19 _____

My times are in thy hand (Ps. 31:15).

> In the second month the peachtree blooms,
> But not until the ninth the chrysanthemums—
> So each must wait till his own time comes.
>   *Japanese proverb*

There is some great hope, some burning desire, to serve your
Lord? There are places to go and precious persons to reach before
it is too late? You must needs be up and doing *now?* Earnestly you
seek the will of God. "Where shall it be, dear Lord? When is the
time? How shall I prepare?" Before you take the first step, dear
worker, you must have constant assurance that He is guiding, that
your Father is at the helm of your ship on the sea of life. Hear from
Him, "Behold I have set before thee an open door." And finally,
"Speak to the children of Israel that they go forward."

295

This unrepealed charge of Jehovah rings down the ages to all children of faith. When all outward circumstances say that it is impossible to go forward, then it is God's time to do it. When it requires a miracle to go forward, that is God's time. Cromwell said to his soldiers just before a great battle: "Know ye soldiers all, that God always comes to man's help in the nick of time."

O, for grace to wait and watch for God! His "set time" will come. "Ye have need of patience." Answers to prayer are delayed at times for the strengthening of our confidence in God. Abraham waited twenty-five years for the answer to the promise that a son would be given him. Daniel waited twenty days for the answer to a petition for the interpretation of a vision. The sisters of Lazarus waited some days for Jesus to answer their request concerning their brother and He answered it in such a different manner from that they had expected.

God's set time will come. It will come quietly and gently as a sunbeam stealing through an open window on a summer's morn and a precious experience is ours that will be ours forever.

Mrs. Charles E. Cowman

OCTOBER 20

Every good gift and every perfect gift is from above . . . (James 1:17).

Every good gift of God is a "perfecting" gift as well as a gift which is sound and one which is flawless.

The heart may cry out in the darkness, "God's gifts have been anything but good and perfect to me! He has instead robbed me of health and hopes and loved ones. Faith is a mockery, and providence a fool's dream." Dear sufferer, look again at the text. "Every good gift and every perfect gift is from above, and cometh down from the Father of Lights, with whom is no variableness, neither shadow of turning." Are these not wonderful words! The writer of James might have been a student of astronomy today. The word "variableness" is parallax, and that means a difference due to a change in the point of view. "But that is what I mean," you exclaim; "God has changed toward me. See how He treated me once; see my happy young days, my glorious buds and blossoms, and now see my luxuriance cut away, my exuberance gone; my branches bleeding from His knife."

Dear heart, every gift of God is a perfecting gift. The plow and the harrow and the pruning knife are as much His gifts as the sun and the rain. Grapes are better than mere luxuriant leaves and a tangle of twiners. For that is all they would be without the pruning step. Character is worth all it costs, and since God is ceaselessly, changelessly bent upon building character, the denial or trial that helps to bring it to pass is as much a tool of His invariable purpose as the gift that makes you laugh with joy.

The shadow on your life came not from His turning, but from yours. God has never changed His mind of love toward you, and never a shadow falls because He turned His face away. Every good gift and every perfect gift is from above. Someday the gold will be thankful for the crucible, the steel for the furnace of pain, the purple clusters for the knife that cuts.

Maltbie Davenport Babcock,
from Thoughts for Every-Day Living

OCTOBER 21

. . . and yet show I unto you a more excellent way (1 Cor. 12:31).

> I carefully laid every plan:
>   The future seemed so bright.
> My hopes and dreams they towered high—
>   I saw no trace of night.
>
> And then at closing of the day
>   I knelt in usual prayer,
> And prayed; "Dear Lord, bless every plan—
>   All that I hope and dare."
>
> But day by day my plans all failed,
>   My hopes came tumbling down.
> All my ambitions disappeared,
>   And FAILURE was my crown.
>
> Perplexed—I could not understand,
>   Had I not knelt in prayer?
> And asked that every plan and hope
>   Would find a blessing rare?
>
> Then in the stillness of the night,
>   Out from the shadows dim,

I heard a sweet persuading voice
  That called me close to Him.

"Why don't you let Me make your plans?
  I've trod the path before.
Just leave the future in My hands,
  I'll lead thee o'er and o'er."

In shame, I bowed my humble head;
  My spirit low was brought,
For I had caught a strange new light,
  By His own Spirit taught.

No longer do I pray as once,
  "Dear Lord, bless all my plans."
But now I pray: "Lord, plan for me,
  The future's in Thy hands."

Selected

OCTOBER 22

We hanged our harps upon the willows. . . . How shall we sing the Lord's song in a strange land? (Ps. 137:2, 4).

A thousand full-stringed harp is man,
And each cord gives a jarring sound,
Till God, the mighty harmonist,
The proper note for each has found.

By no small work can all be tuned.
How skilled and patient He must be
To bring the thousand jangling notes
In sweetest heavenly harmony.

Count not our Father's chastening sore.
But yield thine all to His kind hand;
The strains and tests and pulls and turns
In heaven's song we'll understand.

No human power can master all
The compass vast of harp so fine;
The pierced hand of Christ and God
Alone can make its praise divine.

C. H. P.

I lived in an old house in the country once, where the wind would sometimes whistle around so that I thought I would have some music if it must blow like that. So I made a rude aeolian harp of mere sewing-silk strung across a board, and placed it under the slightly lifted sash of a north window, and the music was so sweet through all the house when the wild storms came!

Is there any north window in your life? Could you not so arrange the three wires of faith, hope, and love that the storms of life should only bring more music into this sad world? Many are doing it, and perhaps more music than we dream of comes this way. God has many an aeolian harp.   *From* Crumbs

If you have hung your harp upon the willow, take it down and let the Lord blow blessings across its strings—even though you be in a strange land.

OCTOBER 23

. . . for the prince of this world cometh, and hath nothing in me (John 14:30).

Suppose I own 10,000 acres of land. You come into the market as a purchaser and I sell you 9,999 of those acres, but retain for my own pleasure a plot of one acre in the very center of that holding. I have the right to cross your broad acres to get to my property, and you can't keep me out. The law is on my side. If, when you gave yourself to God you retained anything for your own delectation at the center of your dedicated life, the devil has the right to cross acres of your best resolutions and purposes to get to his property, and you can't keep him out. The law of possession is on his side. Jesus said: "The prince of this world cometh, and hath nothing in me." He had no property in Jesus Christ.

Every child of God ought to be able to look the devil squarely in the face and say: "You have nothing in me—no territory over which I acknowledge your dominion—none over my tongue, none over my temper, none over my will. You do not control me by greed; you do not control me by selfishness; you do not control me by worldliness. I am the Lord's property. Begone, thou seducer and tempter!" Dispute him right on the border of your life over which he knows he has no control, if that life of yours is wholly God's.

Be sure that if you are after ambition, after position, after power, after influence among men, after human applause, the devil has territory in you; but after you study to show yourself approved unto God, and don't care whether you are in a low, or up in a high, position, the devil loses hold on you.

Be wholly God's—that's all; *wholly God's.* On that holiness depends; on that service depends. *Arthur T. Pierson*

> To grow a little wiser day by day,
> To keep my inner life both clean and strong,
> To free my life from guile, my heart from wrong,
> To shut the door on hate and scorn and pride,
> To open up to love the window wide,
> To meet with cheerful heart what comes to me,
> To turn life's discords into harmony.
> To share some weary worker's heavy load,
> To point some straying comrade to the road,
> To know that what I have is not my own,
> To feel that I am never quite alone—
> This would I pray from day to day,
> For then I know my life would flow
> In peace until it be God's will I go. *Unknown*

OCTOBER 24

For it is God which worketh in you both to will and to do of his good pleasure (Phil. 2:13).

It is said that once Mendelssohn came to see the great Freiburg organ. The old custodian refused him permission to play upon the instrument, not knowing who he was. At length however, he reluctantly granted him leave to play a few notes. Mendelssohn took his seat, and soon the most wonderful music was breaking forth from the organ. The custodian was spellbound. He came up beside the great musician and asked his name. Learning it, he stood humiliated, self-condemned, saying, "And I refused you permission to play upon my organ!" There comes One to us, who desires to take our lives and play upon them. But we withhold ourselves from Him, and refuse Him permission, when, if we would yield ourselves to Him, He would bring from our souls heavenly music. *From* Sanctification—What It Really Is

It is a very significant thing that in the Epistles, in which we have the maturest Christian experience, we are not told to wait for the

Spirit, but to "Walk in the Spirit," and we are not told to receive the Spirit, but to be "filled with the Spirit." We are expressly warned against resisting the Holy Ghost whom we have received, against grieving the Holy Ghost who dwells in us, and against quenching the fire which the Holy Ghost has kindled in our hearts.

I believe it is just here that the root cause of so much of the disappointment and defeat in the Christian life is to be found. We are somewhere, somehow, limiting the Holy One, so that He cannot possess us as He longs to do.   *F. C. Gibson*

OCTOBER 25

We believe and know that Jesus is the Christ (John 6:68).

Dr. W. B. Hinson speaks from one of his memorable sermons regarding the fact of Jesus in history. "I seem to stand on the top of a hill up which I have been climbing all my life; and I seem to be about to tell you that which I have been all my life learning. He is a fact and not a fiction on the pages of history. Tacitus, a Roman historian in the first century, spoke of Jesus in this fashion: 'There appeared one Jesus.' He incidentally alluded to the Christ. But nineteen centuries have emphasized the adjective there, and they have spoken of *one* Jesus. In the second century, Lucius, a Greek satirist, gave his brief mention of Jesus when he satirically said—'Jesus the Great.' But those same nineteen centuries have underscored again and again the adjective in that phrase, and they call Jesus the Great. And in century one, four men—Matthew, Mark, Luke and John—wrote the story of Jesus, an altogether wonderful story. They tell of His birth, babyhood, boyhood, young manhood. They tell how He talked, indeed how He looked. They tell how he acted, walked, and gestured, sat down, stood up. They tell all about Him. It is the most intimate story of a life. They tell how He died, how He was buried and where, how He rose again, how He ascended to heaven. And the wonderful record of that life that occupies only one-fourth of my New Testament has done more in the world than all the other books that were ever written.

"The historian Lecky, certainly an unprejudiced man, has told how there has more good come from this story than from all the words ever spoken by all the others who have talked. Those Gospels are history.

"John Stuart Mill, of England, said, 'It is no use denying the historical Christ.' Not it is little use; but it is no use denying it. And the greatest of all French skeptics said, 'It would take a Jesus to forge a Jesus.' The Apostle Paul has written some history about Jesus. We call them his Epistles. And he stands at the head of an army so large I cannot stop even to mention the names of its officers, who eulogize the Christ. For if you go to Shakespeare, who they say is the greatest uninspired man who ever lived, Shakespeare talks about 'the acres over which walked the blessed feet of Him who for our advantage was nailed to the bitter cross.' And if you listen to Gladstone he tells you how in the New Testament the soft note swells to a mighty paen affirming that Jesus is God's Son and the world's Savior. And if you listen to the great German you will find him saying, 'Christ is the holiest among the mighty, and the mightiest among the holy.'

"But most of all I think I love to remember Charles Lamb, the gentle and much afflicted soul. He said, 'Yes, if Shakespeare came in, we should all stand up, but if Jesus Christ came in we should all kneel.'

"Ah, yes, He is a fact. It does not matter what some little professor in some little school says to the contrary. He is a fact and not a fiction, on the pages of history!"

Adapted from The Christ We Forget, *by W. B. Hinson*

OCTOBER 26 _____

If any man thirst, let him come unto me, and drink (John 7:37).

A most unusual story is found in the first chapter of Judges. Achsah had received a gift of land from her father. As she surveyed her new holdings, she discovered, much to her consternation, that there were no water wells—the land was a barren waste.

Achsah sent word to her father Caleb that she would like to see him. She was called into his presence and was greeted with the question, "What wilt thou, my daughter?" Her reply was definite. "Thou hast given me a south land; give me also springs of water."

Her request was granted immediately. Caleb gave her the "upper and the nether springs."

This generous gift exceeded her fondest expectations; the land would now become fruitful and fertile. It was then evident that she learned early one of life's greatest lessons—if a blessing is to be enjoyed, it must be shared. Others should have the opportunity of quenching their thirst from these flowing springs. She sent out this invitation to her neighbors, "Come ye to the waters, come, and drink abundantly. . . ."

Achsah might have been content with a dry, barren land, but how much better that she had the faith to say, "Give me a blessing."

No simpler, stronger symbol of the Spirit could be found than this, a spring—a wellspring—never dry—never turbid; from its clear depths, fed through the secret veins of earth, it gushes ever into life. It goes not downward, but it springs up and it flows out.

"All my fresh springs are in thee," said David. The soul that has found all its springs in God never knows its supply to fail or vary; we need both *upper and nether springs*. The Spirit of God in the highest regions of life and down to its lowest level—the need is still the same. *Mrs. Charles E. Cowman*

OCTOBER 27 —————————————————————

Not that I speak in respect of want: for I have learned, in whatsoever state I am, therewith to be content (Phil. 4:11).

I once read a parable which so beautifully relates what the writer of Philippians has so capably put into the inspired Word. "Once upon a time in the wilderness there was a thorn bush. It looked at its surroundings and sighed. Could anything be more unfortunate? Above was a heaven of brass whence the sun shot out its fiery darts; about it danced the quivering air like the heat of a furnace. And below was the wilderness; here the barren rock cropped up from the ground; here the sand of the desert lay without a grass blade; there some stunted shrub struggled for existence; and yonder there was a patch of scanty herbage. 'Ah, if I were only in the king's garden,' it sighed, 'such as I have heard the travelers tell of, cared for and tended, there might be some hope for me. Or if, indeed, I were worth anything—hung with luscious fruit like the fig tree, or the vines which grow about the cottages of the people, and make glad the sons of men. Or if I were like the stately cedar of Lebanon, or the oak or ash. Or if I could distill some balm for the healing of the nations; or could crown the year with gladness like the gold corn. But a thorn bush; where there is never so much as a bird to build its nest in my branches!'

So the thorn bush whispered to the night winds, and told its sorrow to the stars when the nights were very still.

But lo! it chanced one day that Moses led his sheep to the back of the desert, and the thorn bush burned with fire, yet was unconsumed. And God dwelt in the bush. And forth from it there went the great commission for the deliverance of Israel; and all the ages have been lit up and blest by the vision and by the message that came from the bush on fire."

Mark Guy Pearse, from Thoughts for the Thoughtful

OCTOBER 28 ―――――――――――――――――――――――

. . . having loved his own which were in the world . . . (John 13:1).

We should be gentle above all to those we love the best," J. R. Miller stated in his enlightening little book entitled *A Gentle Heart.* "There is an inner circle of affection to which each heart has a right without robbing others. While we are to be gentle unto all men—never ungentle to any—there are those to whom we owe special tenderness. Much is said of the importance of religion in the home. A home without religion is dreary and unblest indeed. But we must make sure that our home religion is true and real, that it is of the spirit and life, and not merely in form. It must be love—love wrought out in thought, in word, in disposition, in act. It must show itself not only in patience, forbearance, and self-control, and in sweetness under provocation, but also in all gentle thoughtfulness, and in little tender ways in all the family intercourse."

No amount of religious teaching will ever make up for the lack of affectionateness in parents toward children. A gentleman once said, "My mother was a good woman. She insisted on her boys going to church and Sunday school, and taught us to pray. But I do not remember that she ever kissed me."

It matters not how much Bible reading and prayer and catechism saying and godly teaching there may be in a home, if gentleness is lacking, that is lacking which most of all the young need in the life of their home. A child must have love. Love is to its life what sunshine is to plants and flowers. No young life can ever grow to its best in a home without gentleness. The lack is one which leaves an irreparable hurt in the lives of the children.

OCTOBER 29

Now the God of hope fill you with all joy and peace in believing, that ye may abound in hope, through the power of the Holy Ghost (Rom. 15:13).

Be filled with the Spirit (Eph. 5:18).

> Fill'd with this sweet peace forever,
> On we go through strife and care,
> 'Til we find that peace around us
> In the Lamb's high glory there.   *Selected*

The glory of the tabernacle was not its rich tapestries, but the mysterious Presence, the Divine Shekinah, that abode above the mercy seat. Just so that which makes a Christian's body of more value and importance than the earth or moon or sun or stars is the truth that the Spirit of the living God has set up His throne therein. It invests our bodies with a wonderful dignity and sanctity to remember this awful truth, that they are nothing less than the very house of God.

> Lord, I ask it, hardly knowing
>   What this wondrous gift may be,
> But fulfil to overflowing,
>   Thy great meaning let me see.   *Unknown*

There is more room in Christ, in God, in heaven, to give me rest and peace and joy, than in the whole universe to disquiet, trouble and grieve me. But the Holy Spirit alone can fill me with it.
                                                            G. V. W.

> I take the promised Holy Ghost,
> I take the power of Pentecost,

To fill me to the uttermost.
I take; He undertakes. *A. B. Simpson*

OCTOBER 30 —————————————————————

If we walk in the light, as he is in the light, we have fellowship one with another (1 John 1:7).

It was Henry Ward Beecher's last Sunday in the pulpit of Plymouth Church, Brooklyn. Within a week he was stricken with his final illness. When the evening service was over, the illustrious preacher lingered in the aisle and gazed around at the building which he loved so well. Turning to leave, he saw two little newsboys who had wandered in for the services. Dr. Beecher had a fondness for newsboys. He put an arm around each of the lads and talked with them, as they walked down the aisle and out of the church.

Forty-one years afterwards, at a celebration in honor of the ministry of Henry Ward Beecher, one of the speakers, a distinguished minister, told the story of that evening in Plymouth Church, adding, "I was one of those newsboys." Throughout his life, the memory of the arm of Henry Ward Beecher about his shoulders had given him inspiration and strength. A great man had bestowed his friendship.

God offers His friendship to us. Just as those newsboys found a friend, so we, as we walk in the light, may find a fellowship divine.

Selected

> I wish that His hands had been placed on my head,
> That His arms had been thrown around me,
> And that I might have seen His kind look when He said,
> Come, sit, and have fellowship with Me. *Anonymous*

Fellowship with God means walking where He is—in the light.

> In this little while doth it matter,
>   As we work, and we watch, and we wait,
> If we're walking the path He assigns us,
>   Be it service small or great? *Dr. James Vaughn*

"That ye also may have fellowship with us: and truly our fellowship is with the Father, and with his Son Jesus Christ" (1 John 1:3).

306

But now are they many members, yet but one body (1 Cor. 12:20).

God's glory is expressed through the harmony of variety. We do not need sameness in order to gain union. I am now looking upon a scene of surpassing loveliness. There are mountains, and sea, and grassland, and trees, and wide-stretching sky, and white pebbles at my feet. And a white bird has just flown across a little bank of dark cloud." Mark Guy Pearse tells of an experience of variance one bright sunny afternoon while coming down a mountainside in Switzerland many years ago. "A black thunderstorm blotted out the day, and all things were suddenly plunged into darkness. We could only dimly see the narrow, dusty footpaths, and the gloomy sides that were swallowed up in deeper gloom. What, then, of the majesty all about us, heights, and depths, and wonders? All was darkness. Then came the lightning—not flashes, but the blazing of the whole sky, incessant, and on every side. What recesses of glory we gazed into! What marvels of splendor shone out of the darkness!"

Mr. Pearse draws a simile for us by continuing, "Think how with us, in us, is One who comes to make the common, dusty ways of life resplendent, illuminating our dull thoughts by the light of the glory of God; clearing the vision of the soul, and then revealing the greatness of the salvation that is ours in Christ."

From Thoughts for the Quiet Hour

What variety! And when I look closer the variety is infinitely multiplied. Everything blends into everything else. Nothing is out of place. Everything contributes to finished power and loveliness. And so it is in the grander sphere of human life. The glory of humanity is born of the glory of individuals, each one making his own distinctive contribution.

And thus we have need for one another. Every note in the organ is needed for the full expression of noble harmony. Every instrument in the orchestra is required unless the music is to be lame and broken. God has endowed no two souls alike, and every soul is needed to make the music of "the realm of the blest."

J. H. Jowett, from My Daily Meditation

What shall I render unto the Lord for all his benefits toward me? (Ps. 116:12).

> Aye, goodman, close the great barn door;
> The mellow harvest time is o'er,
> The earth has given her treasure meet
> Of golden corn and bearded wheat.
> Ring out the words, "Who of his hoard
> Doth help God's poor, doth lend the Lord!"
> Go, get your cargoes under way—
> The bells ring out Thanksgiving Day!
>
> *From* Harper's Weekly

Like a rare jewel in a tarnished setting, Thanksgiving month gleams out brightly from its dull environment of somber skies and frost-swept earth—the gladdest and the saddest month of twelve. Another year, with its blessings and its burdens, has slipped backward from our grasp, and, with hands and hearts full of varied experiences, we gather once more for the annual festival. In some faces only peace and contentment and quiet joy are visible. God has been good to you, and your happy hearts overflow with gratitude as you grasp the cup which is pressed down and running over. Across other faces is thrown the shadow of a great grief, and you murmur rebelliously through blinding tears, "How can I be thankful?" Dear one, in the midst of your bitter sorrow, do not forget that it is those whom He loves that the Lord chastens.

To many this time is one of sacred "anniversaries of the heart," of which no word can be spoken except to the One to whom all secrets are open. There are others whose living trouble is well-nigh greater than they can bear—to whom the sweep of the death angel's wings would be rapture. And for those on beds of weariness and pain; those widowed and fatherless, keeping poverty at bay; those fiercely assailed by temptation; those whose lives are hard and bare and unlovely—what can this day of praise bring? Shall not we whom goodness and mercy have followed, we who have much, share generously with the less fortunate, the less blessed, and make our lives one long Thanks-giving, Thanks-doing, and Thanks-living Day? *From* Thoughts for the Thoughtful

. . . and we all do fade as a leaf . . . (Isa. 64:6).

> The air is full of hints of grief,
> Strange voices touched with pain,
> The pathos of the falling leaf,
> The rustling of the rain.   *Anonymous*

The burden of every sound we hear, the moral of every sight we see, is the old, old truth, which finds a ready response in every human bosom. Numerous have been the times we have heard these words quoted from the pulpit, but from one with a doleful tone in his voice, leaving us with a feeling of sadness when the leaves begin to fall and the summer roses fade. "We all do fade as a leaf."

That is the great commonplace of the world. It is so trite and true that it has lost in a great measure the power of truth; and therefore God is annually illuminating it to us by the many colored lights of autumn, and investing it, by the aid of nature's touching pictures, with new power and impressiveness. Every year, at the fall of the leaf, He is spreading before us a great parable, in which our decay and death are represented.

Hugh Macmillian, from Thoughts for the Thoughtful

But how does the leaf in autumn fade? It is true that certain trees renew in their autumn foliage the same color that marked them in their budding time of spring, but with fuller, brighter hues. Nature does not die drably! She puts on her most gorgeous robes in autumn and dies gloriously. She goes down with her gay banners waving, smiles back to us as she leaves us. God speaks to His own comforting messages at all seasons and at all times.

Why should we have a dread of the transition? God has made the "valley of the shadow" as beautiful as the daybreak. In Charles Kingsley's last hour he was heard to whisper, "How beautiful is God."

> If peace be in the heart
> The wildest winter storm is filled with beauty
> The very trees and stones, all catch a ray of glory
> If peace be in the heart.

He gave us the secret of victory. It is the peace of God, passing all understanding that makes all the way long a good journey. "My peace I give to you."   *Mrs. Charles E. Cowman*

NOVEMBER 3 _____

. . . we should serve in newness of spirit . . . (Rom. 7:6).

How sadly beats the heavy autumn rain;
  How mournful drives the wind among the trees;
  Along the shore the weary sailor sees
The waves roll in that send him out again;
  The birds are restless in the scattered leaves,
The clouds move wildly on in massy fold,
  And all the outer world, or earth, or air,
  But yesterday, so warm, so fair,
Is changed, and in a night, to drear and cold.

Now goes the golden autumn far away;
  Now nearer comes the winter to my door;
  And thus doth Nature, working evermore,
Create new life from changes and decay.
  O Christ! Who in the hall of Pilate bore
For me the scourage and mocking, for Thy sake
  Fill up the daily loss in life of mine
  With Thy life! So shall love divine
Out of the changing the unchanging make.   *Anonymous*

Go to the man who is carving a stone for a building; ask him where is that stone going, to what part of the temple, and how is he going to get it into place, and what does he do? He points you to the builder's plans. This is only one stone of many. So, when men shall ask where and how is your little achievement going into God's plan, point them to your Master, who keeps the plans, and then go on doing your little service as faithfully as if the whole temple were yours to build.   *Phillips Brooks*

NOVEMBER 4 _____

. . . The heavens declare the glory of God; and the firmament sheweth His handiwork (Ps. 19:1).

Who is the guide of nature, but only the God of nature? The things which nature is said to do, are by divine art performed, using nature as an instrument. Nor is there any such art or knowledge divine in nature herself, but in the Guide of nature's work. *Richard Hooker*

The spacious firmament on high
With all the blue ethereal sky,
The unwearied sun from day to day,
Does his Creator's power display,
And publishes to every land
The work of an Almighty hand. *Joseph Addison*

God of all, whose glory and majesty the heavens declare, whose mercy is as limitless as the starry universe, we would come into Thy presence with sincere hearts and consecrated minds, to know Thee and do Thy will. We would be transformed from the sordid reality of selfishness and sin into the sublime experience of communing with the Infinite. We would give up earthbound thoughts of celestial visions. We would break through the barrier of selfish existence to the stars which Thou hast ordained. As Thou hast placed stars in the heavens by which men are guided, so we would have our lives radiate something of the light of Thy presence with us. Beauty of holiness is no less real than beauty of nature. The unstable estimates of men are molded by those whose hearts are filled with righteousness as the tides of the sea follow the moon. As stars are the splendor of heaven, so souls are the glory of character—man's supreme quest on earth, and formed of God. May our constant prayer be, "to cull Thy peace serene from out the far; to yield it all, and be on earth a star."
Prayer by Daniel Walter Morehouse, astronomer

The God who holds the sea in the hollow of His hand, who swings this ponderous earth in its orbit, who marshals stars and guides planets, is this very God who says, "If ye ask, I will do!"
James H. McConkey

NOVEMBER 5 —————————————————————————

. . . and ye were as a firebrand plucked out of the burning (Amos 4:11).

Before Alexander MacKay, with seven others, set out for Uganda, a farewell meeting was held in the rooms of the missionary society in London. "There is one thing which my brethren have not said, and which I wish to say," said Mackay. "I want to remind the committee that within six months they will probably hear that one of us is dead." He paused; there was a solemn stillness in the room. Then he went on, "Yes; is it at all likely that eight Englishmen should start out for Central Africa, and all be alive six months after? One of us at least—it may be I—will surely fall before that. But what I want to say is this: When the news comes, do not be cast down, but send someone immediately to take the vacant place."

From The Missionary Task

"Oh, let me burn out for my God!" cried Henry Martyn, still thinking of the brand plucked from the flames. He plunges, like a blazing torch, into the darkness of India, of Persia and of Turkey. . . . The brand plucked from the blaze has soon burned out. But what does it matter? At its ardent flame a thousand other torches have been ignited; and the lands that sat so long in darkness have welcomed the coming of a wondrous light!

From A Handful of Stars

I saw a human life ablaze with God,
  I felt a power divine
As through an empty vessel of frail clay
  I saw God's glory shine.

Then woke I from a dream, and cried aloud:
  "My Father, give to me
The blessing of a life consumed by God
  That I may burn for Thee."

Anonymous

"Every Quaker," said George Fox, "ought to light up the country for ten miles around him."

Oh Thou Light of Lights, we would be lightbearers! Help us to light our torches from Thee and to keep them ever aflame. Save us from the presumption of attempting to force our light upon others, but that we might light their way to Thee.

NOVEMBER 6

Produce your cause, saith the Lord; bring forth your strong reasons, saith the King of Jacob (Isa. 41:21).

Over in Canada there lived an Irish saint called "Holy Ann." She lived to be one hundred years old. When she was a young girl, she was working in a family for very small wages under a very cruel master and mistress. They made her carry water for a mile up a steep hill. At one time there had been a well dug there, but it had gone dry; but it stood there year after year. One night she was very tired, and she fell on her knees and cried to God; and while on her knees she read these words: "I will open . . . fountains in the midst of valleys: I will make the wilderness a pool of water, and the dry land springs of water." "Produce your cause, saith the Lord; bring forth your strong reasons." These words struck Holy Ann, and she produced her cause before the Lord. She told Him how badly they needed the water and how hard it was for her to carry the water up the steep hill; then she lay down and fell asleep. She had pleaded her cause and brought forth her strong reasons. The next morning early she was seen to take a bucket and start for the well. Someone asked her where she was going, and she replied, "I am going to draw water from the well." "Why, it is dry," was the answer. But that did not stop Holy Ann. She knew whom she had believed, and on she went; and, lo and behold, there in the well was eighty-three feet of pure, cold water, and she told me that the well never did run dry! That is the way the Lord can fulfill His promises. "Produce your cause, bring forth your strong reasons," and see Him work in your behalf.   *Selected*

How little we use this method of holy argument in prayer; and yet there are examples of it in Scripture: Abraham, Jacob, Moses, Elijah, Daniel. All used arguments in prayer, and claimed the divine interposition on the ground of the pleas which they presented.   *Anonymous*

NOVEMBER 7 _____

Base things of the world and things which are despised hath God chosen (1 Cor. 1:28).

The nearer we get to God, the more conscious are we of our own unworthiness; just as the higher a bird flies in mid-heaven, the deeper will the reflection of its snowy pinions in the placid mere beneath. Let the glowworm vie with the meridian sun;

313

let the dewdrop boast itself against the fullness of the ocean bed; let the babe vaunt its knowledge with the intelligence of a seraph—before the man who lives in touch with God shall think of taking any other position than that of the lowliest humiliation and prostration in His presence. Before Him angels veil their faces, and the heavens are not clean in His sight. And is it not remarkable that our sense of weakness is one of our strongest claims and arguments with God. "He forgetteth not the cry of the humble."

F. B. Meyer

"Let us not be desirous of vain glory" (Gal. 6:26).

The highest bidder for the crown of glory is the lowliest wearer of the cross of self-denial.

A. J. Gordon

The man who prayed, "God, be merciful to me, a sinner," went down to his house justified rather than the other. It is written, "He that humbleth himself shall be exalted."

In some of the great halls of Europe may be seen pictures not painted with the brush, but mosaics, which are made up of small pieces of stone, glass, or other material. The artist takes these little pieces, and, polishing and arranging them, he forms them into grand and beautiful pictures. Each individual part of a picture may be a little worthless piece of glass or marble or shell; but, with each in its place, the whole constitutes the masterpiece of art.

So I think it will be with man in the hands of the great Artist. God is picking up the little worthless pieces of stone and brass that might be trodden under foot unnoticed, and is making them His great masterpiece.

Bishop Simpson, from Thoughts for the Quiet Hour

Count no duty too little, no round of life too small, no work too low, if it come in thy way, since God thinks so much of it as to send His angels to guard thee in it.

Mark Guy Pearse, from Thoughts for the Quiet Hour

NOVEMBER 8 _____

For he is thy Lord; and worship thou him (Ps. 45:11).

The worship of God is the soul bowing down before God in absorbed contemplation of Himself. Over and over do we read the words, "They bowed their heads and worshiped"; or "They fell down and worshiped." It has been well said that "In prayer we are occupied with our needs; in thanksgiving we are occupied with our blessings; in worship we are occupied with Himself." God would not have us less occupied with our needs or present them less to Him. Neither would He have us less occupied with our blessings or return thanks less to Him for them; but He would have us, I am sure, more occupied with Himself in intelligent worship.   *R. A. Torrey*

As a bearing on our prayer life, the testimony of the man whom Jesus gave his sight to the importance of worship, is very significant. "If any man be a worshipper of God, him He heareth" (John 9:31). Worship is the atmosphere in which prayer thrives best, and grows most heavenly and divine.

Prayer is the gate to heaven through the atmosphere of worship.
                                                                Selected

The fragrance of prayer is made of the perfume of worship. Golden vials full of the odor are the prayers of worshiping saints.
                                                                Anonymous

The best and sweetest flowers of paradise God gives to His saints when they are upon their knees.   *Thomas Brooks*

Yes! there's a Friend, so strong, and true, and tender,
    One Friend alone, on Whom you can depend;
His love for aye, is fathomless and boundless,
    It knows no measure, and it knows no end.

Would you then know this Friend? His name is Jesus,
    "The Altogether Lovely One, and True,"
This is my Friend, "The Chief among ten thousand,"
    If you but knew Him, you would worship Him too.   *F. B.*

NOVEMBER 9

For who hath despised the day of small things? (Zech. 4:10).

Little masteries achieved,
Little wants with care relieved,

> Little words in love expressed
> Little wrongs at once confessed,
> Little graces meekly worn,
> Little slights with patience borne,
> These are treasures that shall rise
> Far beyond the shining skies.
>
> *Unknown*

It is the little words you speak, the little thoughts you think, the little things you do or leave undone, the little moments you waste or use wisely, the little temptations which you yield to or overcome—the little things of every day that are making or marring your future life.

Selected, from Thoughts for the Quiet Hour

> Be not dismayed whate'er betide,
>   God will take care of you;
> Beneath His wings of love abide,
>   God will take care of you.
>
> No matter what may be the test,
>   God will take care of you;
> Lean, weary one, upon His breast,
>   God will take care of you.
>
> *Civilla D. Martin*

All through the Bible there is a wonderful care of little things, God noticing them and bringing them to perfectness of meaning. "He putteth my tears in his bottle"; that is condescension. "None of his steps shall slide," as if He numbered step by step all the going of His people. One of those people said, "Thou knowest my downsitting and mine uprising," and "Thou hast beset me behind and before."

Joseph Parker

If the firefly's lamp and the cricket's chirp and the sparrow's fall are of interest to Thee, help us to learn from these, Thy creatures, their lesson of trust and service.

Unknown

NOVEMBER 10 _____

Come up in the morning . . . and present thyself unto me in the top of the mount (Exod. 34:2).

> Alone with Thee, amid the mystic shadows,
>   The solemn hush of nature newly born;

Alone with Thee in breathless adoration,
  In the calm dew and freshness of the morn.   *Unknown*

"The morning is the time fixed for my meeting the Lord," said
Joseph Parker. "This very word morning is as a cluster of rich
grapes. Let me crush them, and drink the sacred wine. In the night
I have buried yesterday's fatigue, and in the morning I take a new
lease of energy. Blessed is the day whose morning is sanctified!
Successful is the day whose first victory is won in prayer! Holy is
the day whose dawn finds thee on the top of the mount! The light
is brightest in the morning. "Wake psaltery and harp; I myself will
awake early."   *From* Thoughts for the Quiet Hour

Having communed with the Heavenly Father in the garden of
prayer when the dew of blessing awaits at sunrise reminds me of a
certain valley in Romania where they grow nothing but roses for
the Vienna market. The perfume of that valley in the time of the
rose crop is such that if you go into it for a few minutes, wherever
you go the rest of the day, people know where you have been.
The fragrance goes with you. Meeting Him in the morning causes
the fragrance of His presence to go with you throughout the entire
day.

John Wesley spent two hours daily in prayer. He began his
prayer at four in the morning and it was said of him, "He thought
prayer to be more his business than anything else and I have seen
him come out of his closet with a serenity of face next to shining."
It is said of John Fletcher that the walls of his room were stained
with the breath of his prayers. His whole life was a life of prayer.
Luther said, "If I fail to spend two hours in prayer each morning,
the devil gets the victory through the day."   *Selected*

NOVEMBER 11

*Canst thou by searching find out God? . . . O that I knew where I might
find him. . . . I have heard of thee by the hearing of the ear: but now mine
eye seeth thee (Job 11:7; 23:3; 42:5).*

Speak to Him, thou, for He hears, and
Spirit with Spirit shall meet—
Closer is He than breathing, and
Nearer than hands and feet.   *Tennyson*

317

According to Tennyson's lines it is a very simple thing to find God. He is near at hand; speak to Him! Would that it were as easy as that. But for most of us the reality and nearness of God is a "discovery."

An illustration of this "discovery" is found in the Book of Job. It is the cry of a baffled man who finds his inherited religion insufficient. He cried, "O that I knew where I might find Him."

Then follows the everlasting quest; and the great "discovery": "I had heard of thee by hearsay but now mine eyes have seen thee." Oh, it is a monumental moment in any life when the eyes of the spirit come open and "hearsay" religions give place to the first-hand experience of the Presence.

After the "discovery" and after the first-hand experience, Spurgeon makes this admonition: "A Christian should be a striking likeness of Jesus Christ. You have read lives of Christ, beautifully and eloquently written, but the best life of Christ is His living biography, written out in the words and actions of His people. If we were what we profess to be, and what we should be, we would be pictures of Christ; yea, such striking likenesses of Him that the world would not have to hold us up by the hour together, and say, "Well, it seems somewhat of a likeness": but they would, when they once beheld us, exclaim, "He has been with Jesus; he has been taught of Him; he is like Him; he has caught the very idea of the holy Man of Nazareth, and he works it out in his life and everyday actions."

"They took knowledge of them that they had been with Jesus" (Acts 4:13).

NOVEMBER 12 —————————————————————————————

I beseech you therefore, brethren, by the mercies of God, that ye present your bodies a living sacrifice, holy, acceptable unto God, which is your reasonable service (Rom. 12:1).

All for Jesus, all for Jesus!
All my being's ransomed pow'rs:
All my thought and words and doings,
All my days and all my hours.   *Mary D. James*

A missionary to the Indians from the north country related the following incident which took place during a consecration service. As he was speaking an old Indian chief arose, walked forward and laid his tomahawk at the feet of the missionary. "Indian chief give his tomahawk to Jesus Christ," he said, and sat down. Still the missionary spoke on of the love of God in Christ Jesus; of the gift of His Son for us and of His claim upon our lives. Rising from his seat the old chief walked forward once more to the front. Unwrapping his blanket from his shoulders he laid it at the preacher's feet, saying: "Indian chief give his blanket to Jesus Christ." Again he sat down. But still the messenger preached on concerning the love of God in Christ. Still he showed how God had rifled heaven of its choicest gift and sent Him to earth to redeem us lost men and give Himself for us. Presently the old chief was seen to disappear from the meeting. By and by he came leading his pony to the tent door. He tied it to a stake and again walked up the aisle. Facing the missionary, he said, "Indian chief give his pony to Jesus Christ." Once more he took his seat. He had given about all he had—all the things he had. Have some of us too given Him things instead of ourselves? And now as the missionary preached of God who spared not His only Son, but freely gave Him up for us, he pressed upon his hearers the claim of Jesus Christ upon the life. Still the message kept sinking into their hearts. And then the old chieftain arose for the last time. He walked forward with tottering steps to the front of the tent. He kneeled down reverently before the missionary. With tears streaming down his bronzed cheeks he said, with trembling lips, "Indian chief give himself to Jesus Christ." Then and there through the open portal of a yielded will he took the first blessed step into consecration. *James H. McConkey*

NOVEMBER 13 ——————————————————

. . . he shall be a vessel unto honor, sanctified, and meet for the master's use and prepared unto every good work (2 Tim. 2:21).

L ife is not a diamond, but a seed, with possibilities of endless growth.

Dr. Lyman Abbott has used this illustration: "I pluck an acorn from the greensward, and hold it to my ear; and this is what it says to me: 'By and by the birds will come and nest in me. By and by I will furnish shade for the cattle. By and by I will provide warmth for the home in the pleasant fire. By and by I will be shelter from the storm to those who have gone under the roof. By and by I will be the strong ribs of a great vessel, and the tempest will beat against me in vain, while I carry men across the Atlantic.' " "O foolish little acorn, wilt thou be all this?" I ask. And the acorn answers, "Yes; God and I."

I look into the faces of a company of children and I hear a whisper, saying: "By and by I will be a great blessing to many. By and by other lives will come and find nest and home in me. By and by the weary will sit in the shadow of my strength. By and by I will sit as comforter in a home of sorrow. By and by I will shine in the full radiancy of the beauty of Christ, and be among the glorified with my Redeemer." "You, frail, powerless little one?" I ask; and the answer is, "Yes; Christ and I." And all these blessed possibilities that are in the life of the young person must go upon the altar in the living sacrifice."

J. R. Miller, from Making the Most of Life

Expose water to fire and it dissolves in vapor; wood, and it vanishes in smoke and flames, leaving but gray ashes behind; iron, and it is converted into rust; but fire may play on gold for a thousand years without depriving it of a degree of its lustre or an atom of its weight.

Beautiful emblem of the servants of God! They, like gold, cannot perish, and their trials, like the action of fire on this precious metal, but purify what they cannot destroy.   *Thomas Guthrie*

NOVEMBER 14 _____

. . . *that ye through His poverty might be rich (2 Cor. 8:9).*

And daily, hourly, loving and giving
In the poorest life make heavenly living.
Rose Terry Cook, from Thoughts for the Thoughtful

"One September," recalls Rev. Hugh Macmillan, "in an afternoon walk on the shore of Loch Awe, I saw an aspen tree that reminded me of the burning bush of the desert. Its foliage was one blaze of the most vivid scarlet. I never saw such a wonderful display of color. The leaves were not dead like the usual sere leaves of autumn; they were, on the contrary, quite fresh and full of life. I drew nearer to see the cause of this strange transformation, why the bush burned and was not consumed, and I found that the tree grew on a little mound, from which the waters of a rill that existed only in rainy weather had washed away the soil, leaving the roots to a large extent exposed. The conditions of life were thus unfavorable; but instead of being made less beautiful, it became more beautiful in consequence. The poverty of its soil had changed the ordinary dull green of its leaves into the most brilliant red, as if each separate leaf were a flame in the heart of a furnace.

A soft breeze of evening whispered through the trembling, fiery tongues of the transfigured aspen, and in my awe-stricken soul I heard the still small voice as of old from the burning bush, telling me that thus it is with human life, from which the stream of circumstances washes away all its worldly good things in which it trusted, leaving its roots bare and exposed. God's breath kindles in it a beauty unknown before, which no mere prosperous worldly condition could have developed; and the poverty and sorrowfulness of its state, which worldly men pity, only make it glow with the light of heaven, and its cross becomes its crown.

From Thoughts for the Thoughtful

The serene beauty of a holy life is the most powerful influence in the world next to the might of God. *Pascal*

NOVEMBER 15 _____

The barrel of meal shall not waste, neither shall the cruse of oil fail (1 Kings 17:14).

What marvelous "coincidences" are prepared by providential grace! The poor widow is unconsciously ordained to entertain the prophet! The ravens will be guided to the brook Cherith! "I have commanded them to feed thee there." Our road is full of surprises. We see the frowning, precipitous hill, and we fear it, but when we arrive at its base we find a refreshing spring! The Lord of the way had gone before the pilgrim. "I go to prepare . . . for you."

But how strange that a widow with only "a handful of meal"

321

should be "commanded to offer hospitality! It is once again "the impossible" which is set before us. It would have been a dull commonplace to have fed the prophet from the overflowing larder of the rich man's palace. But to work from an almost empty cupboard! That is the surprising way of the Lord. He delights to hang great weights on apparently slender wires, to have great events turn on seeming trifles, and to make poverty the minister of "the indescribable riches of Christ."

The poor widow sacrificed her "handful of meal," and received an unfailing supply. And this, too, is the way of the Lord.

J. H. Jowett, from My Daily Meditation

Let me tell you how I made His acquaintance.

I had heard much of Him; but took no heed. He sent daily gifts and presents, but I never thanked Him. He often seemed to want my friendship, but I remained cold. I was homeless, wretched and starving, in peril every hour, and He offered me shelter, comfort, food and safety, but I was ungrateful still.

At last He crossed my path, and with tears in His eyes He besought me, saying, "Come and abide with Me."

Let me tell you how He treats me now.
He supplies all my wants.
He gives me more than I dare ask.
He anticipates my every need.
He begs me to ask for more.
He never reminds me of my past ingratitude.
He never rebukes me for my past follies.
Let me tell you further what I think of Him.
He is as good as He is great.
His love is as ardent as it is true.
He is as lavish of His promises as He is faithful in keeping them.
He is as jealous of my love as He is deserving of it.
I am in all things His debtor, but He bids me call Him, Friend.   *From an Old English manuscript*

NOVEMBER 16 —————————————————————————

Said I not unto thee, that if thou wouldst believe, thou shouldest see the glory of God? (John 11:40).

The world says seeing is believing. Jesus Christ says believing is seeing. The man who sees believes. We come to knowledge through the channel of vision. We know the sky, the stars, the clouds, the sea, because we see them with our eyes. Yet just as real, and quite as simple, is the truth that the man who believes shall see. Faith ever issues into vision. The believer becomes a seer.

Here is a plain strip of canvas. Before it stands the Master Painter. He says, "Do you see that golden sunset? Trust yourself to me and I will paint its glory in your face." And the canvas says, "I am coarse in texture. I am scant in size. I do not see how you can fill me with the glory of that sunset sky." And the Master says, *"Yield, and you shall see."*

Here is a black mass of ore, fresh dug from the grime of the earth. It is soiled, stained, and misshapen. The Master Workman takes it in His hand. "There is naught in me for you," says the ore. And the Goldsmith says, "I will take you and melt you, and mold, and carve, and chase you, until there shall be wrought from your blackness a precious cup of gold fit to grace the feast day of a king. *Yield and you shall see."*

And here is a plain, everyday life—your life. The Master stands before it, and speaks, "Give me your life. It matters not how humble it is, give it to Me. And I will chasten it, and enrich it, and anoint it with My Spirit, and glorify My Father in heaven through it." And you are saying, "I do not see all that consecration means. I do not see any niche of Christian service into which I can fit." And to all this the Master of our lives has still the same answer, *"Yield —and you shall see!"*

James H. McConkey, from Believing Is Seeing

NOVEMBER 17 ─────────────────────────────

For whom he did foreknow, he also did predestinate to be conformed to the image of his Son (Rom. 8:29).

There is more cause for joy than for complaint in the hard and disagreeable circumstances of life. Browning said, "I count life just a stuff to try the soul's strength on." Spell the word "discipline" with a final g, —"discipling." We are here to learn time's lesson for eternity's business. What does it signify if the

circumstances about us are not of our choice, if by them we can be trained, learning the lessons of patience, fortitude, perseverance, self-denying service, acquiescence with God's will, and the hearty doing of it? Circumstances do not make character. The noblest character can emerge from the worst surroundings, and moral failures come out of the best. Just where you are, take the things of life as tools, and use them for God's glory; so you will help the kingdom come, and the Master will use the things of life in cutting and polishing you so that there shall some day be seen in you a soul conformed to His likeness.   *Maltbie Davenport Babcock,*
from Thoughts for Every-Day Living

God wants our best. He in the far-off ages
Once claimed the firstling of the flock, the finest of
    the wheat;
And still He asks His own, with gentlest pleading
To lay their highest hopes and brightest talents at
    His feet.
He'll not forget the feeblest service, humblest love;
He only asks that of our store, we give to Him the best
    that we have.

Christ gives the best. He takes the hearts we offer
And fills them with His glorious beauty, joy and peace,
And in His service as we're growing stronger
The calls to grand achievement still increase.
The richest gifts for us, on earth or in the heaven above,
Are hid in Christ. In Jesus, we receive the best we have.

And is our best too much? O friends, let us remember
How once our Lord poured out His soul for us,
And, in the prime of His mysterious manhood,
Gave up His precious life upon the cross.
The Lord of lords, by whom the worlds were made,
Through bitter grief and tears, gave us the best He had.
                            Selected

NOVEMBER 18 _____

It is a good thing to give thanks unto the Lord (Ps. 92:1).

The remorse of memory is the pain of having failed to enjoy yourself. Have you ever felt that kind of remorse? Have you ever come to a time in which you looked back upon the past, and learned how little you had valued it? To find that days were happy when the days are gone, to learn that one is passing through Elysium and not know it, to see the light on the hill only when it is setting—that is one of the saddest of all experiences. It is the climax of pain when I must say with the poetess,

Oh, while my brother with me played,
Would I had loved him more!

My soul, wouldst thou be free from that pain—that remorse of memory? Thou mayst be so; live in present thanksgiving! Count thy sunbeams now! Treasure today the gems that are strewn upon thy path! The love that is merely retrospective is a very painful thing. I would not have thee wake to the glory of a past only when it is past—desire one of the days of the Son of Man after He has ascended. If thy days of sorrow at any time should cloud thy days of joy, I should like thee to be able to say, "Well, while they lasted, I did appreciate them." There are some who want to feel at death that their life has been a vain show. I would not have it so with thee, O my soul. I should like when death comes, to feel that I had thoroughly enjoyed life—taken the honey from the flower as God meant me to take it. I should like to know that I had not defrauded myself of my birthright, that I made room for others because I had had my share. The cup of gladness which my Father has given me shall I not drink it, even unto the dregs! I shall thank Him for every bird that sings. I shall praise Him for every flower that blows. I shall bless Him for every stream that warbles. I shall love Him for every heart that loves. I shall see the sparkling of the cup ere it passes to the hand of my brother. There shall be no remorse of memory when I have thanked God for today.

George Matheson, from Leaves for Quiet Hours

NOVEMBER 19 _____

And let them sacrifice the sacrifices of thanksgiving . . . (Ps. 107:22).

What is a sacrifice? It is an offering to God. A "sacrifice of thanksgiving" is to praise God when you do not feel like it; when you are depressed and despondent; when your life is covered with thick clouds and midnight darkness. While we are admonished to "pray without ceasing," are we not also commanded to "rejoice evermore"?

Many homes display the motto, "prayer changes things," and great blessing has resulted from this simple statement. We are all aware that prayer does change things. We know, also, that many times the enemy has not been moved one inch from his stronghold, although we have persisted in prayer for days, months—yes, often years.

Such was my own experience when passing through a time of very great pressure, and prayer did not change things. I came into possession of a wonderful secret. That secret is simply this: after we have prayed and believed, "praise changes things."

One morning during the summertime a fellow-missionary, who was then a guest in our home, went out into the garden for a stroll among the flowers. He returned after a short time holding in his hand a lovely white pigeon that he had found beside the garden walk. One of its wings was injured and it could not fly. The missionary became greatly interested in its welfare, building a coop from an old wooden box to shelter it from the weather, and feeding it morning, noon, and night. As the days passed, the pigeon became quite tame. It would watch its mates as they soared away up through the heaven's blue, making no attempt to use its wings and follow them in their flight. Poor little bird with a broken wing! Our hearts were knit to the wee thing in tender sympathy, for were we not also prisoners!

Prayer had gone up from our hearts almost unceasingly: one long, yearning cry for deliverance from the bondage which held us. Not one rift in the cloud could we discern. Although our "prayer wing" was fully developed, we were like the little bird—BOUND. We do praise God, that throughout those dark days we were kept from fainting. Faith ever beheld a star of hope!

Our loving Lord drew our attention at this time to an altogether new line of attacking the enemy. His Word unfolded step by step, and such a revelation of the secret of obtaining victory was given that our prayer life underwent a complete transformation. We discerned that two wings were necessary to mount the soul Godward: prayer, praise. Prayer asks. Praise takes, or obtains the answer.
                                              Mrs. Charles E. Cowman

To know the love of Christ, which passeth knowledge (Eph. 3:19).

A little child was playing by the shore of the broad
blue sea.
And oft he looked away across the waves, so wonderingly.
It was a new entrancing sight to him, that watery waste,
The tossing billows breaking on the sand with foam
wreaths graced.
And often in his distant inland home, with childish glee,
The boy would say to young and older friends, "I have
seen the sea!"
And so he had; the child made no mistake, his words
were true;
But yet, how much of ocean's vast expanse had met
his view?
Only the waves that rippled on the shore; while far away,
The broad Atlantic in its depth and strength beyond him
lay.
And thus we say we know the love of Christ, and so we
do;
'Tis no exaggeration or mistake, but sweetly true.
But ah! how much of that unfathomed love do we yet
know?
Only the ripples on the shores of time, the nearer flow.
The mighty ocean of redeeming love rolls deep and wide,
Filling eternity, and heaven, and earth, with its vast tide.
We know it by a sweet experience now; yet shall explore
Its breadth and length, its depth and height of grace,
for evermore.   *E. R. V.*

Frances Ridley Havergal once said, "We talk about the
telescope of faith, but I think we want even more the microscope
of watchful and grateful love. Apply this to the little bits of our daily
lives, in the light of the Spirit, and how wonderfully they come
out!"

"God is love; and it is good, as it is true," stated Mark Guy
Pearse, "to think that every sun-ray that touches the earth has the
sun at the other end of it; so every bit of love upon God's earth
has God at the other end of it."

For we are his workmanship, created in Christ Jesus unto good works, which God hath before ordained that we should walk in them (Eph. 2:10).

You remember the story of the engineer of the Brooklyn Bridge. During its building he was injured. For many long months he was shut up in his room. His gifted wife shared his toils, and carried his plans to the workmen. At last the great bridge was completed. Then the invalid architect asked to see it. They put him upon a cot, and carried him to the bridge. They placed him where he could see the magnificent structure in all its beauty. There he lay, in his helplessness, intently scanning the work of his genius. He marked the great cables, the massive piers, the mighty anchorages which fettered it to the earth. His critical eye ran over every beam, every girder, every chord, every rod. He noted every detail carried out precisely as he had dreamed it in his dreams, and wrought it out in his plans and specifications. And then as the joy of achievement filled his soul, as he saw and realized that it was finished exactly as he had designed it; in an ecstasy of delight he cried out: "It's just like the plan; *it's just like the plan.*"

Someday we shall stand in the glory and looking up into His face, cry out: "O God, I thank Thee that Thou didst turn me aside from my willful and perverse way, to Thy loving and perfect one. I thank Thee that didst ever lead me to yield my humble life to Thee. I thank Thee that as I day by day, walked the simple pathway of service, Thou didst let me gather up one by one, the golden threads of Thy great purpose of my life. I thank Thee, as, like a tiny trail creeping its way up some great mountainside, that pathway of life has gone on in darkness and light, storm and shadow, weakness and tears, failures and falterings. Thou hast at last brought me to its destined end. And now that I see my finished life, no longer "through a glass darkly" but in the face-to-face splendor of Thine own glory, I thank Thee, O God, I thank Thee that, it's just like the plan; *it's just like the plan.*"

James H. McConkey, from The God-Planned Life

. . . also sat at Jesus' feet and heard His word (Luke 10:39).

Christ never looks greater than when you put some great man by His side.

"I paint," cried Raphael.

"I build," was the boast of Michaelangelo.

"I rule," cried Caesar.

"I sing," cried Homer.

"I conquer," cried Alexander.

"I *seek and save*," cried Jesus Christ.

At Jesus' feet—that is our place of privilege and of blessing, and here it is that we are to be educated and fitted for the practical duties of life. Here we are to renew our strength while we wait on Him, and to learn how to mount on wings as eagles; and here we are to become possessed of that true knowledge which is power. Here we are to learn how real work is to be done, and to be armed with the true motive power to do it. Here we are to find solace amidst both the trials of work—and they are not few—and the trials of life in general; and here we are to anticipate something of the blessedness of heaven amidst the days of earth; for to sit at His feet is indeed to be in heavenly places, and to gaze upon His glory is to do what we shall never tire of doing yonder.

W. Hay Aitken, from Thoughts for the Quiet Hour

All things are possible if men but pray,
And if God did but limit to a day,
The time in which He'd note the upward glance,
Or fix the place, or name the circumstance,
When, where or why petitions could be brought,
Their presence would at His feet be sought.

But since He heareth prayer any time,
For anything, in any place, or clime,
Men lightly value heaven's choicest gift,
And all too seldom do their souls uplift
Pleading at the foot of the Throne of Grace.   *Unknown*

NOVEMBER 23

O give thanks unto the Lord; for he is good; for his mercy endureth forever (1 Chron. 16:34).

Martin Luther once wrote these words, "When I cannot pray, I always sing."

It is said that there is not one despondent note to be found in the New Testament.

In Chronicles there is a thrilling narrative concerning a battle won through praise. Jehoshaphat was told that a great multitude was coming against him from across the sea. He fully realized the difficulty of the situation and went to the Lord with his trouble. His was a humble prayer: "We have no might against this great company . . . neither know we what to do: but our eyes are upon thee." Not upon the greatness of the difficulty, but upon Him. It was a crucial test, but the Lord did not leave Jehoshaphat in doubt as to His will. He made it known through one of the young men who spoke these words of the Lord: "The battle is not yours but God's . . . ye shall not need to fight . . . fear not, nor be dismayed."

Fear is a deadly enemy. Let us remember, when we are tempted to tremble, that "God hath not given us the spirit of fear; but of power, and of love, and of a sound mind" (2 Tim. 1:7).

Then, Jehoshaphat appointed singers who should go forth before the army singing, "Praise the Lord, for his mercy endureth forever." They did this even though there was not one visible sign of the promised salvation of the Lord. Right in the very face of battle—against an army mighty in number, they sang, "Praise the Lord!" The inspired record says: "When they began to sing and to praise, the Lord set ambushments against the children of Ammon, Moab, and Mount Seir . . . and they were smitten." Two of the allied opposing armies began to fight the third, and when they had demolished them, they turned upon each other until the valley was filled with dead bodies and "none escaped." They had more than victory, for we read, "Jehoshaphat and his people . . . were three days in gathering of the spoils, it was so much." They were much richer at the end of the trial than at the beginning. They had added good which they had never dreamed of possessing.

There are two songs in Jehoshaphat's great battle: the song of praise before; the song of deliverance afterwards. We also should have two songs: a song in the valley of Berachab (blessing), praising God for the fulfillment of all that He has promised; but it is more precious to have the song of praise before—praising Him without sight or feeling while we see Him set ambushments against the enemy and complete the victory.   *Mrs. Charles E. Cowman*

The cup which my father hath given me, shall I not drink it? (John 18:11).

J. R. Miller commented that the "cup" is our portion, embracing all the experiences of our earthly lives. Our Father gives us the cup, therefore it must be the very best that the wisest love can provide. When death enters a Christian home there is sweet comfort in the thought that God has really done the best possible for the friend whom He has taken away. We prayed Him to crown our loved one with His richest blessings, and is not that just what He has done?

> Give her, I pray, all good:
>   Bid all the buds of pleasure grow
> To perfect flowers of happiness
>   Where'er her feet may go;
> Bid Truth's bright shield and Love's strong arm
> Protect her from all earthly harm.
>
> Lest there should be some other thing,
>   Better than all the rest,
> That I have failed to ask, I said,
>   "Give Thou the very best
> Of every gift that Thou dost deem
>   Better than aught I hope or dream."
>
> "Better than I can ask or dream!"
>   This was my prayer, and now
> That she is lying still and pale,
>   With God's peace on her brow,
> I wonder, sobbing, sore dismayed,
> If this be that for which I prayed.   *Anonymous*

Bless the Lord, O my soul, and forget not all his benefits (Ps. 103:2).

Harvest is ended. There is a song in the air—a song of joy-filled hearts and thanksgiving. Goodness and mercy have followed throughout every day of the year. We have been loaded, yea, overloaded with His benefits and manifold tokens of His love and mercy. "He careth for us." Our testings and trials have been buried beneath His mercies which outnumber the waves of the sea. We praise God that He saw us through the tempests we thought would pull us under. He is our own God; we are the flock of His pasture and the people of His hand. "Let the people praise thee, O God; let all the people praise thee. Then shall the earth yield her increase; and God, even our own God shall bless us. God shall bless us; and all the ends of the earth shall fear him" (Ps. 67:5–7).

Thanksgiving Day is a sacred day for retrospection—a day also for spiritual inventory—a day for family reunions, fellowship with old friends and neighbors, sharing our bounties with those less favored. If throughout the past year earthborn clouds have blotted out the sunshine in your spiritual sky, may there be a rift in the clouds today so that you can see through to the land of pure delight where saints immortal reign.

This story is told of Sir Michael Costa. He was holding a rehearsal one night with his vast array of musicians and hundreds of voices. The mighty chorus rang out with thunder of organ, sounding of horns and clashing of cymbals. Far back in the orchestra one who played the piccolo said to himself, "In all this din it matters not what I do." Suddenly, all was still! The great conductor had stopped. Someone had failed to take his part! The sweet note of the piccolo had been missed.

Let all the people praise thee, O God; let all the people praise Thee. Then shall the earth yield her increase and God, even our own God shall bless us." Try thanksgiving! Let this Thanksgiving Day mark the beginning of a new life of victory, the "praise life!"

Mrs. Charles E. Cowman

NOVEMBER 26 _____

And the gates of it shall not be shut (Rev. 21:25).

The evening shadows lie stretched across the dusty street; at the far end of their wired enclosure, the chickens wait for their evening meal. They are giving desultory pecks here and there as they wait the appearance of their faithful provider. Presently he opens the gate, and they flock to him in headlong haste from every quarter—as in the manner of chickens.

A commonplace sight? Yes, but is there no luminous thought for us in the widely opened gate which the man has not stayed to close? Not a chick is running outside, not an eye is even turned that way; all are crowded about his feet, all absorbed in the one paramount occupation. The gate is as well open as shut, they have no interest in it. Why? Because all they desire is within!

All the redeemed heart can wish for or imagine will be within. Heaven is the heart of our Father; having tasted His love, who would wish to run, as it were, from the heart of God?—"in the temple of God; and he shall go no more out" (Rev. 3:12). But is not the open gate a menace to the safety of the city? "And there shall in no wise enter into it anything that defileth" (Rev. 21:27). The same light and heat that constitute the life and delight of the gathered children of God is a consuming fire to all without that would enter and hurt them—a flaming and invisible sword "which keeps the way of the tree of life." "I, the Lord, will be a wall of fire round about, and the glory in the midst." He fills heaven with the lightning of His terrible holiness, which is death to all that defiles; but His own children are "at home in the splendor," having been made like Him! The open gate! beautiful symbol of the liberty that is in Christ! "He shall go no more out," having reached the heart of God, we are at home—finding there all the heart desires!
Mary E. Quayle, from A Message From God

Build a little fence of trust around today,
Fill the space with loving deeds and therein stay;
Look not through the sheltering bars upon tomorrow,
God will help thee bear what comes of joy or sorrow.
Butts

NOVEMBER 27 _____

Looking for that blessed hope, and the glorious appearing of the great God and our Saviour Jesus Christ (Titus 2:13).

Until the day break and the shadows flee away (Song of Sol. 2:17).

Have you ever watched the dawn as it slowly and gradually develops until it becomes day? I have, and one midsummer night in Sweden I stayed up looking out of my window until twelve o'clock and by the glow of the western sky read the twenty-first chapter of the Book of Revelation, which contains that wonderful description of the New Jerusalem culminating in the words,

333

"There shall be no night there." Scarcely could it be called "night" there in Sweden—only two hours of semidarkness between sunset and sunrise, but the "no night" of the new heaven and the new earth means so much more than this earthly absence of night. No night of sorrow, for "God shall wipe away all tears from their eyes"; no night of death, for death shall be "swallowed up in victory."

I went to bed then, without having had to use artificial light. I awoke at three, and got up to see the dawn. Oh, how still and hushed it was! It was just as though God had said, "let there be peace!" and there was peace. A great calm lay upon everything.

The waters of the island-studded lake had not a single ripple on their surface; they were as a "sea of glass," whilst nature all around—the opposite wooded shore, and the nearer rocky and richly vegetated isles—seemed silent with a great expectation and anticipation. The sky was clear and blue, without the hint of a cloud. The morning star shone in the south, while in the east there was the faint, faint promise of day!

It was utterly unearthly looking, and more as if one had gotten a sudden and beautiful glimpse into heaven! After that, my morning's text was a revelation to me: "He shall be as the light of the morning when the sun ariseth, even a morning without clouds!" His coming is as certain as the dawn! *Anonymous*

NOVEMBER 28 ⎯⎯⎯⎯⎯⎯⎯⎯⎯⎯⎯⎯⎯⎯⎯⎯

The Lord is good unto them that wait for Him (Lam. 3:35).

The helpless must wait. The patient do wait. But the strong, and the eager—how hard it is for them to wait! To wait for the salvation of a soul when your heart is breaking with suspense; to wait for the consecration of a life while you see the world laying waste its preciousness; to wait for laborers to be thrust forth while the harvest is whitening in death; to wait for God to bring things to pass and see Satan's ravages while you wait; such waiting takes a mighty faith. And yet faith which waits shall surely see. The glory of God comes to the waiting one.

You have been taking a long and wearisome railroad journey. For hours you have been traveling through the dust and heat. You are nearing home, and brook with impatience each delay. At midnight you are awakened by the slowing of your train. It bumps, jars and creaks, and finally comes to a standstill. You wait, and wait. You peer out into the gloom with your face pressed against the car window. Five, ten, twenty minutes pass. Still all is quiet, with no sign of a move. You drum at the windowpane. You turn wearily in your berth. You wonder when the weary wait will end. Presently there is a sound in the distance. The rattle and clatter come nearer. Then there is a rush, a roar, the red glare of a great fiery eye and the monster engine and its trail of coaches sweeps by you in an instant and is swallowed up in the encircling darkness. You have *waited* long. Now you can *see*. You see in vision the awful death which would have come to you had you gone on. You see the wise forethought which kept you waiting on that track. It was a passing siding and the one safe thing to do was to wait. Had you gone on it would have been to the wreckage and death of a collision.

Is your heart there and your body here? Are you eager for service and yet hindered on every side? Is the horizon of life so narrowed by circumstances as to become almost unbearable? Yet God's waiting time is best for you. Wait—and you will see barriers razed. Wait—and you will see circumstances change. Wait—and you will see God bringing things to pass beyond all your dreams. Wait and you shall see. For "He worketh for him that waits for Him."   *James H. McConkey, from the tract* Believing is Seeing

"I wait for the Lord, my soul doth wait, and in His word do I hope" (Ps. 130:5).

NOVEMBER 29 _____

Sit still, my daughter, for the man will not rest, until he have finished the thing this day (Ruth 3:18).

Paradise has vanished from our world, as the picture of a landscape vanishes when swept by storm. And our race stands in much the same plight as did Naomi and Ruth in this old-world story. We have lost our inheritance, and the one barrier which stands between us and despair is the Person and work of our Lord Jesus Christ. But, thank God, we need have no doubt as to the sequel. For as Boaz claimed back the estate for Ruth, so may we be confident that Jesus Christ will never be at rest till this sin-stained and distracted world is restored to her primitive order and beauty, as when the morning stars sang for joy.

Jesus is our near Kinsman by His assumption of our nature. He is the nearest and dearest Friend of our race, who stooped to die for our redemption. And the fact that He carried our nature in Himself to heaven, and wears it there, is an indissoluble bond between us. Sit still! Do not fret! He will never fail, as He will certainly never forsake!

Let us seek the quiet heart in our prayers. Prayer must arise within us as a fountain from unknown depths. But we must leave it to God to answer in His own wisest way. We are so impatient and think that God does not answer. A child asked God for fine weather on her birthday, and it rained! Someone said, "God didn't answer your prayer." "Oh, yes," she replied, "He did. God always answers, but He said no!" God always answers! He never fails! Be still! If we abide in Him, and He abides in us, we ask what we will, and it is done. As a sound may dislodge an avalanche, so the prayer of faith sets in motion the power of God.

In times of difficulty—be still! Thine enemies are plotting thine overthrow! They laugh at thy strong confidence! But has thou not heard His voice saying: "This is the way, walk ye in it"? Then leave Him to deal with thy foes from whatever quarter they come. He is thy rock, and rocks do not shake. He is thy high tower, and a high tower cannot be flooded. Thou needest mercy, and to Him belongeth mercy. Do not run hither and thither in panic! Just quietly wait, hushing thy soul, as He did the fears of His friends on the eve of Gethsemane and Calvary. "Rest in the Lord, wait patiently for Him." "Be still, for He will not rest, until He hath finished the thing this day."   *Mrs. Charles E. Cowman*

NOVEMBER 30 ─────────────────────────────

Whoso offereth the sacrifice of thanksgiving, glorifieth me, and prepareth a way that I may show him the salvation of God (Ps. 50:23 MARGIN RV).

We read in the Book of Joshua how the walls of Jericho fell flat after they were compassed about seven days. God had declared that He had given them the city. Faith reckoned this to be true, so they began their march around the walls using as their only weapon that which indicated triumph—a ram's horn! Unbelief might have prayed this kind of prayer, "O Lord, make the walls totter just a little, or loosen a few stones so that we may have a sign that Thou art going to answer our prayer, and then we will praise Thee." Prudence might have said, "It is not safe to shout until the victory is actually won, lest the Lord be dishonored before the people and be greatly humiliated." This would not have been faith at all. They acted on the authority of God's Word and shouted the shout of faith before there was a sign of encouragement, and the Lord accomplished the rest. It is after we make a full committment that "He will bring it to pass."

How many walls of difficulty would fall flat were we to simply march around them with shouts of praise? As we compass walls with praise, the Lord has promised to "compass us about with songs of deliverance."

There is a legend which tells of two angels who come from Heaven every morning and go on their rounds all the day long. One is the angel of requests. The other is the angel of thanksgiving. Each carries a basket. The one belonging to the angel of requests is soon filled to overflowing, for everyone pours into it great handfuls of requests; but when the day is ended, the angel of thanksgiving has in his basket only two or three small contributions of gratitude. *Mrs. Charles E. Cowman*

DECEMBER 1 _____

With good will doing service, as to the Lord, and not to men (Eph. 6:7).

L ittle self-denials, little honesties, little passing words of sympathy, little nameless acts of kindness, little silent victories over favorite temptations—these are the silent threads of gold which, when woven together, gleam out so brightly in the pattern of life that God approves. *F. W. Farrar*

> Twas but a little light she bore,
> While standing at the open door;
> A little light, a feeble spark,
> And yet it shone out through the dark
> With cheerful ray, and gleamed afar
> As brightly as the polar star.

A little light dispels the gloom
That gathers in the shadowed room
Where want and sickness find their prey,
And night seems longer than the day,
And hearts with many troubles cope
Uncheered by one slight ray of hope.

It may be little we can do
To help another, it is true;
But better is a little spark
Of kindness when the way is dark,
Than one should miss the road to heaven
For lack of light we might have given.   *Anonymous*

Let us be thankful that the privilege is given us in this world of
rebuilding our altars and reconsecrating our lives to God; and
though we may grieve over the poverty and tameness of present
opportunity as compared with the affluence of earlier and
neglected privileges, let us still pour out our hearts in praise that
our chastening was but for a time, and that a fresh beginning is in
mercy granted to us.   *W. C. Holway*

"It's a stumpy world," said Luclarion Grapp, "but some folks
step right over their stumps without scarcely knowing when!"

DECEMBER 2 _____

*Weeping may endure for a night, but joy cometh in the morning (Ps.
30:5).*

Paul did not take pleasure in infirmities. He tells us that he was
anxious to get rid of the infirmity that clouded his life. But
when he saw that God supplied the grace he began to love the
supply better than freedom from infirmity. He saw that it was
better to have darkness with stars brought out by it, than all
sunshine and no stars; that the cold winds of winter are as
necessary for the world's development as the cheerful warmth of
spring and summer; that the mantle of snow is as good for earth as
its mantle of grass and flowers. But for the snow mantle the mantle
of flowers might not be. When a man learns that God's strength is
perfected through his infirmity, necessities, persecutions, and

distresses, he will by and by begin to welcome them as an angel
sent from heaven to minister to him. *A. C. Dixon*

Any man can sing by day; but only he whose heart has been
tuned by the gracious hand of Jehovah can sing in the darkness.
The things of earth may satisfy for the hours of prosperity; but only
the peace of God can give gladness in the darkness of adversity.
God gives joy in sorrow; and when the sad one sings through his
tears, then the Lord comes out to him with new and more tender
assurances, so that by his very hymn he is made more gladsome.
That which is born of trust rises in rapture. *Wm. M. Taylor*

> A dreary month of weeping,
>   Of cloud and fog and rain,
> Is sorrowful December,
>   And all the winds complain.
> For trees are bare and flowers are gone,
>   And birds have hushed all song,
> And days are short and sunless,
>   And nights are dark and long.
>
> But let us wait in patience,
>   The days are swift to go,
> And even sorrow does not stay
>   Long on the earth below;
> Some days must be for weeping,
>   But God and heaven remain,
> And after nights of darkness
>   The sun will shine again. *Marianne Farningham*

DECEMBER 3

*And I will give thee the treasures of darkness, and hidden riches of secret
places, that thou mayest know that I, the Lord, am the God of Israel (Isa.
45:3).*

Years ago, before the city of London had modern paved
streets, the story is told of an incident in Ruskin's life. He was
known during his lifetime for never having missed an opportunity
to relate the goodness of his God. While walking down one of the
streets of London with a friend, the friend turned and disgustingly
commented to Ruskin, "What dirty, dreadful, loathsome stuff!"
He was referring to the peculiarly unpleasant compound, the mud

of London streets. "Hold, my friend," said Ruskin. "Not so dreadful after all. What are the elements of this revolting substance? First there is sand, but when its particles are crystallized according to the law of its nature, what is nicer than clean white sand? And when that which enters into it is arranged according to a still higher law, we have the matchless opal. What else have we in this mire? Clay. And the materials of clay, when the particles are arranged according to their higher laws, make the brilliant sapphire. What other ingredients enter into the London muck? Soot. And soot in its crystallized perfection forms the diamond. There is but one other—water. And water when distilled according to the higher law of its nature, forms the dewdrop resting in exquisite perfection in the heart of the rose. So in the muddy, lost soul of man is hidden the image of his Creator, and God will do His best to find His opals, His sapphires, His diamonds and dewdrops."

The heavenly treasury contains graces which can only be gathered one by one.

A vague desire to be better, stronger, holier, will come to nothing. Character is built, like the walls of an edifice, by laying one stone upon another.   *T. L. Cuyler*

DECEMBER 4 _____

Let the saints be joyful in glory: let them sing aloud upon their beds (Ps. 149:5).

Yes, said Amos R. Wells, let all Christians sing, even on beds of pain. Let all Christians sing, even songs in the night, even songs in prison, like Paul and Silas. Few lives are so songful as they might be and should be. Most lives are groanful. Most lives are full of complaint, meditated if not uttered aloud.

As Phillips Brooks once cheerily said, "True religion sings here, and will sing more hereafter. Distrust your religion unless it is cheerful, unless it turns every act and deed to music, and exults in attempts to catch the harmony of the new life." We read of the mystical "music of the sphere," that unheard anthem of praise made by the stars in their majestic march through the sky. May it not be made, not by the stars at all, but by praiseful human hearts?

It is always possible to find an excuse for good cheer, a fine reason for singing. Here is an excuse that Oliver Herford once thought up:

> I heard a bird sing
>   In the dark of December;
> A magnificent thing
>   And sweet to remember:
> "We are nearer to spring
>   Than we were in September."
> I heard a bird sing
>   In the dark of December.

Yes, and in that same vein, however gloomy our surroundings may be, we can always remember that we are one day nearer heaven than we were yesterday—one day nearer our eternal joy and peace.

What if it is dark around us now, and cold, and stormy? The endless spring is drawing near! Flowers are coming, bird songs are coming, soft breezes and blue skies are coming! Every dark day brings the bright days nearer.

We cannot weigh or number our blessings, neither can we weigh or number our feelings of gratitude to Thee, O God.

DECEMBER 5

Thou hast given me a south land; give me also springs of water. And he gave her the upper springs, and the nether springs (Josh. 15:19).

My Father," said Abbie Mills in her book, *Quiet Hallelujahs,* "has given me a more glorious inheritance than Caleb could bestow upon Achsah, even this south land of perfect love.

"My rich inheritance was a gift from my Heavenly Father, and Jesus gave me a ticket for my journey over, but there was no 'return' attached. Though in some respects I had to change my diet, yet so plenteous was the store, and so delicious the fare, that my soul grew fat and flourishing. The air is most exhilarating, and at the same time so full of rest, that it is refreshing to breathe it by night or by day. One revels in it, eats it, drinks it, bathes in it, and grows glad; becomes full of gladness, rejoices always. It is a joy to work, and there is always plenty to do. Blessed service planned by the chief Husbandman, who brought me into this land, the glory of all lands! The scent of the trees here is like Lebanon.

"This south land of mine has also springs of water. All the sources are in God Himself; so no stagnant pool can be found. No undercurrent of worldliness has warmed the waters in a feverish way, rendering them unpleasant to the taste, and thirst-producing, rather than thirst-assuaging. From the nether springs of love's bottomless abyss, flow the life-giving waters, and all may freely drink and drink again, until all soul-malaria is cleansed, and the old-time thirst need be known no more; for he who drinks abundantly shall find a well of water springing up within him.

"On the beauteous expanse of the river of peace we may spread our sails, and celestial breezes shall waft us toward the shores of heaven; and oh, how sweet the flowers that line the shores, and bloom everywhere. The soul that obeys God, and leaving all behind, at once resolves to go up and possess the Canaan of perfect love, finds life and health and peace.

"I cannot say that all the best of the land is being preempted, and that you will have to take up with some swampy spot if you do not haste to come," continued Abbie Mills, "but it is certain that you will lose much by delay, on your own part. The time for laying up treasures in heaven is so short, we want to work at the greatest advantage, so that our talent may gain ten talents. We cannot afford to remain in a state where we are not fitted for the most complete service we may render. Why tarry amid chilling influences, when there is plenty of sunshine? Why take a sort of grim pleasure in talking about your spiritual rheumatism, when you may be rid of it at once, and forever?"

DECEMBER 6

. . . But by love serve one another (Gal. 5:13).

The old Quaker was right: "I expect to pass through this life but once. If there is any kindness or any good thing I can do to my fellowbeings, let me do it now. I shall pass this way but once."

> Lord, help me to live from day to day
> In such a self-forgetful way,
> That even when I kneel to pray,
> My prayer shall be for OTHERS.

Help me in all the work I do
To ever be sincere and true,
And know that all I'd do for you,
Must needs be done for OTHERS.

Let "Self" be crucified and slain,
And buried deep; and all in vain
May efforts be to rise again,
Unless to live for OTHERS.

And when my work on earth is done,
And my new work in Heaven's begun,
May I forget the crown I've won,
While thinking still of OTHERS.

Others, Lord, yes others
Let this my motto be.
Help me to live for others,
That I may live like Thee.

Charles D. Meigs

DECEMBER 7

Whosoever shall give you a cup of water to drink in My name, because ye belong to Christ, verily, I say unto you, he shall not lose his reward (Mark 9:41).

It seems wonderful indeed that God should keep note of such a little thing as the giving of a cup of water to a thirsty Christian. It shows how dear to Him are His people, since the smallest things done to one of them He accepts, remembers, and rewards. The mention here of the giving of a cup of water suggests that this promise is for little, commonplace acts, rather than for great deeds. We are too niggardly with our helpfulness. God has put His gifts of love into our hearts that they may be given out. We would call a man selfish who should refuse a cup of water to one who was thirsty. Yet many of us do this continually: it is the heart that thirsts, and the water we refuse to give is human kindness.

'Tis a little thing
To give a cup of water, yet its draught
Of cool refreshment drained by fevered lips
May give a shock of pleasure to the frame
More exquisite than when nectarean juice
Renews the life of joy in happiest hours.

It is a little thing to speak a phrase
Of common comfort, which by daily use
Has almost lost its sense, yet on the ear
Of Him who thought to die unmourned
'Twill fall like choicest music.

Kindness is just the word for these small acts. Kindness is love flowing out in little gentlenesses. We ought to carry our lives so that they will be perpetual benedictions wherever we go. All we need for such a ministry is a heart full of love for Christ; for if we truly love Christ we shall also love our fellowmen, and love will always find ways of helping. A heart filled with gentleness cannot be miserly of its benedictions.   *J. R. Miller, from* Come Ye Apart

DECEMBER 8 _____

And it shall come to pass, that before they call, I will answer; and while they are yet speaking, I will hear (Isa. 65:24).

Did you ask the Lord for patience?
Did you plead for it in prayer,
Then tribulations great befell you,
And you thought He didn't care?
Oh, my child, He heard and answered,
Answered full your prayer;
"Tribulation worketh patience,"
That's the gem you longed to wear.

Did you ask Him for submission?
Did you plead for it in prayer,
And such suffering great o'ertook you
That you thought He didn't care?
Ah, my dear, He heard and answered
That true prayer with bitter tear;
For we only learn obedience
By things we suffer here.

'Twas unselfishness you wanted,
Asked for it in prayer,
And the sacrifices He asked for
Seemed too great for you to bear?
Ah, He cared, He heard and answered,
Answered full your prayer;

For we learn to be unselfish
By the sacrifice we bear.

Did you ask the Lord for victory,
Plead for it in prayer,
And life's battle surged around you,
Hid His face so fair?
Ah, my child, He heard and answered,
Answered your own prayer;
For we learn to be victorious,
By the daily cross we bear.

Did you ask to be made humble,
And for strength its fruit to bear;
Then the way you were tormented
Made you feel He didn't care?
Well, my child, He heard and answered,
Answered deepest prayer;
Humility and strength to bear it
Come to those who know life's care.

We count not things we're seeing,
But the things which are above,
For things we see are fleeting,
But above is God and love.
The big things beyond this earth life
Are unseen by us today;
But there everlasting beauty
Will be ours to keep for aye.   *Josephine Hope Westervelt*

DECEMBER 9

David enquired of the Lord (2 Sam. 5:19).

Christian, if thou wouldst know the path of duty, take God for thy compass; if thou wouldst steer thy ship through the dark billows, put the tiller into the hand of the Almighty. Many a rock might be escaped if we would let our Father take the helm; many a shoal or quicksand we might well avoid if we would leave it to His sovereign will to choose and to command. The puritan said, "As sure as ever a Christian carves for himself he'll cut his own fingers." "I will instruct thee and teach thee in the way which thou shalt go," is God's promise to His people. Let us, then, take all our perplexities to Him and say, "Lord, what wilt thou have me to do?" Leave not thy chamber this morning without *inquiring of the Lord.*   *C. H. Spurgeon*

The great gulf fixed by sin and death is crossed again and again by prayer, over Christ as the bridge.

On the field of prayer, through the power of the precious blood Satan, self, and the world meet their Waterloo.

DECEMBER 10 _____

Be careful for nothing (Phil. 4:6).

Do you cross rivers before you come to them, dread troubles that never come, expect evil from the Lord instead of good? In other words is your soul full of unnecessary care? For that is what the word "careful" means—unnecessary care.

"Do not worry" is a plain and simple command, but it is such a difficult one to follow. M. D. Babcock has given a few beneficial suggestions for the person who feels defeated because of the common ailment of worry. "The anxious Christian hurts more than himself; he hurts the faith of those who know him and the good name of his Lord who has promised to supply all his needs. There is nothing which we cannot pray about. Go deeper into the text: "But in everything by prayer and supplication let your requests be made known unto God." What we can take to God we can trust to God. What we put our fidelity into, He will perfect by His faithfulness. While we work for the best, He works the best for us. We may not succeed as we hoped; we may have discipline we little expected, but the Father knows what His child needs. What God has for us to do we can do, or to bear we can bear. Is there not enough in His ocean to fill our pitcher? With the need of every day will come His promised supply—"My grace is sufficient for thee."

Do not forget the words further on in the text: "with thanksgiving." Be on the lookout for mercies. Blessings brighten when we count them. Out of the determination of the heart the eyes see. If you want to be gloomy, there's gloom enough to keep you glum; if you want to be glad, there's gleam enough to keep you glad. Better lose count in enumerating your blessings than lose your blessings in telling your troubles.

Unbraid the verse into three cords and bind yourself to God with them in trustful, prayerful, thankful bonds—anxious for nothing, prayerful for everything, thankful for anything—"and the peace of God which passeth all understanding shall keep your hearts and minds through Christ Jesus."

From Thoughts for Every-Day Living

DECEMBER 11

Are not five sparrows sold for two farthings, and not one of them is forgotten before God (Luke 12:6).

It was a beautiful winter day," relates J. H. McConkey. "I was sitting on the veranda of a southern hotel enjoying the sunshine and sky. Suddenly I became conscious of the swift flight of some small object before my eyes. Then came a dull thud as of something falling. There before my eyes, not ten feet away, lay the crumpled body of a sparrow. He turned on his back, little claws stretched appealingly toward the sky, then the tiny eyelids closed over his death-dimmed eyes. His swift flight through the air had evidently brought him into a death collision with a pole or buttress and his sparrow life had been the price. It was only a passing incident, this death of a tiny sparrow. Seemingly no one but myself, sitting there alone, had noticed it. But like a flash came to mind a wondrous text, with its marvelous truth—'Not a sparrow falleth without your Father.'

"I was overwhelmed with the thought of how far we failed to believe in, and realize, the tender care of the God of the universe over the tiniest and most insignificant objects of His creation, and much more over the most trivial and passing affairs in the lives of His own dear children.

"Have you ever noted the Master's mathematics in these two sparrow texts—Matthew 10:29 and Luke 12:6? The sparrow was sold as an article of food in the Palestine markets. So cheap was the little bird that two of them were sold for the paltry pittance of a farthing. 'Are not two sparrows sold for a farthing?' 'Are not five sparrows sold for two farthings?' Naturally four of them would be sold for two farthings. But so insignificant were they in the sight of the vendor that, when a buyer came along with two farthings, the seller threw in an extra one, giving five for two, instead of four. Yet of this extra sparrow—almost worthless in the sight of the vendor, the Lord utters this wonderful word, 'Not one of them is forgotten before God.'

"We have been missing a wondrous truth. The God of the universe is also the God of the tiny sparrow. As that sparrow is ever before the face of God, and in His tender care so the most trivial details of our lives are ever present, unforgotten, and tenderly cared for before our Father in heaven. He wants us to bring every such detail, however insignificant, in the happy confidence that He is ever watching and waiting to meet our every need however humble."

From The Fifth Sparrow

DECEMBER 12

Ye shall receive power after that the Holy Ghost is come upon you, and ye shall be witnesses unto Me (Acts 1:8).

> Breathe on me, Breath of God,
> Till I am wholly Thine,
> Till all this earthly part of me,
> Glows with Thy fire divine.
>
> *Edwin Hatch*

Look at it! Think of it! A hundred and twenty men and women having no patronage, no promise of any earthly favor, no endowment, no wealth—a company of men and women having to get their living by common daily life—and yet they are to begin the conquests of Christianity! To them is entrusted a work which is to turn the world upside down. None so exalted but the influence of this lowly company shall reach to them, until the throne of the Caesars is claimed for Christ. None so far off but the power of this little band gathered in an upper room shall extend to them until the whole world is knit into a brotherhood! Not a force is there on earth, either of men or devils, but they shall overcome it, until every knee shall bow to their Master, and every tongue shall confess that He is Lord.

A thing impossible, absurd, look at it as you will, until you admit this—they are to be filled with the Holy Ghost. Then difficulties melt into the empty air. Then there is no limit to their hopes, for there is no limit to their power. Their strength is not only "as the strength of ten," it is as the strength of the Almighty.

This is Christ's idea of Christianity; the idea not of man—it is

348

infinitely too sublime—the idea of God!

Mark Guy Pearse, from Thoughts for the Quiet Hour

DECEMBER 13

Thou shalt love . . . (Matt. 22:37).

There is a beautiful legend of the sweet-toned bell of the angels in heaven which softly rings at twilight. Its notes make a music supremely entrancing. But none can hear it save those only whose hearts are free from passion and clear of unlovingness and all sin.

This is only a legend. No one on earth can hear the ringing of the bells of heaven. But there is a sweeter music which the lowliest may hear. Those who live the gentle life of patient, thoughtful, selfless love make a music whose strains are enrapturing.

> The heart that feels the approval
>   That comes from a kindly deed
> Knows well there's no sweeter music
>   On which the spirit can feed.
>
> In sweet'ning the life of another,
>   In relieving a brother's distress,
> The soul finds its highest advancement
>   And the noblest blessedness.
>
> That life is alone worth the living
>   That lives for another's gain;
> The life that comes after such living
>   Is the rainbow after the rain.
>
> *J. R. Miller, from* A Gentle Heart

Angels are not fitted for sympathy, for they know nothing about human life. In a picture by Domenichino, there is an angel standing by the empty cross, touching with his finger one of the sharp points in the thorn-crown which the Savior had worn. On his face there is the strangest bewilderment. He is trying to make out the mystery of sorrow. He knows nothing of suffering, for he has never suffered. There is nothing in the angel nature or in the angel life to interpret struggle or pain. The same is measurably true of untried human life. If we would be sons of consolation, our natures must be enriched by experience. We are not naturally gentle to all men. There is a harshness in us that needs to be mellowed. We are apt to be heedless of the feelings of others, to forget how many hearts are sore, and carry heavy burdens. We are not gentle toward sorrow, because our own hearts never have been ploughed. The best universities cannot teach us the divine art of sympathy. We must walk in the deep valleys ourselves, and then we can be guides to other souls. We must feel the strain, and carry the burden, and endure the struggle ourselves, and then we can be touched, and can give help to others in life's sore stress and poignant need.

DECEMBER 14 _____

The spirit of a man will sustain his infirmity; but a wounded spirit who can bear? (Prov. 18:14).

A lovely story is told about a very poor family who had the faculty of making the best of everything. A rich woman was interested in helping them, and one day a neighbor of the poor family told her that they were imposing on her.

Said the neighbor, "I often hear the children of that family talking about the good things they have to eat, luxuries that I can't afford at all." The rich woman thereupon called on the poor family at noon, and as she stood outside the door she heard a little girl ask, "Will you have roast beef today?" Then another girl's voice answered, "No; I guess I'll take cold chicken."

Thereupon the rich woman rapped at the door and entered at once, finding the two girls seated at a table on which were a few slices of dry bread, two cold potatoes, a pitcher of water, and nothing else. In answer to her questions, the girls explained that they pretended their poor fare was all sorts of good things and the play made it really seem like a feast. "You don't know," said one, "how good bread tastes when you call it strawberry shortcake!" "But it tastes a lot better when you call it ice cream," said the other little girl.

The rich woman went away with new ideas of contentment. She had discovered that happiness is not in things but in thoughts. She had learned what Solomon said so long ago, that the spirit can be made to sustain infirmities; but when the spirit is broken, all is lost.

J. R. Wells, from Think on These Things

Ask not for our lot to be transformed; rather that we be transformed instead. Then we will see in our lot the blessings awaiting there for us.

DECEMBER 15 _____

They shall walk with me in white (Rev. 3:4).

It is an interesting study to trace the marks and footprints on the new fallen snow. There God has wiped out the ordinary marks of nature, and provided a spotless, unwritten page on which new marks may be inscribed. Early as you go out to the fields you will find that a great many creatures have gone there earlier than you, whose traces betray them as plainly as if you had seen them passing. Each creature leaves a distinct mark on the snow by which you can identify it.

The spiritual world is a world of purity, where nothing that defileth ought to enter. And the goodness of this pure world, compared with the goodness of the ordinary world, is like a piece of the finest linen cloth ever made by man, which looks dingy and yellow when put beside a patch of new fallen snow.

If at any time you turn aside into the miry ways of sin, when you come back, to the pure snow of the right path, you bring the stains of these miry ways to defile its purity; and your footsteps for a long distance can be traced by their brown muddy prints, and it will be a long ways before the mud finally is washed off, and you make clean footprints in the snow once more.

The footprints in the snow, though they are very distinct, are very evanescent. They disappear with the melting of the snow. And if the footprints you are making in God's pure world were as fleeting as these, you might not need to concern yourself much about the nature of them. But they are enduring as your own nature, enduring as God's Word and God's righteousness. We see in the hard slabs of the sandstone quarry the footprints of birds and reptiles that passed over the sandy shores of seas which vanished millions of years ago; and from these footprints the naturalist can tell you the shape and size and nature of those long extinct creatures, though nothing is left of them but these fossil tracks in the sandstone. And so everyone is leaving footprints on the sands of time, to be hardened into enduring fossils and to be deciphered long after they have passed away. We know the nature of the Christian walk and conversation of the saints in Sardis, from the footprints they have left behind in God's Word, as they walked with Christ in white. Everything else about them has perished; but those footprints make them real and living among us once more. And so, as you walk with Christ, your Christian walk will testify of you when nothing else of you remains in the living world.

"Teach me thy way, O Lord and lead me in a plain path, because of mine enemies." The margin reads "because of them that observe me."

Your path through life lies across the untrodden snow. No one has gone this way before. Let Jesus take your hand as you walk with Him in the white of a soul that trusts only in His righteousness and that loves His law. Let Him make your way clean before you, and enable you to keep it clean, and leave such clear, distinct, characteristic footprints of godliness on it that others may walk in your traces, and be followers of you, as you are a follower of the Lord Jesus.   *Hugh M'Millan*

DECEMBER 16 _____

. . . whether there be knowledge, it shall vanish away (1 Cor. 13:8).

Lessing, a German dramatist and critic of the eighteenth century, once told this parable regarding the limited knowledge of man. "Once upon a time a certain king of a great realm built himself a palace, the most gorgeous that ever had been planned, the wonder of the whole earth. A strife arose among certain connoisseurs as to some of the obscure ground plans upon which the palace was constructed. The conflict lasted through a great many years. While this conflict was going on, it happened upon a time that a watchman one night cried out, 'Fire!' And the architects began running hither and thither, each with his plan, squabbling as to whether the fire had broken out in this place, or whether it had broken out in that place, and as to what was the best spot to apply the engines. And its friends all took to wrangling. Alas! Alas, the beautiful palace will be burned! But it stood there; and presently they discovered that it was not on fire at all. Behind it there was an extraordinary display of northern lights, which shone through it with such brilliancy that the palace itself seemed to be full of flame."

So we say, let knowledge increase, let it run to and fro, let it light up the world all it will, it will only illuminate, because it cannot destroy the city of our God.

We are a generation today of exhausted, overly particular people. We are experts but not examples. We know so much—too much. We want to be thought of as philosophers, not little children; scholars, not babes. Childlike? Never! We miss the secrets God has hidden from the wise and prudent and revealed unto babes. We go on trying to be wise, noble, mighty; but not many wise, noble and mighty have been chosen by God. It is possible for a wise man to become as a little child, but not many of them do it. How often theologians even miss some deep truths but the simple soul among the saints of God has received the hidden lesson and applied it and pressed through to heaven's best. Verily, I say unto you, "We know too much!"

> What does it matter if I go not to God's Word to seek
> The truth, of that which I so glibly speak,
> And the need for His guiding hand on my earthly way—
> Does it really matter just what I may say?   *Selected*

DECEMBER 17 _____

Therefore I will look unto the Lord (Micah 7:7).

Several years ago while visiting certain of the Northern European countries, it was necessary for me to cross the North Sea in a large ocean liner. During the first days of the voyage we sped along over calm seas, but suddenly we were overtaken by a frightening tempest. The waves were like great mountains, and we were lifted to their heights. The great ship rocked and rolled, creaked and groaned. The faces of the passengers were blanched white with fear. Even the little ones clung to their mothers, sensing the nearness of danger—the very air was surcharged by an ominous foreboding of impending destruction. When it seemed that surely the ship had endured to the very limit, a man appeared on the scene. There was no trace of anxiety or concern on his face. His presence radiated calmness, rest and peace. With a voice full of gentleness he assured us, "all's well," and our fears disappeared.

Who was that man? The captain. He had taken that vessel through many a long voyage, plowed rough seas, met terrible storms, and had always arrived safely into port—flags of victory flying at top mast.

What have we to fear? Why do we look down? Where now is thy God? Is not our Captain on board, and with one word can He not say to the waves and winds, "Peace be still," and they obey Him? With hushed hearts let us listen for His sweet whisper of assurance, "All's well. It is I; be not afraid." With Christ in the vessel we smile at the storm.

Yes, one whose faith is continually stimulated by the *upward look* gives no ground to the attempted encroachment of despair. No matter how great the trouble or how dark the outlook, a quick lifting of the heart to God in a moment of real actual faith in Him will completely alter any situation and turn the darkness of midnight into glorious sunrise.   *Mrs. Charles E. Cowman*

DECEMBER 18 _____

Commit thy way unto the Lord; trust also in him; and he shall bring it to pass (Ps. 37:5).

> "Commit thy way unto the Lord and trust!"
>   Ah, it is here we fail! We give the wheel
> Of our small bark to Him; but then we trust
>   Our hand upon His hand,
>   And dare to stand
> Beside our Master, lest He wreck our keel.
>
> "Commit thy way unto the Lord and trust!"
>   Leave all to Him; believe He knows thy course,
> Thy dangers, and thy safety—all—then just
>   Abandon all to Him:
>   So shalt thou skim,
> Borne briskly on before the Spirit's force.
>
> "Commit thy way unto the Lord and trust!"
>   There is an "also" we too oft forget,
> And so are plagued and worried. Oh, we must
>   "Trust also," then our soul

Shall cease to roll
In restlessness and reason and regret!

Commit! and then, committed, trust His Word!
   Has He not said that He will bring thee through?
Trust His strong arm; and when wild storms are heard,
   Believe He holds them still
   By His strong will.
Trust Him, the Wise, the Faithful, and the True.

Trust Him to manage all that thou dost now
   Commit to Him—the ship—the sails—the sea—
The sailors, thy strange crew. And ask not how
   He will do all for thee,
   But trustful be.
Lie down and rest from anxious worry free.   *Unknown*

DECEMBER 19 _____

*And the angel said unto them, Fear not; for, behold, I bring you good
tidings of great joy, which shall be to all people (Luke 2:10).*

What a beautiful message spoken by the angels to the humble
shepherds as they watched over their flocks that night! How
startled they must have been when out from the heavens there
burst upon them the strains of sweetest music! Little wonder that
they trembled at this unusual happening and were "sore afraid."
How tender and assuring must have been the voice that bade
them, "Fear not." And thus the angel's announcement was made
on that night of all nights; that holy night; and Bethlehem's
manger cradled a King! Your King! My King! The wide world's
King! The God-sent King, from "out of the ivory palaces, into a
world of woe"—because "God so loved!"

A number of years ago Dr. Cortland Myers, then pastor of
Tremont Temple, Boston, when preaching from the text, "Fear
Not!" made several never-to-be-forgotten remarks, so applicable
to this strange hour in the history of our stricken world. He said:
"The two words, 'Fear Not' are the *thrush-notes* of the Bible! The
thrush sings in the depths of the forest; a bit of music like that
which occurs nowhere else in all the bird-world. It is marvelously
sweet. It is unique, and absolutely alone. There is nothing else like
it—and man's genius has many times tried to capture it and thrust

355

it within the bars of music, and always failed in the attempt. It seems almost as if this is the note that was dropped out of the angel's music. Maybe they left it in the world the night they sang at Bethlehem; for, they had it in the Christmas anthem. Maybe they forgot it and left it here! It is a part of the angel's music. But is it a part of real life? Does it belong in reality, to every man's life and to *all* conditions of life? Is it a certainty? Something substantial? It *is* a positive reality! It *is* a part of the music of life; one of the high notes of the music! "Fear Not!"   *Mrs. Charles E. Cowman*

DECEMBER 20 _____

Who art thou that judgest another? (James 4:12).

One Christmas someone sent Mr. Whittier a gentian flower pressed between two panes of glass. Seen from one side it appeared only a blurred mass of something without beauty. But seen from the other side of the glass the exquisite beauty of the flower appeared, in all its delicate loveliness. Whether the gift was lovely or not to the view depended on the side from which one looked at it. The poet hung the gift on the windowpane, putting the blurred side out and the lovely flower side toward his room. Those who passed by without looking up, marked only a "gray disk of clouded glass," seeing no beauty; but the poet, sitting within, looked at the token, and saw outlined against the winter sky all the exquisite loveliness of the flower:

> They cannot from their outlook see
> The perfect grace it hath for me;
> For there the flower, whose fringes through
> The frosty breath of autumn blew,
> Turns from without its face of bloom
> To the warm tropic of my room,
> As fair as when beside its brook
> The hue of bending skies it took.
>
> But deeper meanings come to me,
> My half-immortal flower, from thee;
> Man judges from a partial view,
> None ever yet his brother knew;
> The Eternal Eye that sees the whole
> May better read the darkened soul,

And find, to outward sense denied,
The flower upon its inmost side.   *John Greenleaf Whittier*

Too often we look upon the blurred side of actions—yes, of people too. We do not see the loveliness that there is on the other side. We are all continually misinterpreting others. There is a flower side in many an act which we condemn because we see only the blurred side. Let us train ourselves to believe the best always of people and of actions, and find some beauty in everything.   *J. R. Miller, from* Thoughts for the Thoughtful

DECEMBER 21

. . . Let us now go even unto Bethlehem (Luke 2:15).

Yet in thy dark streets shineth
  The everlasting Light;
The hopes and fears of all the years
  Are met in Thee tonight.   *Phillips Brooks*

It isn't far to Bethlehem town—
It is anywhere that
Christ comes down
And finds in some one's
Shining face
A welcome, and a biding place.
The road to Bethlehem
Runs right through
The homes of people
Like me and you.   *Anonymous*

The birth of Jesus is the sunrise of the Bible. Toward this point the aspirations of the prophets and the poems of the psalmists were directed as the heads of flowers are turned toward the dawn. From this point a new day began to flow very silently over the world—a day of faith and freedom, a day of hope and love. When we remember the high meaning that has come into human life and the clear light that has flooded softly down from the manger-cradle in Bethlehem of Judea, we do not wonder that mankind has learned to reckon history from the birthday of Jesus, and to date all events by the years before or after the nativity of Christ.

'Twas not the angel's message
  That gave the Christmas thought

Nor yet the gold and incense
Which the Wise Men had brought.

'Twas not the star that led them
Upon the unknown way;
It was the birth of Jesus
That makes the Christmas day!   *Annie Johnson Flint*

Even the centuries obey Him and swing their orbits around His cradle and date their calendar from His birth.   *Selected*

DECEMBER 22

For unto you is born this day in the city of David, a Saviour, which is Christ the Lord (Luke 2:11).

"Unto you is born this day a Saviour"
Which is Jesus Christ the wondrous Lord;
Not a "teacher," not a "good example,"
But the Son of God, the Living Word.

No "philosopher," his fancies weaving,
Warp of dreams and woof of visions vast,
Not a "prophet," peering down the future,
Not a "scholar," delving in the past.

BUT

"Unto you is born this day a Saviour,"
Earth's one hope, the Life, the Truth, the Way;
Mighty God and glorious Redeemer,
Jesus Christ the Lord is born today.

Annie Johnson Flint

Jesus Christ was born in the meanest of circumstances, but the air above was filled with the hallelujahs of the heavenly hosts. His lodging was a cattle pen, but a star drew distinguished visitants from afar to do Him homage.

His birth was contrary to the laws of life. His death was contrary to the laws of death. No miracle is so inexplicable as His life and teaching.

He had no cornfields or fisheries, but He could spread a table for 5,000 and have bread and fish to spare. He walked on no beautiful carpets, but He walked on the waters and they supported Him.

358

His crucifixion was the crime of crimes, but, on God's side, no lower price than His infinite agony could have made possible our redemption. When He died few men mourned, but a black crepe was hung over the sun. Though men trembled not for their sins, the earth beneath shook under the load. All nature honored him; sinners alone rejected Him.

Sin never touched Him. Corruption could not get hold of His body. The soil that had been reddened with His blood could not claim His dust.

Three years He preached His gospel. He wrote no book, built no church, had no money back of Him. After 1,900 years, He is the one central character of human history, the perpetual theme of all preaching, the pivot around which the events of the age revolve, the only Regenerator of the human race.

Was it merely the son of Joseph and Mary who crossed the world's horizon nearly 2,000 years ago? Was it merely human blood that was spilled on Calvary's hill for the redemption of sinners and which has worked such wonders in men and nations through the centuries?

What thinking man can keep from exclaiming: "MY LORD AND MY GOD!"   *Keith L. Brooks*

DECEMBER 23 _____

Where is He that is born King . . . (Matt. 2:2).

Unbelieving people say that this ancient story of the Wise Men, the star, and the shepherds is not common sense—how could three sages pick out one star from a full sky of countless stars, and follow its gleam to a little town in Palestine? Is it common sense that a virgin should bring forth a child? Is it common sense, the unbeliever asks, that shepherds should find the King of Kings in a barn in Bethlehem, the hope of all the ages born in a stall? Perhaps it is not common sense, but it is *true,* for Christ, the King of Kings *was* born in that barn; and today Herod (who seemed so important then) is only remembered because he tried to kill the Babe. Let your mind run swiftly over the thirty years of His life on earth, to its closing scene, on Golgotha—He is dying nailed to a hard cross; and common sense says He is done for, finished. Common sense said just that, at the foot of the cross,

359

and went back to the city for another drink, and an evening's entertainment. But common sense once more was wrong—for He was not finished. He had only *begun!*

It is humbling to discover that our human common sense is so mistaken so often, in such important matters. But it is a healthy discovery to make, for then we face the fact that God made us with limited sense, needing His counsel, needing His star in the dark night of life, to guide us to the truth.

From a Christmas letter to
Streams in the Desert *fellowship members*
by Mrs. Harriett Thatcher

". . . for we have seen his star in the east, and are come to worship him" (Matt. 2:2).

DECEMBER 24 _____

. . . shepherds abiding in the field, keeping watch over their flock by night (Luke 2:8).

Jesus said: I am the Good Shepherd: the Good Shepherd giveth His life for the sheep (John 10:11).

It was Christmas Eve, 1875. Ira D. Sankey was traveling by steamboat up the Delaware River. It was a calm, starlit evening, and there were many passengers gathered on deck. Mr. Sankey was asked to sing. He stood leaning against one of the great funnels of the boat, and his eyes were raised to the starry heavens in quiet prayer. It was his intention to sing a Christmas song, but he was driven almost against his will to sing "Savior Like a Shepherd Lead Us."

There was a deep stillness. Words and melody, welling forth from the singer's soul, floated out over the deck and the quiet river. Every heart was touched.

After the song was ended, a man with a rough, weatherbeaten face came up to Mr. Sankey and said, "Did you ever serve in the Union army?"

"Yes," answered Mr. Sankey, "in the spring of 1860."

"Can you remember if you were doing picket duty on a bright, moonlit night in 1862?"

"Yes," answered Mr. Sankey, very much surprised.

"So did I," said the stranger, "but I was serving in the Confederate army. When I saw you standing at your post I said to myself, 'That fellow will never get away from here alive.' I raised my musket and took aim. I was standing in the shadow, completely concealed, while the full light of the moon was falling upon you. At that instant, just as a moment ago, you raised your eyes to heaven and began to sing. Music, especially song, has always had a wonderful power over me, and I took my finger off the trigger.

" 'Let him sing his song to the end,' I said to myself. 'I can shoot him afterwards. He's my victim at all events, and my bullet cannot miss him.' But the song you sang then was the song you sang just now. I heard the words perfectly:

> We are Thine, do Thou befriend us,
> Be the guardian of our way.

"When you had finished your song it was impossible for me to take aim at you again. I thought, 'The Lord, who is able to save that man from certain death, must surely be great and mighty,' and my arm of its own accord dropped limp at my side.

"Since that time I have wandered about, far and wide, but when I just now saw you standing there praying as on that other occasion, I recognized you. Then my heart was wounded by your song. Now I ask that you help me find a cure for my sick soul."

Deeply moved, Mr. Sankey threw his arms about the man who in the days of the war had been his enemy. And that night the stranger found the Good Shepherd as his Savior.

From It Happened on Christmas Eve

DECEMBER 25

And she brought forth her firstborn son, and wrapped him in swaddling clothes, and laid him in a manger (Luke 2:7).

The wonder of Christmas is its simplicity.

There is Mary the mother; and there is Joseph to whom she was betrothed. Plain and simple folks, these, even as you and I. There are the shepherds—the first Christmas congregation. Humble folks, these, folks who lived close to the things God made—the earth the carpet for their feet, the sun and stars their coverings.

From a Christmas letter to
Streams in the Desert *fellowship members*
by Mrs. Harriett Thatcher

These are "The Shepherds" in His sight
  Who keep watch over flocks by night;
The milkman, watchman, paper-boys,
  Who forego many of life's joys
To stay on watch beside their "sheep,"
  And to their tasks devotion keep.
The nurses, mothers, those who make
  Our comforts real and never take;
It is to them God's angels sing.

Julien C. Hyer, from the same source

Yes, and the child, too. Nothing here of the pomp and circumstance of life; only the simplicity of the divine.

It is this simplicity which makes Christmas wonderful.

Here may we all come, suppliant. Not to a throne of human exaltation, but to a throne of divine simplicity.

Here may we worship recognizing in the simplicity of the Child the meaning of God's redeeming love.

Here may we bring our joys and our sorrows; our joys will be hallowed, and our sorrows will be lightened.

Here may we receive strength for the days to come, light for the time that shall be. And the Light that shines from a humble manger is strong enough to reach to the end of our days.

Here, then, we come—the young, the old; the rich, the poor; the mighty, the servant—worshiping in the beauty of divine simplicity, marveling at its simple love.

This is the wonder of Christmas. Selected from the same source

"Unto you," yes, even you, O weary heart and worn,
Unto you whose feet are tired, whose trembling hands
    are torn:
"Unto you," this sacred morn, come tidings from above
Which whisper of a Saviour born, and speak His tones
    of love.

"Unto you," yes, even you, is Jesus born today,
If you will meekly give Him room, and bid your sweet
    Guest stay;
Though all the world may have their share, yet He is all

for you,
He'll rest His head within your heart, and shed His love
so true.

He does not ask for palace rare, to make His royal home,
He does not seek for costly fare, but love's sweet bidding,
"Come";
He seeks a subject fond and true to yield to His blest
sway,
To let the brightness of His smile light up your weary way.

"Unto you," though least of all His little ones today,
The star of Bethlehem doth shine, with gladness in its ray;
"Unto you," though small your strength, and weak the
praise you bring,
"Unto you," dear trembling one, He comes your Lord
and King.

"Unto you," this Christmas-tide; with your longing heart
The angels sing their song again, with all their heavenly
art,
Nay, sweeter far than their sweet song, the Spirit from
above
Shall bring the tidings of your King, and whisper of His
love.

Carrie Judd Montgomery

DECEMBER 26 _____

*Though an host should encamp against me, my heart shall not fear;
though war should rise against me, in this will I be confident. Why art thou
cast down, oh my soul? Hope thou in God for I shall yet praise Him (Ps.
27:3; 42:5).*

Take away faith, and in vain we call to God. There is no other
road betwixt our souls and Heaven. Blockade that road and
we cannot communicate with the Great King. Faith links us with
Divinity.

An outstanding minister said that one evening he found himself
staggering along under a load that was heavy enough to crush half
a dozen strong men. Out of sheer exhaustion he put it down and
took a good look at it. He found that it was all borrowed. Part of it
belonged to the following day; part of it belonged to the following

week, and here he was borrowing it that it might crush him *now* —a very stupid but a very ancient blunder.

Never yield to gloomy anticipations. Who told you that the night would never end in day? Who told you that the winter of your discontent should proceed from frost to frost, from snow and ice and hail to deeper snow? Do you not know that day follows night, that flood comes after the ebb, that spring and summer succeed winter? Place your hope and confidence in God. He has no record of failure.

Mrs. Charles E. Cowman

How privileged indeed are those who experience the admonitions of advice from individuals who are concerned that the road is not an easy road. Those who have walked many a weary mile on the journey have given the most welcome words of comfort to the stumbling, exhausted initiate. Such words were passed on by a seasoned traveler:

All dem roses gwine ter fade;
    Honey, doan' yo' sigh.
Gwine ter be mo' roses made
    Foh yo' bye-an-bye;
Gwine ter be mo' roses grow—
    Doan' yo' worry, child.
'Bout dem tho'ns dat hu't yo' so;
    Roses—afteh' while.

We dess 'bleeged ter hab some night
    Sho' as yo' is bo'n;
Afteh 'while hit gwine be light—
    Finest kin' o' mo'n.
Dahkes' clouds dat eveh was
    Hangin' 'roun' dis chile;
Doan' yo' worry none because—
    Sunshine, afteh while.

All dem teahs dat come today
    Has dey puppose, too;
Afteh while dey's gwine erway—
    Hit's de way dey do.
Teahs dess wash erway yo' woe;
    Doan' yo' worry, chile.
Sunshine bring de rose, yo' know—
    Afteh while, a smile!

Anonymous

Thou wilt cast all their sins into the depths of the sea (Micah 7:19).

A s a child you have stood by the banks of the tiny brook which rippled through the meadow. How shallow it is! The stream is but a film of water. The depths are but shoals. In those shallows all things are open and revealed. Every grain of sand is bare. Each bit of shining mica is as clear as if in the open. Every tiny pebble is uncovered. Nothing in the shallows is hidden. Somewhat after this fashion do we too often view God's covering of our sins. It is as though He had cast them only into the shallows. But this is not where God in His grace has put them. For the Holy Spirit says of them, "Thou wilt cast all their sins into *the depths of the sea.*"

Why has He chosen this figure? Just what does it signify? When we were college boys, our old professor used to tell us of a spot in the sea off our western coast which was five miles deep. Think of a solid mile of depth. Then add another mile to that. Then double this, and finally climax it with another mile on top of these four. Five miles deep! Into those almost fathomless deeps nothing which sinks ever comes back. All is shrouded in dense and impenetrable darkness. No eye can pierce into those black deeps of the ocean. No ray of light illumines the darkness. No message ever comes back from that which is swallowed up in this abyss. And into such a gulf of oblivion has God cast all the sins of those who accept His Son as their sin-bearer. *In Christ* His work of remission of sins is complete. Not as into the shallow depths of the brook which murmurs through the field and valley where the eye can rest upon them and the heart grieve for them, has He cast them. Nor does it please His heart of love, nor do honor to the riches of His grace that we should sorrow over them as though they were still upon our own hearts and staining our own innermost souls.

James H. McConkey

Goodness and mercy shall follow me all the days of my life (Ps. 23:6).

B ut why *"follow"* me? Why not "go before"? Because some of my enemies are in the rear; they attack me from behind. There are foes in my yesterdays which can give me fatal wounds.

They can stab me in the back! If I could only get away from the past! Its guilt dogs my steps. Its sins are ever at my heels. I have turned my face toward the Lord, but my yesterdays pursue me like a relentless hound! So I have an enemy in the rear.

But, blessed be His name, my mighty God is in the rear as well as my foe. "Goodness and mercy shall follow me!" No hound can break through that defense. Between me and my guilt there is the infinite love of the Lord. The loving Lord will not permit my past to destroy my soul. I may sorrow for my past, but my very sorrow shall be a minister of moral and spiritual health. My Lord is Lord of the past as well as of the morrow, and so today "I will trust and not be afraid." *J. H. Jowett, from* My Daily Meditation

> Most of my ills I have cured,
> And the worst I have always survived.
> But the very worst ones I've endured—
> Were those that never arrived. *Anonymous*

And so I am not to worry about the coming crisis! "God is never before His time, and never behind!" When the hour is come, I shall find that the great Host hath made "all things . . . ready." When the crisis comes He will tell me how to rest. The orders are not given until the appointed day. Why should I fume and fret and worry as to what the sealed envelope contains? It is enough that He knows all, and when the hour strikes the secrets shall be revealed. *J. H. Jowett*

"It shall be given you in that same hour" (Matt. 10:19).

DECEMBER 29

. . . tomorrow shall be as this day, and much more abundant (Isa. 56:12).

> December's sun is low; the year is old;
>   Through fallen leaves and flying flakes of snow
> The aged pilgrim climbs the mountain cold—
>   But look! the summit's in the afterglow.
>
> The fierce winds hold their breath; the rocks give way;
>   The stars look down to guide her up the heights
> And all around her lonely footsteps play
>   Auroral waves of spiritual light.

Nothing before her but the peak, the sky!
Nothing? Ah, look! beyond is everything!
Over those mountains greener valleys lie;
A happier New Year, an eternal spring!
Lucy Larcom, from Thoughts for the Thoughtful

Whereas *ye know not what shall be on the morrow (James 4:14).*

A friend stands at the door;
In either tight-closed hand
Hiding rich gifts, three hundred and threescore;
Waiting to strew them daily o'er the land
Even as seed the sower.

Friend, come thou like a friend,
And whether bright thy face,
Or dim with clouds we cannot comprehend,
We'll hold our patient hands, each in his place,
And trust thee to the end;
Knowing thou leadest onward to those spheres
Where there are neither days, nor months, nor years.
Dinah Muloch Craik, from Thoughts for the Thoughtful

How often have you found yourself at the entrance into a duty, becalmed as a ship, which at first setting sail had hardly wind to swell its sails while under the shore and shadow of the trees, but meets a fresh gale of wind when out into the open sea! How like the new year which lies before us. It is a responsibility—a trust. Did you ever launch out into duty as the apostles to sea with the wind in your face, as if the Spirit of God, instead of helping you on, meant to drive you back, and yet had found Christ walking to you before the duty was done?

Abraham did not see the ram which God had provided for His sacrifice until he was in the mountain. Climbing the mountain toward the new year God is there. The Christian often goes up that mountain toward his charge with a heavy heart because before he reaches the top he can have no sight of Him who is to lead into the unknown. Turn not back. Go on with courage. He may be nearer than you think.

DECEMBER 30 _____

. . . *Jesus Himself drew near and went with them (Luke 24:15).*

The road often leads through green pastures and beside the still waters, more often through long valleys, shadowless and deep, over mountains unscalable; but let us ask not questions concerning the road as we journey, for the road leads home. He Himself walks with us.

We cannot see beyond the door,
We know not what He hath in store
　For us;
We can but bow our hearts and pray
For strength to serve Him day by day,
　And work and trust.

Pain, dread, and doubt do us pursue:
We wonder what He hath in view
　For us;
And then by faith we pierce the haze
And on His face one moment gaze—
　And love and trust.

We blaze our trail through desert sand,
We know there is a better land
　For us;
Its fields and flowers we cannot see,
But Jesus promised it, and we
　Just pray and trust.

Some day we'll reach the mountain height
And see the land that's ours by right
　Through grace;
Then we'll praise God for desert sands,
For blinded trails and barren lands,
　Before His Face.

Selected

Today is a slender bridge which will bear its own load, but it will collapse if we add tomorrow's. In every year there are 365 letters from the King, each with its own message—"Bear this for Me." What shall we do with the letters? Open them a day at a time. Yesterday's seal is broken; lay that letter reverently away; yesterday's cross is laid down, never to be borne again. Tomorrow's letter lies on the table; do not break the seal. For when tomorrow becomes today, there will stand beside us an unseen Figure; and His hand will be on our brow, and His gaze will be in our eyes, as He says with a loving smile, "As thy days, so shall thy strength be." The golden summary of our life is to be this: as to the

368

past, a record of gratitude; as to the present, a record of service; and as to the future, a record of trust.   *D. M. Panton*

DECEMBER 31 _____

Forgetting the things which are behind (Phil. 3:13).

Thou shalt remember all the way which the Lord thy God led thee (Deut. 8:2).

> Forgetting ills behind me, the sorrows past and gone,
> Forgetting all my wanderings, too sad to dwell upon,
> Remembering God's great goodness, in times of stress
>   and strain,
> Remembering His restorings, I praise my God again.

We stand together at the gateway of another year. It may be a year of many blessed experiences. Follow Him who goes before— the One who went before His people of old—a guiding light, a constant protection, an unfailing Friend and Counselor, and almighty Savior.

When shadows deepen, and fear rides on the moaning wind; when sorrow comes, and we wander in the misty vale of grief; when joy beckons, and our way is sunlit—*"remember"* His past leading and know that all is well. When spectres rise hauntingly from the past, when old heartaches and sorrows seem to weigh us down and blot out the sunshine *forget* "those things which are behind," and reach forward to the joys before us. Paul says, "I press toward the mark"—here there is urgency, and nothing must be allowed to hamper the runner's progress.

We make our own hindrances many times—our Master has done all He can to free us from every weight, giving us forgiveness for the past, help in the present, and assurance for the future. So, dear pilgrim, as we face the coming days of a new year, knowing that each one brings our Master's return nearer, let us "lay aside every weight . . . and press toward the mark," with singleness of heart "looking unto Jesus."

> Forgetting all my doubtings, which dimmed faith's vision
>   bright,
> Forgetting all the earth-clouds, the darkness, gloom
>   and night,
> Remembering God's bright sunshine, and radiance of

His face,
Remembering His long patience, I praise my God
for grace.

Forgetting all unkindness which friends and foes
have shown,
Forgetting and forgiving the wrongs that I have known,
Remembering God provided, unsought, each faithful friend,
Remembering love's devotion, I'll praise Him to the end.

Forgetting my repinings when disappointments came,
Forgetting all the murmurings, which filled my soul
with shame,
Remembering God was ever true to His Holy Word,
Remembering He was faithful, I praise my sovereign Lord.

A. G.

ACKNOWLEDGMENTS

The compiler expresses appreciation to the following publishers and authors for permission to quote extracts from their publications:

Moody Press, Chicago, Illinois, for permission to quote a stanza from one of Martha Snell Nicholson's poems; Evangelical Publishers, Toronto, Canada, for permission to quote from the poems of Annie Johnson Flint; Dr. Alfred Price for permission to quote from the bulletins of St. Stephen's Church, Philadelphia, Pennsylvania; Mr. Paul Meyers of *The Log of the Good Ship Grace* for permission to quote from its columns; Zondervan Publishing House for permission to quote a selection from The Amplified Old Testament, Part Two, Job Through Malachi, copyright 1962, Zondervan Publishing House; The Lockman Foundation for permission to quote a selection from The Amplified New Testament, copyright 1958 by the Lockman Foundation.

In addition, the works of such writers of a past generation as Andrew Murray, F. B. Meyer, J. R. Miller, and J. H. Jowett were extremely valuable and yielded much helpful material.

Indulgence is begged in case of failure to reach any other author or holder of copyrighted portions.

ACKNOWLEDGMENTS